African Americans and the Presidents

African Americans and the Presidents

Politics and Policies
from Washington to Trump

F. Erik Brooks and Glenn L. Starks

GREENWOOD™

An Imprint of ABC-CLIO, LLC
Santa Barbara, California • Denver, Colorado

Library of Congress Cataloging-in-Publication Data

Names: Brooks, F. Erik, author. | Starks, Glenn L., 1966- author.
Title: African Americans and the presidents : politics and policies from Washington to
    Trump / F. Erik Brooks and Glenn L. Starks.
Description: Santa Barbara, CA : Greenwood, An Imprint of ABC-CLIO, LLC, [2019] |
    Includes bibliographical references and index.
Identifiers: LCCN 2018049999 (print) | LCCN 2018051113 (ebook) | ISBN 9781440862120
    (ebook) | ISBN 9781440862113 (cloth)
Subjects: LCSH: Presidents—United States—Racial attitudes—History. | African
    Americans—Politics and government. | African Americans—Government policy. |
    United States—Race relations—Political aspects—History.
Classification: LCC E176.472.A34 (ebook) | LCC E176.472.A34 B76 2019 (print) |
    DDC 323.1196/073—dc23
LC record available at https://lccn.loc.gov/2018049999

ISBN: 978-1-4408-6211-3 (print)
        978-1-4408-6212-0 (ebook)

23 22 21 20 19   1 2 3 4 5

This book is also available as an eBook.

Greenwood
An Imprint of ABC-CLIO, LLC

ABC-CLIO, LLC
147 Castilian Drive
Santa Barbara, California 93117
www.abc-clio.com

This book is printed on acid-free paper ∞
Manufactured in the United States of America

Contents

Introduction

The American president is arguably the most recognized and powerful individual in the United States. While the United States has a federal government based on three branches with checks and balances to ensure constitutional equality, the president has tremendous influence over laws passed and the political stance of the government. Additionally, the president's real authority lies in the power over how legislation and court orders are executed.

The legal, social, cultural, and political history of African Americans has been driven by policies and programs implemented by presidents of the United States over the course of America's history. From slavery through emancipation to the current day, how presidents have addressed such issues as civil rights, policies supporting equality, funding for education, and support for social improvement programs at the federal level have been catalysts for subordinate programs at the state and local levels. For example, the Bill of Rights was added to the U.S. Constitution in 1791 to guarantee such liberties as free speech and the right to property for all Americans. However, those rights were not fully granted to African Americans until centuries later and came into being in a piecemeal fashion as individual laws were passed under various presidential administrations. At times, the guarantees to African Americans per federal laws took decades to be fully realized due to resistance from federal, state, and local government and private establishments as well as groups and individuals.

African Americans have always been politicized in terms of being a part of the political process and being recognized by presidents. The nation's first president, George Washington, recognized the need to address the condition of blacks in slavery. This was an issue on the agenda of the next 15 presidents. However, it is the stance that different presidents took to address the condition of African Americans and how the rights guaranteed in the Constitution should be applied that has driven the course of African American development. At times, African Americans had to take aggressive stances to gain even the most basic liberties such as the rights to vote and hold political office. The position of some presidents seemed not only based on legal foundations but also on their moral position of the treatment of human beings based on the color of their skin. In some cases, the morality of their positions was pushed by the actions of others as a test of their presidential stance in the wake of national scrutiny.

This book explores the relationship of African Americans to each president of the United States. The purpose of the book is to analyze the policies, programs, agendas, and even moral positions each president has taken in addressing the social, cultural, political, and legal concerns and rights of African Americans. The book also explores how African Americans as a community viewed each president in terms of political support. Movements to gain racial equality and end discrimination were often centered on the president by African Americans in the hope that the federal government would take actions to deal with issues at the state and local levels. For example, demands for civil rights, equality in voting, and an end to housing discrimination were targeted for change by presidents as a catalyst for equality at all levels of government.

This book aims to explore the American presidency and the issue of race through the lens of the African American community. Specifically, separate entries examine and analyze each of the 45 American presidents' policies, cabinet appointments, and handling of race matters in the United States. This work is intended for a general audience, professionals, and scholars. Each entry takes an incisive look at each American president by distilling his life, career, and the policies enacted under his presidency in relationship to the African American community. The entries utilize their personal writings, memoirs, news articles, autobiographies, and biographies to frame their views on the issue of race and how they dealt with the issue of race before, during, and after their presidency. In-text citations within each entry can be found in the Further Reading section at the end of each entry or in the Bibliography in the back matter.

For two reasons, this book is divided into discrete time periods to address the relationship of African Americans to each president. First, the history of African Americans can be categorized into time periods based on the evolution of their political rights as well as social and cultural progression. Second, the stances and actions that presidents took to address their positions toward African Americans coincide with these categorical timelines. Presidents did not act alone based on their individual political and personal agendas but instead acted in concert with the political and social climate of their time. Some took actions that directly reflected the demands and perceptions of society and the national political climate. Others took actions to advance the condition of African Americans in the hope of moving society forward even if the political climate was deemed not ready to progress. To these ends, this book addresses each president's relationship with African Americans and vice versa within these categorical periods: slavery, the American Civil War, emancipation, post–Reconstruction, the civil rights era, and the post–civil rights era.

Slavery Era

Politically, slavery was a contentious issue during the founding of the United States, mostly on moral grounds. The Declaration of Independence was completed in 1776, and the Constitution was ratified in 1788. When George Washington became the first president of the United States, there were nearly 800,000 blacks in the new country, 19 percent of the population. Of all blacks, 91 percent were slaves, with the majority being in Virginia followed by South Carolina, Maryland, and North Carolina. The slave trade had been in place in the original 13 states since 1719, and slavery was a primary factor driving the economy.

When the nation was founded, the founding fathers had questions on the plight of slavery. This was evident in the Declaration of Independence stating "all men are created equal" without any qualifiers for race. Yet no agreement could be reached on how to handle the issue, even though the United States was to be a country based on religious, social, and political liberty. The greatest opposition to any forms of freedom for blacks came from southern leaders and landowners, who resisted due to a combined reliance on slavery to support their agriculturally based economy and a strong racial prejudice for nonwhites. Most of the founding fathers could at least relate to the first concern, given the majority of the founder fathers had owned slaves at some point (see Table 1).

The morality of slave ownership is evidenced by personal statements of some of the founding fathers. Patrick Henry once stated in a letter "I am drawn along by the general inconvenience of living without them. I will not—I cannot justify it, however culpable my conduct." George Washington wrote to a friend, in part stating "I can only say that there is not a man living who wishes more sincerely than I do to see a plan adopted for the abolition of [slavery]." George Mason, addressing the Virginia Ratifying Convention, stated "As much as I value a union of all the states, I would not admit the southern states into the union unless they agreed to the discontinuance of this disgraceful trade, because it would bring weakness and not strength to the union" (Cushing 1843, 393).

Table 1   U.S. Founding Fathers Slave Ownership

| Slaveholder (at Some Point in Their Lives) | | Never Owned Slaves | |
Name	State	Name	State
Charles Carroll	Maryland	John Adams	Massachusetts
Samuel Chase	Maryland	Samuel Adams	Massachusetts
Benjamin Franklin	Pennsylvania	Oliver Ellsworth	Connecticut
Button Gwinnett	Georgia	Alexander Hamilton	New York
John Hancock	Massachusetts	Robert Treat Paine	Massachusetts
Patrick Henry	Virginia	Thomas Paine	Pennsylvania
John Jay	New York	Roger Sherman	Connecticut
Thomas Jefferson	Virginia		
Richard Henry Lee	Virginia		
James Madison	Virginia		
Charles C. Pinckney	South Carolina		
Benjamin Rush	Pennsylvania		
Edward Rutledge	South Carolina		
George Washington	Virginia		

Efforts were taken to limit slavery by prohibiting the importation of foreign slaves to individual states and banning slavery in the Northwest Territory (Pennsylvania, north of the Ohio River, east of the Mississippi River, and south of the Great Lakes). Yet compromises quelled any actions to abolish slavery, ending in the three-fifths compromise whereby congressional seat appointments to each state were based on all of states' white population and three-fifths of their slave population. While this at least recognized the existence of blacks, it really gave greater political power to southern states, where most slaves were located.

Another issue was the actions by the founding fathers to limit the power of the newly established central government. This was done to ensure the government of the new nation would not face the same tyranny seen in Europe. Thus, each state was given power to determine how the treatment of the future of slaves would be addressed.

The stance of each president in regard to blacks and slavery reflects his moral views of the issue, less so than the social and political climate of the time. This is because slavery was well established before the United States was established. Many of the founding fathers were born into families where slaves had been used for generations. Yet the founding of a nation based on the guarantees of life, liberty, and the pursuit of happiness caused a moral dilemma for many of the early presidents of the United States. None of the founding fathers who became president lived long enough to see the abolishment of slavery. However, it is the actions of many of them that led to the ultimate legal end of slavery in the United States.

George Washington

1st President of the United States
Presidential Term: April 30, 1789–March 4, 1797
Political Party: Independent Politician
Vice President: John Adams

George Washington was born on February 22, 1732, in Pope's Creek, Westmoreland County, Virginia. He did not receive any formal education after age 17. Washington was elected president in 1789 and received 69 votes in the Electoral College, while John Adams received 34 votes. John Adams became vice president as a result of his second-place finish in the Electoral College. Washington and Adams were unanimously reelected in 1792.

Washington became a slaveholder at age 11. When his father Augustine Washington died in 1743, he bequeathed his son the 280 acre family farm near Fredericksburg, Virginia, which included 10 slaves. As a young adult, Washington purchased at least eight more slaves in 1755. This purchase included four men, two women, and a child. Washington continued purchasing more slaves during his life. When he married Martha Dan-

As president, George Washington signed the Naturalization Act of 1790, which restricted citizenship to "any alien, being a free white person" who had been in the United States for two years. This law cemented the institution of slavery in the new republic. (Chaiba Media)

dridge Custis in 1759, his slaveholdings increased significantly. In 1757 Daniel Parke Custis, Martha's first husband, died without having a will. Martha received one-third of Custis's estate, which included slaves (Chernow 2010). She brought 84 slaves with her to Washington's estate when they were married. At the time of Washington's death, he and his wife had at least 317 enslaved people living and working on their estate at Mount Vernon, and he had been a slave owner for 56 years of his life (Thompson 2018). Under the law, neither George nor Martha could free the enslaved people gained through the Custis estate. Upon the death of George and Martha Washington, the law stipulated the more than 150 enslaved people would be returned to the Custis estate and be dispersed to the grandchildren.

Virginia law stipulated these slaves could not be freed without compensating the Custis heirs.

Washington used harsh physical and psychological treatment against his enslaved people, including whippings and threats of violence. He instituted a system of review in order to determine if slaves should receive corporal punishment. This system was usually aided by some form of verbal abuse or threat. Since the work of more highly skilled laborers and house servants was less physically demanding than that of field-workers, Washington could threaten to demote the former to more backbreaking fieldwork. The most severe threat involved telling enslaved individuals that he would sell them to a slave buyer on a distant plantation so they would not see their family members at Mount Vernon again. On numerous occasions this threat became reality as Washington wrecked families by selling away individuals. He also ignored laws that would allow his slaves to gain freedom if they were to escape to a nearby state.

There were several occasions when people held in slavery by Washington escaped. One of the most noted cases of an escaped slave from Washington's plantation was that of Ona Judge. In some accounts she was also called Oney Judge. Ona was described as light-skinned with freckles. As a child, she was a playmate with George Washington's grandchild, Nelly. Ona also was tasked with several chores such as churning butter, cooking food, making candles, and washing clothes. As was the customs and laws of the time, Ona did not receive any educational or religious training. She moved into the Washingtons' mansion when she was just nine years old and became a seamstress, just like her mother. Ona became Martha Washington's personal servant. Ona and a master chef named Hercules were two of the Washingtons' most prized slaves. In 1798 when George Washington headed to New York for his inauguration as president, he took a few slaves with him (Dunbar 2017). Ona was among those laborers who accompanied Washington to New York. When the nation's capital repositioned from New York to Philadelphia, Ona transitioned also.

Washington, like many other slave owners, was aware of slave residency laws enacted in Pennsylvania. If enslaved blacks stayed in Pennsylvania a certain period of time, they could be granted freedom. To obfuscate these residency laws in Pennsylvania, Washington made sure to rotate his slaves in and out of the state every six months to avoid establishing residency. They also would travel out of state to make sure residency could not be established. While staying in Philadelphia, Ona met and made friends with free blacks, and after meeting these individuals, she began to thirst for freedom also. In 1796 near the end of Washington's term in office, he was preparing to return to private life in his native Virginia. Ona planned her escape, and while the Washingtons were eating dinner she slipped out of the house and went into hiding. Washington placed an advertisement in the *Pennsylvania Gazette* offering $10 for her capture and return. Abolitionists aiding in Ona's escape searched the docks in Philadelphia and found Captain John Bowles who was willing to let her stow away on his ship. The ship was bound for Portsmouth, New Hampshire. Once in New Hampshire, Ona found refuge in the northeast coastal city. She made friends in the African American community in Portsmouth. Ona was spotted in Portsmouth, and this information was relayed back to Washington. He attempted to persuade some influential members in the white community of Portsmouth to return Ona. She had begun her new life, yet Washington refused to grant her freedom. He was deterred with the difficulty of capturing Ona. In 1798, Washington sent his nephew Burwell Bassett to bring Ona back to Mount Vernon (Dunbar 2017). By this time Ona had married John Staines and had become a mother. Washington spent at least three years trying to capture and force Ona Judge back into slavery.

Washington believed black people were too inferior to enlist for military service. In 1775 he issued a general ban barring the recruitment and enlistment of black men in the Continental Army. Enslaved blacks were not permitted to serve in the military because of the fear they would retaliate against those who had enslaved them. Washington barred the recruitment of black people even though black soldiers had fought in battles with white soldiers in Lexington, Concord, and Bunker Hill. In fact, one of the first soldiers to be killed at the Boston Massacre was Crispus Attucks. Eventually the policy barring black men from military service of any kind was reversed due to troop shortages among white men. Washington relented and allowed black men to serve in the Continental Army. In January 1776 he began allowing the use of free black men with prior military experience, and eventually this was extended to all free black men with or without prior military experience (Kennedy 2014). By 1777, Congress had authorized the use of all black men in the Continental Army to help fill quotas. During the Battle of Bunker Hill approximately 5 percent of the American soldiers were black. The Continental Army then offered a promise of freedom to all slaves who fought in the American Revolutionary War. The 1st Rhode Island Regiment raised the idea of using black men in the army. In February 1778, Rhode Island voted to allow the enlistment of every able-bodied Negro, mulatto, or Indian man slave (Kornblith 2010). The 1st Rhode Island Regiment was created to help defend Massachusetts and its coast from the British. The regiment was made up of about 200 men consisting of 140 black men and 60 white men and Native Americans.

As president of the United States, George Washington signed several pieces of legislation that helped cement the institution of slavery in the new republic and secured second-class status for blacks in America. The Naturalization Act of 1790 restricted citizenship to "any alien, being a free white person" who had been in the United States for two years. This wording specified citizenship for "a free white person" and excluded Africans (U.S. Congress 1790). Asians were also not eligible to be naturalized. The legislation did not address the citizenship status of non-white people born on American soil. The Naturalization Act of 1790 set the criteria for naturalization as two years of residency, proof of good moral character, and an oath to protect the U.S. Constitution. The Fugitive Slave Act of 1793 was federal law that allowed for the capture and return of any slave within the United States.

On February 12, 1793, George Washington signed the Fugitive Slave Act of 1793 into law. This law was enacted in response to a disagreement between Pennsylvania and Virginia over the return of a fugitive slave named John Davis. The law charged that each individual state had the responsibility to return fugitive slaves. The enactment of the law resulted in many free blacks being illegally captured and sold into slavery. The Fugitive Slave Act of 1793 was immediately met with heavy criticism. Many critics of the legislation argued that this authorized government-sanctioned kidnapping. The act allowed slave owners and their agents to search for slaves anywhere within the borders of free states. Under these draconian practices, all the slave hunters had to do was capture suspected slaves and take them to a judge. This was often done with scant or no evidence. If the owner was granted custody of the slave, they were allowed to return to their home state. Persons assisting slaves, hiding slaves, or withholding information about escaped slaves were fined. Section 3 of the Fugitive Slave Act of 1793 specially reads:

> And be it also enacted, That when a person held to labor in any of the United States, or in either of the Territories on the Northwest or South of the river Ohio, under the laws thereof, shall escape into any other part of the said States or Territory, the person to whom such labor or service may be due, his agent or attorney, is hereby empowered to seize or arrest such fugitive from labor, and to take him or her before any Judge of the Circuit or District Courts of the United States, residing or being within the State, or before any magistrate of a county, city, or town corporate, wherein such seizure or arrest shall be made, and upon proof to the satisfaction of such Judge or magistrate, either by oral testimony or affidavit taken before and certified by a magistrate of any such State or Territory, that the person so seized or arrested, doth, under the laws of the State or Territory from which he or she fled, owe service or labor to the person claiming him or her, it shall be the duty of such Judge or magistrate to give a certificate thereof to such claimant, his agent, or attorney, which shall be sufficient warrant for removing the said fugitive from labor to the State or Territory from which he or she fled. (U.S. Congress 1793)

Section 4 of the law reads:

> And be it further enacted, That any person who shall knowingly and willingly obstruct or hinder such claimant, his agent, or attorney, in so seizing or arresting such fugitive from labor, or shall rescue such fugitive from such claimant, his agent or attorney, when so arrested pursuant to the authority herein given and declared; or shall harbor or conceal such person after notice that he or she was a fugitive from labor, as aforesaid, shall, for either of the said offences, forfeit and pay the sum of five hundred dollars. Which penalty may be recovered by and for the benefit of such claimant, by action of debt, in any Court proper to try the same, saving moreover to the person claiming such labor or service his right of action for or on account of the said injuries, or either of them. (U.S. Congress 1793)

The Slave Trade Act of 1794 was a law passed by the U.S. Congress to limit America's involvement in the slave trade. The bill was introduced in the Third Congress and was passed in March 1794. Specifically, the law banned the transporting of slaves from the United States to any foreign places or country. Oddly, the legislation did not address the importation of slaves into the country and only addressed ships from other countries. Section 1 of the law stated the following:

Be it enacted by the Senate and House of Representatives of the United States of America in Congress assembled, That no citizen or citizens of the United States, or foreigner, or any other person coming into, or residing within the same, shall, for himself or any other person whatsoever, either as master, factor or owner, build, fit, equip, load or otherwise prepare any ship or vessel, within any port or place of said United States, nor shall cause any ship or vessel to sail from any port or place within same, for the purpose of carrying on any trade or traffic in slaves, to any foreign country; or for the purpose of procuring, from any foreign kingdom, place or country, the inhabitants of such kingdom, place or country, to be transported to any foreign country, port, or place whatever, to be sold or disposed of, as slaves: And if any ship or vessel shall be so fitted out, as aforesaid, for the said purposes, or shall be caused to sail, so as aforesaid, every ship or vessel, her tackle, furniture, apparel and other appurtenances, shall be forfeited to the United States; and shall be liable to be seized, prosecuted and condemned, in any of the circuit courts or district court for the district where said ship or vessel may be found and seized. (U.S. Congress 1793)

The law also called for stiff penalties, which included forfeiture of the ship and possibly a $2,000 fine being levied against the owner, and also called for the forfeiture of any slaves on board the ship and a fine of $200 per slave. Slavery would later be banned with the adoption of the Thirteenth Amendment in 1864, although discriminatory practices continued against blacks.

George Washington's last will and testament does not clarify his stance on the issue of slavery. There was contradictory language in the will regarding the freedom of his slaves upon his death. His will dictated an order to free his slaves upon his death but also stipulated they remain with Martha for as long as she wished. The only slave Martha immediately freed was William Lee. This was probably due to his heroics during the American Revolutionary War, and George Washington specified William Lee should be given his freedom immediately after Washington's death. Martha freed a few other slaves owned by her husband in 1801. Two reasons have emerged as to why she freed some slaves and not others. One theory holds that she freed some slaves whom she believed were conspiring to murder her. Another theory holds that she freed the slaves previously owned by her husband because she was convinced that freeing those slaves would adversely impact her children's inheritance. Martha Washington never freed any of the slaves she directly owned.

Bushrod Washington, future U.S. Supreme Court justice and nephew of George Washington, inherited the mansion at Mount Vernon and the 4,000 acres of the estate (Baptist 2014). Bushrod did not emancipate the enslaved people of Mount Vernon and in fact proved to be harsher than George Washington in his treatment of them.

FURTHER READING

Baptist, Edward. 2014. *The Half Has Never Been Told: Slavery and the Making of American Capitalism*. New York: Basic Books.

Chernow, Ron. 2010. *Washington: A Life.* New York: Penguin Group.

Dunbar, Erica Armstrong. 2017. *Never Caught: The Washingtons' Relentless Pursuit of Their Runaway Slave Ona Judge.* New York: Atria Publishing.

Ellis, Joseph. 2003. *His Excellency: George Washington.* New York: Vintage Books.

Flexner, Thomas James. 1975. *Washington: The Indispensable Man.* New York: Collins Books.

Kennedy, Frances H. 2014. *The American Revolution: A Historical Guidebook.* Oxford: Oxford University Press.

Kornblith, Gary J. 2010. *Slavery and Sectional Strife in the Early American Republic.* Landham, MD: Rowman and Littlefield, 2010.

Thompson, Mary V. 2018. "George Washington: The Only Unavoidable Subject of Regret." Mount Vernon, https://www.mountvernon.org/george-washington/slavery/the-only -unavoidable-subject-of-regret/.

John Adams

2nd President of the United States
Presidential Term: March 4, 1797–March 4, 1801
Political Party: Federalist
Vice President: Thomas Jefferson

John Adams was born on October 30, 1735, in Braintree, Massachusetts (now Quincy, Massachusetts). A portion of Braintree was renamed in honor of Adams's son John Quincy Adams, who later became the sixth president of the United States. John Adams was admitted to Harvard University at age 15. He served as vice president of the United States and was elected president of the United States in 1796 by defeating Thomas Jefferson by three votes, with a 71 to 68 margin in the voting in the Electoral College. Jefferson became vice president as a result. Adams became the first president of the United States to live in the White House. He was 61 years old when he became president and would lose his reelection bid to Jefferson in 1800. Adams and Jefferson would become bitter rivals. Of the first five presidents of the United States, Adams was the only president who did not own slaves.

Adams was a signatory on the Declaration of Independence and showed his antislavery sentiments throughout the crafting of the document. He stated, "There is one resolution I will not omit. Resolved that no Slaves be imported into any of the Thirteen Colonies" (Adams 1851). He was pleased with an earlier draft of the Declaration of Independence where Thomas Jefferson had a passage referencing slavery even though he knew the southern delegates would object to it and that it had little chance of surviving the revision process. During the Continental Congress, Adams argued against the southern position that blacks should not be included in the census for taxation purposes.

The petitioners condemned racism that prevented colonists from including Africans in conceptions of American liberty. A petition from 1777 submitted by eight black Bostonians, including Prince Hall, the founder of black Masonry, while repeating the language of earlier petitions, expressed "Astonishment that It have Never Bin Considered that Every Principle from which America has Acted in the Cours of their Unhappy Difficulties with Great Briton Pleads Stronger than A thousand arguments . . . that they may be Restored to the Enjoyments of that which is the Naturel Right of all men." A group of Connecticut blacks declared in their petition of 1779 that it was a "flagrant Injustice" that those "contending, in the Cause of Liberty," deny what "Reason and Revelation join to declare, that we are the Creatures of that God, who made of one Blood, and Kindred, all the Nations of the Earth" (Harding 1981, 43). Prince Hall's petition of 1777, which asked that all slaves be freed at the age of 21, generated an abolition bill in the General Court, but it too was allowed to die.

In 1777, Adams was approached by a few Massachusetts legislators seeking advice on how to gradually end slavery in the state. After the slave rebellions in Haiti in 1791, Adams and other whites were terribly afraid that if black people were freed, they would band together and kill white people. While Adams did not own slaves and espoused antislavery sentiments, he was reluctant to become a full-fledged abolitionist. In fact, he did not devote his political life to addressing slavery but did engage in discussions of slavery issues through his letters. He believed slavery should be incrementally eradicated and also believed that immediately eliminating slavery would be perilous and disrupt the progress of the country. He thought that a cautious, gradual, and intentional method of freeing enslaved people was best for a country that was just forming. While serving as a member of the Massachusetts legislature, Adams opposed legislation on the abolition of slavery in the state because he believed the issue was too divisive and this legislation should be proposed at a later date when the issue of slavery was not so divisive. He publicly spoke out against the institution of slavery. Adams stated, "Negro slavery is an evil of colossal magnitude." He also stated, "Slavery in this Country I have seen hanging over it like a black cloud for half a century" (Kaplan 1991). Adams continued to speak out against slavery in part because he feared there would be an insurgence where blacks would slaughter whites in mass acts of revenge like had taken place in Haiti: "I shudder when I think of the calamities which slavery is likely to produce in this country. You would think me mad if I were to describe my anticipations. . . . If the gangrene is not stopped I can see nothing but insurrection of the blacks against the whites" (Coffman 2012).

Adams and his wife Abigail Adams did not utilize slave labor in the White House or during their time prior to his presidency. Instead, they hired free blacks as domestics and laborers. After their time in the White House, they employed free white people as servants to assist them in their house. Abigail's father practiced slavery, but she refused to engage in these practices.

During the American Revolutionary War, Adams was opposed to using black soldiers in the Continental Army. He feared doing so would divide the young country and that southerners would withdraw their support for the Continental Army. Toward the latter part of his life, his views and comments against slavery became more poignant. In January 1801 after he left public life and had become somewhat of a recluse, he responded to a letter in a Quaker antislavery pamphlet. In his response letter, he professed his ardent opposition to slavery and reaffirmed the fact that he never owned a slave:

Although I have never Sought popularity by any animated Speeches or inflammatory publications against the Slavery of the Blacks, my opinion against it has always been known and my practice has been so conformable to my sentiment that I have always employed freemen both as Domisticks and Labourers, and never in my Life did I own a Slave. The Abolition of Slavery must be gradual and accomplished with much caution and Circumspection. (Scherr 2018)

In June 1819, Adams responded by letter to Robert Evans and reaffirmed his opposition to slavery, writing, "Every measure of prudence, therefore, ought to be assumed for the eventual total extirpation of slavery from the United States. . . . I have, throughout my whole life, held the practice of slavery in . . . abhorrence" (Adams 1819). Adams's view was inconsistent on slavery, and although he proclaimed his opposition to slavery, he did not publicly raise opposition to slavery at the Constitutional Convention. He later used the plight of Africans in America as a metaphor to illustrate England's oppression of people in the colonies.

In 1823, Adams wrote a letter to John Yates and stated the following:

Superstitions and tyrannical dominations oppress mankind all over the World[;] we cannot relieve them all we shall receive with open Arms. I hope, all who can seek refuge and protection under our mild Government, And if public charities could be applied to assist emigrants from Slavery to Liberty it would be more usefully employed than in some other enterprises of less promising beneficence—I hope nothing will be done which may embarrass our National Government, sound political prudence ought not to be banished from our deliberations. (Adams 1823)

Adams advocated an incremental gradual approach to ending slavery in the United States. His son John Quincy Adams would take a more aggressive approach to upending slavery in the United States.

FURTHER READING

Adams, John. 1819. "From John Adams to Robert J. Evans, 8 June 1819." Founders Online, National Archives, http://founders.archives.gov/documents/Adams/99-02-02-7148.

Adams, John. 1851. *The Works of John Adams, Second President of the United States*, Vol. 3. Boston: Bolles and Houghton Publishing.

Coffman, Steve. 2012. *Words of the Founding Fathers*. Jefferson, NC: McFarland.

Diggins, John Patrick. 2004. *The Portable John Adams, 1735–1826*. New York: Penguin Group.

Howe, John R. 1964. "John Adams's View of Slavery." *Journal of Negro History* 49, no. 3 (July): 201–206.

Kaplan, Sidney. 1991. *American Studies in Black and White: Selected Essays, 1949–1989*. Amherst: University of Massachusetts Press.

McCullough, David. 2002. *John Adams*. New York: Touchstone Publishing.

Scherr, Arthur. 2018. *John Adams, Slavery, and Race: Ideas, Politics, and Diplomacy in an Age of Crisis*. Santa Barbara, CA: ABC-CLIO.

Sheffelton, Frank. 2003. *The Letters of John and Abigail Adams.* New York: Penguin Group.

Wood, Gordon S. 2016. *John Adams: Writings from the New Nation 1784–1826.* New York: Library of America.

Thomas Jefferson

3rd President of the United States
Presidential Term: March 4, 1801–March 4, 1809
Political Party: Democratic-Republican
Vice President: Aaron Burr (1801–1805), George Clinton (1805–1809)

Thomas Jefferson was born on April 13, 1743, in Shadwell, Goochland County (now Albemarle County, Virginia). He was educated at the College of William & Mary. Jefferson was elected vice president in 1796 after coming in second in the Electoral College to John Adams and was then elected president of the United States in 1800 by defeating John Adams. Jefferson and his running mate Aaron Burr each received 73 electoral votes. This sent the election to the House of Representatives, where it was resolved by the 36th ballot. Jefferson was reelected in 1804. He was married to Martha Wayles Skelton in 1772, and they had six children together. Jefferson also fathered several children with his slave named Sally Hemings. He was a slave owner and at some intervals was one of the largest slave owners in Virginia. He established a 5,000-acre working plantation known as Monticello located near Charlottesville, Virginia. Monticello, along with the enslaved people who worked it, was an engine that fueled Jefferson's economic gains and wealth. Mulberry Row was a row of shanties on the Monticello properties that housed slaves. At the height of its operation, there were about 17 structures on Mulberry Row.

Jefferson's views on slavery, as with many things in his life, appeared to have been self-contradictory. Jefferson hated debt but carried large amounts

In 1776, Thomas Jefferson openly criticized slavery within an early draft of the Declaration of Independence. This paragraph was removed from the final draft of the document. (Library of Congress)

of personal debt because he was not a good financial manager. As a means of getting out of debt, he put young slave boys to work in the blacksmith's shop to make nails. Those who proved to be excellent, compliant, and skilled workers in the blacksmith's shop were trained for less backbreaking work as house slaves, skilled workers, or overseers on the plantation. When Jefferson was not being consumed by his personal debt, he was engaged in intellectual activities of his time. Among the many of his invention projects in which he attempted to find scientific methods that would increase the productivity of the boys in the blacksmith shop, Jefferson realized the production of nails was a way to create income and to pay some of his debtors.

In 1776 while Jefferson was writing a draft of the Declaration of Independence, he made a reference to slavery in a paragraph that was voted down by others and removed from the final draft of the document (Davis 1999). Slaveholders from Georgia and South Carolina fought vehemently to remove antislavery passages from the Declaration of Independence. It should be noted that some northerners also owned slaves and benefited and profited from slave labor. Some northern manufacturers profited from the cotton and other agricultural products produced in southern colonies. Later, Jefferson blamed delegates from Georgia and South Carolina for the removal of the passages from the final document. The paragraph removed from the Declaration of Independence read as follows:

> [King George III] has waged cruel war against human nature itself, violating its most sacred rights of life and liberty in the persons of a distant people who never offended him, captivating & carrying them into slavery in another hemisphere, or to incur miserable death in their transportation thither. This piratical warfare, the opprobrium of infidel powers, is the warfare of the Christian king of Great Britain. Determined to keep open a market where MEN should be bought and sold, he has prostituted his negative for suppressing every legislative attempt to prohibit or to restrain this execrable commerce: and that this assemblage of horrors might want no fact of distinguished die, he is now exciting those very people to rise in arms against us, and to purchase that liberty of which he has deprived them, by murdering the people upon whom he also obtruded them thus paying off former crimes committed against the liberties of one people, with crimes which he urges them to commit against the lives of another. (Library of Congress 2018)

Jefferson believed black people were inferior to white people. He questioned whether black people's low status was due to inherent inferiority or because of decades of degrading enslavement. When he wrote in the Declaration of Independence that "all men are created equal," he owned 175 slaves. Moreover, Jefferson advocated for scientific proof of blacks' inferiority as justification for their subordination. He also tried to make the case that blacks were less beautiful and were prone to more hypersexual activity. Jefferson believed that blacks held inferior faculties of reason and imagination. He noted that the differences between blacks and whites could be explained not by the different conditions in which they lived but by their nature that produced the difference. In 1790 as a wedding gift, Jefferson gave his newly married daughter and her husband 1,000 acres of land and 25 slaves (Feagin 2001).

In August 1791, black intellectual Benjamin Banneker wrote to Thomas Jefferson to refute that black people were inheritably intellectually inferior to white people and that any intellectual deficiencies could be attributed to the institution of slavery. He challenged Jefferson's views on slavery and black intelligence. Banneker, born to free parents in Maryland, was a celebrated astronomer, mathematician, and publisher of a popular almanac. He also surveyed the land where the nation's capital is located. Banneker's letter read:

SIR,

I AM fully sensible of the greatness of that freedom, which I take with you on the present occasion; a liberty which seemed to me scarcely allowable, when I reflected on that distinguished and dignified station in which you stand, and the almost general prejudice and prepossession, which is so prevalent in the world against those of my complexion.

I suppose it is a truth too well attested to you, to need a proof here, that we are a race of beings, who have long labored under the abuse and censure of the world; that we have long been looked upon with an eye of contempt; and that we have long been considered rather as brutish than human, and scarcely capable of mental endowments.

Sir, I hope I may safely admit, in consequence of that report which hath reached me, that you are a man far less inflexible in sentiments of this nature, than many others; that you are measurably friendly, and well disposed towards us; and that you are willing and ready to lend your aid and assistance to our relief, from those many distresses, and numerous calamities, to which we are reduced. Now Sir, if this is founded in truth, I apprehend you will embrace every opportunity, to eradicate that train of absurd and false ideas and opinions, which so generally prevails with respect to us; and that your sentiments are concurrent with mine, which are, that one universal Father hath given being to us all; and that he hath not only made us all of one flesh, but that he hath also, without partiality, afforded us all the same sensations and endowed us all with the same faculties; and that however variable we may be in society or religion, however diversified in situation or color, we are all of the same family, and stand in the same relation to him.

Sir, if these are sentiments of which you are fully persuaded, I hope you cannot but acknowledge, that it is the indispensable duty of those, who maintain for themselves the rights of human nature, and who possess the obligations of Christianity, to extend their power and influence to the relief of every part of the human race, from whatever burden or oppression they may unjustly labor under; and this, I apprehend, a full conviction of the truth and obligation of these principles should lead all to. Sir, I have long been convinced, that if your love for yourselves, and for those inestimable laws, which preserved to you the rights of human nature, was founded on sincerity, you could not but be solicitous, that every individual, of whatever rank or distinction, might with you equally enjoy the blessings thereof; neither could you rest satisfied short of the most active effusion of your exertions, in order to their promotion from any state of degradation, to which the unjustifiable cruelty and barbarism of men may have reduced them.

Sir, I freely and cheerfully acknowledge, that I am of the African race, and in that color which is natural to them of the deepest dye; and it is under a sense of the most profound gratitude to the Supreme Ruler of the Universe, that I now confess to you, that I am not under that state of tyrannical thraldom, and inhuman captivity, to which too many of my brethren are doomed, but that I have abundantly tasted of the fruition of those blessings, which proceed from that free and unequalled liberty with which you are favored; and which, I hope, you will willingly allow you have mercifully received, from the immediate hand of that Being, from whom proceedeth every good and perfect Gift.

Sir, suffer me to recall to your mind that time, in which the arms and tyranny of the British crown were exerted, with every powerful effort, in order to reduce you to a state of servitude: look back, I entreat you, on the variety of dangers to which you were exposed; reflect on that time, in which every human aid appeared unavailable, and in which even hope and fortitude wore the aspect of inability to the conflict, and you cannot but be led to a serious and grateful sense of your miraculous and providential preservation; you cannot but acknowledge, that the present freedom and tranquility which you enjoy you have mercifully received, and that it is the peculiar blessing of Heaven.

This, Sir, was a time when you clearly saw into the injustice of a state of slavery, and in which you had just apprehensions of the horrors of its condition. It was now that your abhorrence thereof was so excited, that you publicly held forth this true and invaluable doctrine, which is worthy to be recorded and remembered in all succeeding ages: "We hold these truths to be self-evident, that all men are created equal; that they are endowed by their Creator with certain unalienable rights, and that among these are, life, liberty, and the pursuit of happiness." Here was a time, in which your tender feelings for yourselves had engaged you thus to declare, you were then impressed with proper ideas of the great violation of liberty, and the free possession of those blessings, to which you were entitled by nature; but, Sir, how pitiable is it to reflect, that although you were so fully convinced of the benevolence of the Father of Mankind, and of his equal and impartial distribution of these rights and privileges, which he hath conferred upon them, that you should at the same time counteract his mercies, in detaining by fraud and violence so numerous a part of my brethren, under groaning captivity and cruel oppression, that you should at the same time be found guilty of that most criminal act, which you professedly detested in others, with respect to yourselves.

I suppose that your knowledge of the situation of my brethren, is too extensive to need a recital here; neither shall I presume to prescribe methods by which they may be relieved, otherwise than by recommending to you and all others, to wean yourselves from those narrow prejudices which you have imbibed with respect to them, and as Job proposed to his friends, "put your soul in their souls' stead;" thus shall your hearts be enlarged with kindness and benevolence towards them; and thus shall you need neither the direction of myself or others, in what manner to proceed herein. And now, Sir, although my sympathy and affection for my brethren hath caused my enlargement thus far, I ardently hope, that your candor and generosity will plead with you in my behalf, when I make known to you, that it was not originally my design; but having taken up my pen in order to direct to you, as a present, a copy of an Almanac, which I have calculated for the succeeding year, I was unexpectedly and unavoidably led thereto.

This calculation is the production of my arduous study, in this my advanced stage of life; for having long had unbounded desires to become acquainted with the secrets of nature, I have had to gratify my curiosity herein, through my own assiduous application to Astronomical Study, in which I need not recount to you the many difficulties and disadvantages, which I have had to encounter.

And although I had almost declined to make my calculation for the ensuing year, in consequence of that time which I had allotted therefor, being taken up at the Federal Territory, by the request of Mr. Andrew Ellicott, yet finding myself under several engagements to Printers of this state, to whom I had communicated my design, on my return to my place of residence, I industriously applied myself thereto, which I hope I have accomplished with correctness and accuracy; a copy of which I have taken the liberty to direct to you, and which I humbly request you will favorably receive; and although you may have the opportunity of perusing it after its publication, yet I choose to send it to you in manuscript previous thereto, that thereby you might not only have an earlier inspection, but that you might also view it in my own hand writing.

And now, Sir, I shall conclude, and subscribe myself, with the most profound respect, Your most obedient humble servant,

BENJAMIN BANNEKER.

Jefferson may have recognized and understood the evil nature of human slavery, but he failed to vehemently oppose it because he became so tied to the system and its economic benefits. He wrote the following in a 1782 book, *Notes on the State of Virginia:*

God who gave us life gave us liberty. Can the liberties of a nation be secure when we have removed a conviction that these liberties are the gift of God? Indeed I tremble for my country when I reflect that God is just, that his justice cannot sleep forever. Commerce between slave and master is despotism. Nothing is more certainly written in the book of fate that these people are to be free. Establish the law for educating the common people. This is the business of the state to effect and on a general plan.

Like his contemporary George Washington, Jefferson sometimes sold slaves away, breaking up families and friends. He was a proponent of humane punishment for white people while prescribing harsh punishments for slaves and free black people. It is estimated that over the course of Jefferson's lifetime, he owned 600 slaves. He engaged in the commerce of slavery, buying and selling slaves as a source of capital. He freed only three slaves, the children of Sally Hemings. Martha, the daughter of Thomas Jefferson, freed Sally Hemings.

FURTHER READING

Crawford, Alan Pell. 2009. *Twilight at Monticello: The Final Years of Thomas Jefferson.* New York: Random House.
Davis, David B. 1999. *The Problem of Slavery in the Age of Revolution, 1770–1823.* Oxford: Oxford University Press.
Ellis, Joseph J. 1998. *American Sphinx: The Character of Thomas Jefferson.* New York: Vintage Books.
Feagin, Joe. 2001. *Racist America: Roots, Current, Realities, and Future Reparations.* New York: Routledge.
Meacham, John. 2013. *Thomas Jefferson: The Art of Power.* New York: Random House.
Reed-Gordon, Annette. 1998. *Thomas Jefferson & Sally Hemings: An American Controversy.* Charlottesville: University of Virginia Press.
Reed-Gordon, Annette. 2009. *The Hemingses of Monticello: An American Family.* New York: Norton.
Wood, Gordon S. 2017. *Friends Divided: John Adams and Thomas Jefferson.* New York: Penguin Books.

James Madison Jr.

4th President of the United States
Presidential Term: March 4, 1809–March 4, 1817
Political Party: Democratic-Republican
Vice President: George Clinton (1809–1812), None (1812–1813),
Elbridge Gerry (1813–1814), None (1814–1817)

James Madison Jr. was born on March 16, 1751, in Port County, Virginia. He was educated at the College of New Jersey (now Princeton University). Madison was considered the master builder of the U.S. Constitution and served as secretary of state in Thomas Jefferson's administration. Madison and his wife, Dolley Dandridge Payne Todd Madison, did not have children from their marriage, but there were two sons from her previous marriage. Dolley grew up in a family with antislavery sentiments. In 1808, James Madison ran on the Republican ticket with George Clinton of New York. The Madison and Clinton ticket defeated the Federalist Party's ticket by a margin of 122 to 47. In 1812 Madison ran with Elbridge Gerry of Massachusetts as his running mate and won a second term as president, winning 128 electoral votes to 89. While some believed Madison was against slavery like many of the other founding fathers of the United States, his actions on slavery did not match his rhetoric. Madison had aspirational beliefs about the institution of slavery, but his actions were tepid against it. He was a slave owner, and it appears his approach to ending slavery was a gradual one. In 1785 during a session of the Virginia House of Delegates, Carter Harrison, who was proslavery, made a motion to repeal legislation introduced in 1782 that would make it permissible for slave owners to voluntarily free their slaves. Harrison's sponsored bill passed by only one vote. In the wake of this vote, Madison wrote a letter to his brother expressing his displeasure with the bill becoming law. Madison believed that passing this law would bring the issue of slavery to a head and motivate abolitionists to push harder for immediate freedom for all slaves.

Madison's racial attitude was exposed in a 1783 letter to his father. In the letter, Madison stated that he faced a quandary concerning Billey, an enslaved manservant who accompanied Madison when he traveled to serve in Congress in Philadelphia. Billey was once the servant of Madison's father and then became a servant to James Madison. James Madison wrote to his father that he could not bring Billey back to the family plantation at Montpelier. Billey had been exposed to the concepts of liberty and freedom, and Madison was afraid that he would motivate others to rise up and revolt against their slave masters and kill them. Also in the letter, Madison noted that he could not get angry with Billey because he was longing for the same freedoms and the right to liberty as every other human being, the same rights that had been fought for during the American Revolutionary War (Madison 1794).

Madison, along with several other founding fathers of the country, did not believe it was the opportune time to end the practice of slavery. Later in 1785 he supported a bill proposed by Jefferson that called for an incremental approach to ending slavery. The measure did not pass. In 1787, the drafting of the Constitution was at the forefront of building America. Tensions would loom between large states and small states over the issue of slavery, which became one of the central issues in the drafting of the Constitution. Madison had spent months brushing up on political theory before he went to the Constitutional Convention. He and the Virginia delegation arrived first at the convention and began to work on the Virginia Plan, a plan that favored large states. The New Jersey Plan was favorable to smaller states. Two key issues were prevalent in these plans. One issue was how slaves would be counted for representation. The other issue was the call for a stronger central government. The tension was broken by the Great Compromise, also called the Connecticut Plan. The Three-fifths Compromise settled the disagreement over how slaves would be counted. Northerners wanted to count slaves fully in the population count so the southern states would have to pay more taxes. Southerners wanted to count slaves as little as possible because this would reduce their tax contributions. After much debate at the Constitutional Convention, the delegates agreed that three-fifths of all slaves were to be counted for tax purposes based on population and for representation purposes in the House of Representatives. It was also agreed that Congress would limit the number of slaves brought into the country after 1808. The Three-fifths Compromise did not settle the issue of slavery and would be overturned by the Thirteenth and Fourteenth Amendments.

While Madison was in the U.S. Congress, Benjamin Franklin petitioned Congress to abolish slavery and the slave trade. Madison had another opportunity to squarely vote to overturn slavery in the United States but once again would not address the issue head-on. Madison caved to the congressional southern faction and failed to support Franklin's measure to end slavery in the United States and the country's participation in the slave trade. In response to Franklin's proposed measure, Madison stated the issue of slavery concerned him, and he hoped the government would work within the Constitution and find a gradual end to slavery. He knew slavery was wrong and a moral abomination. However, the economic boom of slavery and the wealth accumulated on his family's plantation would not allow him to do what was moral and honorable: end slavery outright. In a letter to Marquis de Lafayette, Madison referred to slavery as "an evil, moral, political, and economic, and a sad blot on our free country" but still did not call for the immediate end to slavery.

Madison proposed ending slavery by sending enslaved blacks to the "interior wilderness" or the "Coast of Africa" as a possible solution after their emancipation. He believed his proposal would be the best hope for the country to put the institution of slavery behind it. Madison believed that this was the best solution because racism was so pervasive in white society that it would be impossible for black people to integrate with whites. In 1789 he crafted a memorandum on an African colony for freed slaves. The memorandum was not a detailed plan but merely a blueprint without any practical method of being implemented. Specifically, the memorandum stated:

> Without enquiring into the practicability or the most proper means of establishing a Settlement of freed blacks on the Coast of Africa, it may be remarked as one motive to the benevolent experiment that if such an asylum was provided, it might prove a great encouragement to manumission in the Southern parts of the U.S. and even afford the best hope yet presented of putting an end to the slavery in which not less than 600,000 unhappy negroes are now involved.

> In all the Southern States of North America, the laws permit masters, under certain precautions to manumit their slaves. But the continuance of such a permission in some of the States is rendered precarious by the ill effects suffered from freedmen who retain the vices and habits of slaves. The same consideration becomes an objection with many humane masters against an exertion of their legal right of freeing their slaves. It is found in fact that neither the good of the Society, nor the happiness of the individuals restored to freedom is promoted by such a change in their condition.

> In order to render this change eligible as well to the Society as to the Slaves, it would be necessary that a complete incorporation of the latter into the former should result from the act of manumission. This is rendered impossible by the prejudices of the Whites, prejudices which proceeding principally from the difference of color must be considered as permanent and insuperable.

> It only remains then that some proper external receptacle be provided for the slaves who obtain their liberty. The interior wilderness of America, and the

Coast of Africa seem to present the most obvious alternative. The former is liable to great if not invincible objections. If the settlement were attempted at a considerable distance from the White frontier, it would be destroyed by the Savages who have a peculiar antipathy to the blacks: If the attempt were made in the neighborhood of the White Settlements, peace would not long be expected to remain between Societies, distinguished by such characteristic marks, and retaining the feelings inspired by their former relation of oppressors & oppressed. The result then is that an experiment for providing such an external establishment for the blacks as might induce the humanity of Masters, and by degrees both the humanity and policy of the governments, to forward the abolition of slavery in America, ought to be pursued on the Coast of Africa or in some other foreign situation. (Madison 1789)

In 1819, Madison proposed selling the lands gained in the Louisiana Purchase to buy and then free all slaves in the United States. Each parcel would go on sale for $3 an acre, and the proceeds would be used to eradicate slavery by purchasing slaves. Edward Coles, Madison's private secretary, was a fervent proponent of ending slavery. Coles constantly lobbied Madison to make a stronger public stand against slavery and vowed to free his slaves shortly after Madison left office in 1817. Making good on the promise, Coles prepared his former slaves by buying land in Illinois to start up farms for them. Madison appreciated Coles backing his convictions with deeds but still worried whether the former slaves were capable of caring for their own affairs. After his presidency, Madison laid out his philosophy on the future of people of African descent in America. He believed that the end of slavery should be gradual; that there should be an agreement between the slave and the master, with the master receiving compensation for loss of property; and that black people should be moved to a region not occupied by white people. Madison's thoughts of slavery continued to evolve over time, but he still withheld freedom from his slaves. In 1829 he wrote:

That peculiar feature in our community. . . . The colored part of our population. . . . It is due to justice; due to humanity; due to truth; to the sympathies of our mature; in fine, to our character as a people, both abroad and at home, that they should be considered, as much as possible, in the light of human beings, and not as mere property. As such they are acted upon by our laws, and have an interest in our laws. They may be considered as making a part, though a degraded part, of the families to which they belong. (Madison 1789)

Throughout his post-presidency, Madison spoke out against slavery and worked for antislavery movements. He later became president of the American Colonization Society, whose mission was to move free black people and former slaves to Liberia, Africa in 1833. In 2018 Liberia was one of the poorest countries in the world, ranking a mere 177th of 188 countries in the Human Development Index compiled by the United Nations Development Program. By the end of his life, Madison sold several of his farms; however, he did not sell his slaves and did not free his slaves in his will.

FURTHER READING

Brookhiser, Richard. 2013. *James Madison.* New York: Basic Books.

Cheney, Lynne. 2015. *James Madison: A Life Reconsidered.* New York: Penguin Books.

Feldman, Noah. 2017. *The Three Lives of James Madison: Genius, Partisan, President.* New York: Random House.

Hunt, Galliard. 1906. *The Writings of James Madison, 1819–1836: Volume IX.* New York: Putnam.

Ketcham, Ralph. 1990. *James Madison: A Biography.* Charlottesville: University of Virginia Press.

Madison, James. 1789. "Memorandum on an African Colony for Freed Slaves, [ca. 20 October] 1789." Founders Online, National Archives, http://founders.archives.gov /documents/Madison/01-12-02–0287.

Madison, James. 1794. "Letter: James Madison to James Madison Sr., 19 May 1794." Founders Online, https://founders.archives.gov.

James Monroe

5th President of the United States
Presidential Term: March 4, 1817–March 4, 1825
Political Party: Democratic-Republican
Vice President: Daniel D. Tompkins

James Monroe was born on April 28, 1758, in Westmoreland County, Virginia. He attended the College of William & Mary, fought in the Continental Army, and later studied law under Thomas Jefferson. He and his wife, Elizabeth Kortright Monroe, had three children. Elizabeth's father was a slave owner in New York. Monroe was elected president of the United States in 1816. His vice president was Daniel D. Tompkins of New York. The Monroe-Tompkins ticket received 183 Electoral College votes to 34 votes for the Federalists' ticket. Monroe and Tompkins were unanimously reelected to office with 231 electoral votes in 1820. Monroe was a Continental Army veteran who was wounded at the Battle of Trenton and later fought at the Battle of Monmouth. He served in the Virginia House of Delegates and was a member of the Virginia Convention to ratify the U.S. Constitution. He also served as U.S. senator from Virginia. From 1799 to 1802, Monroe served three consecutive terms as governor of Virginia. He also served as secretary of state and as secretary of war for President James Madison. James Monroe was the last revolutionary hero and founding father to assume the presidency. Under Monroe's time as president of the United States, the country purchased Florida from Spain for $5 million, and five states—Missouri, Illinois, Alabama, Mississippi, and Maine—were admitted to the union.

When Monroe was 16 years old his father died, and he inherited one male slave named Ralph. In 1793 Monroe purchased a plantation adjacent to Thomas Jefferson's Monticello plantation in Charlottesville, Virginia. Monroe owned 30 to 40 slaves who worked his plantation, called the Highlands (Gianetti and Williams 2017). During his lifetime he owned about 250 slaves. Like several other founding fathers of the United States, Monroe's view of slavery was contradictory. He called for an end to slavery and made reference to the evil associated with it but owned slaves and believed a quick end to slavery would disrupt the social order of society. During his first term as the governor of Virginia, he faced slave revolts. Gabriel, an enslaved man on Thomas Posser's plantation in Henrico County, located west of Richmond, Virginia, incited a slave revolt on a nearby plantation. The slaves aimed to rise up and kill all of the white people located in and around the area. There were exceptions made for white people who identified as Methodist, Quaker, or French (Egerton 1993). Gabriel made an error in his planning of the slave revolt. He erroneously thought that poor whites would join him and create a more democratic government in Virginia. Monroe used the militia to put down the insurrection. He had them protect the state capitol and all strategic locations in the city of Richmond. A rainstorm hit the area, which delayed the commencement of the uprising. This allowed the militia time to strategize and implement a plan of attack. The plan was devised using information they had received from slaves who turned out to be traitors.

A nearby slave patrol responded and captured and immediately killed 10 slaves. They also took five slaves into custody. In considering the punishment of those who participated in the revolt, Monroe wrote to Thomas Jefferson and expressed that he was leaning toward showing mercy to the insurgents. Monroe thought that issuing harsh punishments would cause further uprising and fuel a race war. As a result of the failed slave revolt, four of the five slaves were found guilty. The other captured slave pleaded benefit of clergy and received a lesser sentence (Egerton 1993). This slave was flogged and branded instead. Before the executions took place, Governor James Monroe checked to make sure of their identities and granted a pardon to one and allowed two to hang. The fourth died in jail from exposure to the cold. These events further helped influence and shape Monroe's view that eliminating slavery should be done gradually.

The 1810 census showed that James Monroe owned 49 slaves. As a possible solution to the practice of slavery in America, he supported colonization of enslaved Africans. In 1817 as the president of the American Colonization Society, Monroe discussed repatriating enslaved black people back to Africa. Liberia was established as a place where slaves captured on foreign ships could be freed and resettled. It was settled by former enslaved people from the Caribbean Islands and America (Tucker 2013). Monroe took several slaves with him to Washington, D.C., to serve at the White House from 1817 to 1825. In 1822, the first freed Africans from America arrived in Liberia. Joseph Jenkins Roberts, a freed slave from Virginia, became the first president. For 133 years Liberia was ruled by the True Whig Party, whose government and constitution were modeled after the U.S. Constitution. Liberia, located in the western portion of the continent of Africa, named its capital Monrovia as a tribute to Monroe. In 1847, Liberia declared its independence from the American Colonization Society.

The economic profitability of the Highlands and other plantations like it in Virginia took a nosedive. The land in the Piedmont areas of Virginia was not suitable for large-scale cotton crops. Cotton was solidified as the cash crop in the Deep South. In 1826, Monroe sold his house at the Highlands along with some of the slaves who lived on the plantation (Leibiger 2013). Slaves were a great economic commodity for Monroe, and he did not believe in losing his financial returns on his investments by letting them leave or escape without being compensated. Two of his slaves escaped in 1826. Like George Washington, Monroe launched an expansive search for the two escaped slaves and placed an advertisement in the local paper offering a reward for their return. In 1828 he sold land on the Highlands and many of the slaves to plantation owners in the Deep South. Many of Monroe's enslaved individuals were bought by Colonel Joseph White, a plantation owner in Jefferson County, Florida (Cunningham 2003).

President Monroe signed the Missouri Compromise. Missouri sought to become a part of America as a slave state. By 1818, the Missouri Territory had enough settlers to become a state. Because most of the settlers were from the South, it was probable that Missouri would enter as a slave state. Northerners argued that most of Missouri's landmass was both north and west of the southern boundary of the Ohio River and therefore Missouri should be admitted as a free state. The debate over the status of Missouri spanned two congressional sessions before Maine joined the union in 1820 as a free state, and Missouri was admitted as a slave state in 1821.

The Missouri Compromise is also known as the Compromise Bill of 1820. With the admission of Missouri and Maine to the union, the number of slave states and nonslave states was balanced at 12 each. This presented balance in the U.S. Senate, because both northern and southern state factions gained U.S. senators in this arrangement. Slavery was also forbidden north of the latitude line that ran along the southern border of Missouri to the Louisiana Territory. The Missouri Compromise helped create a total of 9 new states that would not allow slavery. Monroe was a strong supporter of states' rights and allowed Congress to take the lead on the slavery issue in the new territories through debates and the crafting of legislation. He believed it was his duty to make sure the legislation was constitutional. Like Jefferson, Monroe believed that eliminating slavery would dismantle and divide the young country and contribute to its ultimate demise.

During an annual message to Congress in December 1823, President Monroe gave a warning to Europe and all other nations to stay out of the affairs of the United States. This doctrine laid four basic points:

1. The United States would not get involved in European affairs.
2. The United States would not interfere with existing colonies in the Western Hemisphere.
3. No nation could form new colonies in the Western Hemisphere.
4. If a European nation attempted to colonize in the Western Hemisphere, the United States would view this as a hostile act.

These principles became known as the Monroe Doctrine and guided U.S. foreign policy for years to come.

After Monroe left the office of the presidency, he returned to his plantation but eventually moved to another plantation called Oak Hill in Aldie, Virginia, nine miles south of Leesburg, Virginia. He continued to oversee labor of the 77 slaves on his estate. Monroe fell off a horse in 1828, which limited his mobility. He then battled an extended illness but maintained his mental sharpness. In 1829, Monroe began writing his autobiography and actively defended the work of his administration against his critics. After his wife died in 1830, he moved in with his daughter and son-in-law. President James Monroe died on July 4, 1831.

FURTHER READING

Ammon, Harry. 1990. *James Monroe: The Quest for National Identity.* Charlottesville: University of Virginia Press.

Cunningham, Noble E. 2003. *Jefferson and Monroe: Constant Friendship and Respect.* Chapel Hill: Thomas Jefferson Foundation, University of North Carolina Press.

Egerton, Douglas. 1993. *Gabriel's Rebellion: The Virginia Slave Conspiracies of 1800 and 1802.* Chapel Hill: University of North Carolina Press.

Giannetti, Charlene, and Jai Williams. 2017. *Plantations of Virginia.* Lanham, MD: Rowman and Littlefield.

Hart, Gary. 2005. *James Monroe: The American Presidents Series; The 5th President, 1817–1825.* London: Macmillan.

Leiberger, Stuart A. 2013. *Comparison to James Madison and James Monroe.* Malden, MA: Wiley Blackwell.

Tucker, Spencer C. 2013. *American Civil War: The Definitive Encyclopedia and Document Collection.* Santa Barbara, CA: ABC-CLIO.

Unger, Harlow Giles. 2010. *The Last Founding Father: James Monroe and a Nation's Call to Greatness.* Boston: Da Capo.

John Quincy Adams

6th President of the United States
Presidential Term: March 4, 1825–March 4, 1829
Political Party: Federalist, Democratic-Republican, Whig
Vice President: John C. Calhoun

John Quincy Adams was born on July 11, 1767. His father was John Adams, the second president of the United States. The younger Adams was educated at Harvard University and married Louisa Catherine Adams in 1797. They had four children. Adams was elected president of the United States in 1824. In the 1824 presidential election, none of the presidential candidates received the majority of the vote. The election was decided by the House of Representatives during this time based on the candidate receiving the most electoral votes. Although Andrew Jackson received the most popular votes, Adams received the most electoral votes.

Adams was vehemently opposed to slavery in any form. In 1804 as a freshman senator, he claimed that the clause in the U.S. Constitution that counted slaves as three-fifths of a free person when calculating congressional representation created a "privileged order of slave-holding Lords, and a race of men degraded to a lower status, merely because they were not slave-holders. Every planter south of the Potomac has one vote for himself and three votes in effect for every five slaves he keeps in bondage; while a New England farmer, who contributes tenfold as much to the support of the government, has only a single vote" (Hecht and Speirs 1995). Adams was adamant in his stance against slavery.

In 1841, John Quincy Adams appeared before the U.S. Supreme Court to argue on behalf of African slaves who had revolted and seized a Spanish slave ship. This lawsuit is known as *United States v. Schooner Amistad* and is considered one of the most important legal cases involving slavery in the United States. The African slaves won the lawsuit and were declared free. (Library of Congress)

In 1820 Adams stated, "Slavery is the great and foul stain upon the North American Union. . . . A dissolution, at least temporary, of the Union, as now constituted, would now be certainly necessary. . . . The Union might then be reorganized on the fundamental principle of emancipation" (Waldstreicher and Mason 2016). After losing the presidency to Andrew Jackson in 1828, Adams was elected to the House of Representatives, where he served for 17 years representing Massachusetts. As a member of the House, Adams became very vocal in his opposition to slavery. He advocated his abolitionist views and framed his argument against slavery in moral terms. Adams would not allow his fellow House of Representative members to manipulate language in order to adopt unjust laws or shield their own hypocrisy when it came to the issue of slavery.

In 1837, Adams attempted to present to the House of Representatives a petition from free black women of Virginia regarding slavery. A fellow congressman attempted to smear the women, inferring they were "infamous" and prostitutes. Adams reminded them that many of these congressmen had either raped or engaged in sex acts with the women, so they had to look in the mirror if they were questioning the morality of these women. Adams also challenged the hypocrisy of southern preachers who preached that God sanctioned slavery and justified slavery through biblical scriptures.

In 1841, Adams appeared before the U.S. Supreme Court to argue on behalf of African slaves who had revolted and seized a Spanish slave ship, known as the *Amistad* case. In February 1839, Portuguese slave hunters kidnapped a large group of Africans from Sierra Leone. The slave hunters shipped the Africans to Havana, Cuba, which was a hub of the transatlantic slave trade. Two Spanish plantation owners, Pedro Montes and Jose Ruiz, purchased 53 of the Africans. The Africans were them loaded onto a ship named the *Amistad* that transported them to a plantation in the Caribbean Islands. On July 1, 1839, the Africans took control of the ship and killed the captain and the cook. They demanded that Montes and Ruiz sail to Africa. Montes and Ruiz actually steered the ship north, and the ship was seized off of the coast of New York by the USS *Washington*. The ship, its cargo, and all on board were taken to New London, Connecticut. While the slave owners were released from custody, the Africans were charged with murder and placed in jail. The murder charges were later dismissed, but the Africans were held in jail until the case could be heard in the district court. Various factions—plantation owners, the government of Spain, and the captain of USS *Washington*—each claimed rights to the Africans or compensation.

Northern abolitionists raised money to fund the defense of the Africans. They saw this cause as a viable way to bring to the world's attention the evils of the African slave trade. The case made it to the U.S. Supreme Court, and as a former U.S. president and descendant of American revolutionaries, Adams served as the primary lawyer for the Africans. Preparing for his appearance before the court, he requested papers from the lower courts one month before the proceedings opened. For nearly nine hours, the 73-year-old former president of the United States ardently defended the rights of the Africans. He argued the Africans had the right to be free on both legal and moral grounds. Adams strengthened his arguments by making references to and reminding the U.S. Supreme Court of treaties prohibiting the slave trade and to the Declaration of Independence.

The U.S. Supreme Court ruled in favor of the Africans. In its ruling, the Court cited the Africans had never been slaves, as they had been kidnapped and transported illegally. Thus, they were free individuals. Justice Joseph Story wrote and read the decision: "It was the ultimate right of all human beings in extreme cases to resist oppression, and to apply force against ruinous injustice." The opinion asserted the Africans had the right to resist "unlawful" slavery.

Adams's commitment to human equality and his continued opposition to slavery were cemented with his work on the *Amistad* case. His legacy was best summed up when he asked, "What can I do for the cause of God and man, for the progress of human emancipation, for the suppression of the African slave-trade?" (Meacham 2007). He continued: "Yet my conscience presses me on; let me but die upon the breach" (Waldstreicher and Mason 2016). John Quincy Adams died on February 23, 1848, at age 80 after suffering a series of strokes.

FURTHER READING

Hecht, Mary B., and Katherine E. Speirs. 1995. *John Quincy Adams: A Personal History of an Independent Man*. Newtown, CT: American Political Biography.

Kaplan, Fred. 2015. *John Quincy Adams: American Visionary*. New York: Harper Perennial.

Meacham, John. 2007. *American Gospel: God, the Founding Fathers, and the Making of a Nation*. New York: Random House.

Remini, Robert V. 2002. *John Quincy Adams: The American Presidents Series*. New York: Times Books.

Traub, James. 2016. *John Quincy Adams: Militant Spirit*. New York: Basic Books.

Unger, Harlow Giles. 2012. *John Quincy Adams*. Boston: Da Capo.

Waldstreicher, David, and Matthew Mason. 2016. *John Quincy Adams and the Politics of Slavery*. New York: Oxford University Press.

Andrew Jackson

7th President of the United States
Presidential Term: March 4, 1829–March 4, 1837
Political Party: Democratic-Republican
Vice President: John C. Calhoun (1829–1832), None (1832–1833),
Martin Van Buren (1833–1837)

Andrew Jackson was born in Waxhaw, South Carolina, in 1767. Jackson grew up poor in the Carolinas during the American Revolutionary War, but by the end of his life he was a wealthy man because he profited from slavery. He joined the military at age 13 and served as a courier, and by his late teens he understudied law for about two years and passed the bar. He became a noted young lawyer and set up practice in Tennessee. In 1791, Jackson married Rachel Donelson Robards. She was reportedly still married to someone else when she married Jackson, so they married again in 1794. They had no children. Jackson was the first man elected from Tennessee to the House of Representatives, and he also served briefly in the Senate.

Jackson ran for president of the United States in 1824 and captured 153,544 popular votes over John Quincy Adams of Massachusetts and Richard Rush of Pennsylvania. However, Jackson did not win the Electoral College vote, and the House of Representatives awarded the presidency to Adams. Jackson ran for president again in 1832 on the Democratic Party ticket with Martin Van Buren. This time, Jackson won the Electoral College with 219 votes. He was known as the people's president but was also a slave owner. Jackson carried the nickname "Old Hickory" because of his heroic exploits in the Battle of New Orleans during the War of 1812. Remembering the election with Adams, in his first annual message to Congress Jackson recommended eliminating the Electoral College. He also has

Andrew Jackson was the 7th president of the United States. He was an advocate of Manifest Destiny, a romanticized concept without definitive terms, which idealized Puritan exceptionalism and white European morality. President Jackson was a plantation and slave owner who believed he had a patriarchal responsibility to implement legislation that forced American Indians from their land. (Library of Congress)

the distinction of being the first president of the United States to have an assassination attempt on his life. In 1835, a man approached Jackson as he left a funeral at the Capitol building. Richard Lawrence shot at Jackson but missed. Jackson confronted his would-be assassin and clubbed him several times with his walking stick. Lawrence pulled out another gun but missed again and was then roughly ushered away.

Jackson owned multiple properties. He bought his Hermitage Plantation near Nashville, Tennessee, in 1804. Hermitage was a 1,000 acre plantation operated by enslaved individuals. He also operated a plantation in what is modern-day Mississippi and Alabama. Cotton was the cash crop of choice at Hermitage. Initially Jackson only owned 9 slaves but some 25 years later had accumulated over 100 slaves. He bought his first slave, a young woman, in 1788. By 1794, Jackson was fully immersed in slave buying and trading. Like previous slave-owning presidents, he placed advertisements for escaped slaves that promised additional compensation of an extra $10 and up to $300 for every 100 lashes given to an escapee by his slave catcher (Brown 2017).

Jackson was not above issuing corporal punishment to his slaves. In 1821 he threatened to beat one of his wife's slaves and delivered 50 lashes in public for disobedience. Jackson believed that slaves must be psychologically broken before you could treat them well. He also referred to abolitionists who believed slavery was wrong on religious grounds as monsters and vehemently spoke out against the antislavery movement. By the 1820s Jackson owned about 160 slaves. He sold his property in Alabama/Mississippi and moved the slaves and other assets to Hermitage Plantation (Miller and Smith 1997).

Like the other slaveholding presidents of the United States, Jackson was hypocritical on the issue of slavery. He used black people when it was expedient for him. While Jackson did not give his enslaved Africans any rights, when he was a general in the army in 1814 he called for black troops. He solicited black soldiers during the Battle of New Orleans against the British, and he went to nearby plantations to ask another slave owner to allow his slaves to join the army. Jackson wrapped his plea to the slaves in religious language and gave a faint promise of freedom if they defeated the British. He stressed the possibility of freedom to the older males but not the younger males. Jackson reasoned that if the older slaves were killed in battle, they were not as valuable as the younger slaves. Jackson solicited 500 slaves. With limited military combat training, the black troops performed valiantly and helped defeat the British troops. After the Battle of New Orleans, the slaves inquired about their promise of freedom. Jackson called their freedom assertion "very presumptuous" (Roberts 1858). James Roberts, a black man about 60 years old, became very vocal about the promise of freedom. White soldiers and residents of New Orleans heard the exchange between Roberts and Jackson. They suggested that Roberts should be executed because he spoke harshly to a white man. Roberts's anger was rooted in disappointment because he had accompanied his master to fight in the American Revolutionary War, and after his master was killed in battle he was sold to another slave owner and was separated from his wife and children.

Jackson believed Native Americans were uncultured savages and Africans were animalistic beasts. He continued to be a brutal, cruel, and violent slave owner who treated his slaves harshly. In August 1827 Jackson's overseer, Ira Walton, was determined to whip a slave (Cheathem 2014). A common practice of the time, Walton wanted to beat slaves in a public space to send a message to any potential unruly slaves. The slave fought back but was killed as a result of being stabbed with a knife.

Even though Jackson was a brutal slave master, his slaves lived in close proximity to the future president of the United States, some as close as 90 feet from the main house. From 1820 to 1821, Jackson increased his slaveholdings from 20 to 44 to support his financial security; Charles was among these slaves and became a trusted servant of Jackson. Charles became Jackson's personal slave and carriage driver. Jackson's plantation was based on agricultural production. As with other planters in the Deep South, cotton was the primary crop, but Jackson also farmed corn, hemp, and tobacco. Slaves also raised livestock, ran the cotton gin and grain mill on the property, and tended to Jackson's prize racehorses. By the time he was president of the United States, Jackson owned nearly 100 slaves; an estate inventory following Jackson's death counted 161 slaves (Miller and Smith 1997).

Northern abolitionists mailed antislavery tracts to residents of the South. Postmasters refused to deliver the tracts. Moreover, white southerners destroyed the tracts. Destroying mail is against federal law. Seizing the political moment, Jackson failed to punish those who destroyed the mail. Specifically, he responded as follows:

> I have read with sorrow and regret that such men live in our country—I might have said monsters—as to be guilty of the attempt to stir up amongst the South the horrors of a servile war—Could they be reached, they ought to be made to atone for this wicked attempt, with their lives. But we are the instruments of, and executors of the law; we have no power to prohibit anything from being transported in the mail that is authorized by the law. . . . [The postmaster should] deliver to no person those inflammatory papers, but those who are really subscribers for them. . . . The postmaster ought to take the names down, and have them exposed through the public journals as subscribers to this wicked plan of exciting the Negroes to insurrection and to massacre. (Paulus 2017)

Jackson believed westward expansion of the United States would keep the country a strong republic. This expansion came at the expense of Native American tribes, including their land being forcibly taken from them. Jackson supported these actions by signing the Indian Removal Act of 1830 that allowed the government to use force in evicting Native Americans from their land, including members of the Cherokee Nation who had supported the United States in the War of 1812. The Cherokees fought the new law in the U.S. Supreme Court and won the case. Furthermore, Jackson reacted to the abolitionist controversy in purely political terms. He wanted to secure the power for the Democratic Party, and politics became a part of his mode of operation as president of the United States. During Jackson's administration, Congress began adopting annual gag rules to keep discussion of abolition petitions off the House and Senate floors. Jackson did not free any of his enslaved people and was known as the champion of the common white man. In

2016 Donald J. Trump, the 45th president of the United States, hung a portrait of Andrew Jackson in the Oval Office.

FURTHER READING

Brands, H. W. 2006. *Andrew Jackson: His Life and Times.* New York: Anchor Books.

Brown, Deneen. 2017. "Hunting Down Runaway Slaves: The Cruel Ads of Andrew Jackson and the Master Class." *Washington Post,* May 1, https://www.washingtonpost .com/news/retropolis/wp/2017/04/11/hunting-down-runaway-slaves-the-cruel -ads-of-andrew-jackson-and-the-master-class/?noredirect=on&utm_term=.30 7593ea47f2.

Cheathem, Mark R. 2014. "Hannah, Andrew Jackson's Slave." *Humanities* 35, no. 2 (March–April), https://www.neh.gov/humanities/2014/marchapril/feature/hannah -andrew-jacksons-slave.

Inskeep, Steve. 2016. *Jacksonland: Jackson, President Andrew Jackson, Cherokee Chief, John Ross, and a Great American Land Grab.* New York: Penguin Books.

Meacham, John. 2009. *American Lion: Andrew Jackson in the White House.* New York: Random House Trade.

Miller, Randall, and John David Smith. 1997. *Dictionary of Afro-American Slavery.* Westport, CT: Praeger.

Opal, J. M. 2017. *Avenging the People: Andrew Jackson, the Rule of Law and the American Nation.* New York: Oxford University Press.

Paulus, Carl Lawrence. 2017. *The Slaveholding: Fear of Insurrection and the Coming of the Civil War.* Baton Rouge: Louisiana State University Press.

Remini, Robert V. 1990. *The Legacy of Andrew Jackson: Essays on Democracy, Indian Removal, and Slavery.* Baton Rouge: Louisiana State University Press.

Roberts, James. 1858. *The Narrative of James Roberts, a Soldier under Gen. Washington in the Revolutionary War, and Gen. Jackson at the Battle of New Orleans, in the War of 1812: "A Battle Which Cost Me a Limb, Some Blood and Almost My Life."* Chicago: Printed for the Author.

Maarten "Martin" Van Buren

8th President of the United States
Presidential Term: March 4, 1837–March 4, 1841
Political Party: Democratic-Republican Party, Free Soil Party
Vice President: Richard M. Johnson

Maarten "Martin" Van Buren was born on December 5, 1782, in Kinderhook, New York. He did not attend college, but at age 12 he began studying law as an apprentice to a village lawyer in New York. Van Buren completed a law internship and was admitted to the New York bar exam in 1803. His family owned six slaves in New York. As a young man, Van Buren outright owned one slave named Tom. In 1814, Tom escaped but was captured eight years later in Worcester, Massachusetts. Van Buren offered slave catchers $50 if Tom could be returned unharmed and without violence. Slave catchers could not make assurances against violence, and therefore Tom remained free. Like previous U.S. presidents who owned slaves, Van Buren's stance on slavery appeared contradictory.

In 1807 Van Buren married Hannah Hoes, and they had five children. Hannah was a cousin and childhood sweetheart of Van Buren. He was a stalwart in New York politics, having served in the New York State Senate in 1812 and as the New York attorney general in 1816. Van Buren was also one of the key founders of the Democratic Party and helped push the party's prominence in New York. He served as secretary of state in President Andrew Johnson's administration.

In 1836, Van Buren ran for president on the Democratic Party ticket with Richard Mentor Johnson as his running mate. Their ticket ran against three Whig Party candidates. Van Buren received 764,198 popular votes and 170 Electoral College votes, and the Whig Party candidates received almost as many popular votes. Van Buren defeated Daniel Webster, William Henry Harrison, and H. L. White, who were anti–Andrew Jackson candidates. Van Buren's popularity was based on his affiliation with President Jackson. Van Buren was a smooth-talking politician whose supporters deemed him "the Magician." His opponents called him "Martin Van Ruin." Van Buren did not want slavery abolished in the United States. In his inaugural address on March 4, 1837, he further elaborated on the issue of slavery:

> I must go into the presidential chair the inflexible and uncompromising opponent of every attempt on the part of Congress to abolish slavery in the District of Columbia against the wishes of the slaveholding states and also with a determination equally decided to resist the slightest interference with it in the states where it exists. (Richardson 1909)

Van Buren is noted for several political accomplishments. He was the founder of the two-party system in the U.S. political system, the party caucus, the nominating convention, the patronage system, and the process to successfully market a candidate for political positions. He had an impressive political career in the federal government and held several cabinet-level positions. Van Buren was a key political ally of Andrew Jackson and was instrumental in getting him elected as president of the United States. In return for his loyalty, Jackson appointed Van Buren the 10th secretary of state. He became one of Jackson's most trusted advisers and a chief political ally. Van Buren was nominated and elected vice president on the Jackson ticket in 1832, and Jackson endorsed Van Buren for president in 1835.

Van Buren could be a ruthless politician who said and did what was politically expedient for him and his political allies. In 1821 at a convention to create a new constitution for New York, a proposal forbidding free black people the right to vote came forward. Free black people had been able to vote in New York prior to this proposed amendment. While Van Buren opposed this proposed amendment, he did support an amendment that allowed free blacks who paid $250 to vote. He also urged New York's members of Congress to vote against admitting Missouri as a slave state.

Van Buren considered slavery cruel and immoral, yet his family had owned slaves. He opposed the use of cheap black labor because he saw it as unfair competition with white workers. Van Buren called slavery "an evil of first magnitude" but went silent on the matter while running for president. He used dog-whistle politics and stated that he would not interfere with local politics, giving slave owners the message that he would not address the issue of slavery as president of the United States. He used the U.S. Constitution as a mask so that he would not have to address the issue of slavery while he held office. Van Buren was opposed to the advancement of slavery into new territory but supported it where it already existed.

Van Buren addressed the issue of slavery in his presidential inaugural speech. His comments further clarified his stance on slavery and took this issue head-on: "Perceiving, before my election, the deep interest this subject was beginning to excite, I believed it a solemn duty fully to make known my sentiments in regard to it" (Williams 1846). Newspapers published articles and editorials about Van Buren's address in which he recognized the issue of slavery as a divisive one on the national agenda. Van Buren stated, "The last, perhaps the greatest, of the prominent sources of discord and disaster supposed to lurk in our political condition, was the institution of domestic slavery" (Kinealy 2016). Van Buren referred to slaveholders as "sincere friends to the happiness of mankind," and he described abolition as a vicious device "of evil disposed persons to disturb the harmony of our happy Union."

Van Buren was so opposed to abolishing the institution of slavery that he published an antiabolition pamphlet. Two weeks into his presidential term an economic depression hit the United States. As a wave of panic hit the country, banks refused to pay off their depositors, and the money market collapsed. In 1840, the U.S. financial markets took another economic downturn, sealing his fate as a one-term president. Van Buren lost to William Henry Harrison in the presidential election of 1840. In 1848 Van Buren was nominated for president by the Free Soil Party but was soundly defeated.

Toward the end of his life, Van Buren praised the *Dred Scott* decision in which the U.S. Supreme Court denied citizenship to African Americans: "I have read all the opinions given by the judges in the *Dred Scott* case with care, and . . . I am now convinced that the sense in which the word 'citizen' was used by those who framed and ratified the Federal Constitution was not intended to embrace the African race" (Van Buren 1867).

FURTHER READING

Curtis, James C. 1970. *Fox at Bay: Martin Van Buren and the Presidency, 1837–1841.* Lexington: University of Kentucky Press.

Kinealy, Christine. 2016. *Daniel O'Connell and the Anti-Slavery Movement: The Saddest People the Sun Sees.* New York: Routledge.

Mushkat, Jerome. 1997. *Martin Van Buren: Law, Politics, and the Shaping of Republican Ideology.* DeKalb: Northern Illinois University Press.

Niven, John. 1983. *Martin Van Buren: The Romantic Age of American Politics.* New York: Oxford University Press.

Richardson, James D. 1909. *A Compilation of the Messages and Papers of the Presidents: 1789–1902,* Vol. 3. Bureau of the National Literature and Art.

Sibley, Joel H. 2002. *Martin Van Buren and the Emergence of American Popular Politics.* New York: Rowman and Littlefield.

Van Buren, Martin. 1867. *Inquiry into the Origin of Political Parties in the United States.* New York: Hurd and Houghton Publishing.

Widmer, Ted. 2005. *Martin Van Buren: The American Presidents Series; The 8th President, 1837–1841.* New York: Times Books.

Williams, Edwin. 1846. *The Addresses and Messages of the Presidents of the United States,* Vol. 2. New York: Edward Walker Publishing.

William Henry Harrison Sr.

9th President of the United States
Presidential Term: March 4, 1841–April 4, 1841
Political Party: Whig, Democratic-Republican
Vice President: John Tyler

William Henry Harrison Sr. was born on February 9, 1773, on the Berkeley Plantation in Charles County, Virginia. Harrison's father was an original signatory on the Declaration of Independence. Both Harrison's father, Benjamin Harrison, and his grandfather, also named Benjamin Harrison, were slaveholders. Harrison's father served as governor of Virginia for three terms. He forced William to go to college at Hampden-Sydney College for three years. At his father's strong urging, William Harrison studied medicine in Richmond, Virginia, and then at the University of Pennsylvania in Philadelphia, but Harrison joined the military before completing medical school.

In 1840, as a presidential candidate in need of southern votes, William Henry Harrison flip-flopped on the issue of slavery. He claimed he had never been a member of an abolitionist society, and the organization he joined was merely a "humane society." (Chaiba Media)

After his father died in 1791, Harrison began to carve out his own destiny. He left the University of Pennsylvania, joined the military, and fought in the battles against Native Americans in the Northwest Territory. After resigning from the U.S. Army in 1798, he became secretary of the Northwest Territory. He was nicknamed "Old Tippecanoe" because of his leadership at the Battle of Tippecanoe. This nickname would become a part of his catchy presidential campaign slogan of 1840, "Tippecanoe and Tyler Too," that helped him win the presidency. Harrison was a slave owner with approximately 11 slaves and forced these enslaved people into a system of indentured servitude. There was little difference between slavery and indentured servitude.

In 1795 Harrison married Anna Tuthill Symmes. They had eight children together, and his wife had two children from a previous marriage. Harrison ran for president in 1836 and lost to Martin Van Buren but was elected president of the United States in 1840, with 1,275,016 popular votes and 234 votes in the Electoral College. Martin Van Buren received 1,127,781 popular votes and only 60 electoral votes. When Harrison won the presidency in 1840, 78 percent of the eligible males turned out to vote, which was a new high for the country. At age 68, Harrison was the oldest person elected president until Ronald W. Reagan in 1980 and Donald J. Trump in 2016.

Harrison's foray into politics began when he was appointed secretary of the Northwest Territory in 1798. He was also representative of this territory in the U.S. Congress from 1799 to 1801. President John Adams appointed him governor of the Indiana Territory in 1801, where Harrison served for 12 years. This territory included what is modern-day Indiana, Illinois, Wisconsin, and Michigan. The Northwest Ordinance banned slavery north of the Ohio River, and Harrison did not permit slavery outright in the territory. However, indentured servitude became the method by which black and poor white labor was still exploited.

In 1805, the Indiana Assembly passed an act allowing slave owners to convert to indenture servitude. Under this law, blacks under age 15 could be kept in service until age 35. As Indiana's governor, Harrison signed the bill into law. The Indiana Territory simply adopted the indentured servitude codes that the State of Virginia had already been practicing. In 1809, Indiana separated from the rest of the territory; the state legislature not only banned slavery but also banned indentured servitude. Harrison also signed the bill into law. During this time, the Indiana Assembly also ended land ownership as a requirement for white men to vote. In 1812, President James Madison commissioned Harrison a brigadier general in the U.S. Army. Harrison became the top commander in the Northwest Territory. After his military career ended when he resigned in 1814, Harrison, a christened war hero, made his home in Ohio and returned to politics. He represented Ohio in the U.S. House of Representatives from 1816 to 1819, served as a U.S. senator from 1825 to 1828, and held an ambassadorship to Colombia from 1828 to 1829.

In 1820 Harrison, as a member of the Ohio Senate, voted for a measure that would allow petty thieves to be sold into terms of service if they were unable to pay their fines. During a congressional campaign in 1822, Harrison told Ohio voters that he opposed slavery and was a member of the Abolition Society. However, he argued against equal rights for former slaves in 1835. In 1836, Harrison ran as a Whig Party candidate against Martin Van Buren, who was the vice president under Andrew Jackson. During this bid for the highest office in the land, Harrison declared Congress had no power to eliminate slavery in the states or in the District of Columbia. Harrison lost the election. Four years later he was prepared for a rematch. This time he reinvented himself. He emphasized his decorated military career and painted himself as a commoner in an effort to appeal to the populace. In 1840 as a presidential candidate and needing to secure southern votes, he flip-flopped on the issue of slavery. He claimed he never had been a member of an abolitionist society and that the organization he joined was merely a "humane society."

After one of the longest inaugural speeches in history and given in a freezing rain, Harrison developed pneumonia, and after one month into his presidency he died. He was the first president of the United States to die in office.

FURTHER READING

Collins, Gail. 2012. *William Henry Harrison: The American Presidents Series.* New York: Times Books Henry Holt.

Crapol, Edward P. 2002. *John Tyler, the Accidental President.* Chapel Hill: University of North Carolina Press.

Owens, Robert M. 2011. *Mr. Jefferson's Hammer: William Henry Harrison and the Origins of American Indian Policy.* Norman: University of Oklahoma Press.

Civil War Era

For years to come, U.S. presidents would struggle to resolve the contradiction between the country's democratic ideals and the realities of slavery in the United States. Like many of the founders, U.S. presidents failed to adequately deal with the issue of slavery in the United States. As the black population steadily increased in the United States, slavery became a paramount issue of the country's domestic and foreign agenda. Between 1790 and 1860 the slave population grew to include 3,953,760, while there were also nearly 500,000 free blacks living in the United States. Frederick Douglass posited slavery as America's great sin and shame. By 1862, slavery had been outlawed in the District of Columbia and all current and future U.S. territories.

In 1861, several southern states seceded from the United States and formed the Confederate States of America in an attempt to save the institution of slavery. As a result of this rupture between proslavery and nonslavery states, the United States erupted into civil war. Initially, the Confederacy began with delegates voting at the secession convention in Montgomery, Alabama, in February 1861. The Confederacy was formed when seven states (South Carolina, Mississippi, Florida, Alabama, Georgia, Louisiana, and Texas) originally left the United States to form their own country. Later four more states (Virginia, Arkansas, Tennessee, and North Carolina) joined the Confederate States. Missouri and Kentucky were accepted as members of the Confederacy but never declared secession. On February 18, 1861, at the state capitol in Montgomery, Alabama, Jefferson Davis took the oath of office as president of the Confederate States of America. The Confederate capital would move to Richmond, Virginia, in May 1861 and later to Danville, Virginia, in 1865. On April 12, 1861, Confederate troops attacked the Union at Fort Sumter in the harbor of Charleston, South Carolina. This was the beginning of the United States of America being a severed nation, with Americans joining the Union and Confederate militaries to war against each other. Black men had a long history of serving in the military. They had served in the army and navy during the American Revolution. Black men had also served in the War of 1812. Very few black men if any served in the Mexican-American War, as they were not permitted to enlist because of a 1792 law that barred black men from fighting in the U.S. Army.

Many of the U.S. presidents feared blacks serving in the military. President Abraham Lincoln feared that using black troops in the war would cause border states such as Maryland, Kentucky, and Missouri to secede and become a part of the Confederacy. While black men served in the American Civil War for both the Union and the Confederates, most served in the Union forces in support positions. The Union Army consisted of free black men and runaway slaves who joined the military to fight the Confederacy. By early 1865 the South, wanting to turn the tide from defeat, began to allow blacks to enlist, but very few took advantage of this opportunity.

On April 9, 1865, General Robert E. Lee surrendered to Ulysses S. Grant at Appomattox, Virginia, and brought the four-year war to an end. Days earlier Lee had abandoned Petersburg, Virginia, and the Confederate capital of Richmond, Virginia. Many troops continued to fight for several months after the official surrender because of the slow and limited means of communication at the time. After the Confederacy's surrender in 1865, tensions loomed in southern states as occupied troops provided protection for formerly enslaved blacks in the South. Congress passed the Thirteenth Amendment, which ended slavery. President Lincoln was assassinated before the amendment was ratified and thus was not there to guide the country through the Reconstruction period. With the Fourteenth Amendment in 1868, black people were guaranteed equal protection under the law and erased the U.S. Supreme Court's decision in the *Dred Scott* case.

In 1870 Congress passed the Fifteenth Amendment, which guaranteed all citizens of the United States the right to vote. Even with passage of the Thirteenth Amendment, the Fourteenth Amendment, and the Fifteenth Amendment to the U.S. Constitution, targeted racial violence persisted against black people during the Reconstruction period, and postwar intervention ended less than 15 years after the conclusion of the Civil War. The U.S. Congress established the Bureau of Refugees, Freedmen, and Abandoned Lands, also known as the Freedmen's Bureau, to provide support for black people in regard to justice, labor, education, medical aid, and political education in the southern states.

John Tyler

10th President of the United States
Presidential Term: April 4, 1841–March 4, 1845
Political Party: Whig, Democratic-Republican
Vice President: None

John Tyler was born on March 29, 1790, on the family plantation in Charles City County, Virginia. Tyler graduated from the College of William & Mary with a bachelor of arts in 1807. He then studied law with private instructors. Tyler had a vaunted political career, serving in several capacities on the state and federal levels. His political career began in 1811, when he was elected to the Virginia legislature at age 21. He served in the state legislature from 1811 to 1816 and was a member of the U.S. House of Representatives from 1817 to 1821. He returned and served a second stint in the state legislature from 1823 to 1825. Tyler served as governor of Virginia from 1825 to 1827 and in the U.S. Senate from 1827 to 1836. He married Letitia Christian in 1813, and they had eight children together. His wife died after suffering a stroke, making her the first president's wife to die while her husband was still president. Tyler also became the first U.S. president to marry while in office. He married a second time in 1844 to Julia Gardiner. Gardiner was age 24, and Tyler was age 54. They had seven children together.

Tyler assumed the presidency after the death of William Henry Harrison and was a "States' Rights Whig." Tyler was from a slaveholding family and was a

John Tyler was the 10th president of the United States. He was the first vice president to become president following the death of the incumbent, when William Henry Harrison died 31 days into his term. An advocate for states' rights, Tyler supported the secession of southern states to protect the institution of slavery and as a means of avoiding a civil war. (Library of Congress)

staunch supporter of slavery. He was elected to the U.S. presidency in 1841. His policies increased the gulf between the slaveholding and nonslaveholding states, which further propelled the country closer to civil war over the issue of slavery. As a member of Congress, Tyler argued that Congress had no constitutional right to pass a law prohibiting slavery in the territories of the United States. He erroneously rationalized that the expansion of slavery to the territories would improve the condition of slaves because of the increased demand for labor. He also believed free black people should not be allowed the become citizens. Tyler viewed black people simply as commodities. When he was cash-strapped, he sold slaves and rented slaves out to people. To financially support his move to Washington, D.C., he sold a female slave. Tyler had an intense hatred for abolitionists, often referring to abolitionist literature and pamphlets as "evil." As for those who subscribed to an abolitionist philosophy, he said they "deserved the deepest curses of the patriot, for having put in jeopardy the noblest and fairest fabric of government the world ever saw" (Tooley 2015).

In 1838 Tyler was elected president of the Virginia Colonization Society, whose mission was to relocate black people back to Africa. Tyler stated, "The Negro is from Africa, a barbarian, ignorant, idolatrous; he is restored, civilized, and Christian" (Tyler 1884). In 1841 Tyler's entire cabinet resigned, except for Secretary of

State Daniel Webster, because his policies went against the party's platform and also because of his vetoes against the Third Bank of the United States. He operated the rest of his presidency without the support of his political party. In 1844, Tyler made a brief attempt to run as a third-party candidate but withdrew from the race due to a lack of support.

During his post-presidency, Tyler moved to a plantation between Williamsburg and Richmond, Virginia. He chaired a peace conference in Washington, D.C., with the goal of preventing the country from going into a civil war and brokering a compromise between the two factions. Representatives from the northern states and the southern states discussed domestic issues; however, they were unable to reach a compromise and prevent the fracture of the country. After this failed peace conference, Tyler openly supported the Confederacy and lobbied others from Virginia to take his position in supporting the interests of the planters and the institution of slavery. He served as a delegate to the Virginia Secession Convention. Virginia seceded from the Union in 1861, and Tyler was elected to the Confederate Congress. Tyler died in 1862 before he could be sworn in to take his seat in the Confederate Congress.

FURTHER READING

Chitwood, Oliver. 1990. *John Tyler, Champion of the Old South.* Newton, CT: American Political Biography.

Crapol, Edward. 2006. *John Tyler, The Accidental President.* Chapel Hill: University of North Carolina Press.

May, Gary. 2008. *John Tyler, The American Presidents Series; The 10th President, 1841–1845.* New York: Henry Holt.

Monroe, Dan. 2003. *The Republican Vision of John Tyler.* College Station: Texas A&M University Press.

Peterson, Norma Lois. 1989. *The Presidencies of William Henry Harrison and John Tyler.* Lawrence: University Press of Kansas.

Skaggs, David Curtis. 2014. *William Henry Harrison and the Conquest of the Ohio Country: Frontier Fighting in the War of 1812.* Baltimore: Johns Hopkins University Press.

Tooley, Mark. 2015. *The Peace That Almost Was: The Forgotten Story of the 1861 Washington Peace Conference and the Final Attempt to Avert the Civil War.* New York: Nelson Books.

Tyler, Lyon Gardnier. 1884. *The Letters and Times of the Tylers,* Vol. 1. Richmond, VA: Whittet and Shepperson Publishing.

James Knox Polk

11th President of the United States
Presidential Term: March 4, 1845–March 4, 1849
Political Party: Democratic
Vice President: George M. Dallas

James Knox Polk was born in Mecklenburg County, North Carolina, the oldest of 10 children. During his adolescent years his family moved to Columbia, Tennessee. Polk did not attend school until he was 17 years old, and after 2 years of education he enrolled at the University of North Carolina, where he received a bachelor of arts with honors, studying mathematics and the classics, in 1818. In 1824 Polk married Sarah Childress; they did not have any children. He practiced law and later entered politics, having served in the legislature in Tennessee and later in the U.S. Congress. Polk befriended Andrew Jackson and later served as the governor of Tennessee. In 1835 Polk was elected to the U.S. House of Representatives, where he served seven terms. From 1835 to 1839, he was the Speaker of the House. Polk is the only Speaker of the House who also served as president of the United States. He favored states' rights and supported the policies of fellow Tennessean President Andrew Jackson.

Polk was a slave owner his entire life. His father bequeathed 8,000 acres of land and divided up his 53 slaves among his widow and children at his death. Polk took charge of 20 of these slaves and inherited others after his brother's death. Polk was a brutal slave owner, and his slaves ran away to nearby plantations claiming mistreatment. Polk believed in corporal punishment for slaves and that whippings deterred any kind of insolence among other slaves. He stated "A slave dreads the punishment of stripes more than he does in imprisonment and that description of punishment has a beneficial effect upon his fellow slaves" (Sellers 1957). In 1831, Polk became an absentee cotton planter. He sent slaves and a few overseers to clear plantation land near Somerville, Tennessee, that his father had left him. Polk sold his Somerville plantation four years later, and he and his brother-in-law bought 920 acres of land and operated a cotton plantation near Coffeeville, Mississippi. Polk ran this plantation for the rest of his life, eventually becoming the sole owner.

Polk rarely sold slaves, viewing them as a commodity, and when he became president, he bought more. He made a provision in his will that his slaves were to be freed after the death of his wife. The Emancipation Proclamation and the Thirteenth Amendment mandated freedom for slaves. This was well before the death of Polk's wife, who died in 1891.

In 1844, Polk was elected on the Democratic ticket with George Mifflin Dallas of Pennsylvania, with 170 Electoral College votes and 1,337,243 popular votes. The Whig Party chose the mocking campaign slogan "Who Is James Polk?" in an attempt to point to the fact that Polk was a virtual unknown in national politics. During his campaign for the presidency, he promised voters that if he was elected he would pursue expansion of the country's borders westward. Polk also favored statehood for Texas and the Oregon Territory. He had an ambitious presidential agenda. Under Polk's presidency, the United States expanded in size, settling a boundary dispute with England over the Oregon Territory that consisted of Washington, Oregon, Idaho, and portions of Montana and Wyoming. Through the Mexican-American War, the country acquired California and a large portion of the Southwest. Mexico gave up on its claim to Texas, and the United States purchased California, Arizona, Colorado, Nevada, New Mexico, and Utah. Under Polk's administration, America expanded to the Pacific Ocean. The administration lowered tariffs and established an independent federal treasury through the Independent Treasury Act of 1846. Even with the success of expanding the country, the fissure between the slaveholding and nonslaveholding states over the expansion of slavery deepened during Polk's presidency.

In 1846, Democratic congressman David Wilmot of Pennsylvania introduced an amendment to an appropriations bill that reinserted the issue of slavery to the forefront of debate. Wilmot's amendment asserted that slaves would not be permitted in any of the property acquired from Mexico. Wilmot's amendment passed the U.S. House of Representatives but failed in the U.S. Senate. The debate over the amendment was contentious and exposed fractures in the Whig Party and the Democratic Party. This also withered southern support for Polk and gave way to southern politicians developing the "southern rights position," which proposed slavery anywhere in the territories including the modern-day states of Washington, Oregon, Idaho, Nevada, and the northern portion of California.

Abolitionists called Polk an instrument of the slave owners. He believed abolitionists were "fanatical and wicked agitators." In 1848, Polk questioned the motives of abolitionists: "The agitation of the slavery question is mischievous and wicked, and proceeds from no patriotic motive by its authors. It is a mere political question on which demagogues and ambitious politicians hope to promote their own prospects for political promotion. And this they seem willing to do even at the hazard of disturbing the harmony if not dissolving the Union itself" (Ashworth 1995).

In 2015, Polk's memory and name were evoked at a town hall meeting in Sioux City, Iowa, when Republican presidential candidate and former governor of Florida Jeb Bush stated James Polk was one of his favorite presidents. In March 2017, two former slaves who labored on Polk's plantation were provided with tombstones marking their graves at the Nashville City Cemetery. The replacement tombstones are part of an effort to recognize more African Americans buried at Nashville City Cemetery. The Nashville City Cemetery Association is a nonprofit support group that funded the tombstones at about $500 each.

The President James K. Polk Home & Museum collaborated to purchase the new tombstones. There has been considerable information discovered on one of Polk's slaves. Elias Polk served in the White House. He was born into slavery and at age 18 was sent to be the servant of James and Sarah Polk when they married. For the next 25 years, Elias worked for James Polk and became his personal valet. As James Polk ascended political ranks to become a U.S. congressman and Tennessee governor, Elias was with him every step of this journey. When Polk was elected president of the United States in 1844, Elias spent time in both Washington, D.C., and Tennessee doing various work for Polk and his wife (Kinslow 2018).

While campaigning for the presidency, Polk promised not to seek reelection and served only one term as president of the United States. In March 1849 he left the White House in poor health and returned to Nashville, where he died in June, only three months after his term ended. Polk's slave Elias Polk gained his freedom after the American Civil War and became politically active. Elias established several different African American social clubs and was appointed porter in the Tennessee legislature in 1871 (Kinslow 2018). In 1876 he made his way to Washington, D.C., where he worked for House of Representatives clerk George M. Adams. Elias Polk died of pneumonia in December 1886.

FURTHER READING

Ashworth, John. 1995. *Slavery, Capitalism, and Politics in the Antebellum Republic: Commerce and Compromise, 1820–1850,* Vol. 1. Cambridge: Cambridge University Press.

Bergeron, Paul. 1987. *The Presidency of James K. Polk.* Lawrence: University Press of Kansas.

Borneman, Walter. 2009. *Polk: The Man Who Transformed the Presidency and America.* New York: Random House.

Dusinberre, William. 2007. *Slave Master President: The Double Career of James Polk.* Oxford: Oxford University Press.

Kinslow, Zacharie, W. 2018. "Enslaved and Entrenched: The Complex Life of Elias Polk," The White House Historical Society, Washington D.C. https://www.whitehouse history.org/enslaved-and-entrenched.

Zachary Taylor

12th President of the United States
Presidential Term: March 4, 1849–July 9, 1850
Political Party: Whig
Vice President: Millard Fillmore

Zachary Taylor was born on November 24, 1874, in Montebello, Orange County, Virginia. His family's lineage goes all the way back to the Mayflower and separatist preacher William Brewster. Taylor's father, Richard Lee Taylor, served in the Continental Army in the American Revolutionary War. Zachary Taylor did not attend college but studied under tutors and then chose a career in the military. Taylor was a decorated soldier. He commanded troops in the War of 1812, the Black Hawk War in 1832, the Second Seminole War (1835–1842), and the Mexican-American War (1846–1848). His troops nicknamed him "Old Rough and Ready." Taylor's daughter, Sarah, married Jefferson Davis but died of malaria within three months of

Zachary Taylor was the 12th president of the United States. He was elected president on the Whig Party ticket with 163 electoral votes and the majority of the popular vote. As president, Taylor seemed to be indifferent on the issue of slavery. (Chaiba Media)

the marriage. Taylor did not approve of Davis's marriage to his daughter, but over time the two resolved the matter, and Davis became one of Taylor's most trusted advisers. Davis later became the president of the Confederate States of America.

As a youth, Taylor lived in the frontier land in Kentucky. He married Margaret Mackall Smith in 1810, and they had six children. Taylor later settled in Louisiana. He was elected president of the United States on the Whig Party ticket with 163 of the Electoral College vote and 1,360,0999 of the popular vote. Though he ran as a Whig, his political voting record was unknown, and it appears that he never voted prior to casting a vote for himself in 1848. He considered himself a Jefferson-Democrat but ran under the Whig Party political banner (Holt 1999). Taylor's running mate was Millard Fillmore of New York.

When Taylor was elected president of the United States, there were a total of 2,880,572 voters who cast votes in the 30 states of the United States. The amount of votes cast amounted to about 72 percent of the population eligible to vote. These vote totals were down slightly from the previous presidential election in 1844 (Ragsdale 1998). Of course, their totals do not take into account the disenfranchisement of women and blacks who had yet to realize their full rights as citizens of the country. Those who could legally vote were white men over the age of 21. Women did not get the right to vote until 1920. At this time each state determined who was eligible to vote, and in some cases white immigrants who were not classified as citizens were still allowed to vote in U.S. elections.

At the time Taylor was elected president of the United States, the expansion of slavery was the central issue on the presidential campaign trail. Because he owned slaves, many southerners thought he would expand slavery into new territories and be a strong advocate for slavery. Most abolitionists did not vote for Taylor. When elected president, Taylor seemed to be indifferent on the issue of slavery and was more concerned with keeping the country together than expanding slavery. He refused to seize slaves who were held by the Seminoles after the tribe was defeated in Florida. Many of the slaves had escaped from white plantation owners who were furious that slaves were not returned to them after the war. Taylor also thought that Native Americans were savages who needed to be contained and constrained. Taylor found the institution of slavery morally acceptable in part because he believed that he practiced a "humane" brand of slavery even though he believed black people were unequal creatures (Holt 1999).

The issue of slavery overshadowed Taylor's short term as president. Those on the opposing sides of the issue were locked in a bitter battle that dominated most of the public's agenda during this time period. As president of the United States, Taylor allowed California and New Mexico to become states and hold their own conventions. This ensured that nonslave states would hold an advantage over slaveholding states. Because Taylor seemingly supported curtailing the advancement of slavery, some southern leaders threatened to secede in 1850. Taylor forcefully responded to the threat of secession, saying that with any attempt to secede, he would not hesitate to hang the perpetrators. Taylor's son, Richard "Dick" Taylor, would later serve in the Confederate Army during the American Civil War. Zachary Taylor died in July 1850 at age 65 of a stomach condition after eating a bowl of cherries with iced milk. He was the last southerner to be elected president of the United States until Lyndon Johnson, already in office after President John F. Kennedy was assassinated, was elected to the presidency in 1964.

FURTHER READING

Bauer, Jack K. 1985. *Zachary Taylor: Soldier, Planter, Statesman of the Old Southwest.* Baton Rouge: Louisiana State University Press.

Eisenhower, John S. D. 2008. *Zachary Taylor.* New York: Henry Holt.

Holt, Michael. 1999. *The Rise and Fall of the American Whig Party: Jacksonian Politics and the Onset of the Civil War.* New York: Oxford University Press.

Ragsdale, Lyn. 1998. *Vital Statistics on the Presidential Election.* Washington DC: Congressional Quarterly Press.

Millard Fillmore

13th President of the United States
Presidential Term: July 9, 1850–March 4, 1853
Political Party: Whig, Know Nothing, Anti-Masonic
Vice President: None

Millard Fillmore was born on January 7, 1800, in Summerhill, New York. He attended rural schools and was self-educated. He worked on the family farm and was an apprentice to a cloth maker. The two-year apprenticeship was abusive, and Fillmore left and moved to New Hope, New York. A ferocious reader, he educated himself through reading and was later admitted to the bar and practiced law in the state of New York. As a young lawyer, Fillmore joined the Anti-Masonic Party but eventually became a member of the Whig Party. He married his first wife, Abigail Powers, who was one of his former school teachers, in 1826. They had two children. He later married Caroline Carmichael McIntosh in 1858. This union did not produce any children. In 1828, Fillmore won a seat in the New York legislature. After three terms, he was elected to the U.S. House of Representatives in 1832. Fillmore's political platform was primarily centered on supporting a protective tariff and eliminating the slave trade between states.

In 1846, Fillmore was instrumental in establishing the University of Buffalo and became the university's first chancellor with an honorary title. One year later, he ran for public office and became the chief financial officer for New York. In 1848, Fillmore was chosen as Zachary Taylor's vice presidential running mate. Whig politician and party boss Thurlow Weed gave his stamp of approval for Fillmore's ascension to vice presidential candidate. Fillmore became president after Zachary Taylor died while in office in July 1850. Taylor's entire cabinet had resigned (Nelson 1996). In a calculated political move, Fillmore appointed Daniel Webster to be secretary of state as a show of support to the moderate faction of the Whig Party. Fillmore also built an alliance with Illinois senator Stephen A. Douglas.

The issue of slavery ominously loomed over the country, and divisions grew wider over the territories gained in the Mexican-American War. Northern states and southern states searched for a suitable compromise to resolve the issue of balancing slave states and nonslaveholding states into new states coming into the union. One resolution was offered by two long-standing U.S. senators. The Compromise of 1850 was crafted and presented by Senator Henry Clay of Kentucky and was pushed through by Illinois Senator Stephen A. Douglas. The Compromise of 1850 proposed that California would become a part of the United States as a nonslaveholding state and created New Mexico and Utah. These two territories would determine for themselves if they would be slave states or nonslaveholding states. The compromise would also end the slave trade in Washington, D.C., but people could still own slaves. The Compromise of 1850 would also simplify the process for southerners to regain custody of fugitive slaves, requiring abolitionists to return runaways to their slave masters. There were several high-spirited congressional debates about ending or at the least curbing the expansion of slavery.

The Compromise of 1850 consisted of five separate bills. Senator Douglas split the proposed law so that senators could vote separately on each bill. All five bills passed, and President Fillmore signed them into law. He threatened to use federal troops to enforce the Fugitive Slave Act and stated, "God knows that I detest slavery, but it is an existing evil, for which we are not responsible, and we must endure it, and give it such protection as is guaranteed by the constitution, till we can get rid of it without destroying the last hope of free government in the world" (Serverance 1907). During the writing of his last State of the Union Address, Fillmore was set to address the issue of slavery head-on, but his cabinet members convinced him to eliminate the passages dealing with slavery from the draft of the speech. In Fillmore's draft, he made references to the uprising and rebellion in Haiti and fanned the flames of fear by suggesting the same thing could happen in the America. He suggested that sending black people back to Africa would be a feasible policy solution to slavery in America.

Fillmore's support and signing of the Fugitive Slave Act of 1850 was a major victory for southern slave owners but ended his chance of earning a second term as president. He reluctantly accepted the Whig Party nomination in 1852 and then withdrew his name from nomination. When the Whig Party imploded because many of its members joined the Republican Party, Fillmore refused to join the Republican Party. He accepted the nomination for president of the National American Party, also called the Know Nothing Party, in 1856. In this election, the Democratic Party candidate, James Buchanan, defeated the Republican Party candidate, John C. Fremont. Fillmore received only eight electoral votes.

Fillmore later became a civic leader and socialite once he retired from public service. He often provided commentary on politics and political issues during retirement. In 1874, Fillmore died from complications after suffering a stroke. As recently as 2017, debates about his legacy at the University of Buffalo continue. Fillmore's name appears on signs and a building on campus, and a portrait of him hangs in prominent spots in Capen and Abbott Halls. The university stated that the building is named after Fillmore because of his prominent role in the founding of the university and that naming a building after Fillmore does not mean the university endorses his presidential legacy, which includes the Compromise of 1850 and the Fugitive Slave Act. Some students complained that the University of Buffalo did little to educate them on Fillmore's complicated history. The Buffalo chapter of the National Association for the Advancement of Colored People called on lawmakers and city officials to refrain from naming any buildings or streets in honor of Fillmore.

FURTHER READING

Finkelman, Paul. 2011. *Millard Fillmore: The American Presidents Series; The 13th President, 1850–1853.* New York: Times Books, Henry Holt.

Nelson, Michael. 1996. *Guide to the Presidency.* New York: Congressional Quarterly.

Rayback, Robert J. 1992. *Millard Fillmore: Biography.* Newtown, CT: American Political Biography.

Rowland, Thomas J. 2013. *Millard Fillmore: The Limit of Compromise.* UK: Nova Science Club.

Severance, Frank H. 1907. *Millard Fillmore Papers,* Vol. 1. Buffalo, NY: Buffalo Historical Society.

Franklin Pierce

14th President of the United States
Presidential Term: March 4, 1853–March 4, 1857
Political Party: Democratic
Vice President: William R. King

Franklin Piece was born in 1804 in Hillsborough, New Hampshire. He earned a bachelor of arts from Bowdoin College in 1824. Pierce was admitted to the bar and practiced law after college in 1827. At age 24, he was elected to the New Hampshire state legislature and later became the Speaker of the New Hampshire House of Representatives. He served in the state legislature from 1833 to 1837. At age 32, Pierce was elected to the U.S. Senate and served from 1837 to 1842. He was a devoted supporter of President Andrew Jackson and was known as "Young Hickory," which was a play on Jackson's nickname "Old Hickory." In 1834 Pierce married Jane Means Appleton, and they had three children.

Franklin Pierce was the 14th president of the United States. Pierce was a member of the Democratic Party, who saw abolitionists and their movement as a threat to sustaining the United States. Pierce did not own slaves, but consulted with southern states to solve the slavery issue. (Library of Congress)

Pierce's wife did not like political life. Several deaths in the Pierce families triggered Franklin Pierce's penchant for drinking heavily. He served in the Mexican-American War.

At the time Pierce was elected, he was the youngest man to be elected president of the United States, at age 48. Attempting to build a coalition with the southern wing of the Democratic Party, he placated them but filled his cabinet with political extremists on both sides of the slavery issue. His politically savvy friends from New Hampshire put his name forward for president of the United States in 1852. At the Democratic Party convention, the delegates crafted a platform that supported the Compromise of 1850 and supported the status quo on slavery. After 48 rounds, which eliminated more prominent candidates, Pierce emerged with the nomination. He ran on the Democratic Party ticket with William Rufus De Vane of Alabama. Pierce received 254 electoral votes and 1,601,274 popular votes. He failed to effectively provide policy solutions for the country's divide on the issue of slavery but was elected president of the United States in 1852.

Pierce was a northern Democrat who saw abolitionists and their movement as an enormous threat to sustaining the union. This made him an acceptable candidate to many of the constituents in the South. He did not own slaves but sought consultation and policy advice from southern states on how to solve the slavery issue, hoping to keep the union together and avoid a civil war. The policy choices and recommendations from his southern advisers only helped accelerate the drumbeat to civil war in the United States. Pierce's southern advisers wanted to extend slavery into other areas of the United States. They found an opening with the desire to build a transnational railroad. In a bipartisan effort between slave states and nonslaveholding states, a potential policy solution was proposed. Stephen A. Douglas, Illinois senator, and Jefferson Davis, secretary of war, persuaded Pierce to purchase land for a southern railroad to establish a transnational railroad route (Conlin 2014). Under Pierce's administration, the United States purchased parts of what is now Arizona and the southern portion of New Mexico. Senator Stephen Douglas's legislative proposal called for organizing the western territories through which a railroad could operate. Douglas also provided in his legislative proposal that the residents of the new territories could decide if they wanted slavery or not (Rodriguez 2007). The result was a rush into Kansas as southerners and northerners vied for control of the territory. When Pierce signed the Kansas-Nebraska Act, it reopened the expansion of slavery in the Midwest by nullifying the Missouri Compromise. Violent, bloody conflicts erupted between proslavery and antislavery groups over Kansas's slavery status. Northerners were furious over the expansion of slavery and the poor treatment of slaves, free black people, and immigrants (Rodriguez 2007). With the passage of the Kansas-Nebraska Act in 1854 and its bloody aftermath, the formation of new political parties eroded the political power of the Democratic Party. Pierce became the target of great anger and rage. As a result, he became the first U.S. president to utilize bodyguards. The Democratic Party became so disillusioned with Pierce that it refused to nominate him for a second term, and James Buchanan became the next president of the United States.

After leaving the presidency, Pierce traveled internationally. He began drinking heavily again, and his criticisms of the northern abolitionists increased. By 1860, many Democrats wanted to nominate Pierce for president of the United States. They saw him as a compromise for Democratic Party unity. Pierce refused to run for the presidency again. In 1864, his friends attempted to nominate him again. Pierce sent a letter and had it read publicly stating he would not run for president again. He became outspoken about Abraham Lincoln's presidency and in particular Lincoln's suspension of habeas corpus. Franklin Pierce spent his last years in New Hampshire in virtual seclusion. He died in Concord, Massachusetts, on October 8, 1869.

FURTHER READING

Bergeron, Paul. 1987. *The Presidency of James K. Polk.* Lawrence: University Press of Kansas.

Bisson, Wilfred J. 1993. *Franklin Pierce: A Bibliography.* Westport, CT: Greenwood.

Conlin, Joseph R. 2014. *The American Past: A Survey of American History,* Vol. I: To 1877. Boston: Cengage Learning.

Holt, Michael. 2010. *Franklin Pierce: The American Presidents Series; The 14th President, 1853–1857.* New York: Times Books.

Nichols, Roy. 1993. *Franklin Pierce: Young Hickory of the Granite Hills.* Newtown, CT: American Political Biography.

Rodriguez, Junius P. 2007. *Slavery in the United States: A Social, Political, and Historical Encyclopedia,* Vol. 1. Santa Barbara, CA: ABC-CLIO.

James Buchanan Jr.

15th President of the United States
Presidential Term: March 4, 1857–March 4, 1861
Political Party: Democratic
Vice President: John C. Breckinridge

James Buchanan Jr. was born on April 23, 1791, in Cove Gap, Pennsylvania. He was educated for two years at Dickinson College and was later was admitted to the bar and practiced law. Buchanan was elected president of the United States on the Democratic ticket in 1856 and received 174 Electoral College votes and 1,838,169 popular votes over two other presidential candidates. John Breckinridge, a U.S. senator from Kentucky, served as Buchanan's vice president. Buchanan cut his political teeth by serving in the Pennsylvania Legislation from 1814 to 1816. In 1820, he was elected to the U.S. House of Representatives and served for 10 years in this position. He was appointed ambassador to Russia in 1831. After Buchanan's return to the United States, he was elected to the U.S. Senate in 1834. President James K. Polk named him secretary of state, a post he held until 1849. Under Buchanan's term as secretary of state, the country grew by purchasing California, Texas, and most of the present southwest part of the country. Buchannan also served as the minister to Great Britain and helped draft the Ostend Manifesto. This manifesto laid out a plan for the United States to acquire Cuba. The plan was never acted on after strong opposition from antislavery groups who thought Cuba would become a slave state.

When President Franklin Pierce signed the Kansas-Nebraska Act, Buchanan was living abroad and therefore was not forced to take a public stand on the matter. When angry members of the Democratic Party chose not to nominate Franklin Pierce for another presidential term, they turned to James Buchanan as the party's presidential nominee. Buchanan is the only U.S. president who remained a bachelor his entire life.

President Buchanan is often blamed for the American Civil War because he chose not to act on the issue of slavery. During his presidency, seven states seceded from the United States. Buchanan believed that slavery was protected by the U.S. Constitution. He attempted to be a calming force between proslavery and antislavery factions in the country. He chose this approach by constructing his cabinet with both proslavery and antislavery people. Hostilities between these factions only increased in the United States. Two days after Buchanan's inauguration, the U.S. Supreme Court handed down its infamous decision in the *Dred Scott v. Sandford* case.

Dred Scott was a slave who had lived with his owner in a free state before returning to the slave state of Missouri. Scott argued that time spent in a free state entitled him to emancipation. The decision of the Supreme Court was read in March 1857. Chief Justice Roger B. Taney, who was a staunch supporter of slavery, wrote the majority opinion for the court. The court's opinion stated that "because Scott was black, he was not a citizen and therefore had no right to sue." The opinion also noted that the framers of the Constitution believed that blacks "had no rights which the white man was bound to respect; and that the Negro might justly and lawfully be reduced to slavery for his benefit. He was bought and sold and treated as an ordinary article of merchandise and traffic, whenever profit could be made by it." Under Chief Justice Taney's interpretation of the Declaration of Independence, when the framers of the Constitution wrote "all men are created equal," they did not mean African slaves. He stated, "But it is too clear for dispute, that the enslaved African race were not intended to be included, and formed no part of the people who framed and adopted this declaration" (Cornell Law School 2018).

The decision also declared that the Missouri Compromise of 1820, legislation that restricted slavery in certain territories, was unconstitutional. Buchanan thought this ruling would settle the question of slavery. His supporters considered it a final answer to the slavery controversy. Buchanan used his political influence to coerce Justice Robert Grier of Pennsylvania to join the southern majority. The decision in *Dred Scott v. Sandford* outraged abolitionists and widened the gap between proslavery and antislavery factions in the country.

Buchanan faced unyielding gridlock during his presidential tenure. In 1858, the Republican Party took control of Congress and blocked most of his agenda. In retribution, Buchanan vetoed legislation passed by Republicans. He chose not to run for reelection, and at the Democratic National Convention the party was split. Some delegates wanted Breckinridge to become the party's nominee, while others wanted Illinois senator Stephen A. Douglas. The Republican Party nominated Abraham Lincoln. Lincoln won the presidency with less than 40 percent of the vote in 1860. By the time Lincoln was inaugurated as president of the United

States, six more states had left the Union to form the Confederate States of America. President Buchanan maintained that the seceding states did not have the right to do so, but he also believed he did not have the constitutional power or the means to stop them from leaving the United States. Buchanan died on June 1, 1868, in Wheatland, Lancaster, Pennsylvania.

FURTHER READING

DeRose, Chris. 2014. *The Presidents' War: Six American Presidents and the Civil War That Divided Them.* Lanham, MD: Lyon.

Holt, Michael F. 2010. *Franklin Pierce: The American Presidents Series: The 14th President, 1853–1857.* New York: Times Books, Henry Holt.

Nichols, Roy. 1993. *Franklin Pierce: Young Hickory of the Granite Hills.* Newtown, CT: American Political Biography.

Abraham Lincoln

16th President of the United States
Presidential Term: March 4, 1861–April 15, 1865
Political Party: Whig, Republican
Vice President: Hannibal Hamlin (1861–1865), Andrew Johnson (1865)

Abraham Lincoln was born on February 12, 1809, in Hodgenville, Hardin County (now Larue County), Kentucky. Lincoln married Mary Todd from Springfield, Illinois, on November 2, 1842. They had four children. Lincoln was elected president of the United States in 1860 on the Republican ticket, defeating three others: John Bell of the Constitutional Union Party, Stephen Douglas of the Northern Democratic Party, and John Brekinridge of the Southern Democratic Party. Lincoln's running mate was Hannibal Hamlin of Maine.

Lincoln won the presidency over Stephen A. Douglas, receiving 180 Electoral College votes and 1,866,452 popular votes. In 1864, Lincoln was reelected on the Republican ticket with Andrew Johnson of Tennessee, receiving 212 of the Electoral College vote and 2,213,635 of the popular vote. Lincoln became the first U.S. president to be assassinated, shot by John Wilkes Booth, an actor and Confederate sympathizer, on April 14, 1865.

Until the founding of the Republican Party in 1854, Lincoln was a member of the Whig Party. This political party of national conservative modernizers advocated for a strong federal and state relationship. The party also advocated for the improvement of infrastructure in order to improve trade. Most of the members of the Whig Party had protestant religious values and represented the interests of entrepreneurs. Members of the Whig Party emphasized the value of self-education as a means of individual and moral progress. The northern wing of the Whig Party became increasingly critical of the system of slavery. Eventually the slavery question led to the dissolution of the political party in the 1850s.

Abraham Lincoln was the 16th president of the United States. Lincoln served as president during the turbulent years of the American Civil War, and in 1863 signed the Emancipation Proclamation into law. A lifelong opponent of slavery, he was quoted as saying, "As I would not be a slave, so I would not be a master. This expresses my idea of democracy. Whatever differs from this, to the extent of the difference, is no democracy." (Library of Congress)

One of President Lincoln's most vocal critics was Frederick Douglass. Douglass was an author and orator who had been enslaved on the Eastern Shore of Maryland. He escaped slavery and fled to New Bedford, Massachusetts. Lincoln invited Douglass to the White House on three occasions. One of these invitations was to Lincoln's second inauguration. However, the visit was not without controversy. When Douglass approached the door of the White House he was accosted by two policemen, and Lincoln had to order them to allow Douglass into the reception. Douglass requested that Lincoln change a policy that paid black Union Army soldiers less than white Union Army soldiers. "While white soldiers were paid $13 a month with no deductions, blacks received only $10 per month, from which $3 was held back as a clothing deduction, yielding a net pay of only $7" ("Black Soldiers in the U.S. Military during the Civil War" 2017). Lincoln would not commit to equalizing the black soldiers' pay but promised that black soldiers would get equal pay when the time was right. Black soldiers were relegated to segregated units under white officers and had no chance of promotion to become military officers. Also, black soldiers captured by the Confederacy were not treated as prisoners of war but as runaway slaves and were either sent to slavery or killed. Douglass brought all of these issues to Lincoln.

Lincoln is referred to as the "Great Emancipator" but at times was ambivalent about emancipation for black people. In fact, he came late to the abolitionist cause. Early in Lincoln's public service career, he was against the expansion of slavery but did not call for an end to the institution and practice of slavery. He was involved in a host of lawsuits involving slavery in the 1830s and 1840s. As a lawyer, he represented clients on both sides of the issues, including slave owners seeking to have the courts order that slaves be returned to them.

In 1837 while serving in the Illinois General Assembly, Lincoln and a colleague, Dan Stone, expressed their sentiments against the practice of slavery. They believed that slavery was an unjust practice and a bad policy but did not attempt to undo slavery. Lincoln and Stone also believed that the U.S. Congress had no constitutional power to interfere with the institution of slavery in different states. However, they believed that Congress could abolish slavery in the District of Columbia. They further believed this power should be exerted only with the request and explicit consent of the people of the District of Columbia.

In 1854 in a speech in Peoria, Illinois, Lincoln noted that the practice of slavery in the United States made American democracy appear to be contradictory and hypocritical to the rest of the world, but again he was arguing against the spread of slavery, not immediate emancipation for slaves. In this three-hour speech, Lincoln clarified his stance on slavery and expressed his opposition on moral and legal grounds. He also noted that he did not know the proper policy solutions to end the practice of slavery. This view was different from that of leading abolitionists, such as William Lloyd Garrison's stance on slavery. On the repeal of the Missouri Compromise, Lincoln specifically stated:

> When southern people tell us they are no more responsible for the origin of slavery, than we; I acknowledge the fact. When it is said that the institution exists; and that it is very difficult to get rid of it, in any satisfactory way, I can understand and appreciate the saying. I surely will not blame them for not doing what I should not know how to do myself. If all earthly power were given me, I should not know what to do, as to the existing institution. My first impulse would be to free all the slaves, and send them to Liberia, to their own native land. But a moment's reflection would convince me, that whatever of high hope, (as I think there is) there may be in this, in the long run, its sudden execution is impossible. If they were all landed there in a day, they would all perish in the next ten days; and there are not surplus shipping and surplus money enough in the world to carry them there in many times ten days. What then? Free them all, and keep them among us as underlings? Is it quite certain that this betters their condition? I think I would not hold one in slavery, at any rate; yet the point is not clear enough for me to denounce people upon. What next? Free them, and make them politically and socially, our equals? My own feelings will not admit of this; and if mine would, we well know that those of the great mass of white people will not. (Lincoln 1854)

Lincoln continued to speak out against the expansion of slavery and even declared a hatred for the institution of slavery in the United States, but he did not support immediate freedom for Africans held in slavery. Lincoln expressed his dislike in seeing the mistreatment of slaves but felt it was the slave owner's discretion as to how he treated and punished his slaves. Lincoln also recalled watching the treatment of slaves on a steamboat on which he was traveling and how this experience affected him, but he and other northerners would continue to suppress their disdain for the institution of slavery. Lincoln wrote a letter to his good friend Joshua Speed in 1855:

You know I dislike slavery; and you fully admit the abstract wrong of it. So far there is no cause of difference. But you say that sooner than yield your legal right to the slave—especially at the bidding of those who are not themselves interested, you would see the Union dissolved. I am not aware that any one is bidding you to yield that right; very certainly I am not. I leave that matter entirely to yourself. I also acknowledge your rights and my obligations, under the constitution, in regard to your slaves. I confess I hate to see the poor creatures hunted down, and caught, and carried back to their stripes, and unrewarded toils; but I bite my lip and keep quiet. In 1841 you and I had together a tedious low-water trip, on a Steam Boat from Louisville to St. Louis. You may remember, as I well do, that from Louisville to the mouth of the Ohio there were, on board, ten or a dozen slaves, shackled together with irons. That sight was a continual torment to me; and I see something like it every time I touch the Ohio, or any other slave-border. It is hardly fair to you to assume, that I have no interest in a thing which has, and continually exercises, the power of making me miserable. You ought rather to appreciate how much the great body of the Northern people do crucify their feelings, in order to maintain their loyalty to the constitution and the Union.

I do oppose the extension of slavery, because my judgment and feelings so prompt me; and I am under no obligation to the contrary. (Lincoln 1855)

When Lincoln began to make public statements about slavery, he initially advocated for free states and slave states coexisting but remaining separate. He believed that neither political party should interfere with the other's affairs when it came to the issue of slavery. He later advocated for preventing the expansion of slavery into new territories. In a debate with presidential candidate Stephen Douglas in 1858, Lincoln reiterated his hatred for slavery but again insisted that slavery should not be touched where it already existed:

I have always hated slavery, I think as much as any Abolitionist. I have been an Old Line Whig. I have always hated it, but I have always been quiet about it until this new era of the introduction of the Nebraska Bill began. I always believed that everybody was against it, and that it was in course of ultimate extinction.

I have said a hundred times, and I have now no inclination to take it back, that I believe there is no right, and ought to be no inclination in the people of the free States to enter into the slave States, and interfere with the question of slavery at all. (Lincoln 1858)

In a September 1858 speech, Lincoln argued that the phrase "All men are created equal" applied to black people and white people; however, this did not mean that both races should have the same political rights. During the Lincoln-Douglas campaign debates for the Illinois U.S. Senate election, Douglas alleged that Lincoln was advocating for "negro equality" (Good 2009). Lincoln vehemently denied he was advocating for equality between black people and white people. During the fourth of the seven Lincoln-Douglas debates Lincoln stated, "I will say then that I am not, nor ever have been, in favor of bringing about in any way the social and political equality of the white and black races." He went on to say that "he opposed blacks having the right to vote, to serve on juries, to hold office and to intermarry with whites. What he did believe was that, like all men, blacks had the right to improve their condition in society and to enjoy the fruits of their labor. In this way they were equal to white men, and for this reason slavery was inherently unjust."

Lincoln considered several policy solutions to the slavery problem in the United States. For a time, he floated an idea to compensate slave owners for the loss of slaves if slavery was ended. He pursued this idea even after the American Civil War began and urged the State of Delaware to accept a compensation plan. Ultimately, the Delaware legislature failed to act on the offer and defeated the measure.

Lincoln also floated the idea of mass colonization. Under colonization, former slaves would be removed from the United States. The Caribbean and Latin America were two destinations suggested as possible spots. Liberia, Africa, was another possible destination for slaves who would be freed. In his message to the U.S. Congress in 1861, Lincoln requested appropriations to finance the colonization efforts (Bennett 2007). Even late in the Civil War, he held a meeting with African American leaders urging them to get behind the colonization idea. Lincoln did not favor mandatory colonization and maintained that colonization should be voluntary.

In September 1862, President Lincoln issued his preliminary Emancipation Proclamation. In the proclamation, he declared that on January 1, 1863, all states in rebellion against the Union "shall be henceforward and forever free." Lincoln had attempted to issue the proclamation in 1862, but Secretary of State William Seward advised him to wait until Union troops had gained better footing in the war. In September after the Battle of Antietam, Lincoln saw an opening and issued the proclamation. The Emancipation Proclamation was a military policy directive and did not actually free any slaves. Lincoln did not view the Civil War as an opportunity to free the 4 million Africans held in slavery but instead saw it as a matter of holding the United States together and preserving the union. When the war began in 1861, the Union did not have a clear policy on how to deal with the slaves who had crossed over to Union territory or were freed during battles in the South. The Emancipation Proclamation did not apply to border states such as Maryland, Kentucky, Missouri, and Delaware that maintained strong cultural ties with southern slaveholding states (and the institution of slavery) and economic relationships with northern states that sanctioned slavery. The proclamation applied only to southern states fighting against the Union.

As the Civil War came to a close and it became more apparent that the Union would win the war, Lincoln spent a great amount of time lobbying and pushing the Thirteenth Amendment through Congress. In April 1864, the U.S. Senate passed a proposed amendment banning slavery. However, in the House of Representatives, the legislative measure failed to gain support. When Congress reconvened in December 1864, Republicans moved the proposed amendment to the top of their agenda. President Lincoln became more involved in the legislative process to make sure the amendment would pass. He took a hands-on approach and invited individual representatives to his office to discuss the amendment. He also pressured border state Unionists to change their position and pass the legislation. Lincoln used his influence to get his allies to entice members of the U.S. House of Representatives with plum positions and other enticements. Lincoln reportedly stated, "I leave it to you to determine how it shall be done; but remember that I am President of the United States, clothed with immense power, and I expect you to procure those votes" (Samito 2015). On January 31, 1865, the House of Representatives passed the Thirteenth Amendment, 119 votes for to 56 against. The following day, Lincoln approved the joint resolution of Congress and submitted it to state legislatures for ratification. Lincoln was assassinated on April 14, 1965, and some states did not ratify the legislation until December 6, 1965.

In general, African Americans have idolized President Abraham Lincoln as the "Great Emancipator" because of the mythical lessons taught in the American school system. As students have begun to study his speeches and words, Lincoln's legacy has become more complicated. When Barack Obama served in the Illinois Senate, he stared at a painting of President Abraham Lincoln. Obama said that the study of Lincoln's eyes motivated him to write the article "What I See in Lincoln's Eyes." One paragraph of this article deals explicitly with Lincoln's image as the Great Emancipator and how African Americans perceive this legacy. Illinois senator Obama wrote,

> Still, as I look at his picture, it is the man and not the icon that speaks to me. I cannot swallow whole the view of Lincoln as the Great Emancipator. As a law professor and civil rights lawyer and as an African American, I am fully aware of his limited views on race. Anyone who actually reads the Emancipation Proclamation knows it was more a military document than a clarion call for justice. Scholars tell us too that Lincoln wasn't immune from political considerations and that his temperament could be indecisive and morose. But it is precisely those imperfections and the painful self-awareness of those failings etched in every crease of his face and reflected in those haunted eyes—that make him so compelling. For when the time came to confront the greatest moral challenge this nation has ever faced, this all too human man did not pass the challenge on to future generations. (Obama 2005)

In 2009, Obama became the first African American president of the United States. He chose to take the oath of office with two Bibles, those of Abraham Lincoln and Dr. Martin Luther King, Jr. President Obama also hung a portrait of President Abraham Lincoln in the Oval Office.

FURTHER READING

Bennett, Lerone. 2007. *Forced into Glory: Abraham Lincoln's White Dream.* Chicago: Johnson Publishing.

"Black Soldiers in the U.S. Military during the Civil War." 2017. National Archives, https://www.archives.gov/education/lessons/blacks-civil-war.

Donald, Herbert David. 1996. *Lincoln.* New York: Simon and Schuster.

Foner, Eric. 2010. *The Fiery Trial: Abraham Lincoln and American Slavery.* New York: Norton.

Good, Timothy. 2009. *Lincoln for President: An Underdog's Path to the 1860 Republican Nomination.* Jefferson, NC: McFarland.

Goodwin, Doris Kearns. 2006. *Team of Rivals: The Political Genius of Abraham Lincoln.* New York: Simon and Schuster.

Johnson, Michael P. 2010. *Abraham Lincoln, Slavery, and the Civil War: Selected Writing and Speeches.* New York: Bedford/St. Martin's.

Lincoln, Abraham. 1854. Speech on the Repeal of the Missouri Compromise, Peoria, Illinois, October 16, 1854. From Mark Neely, Jr., *The Abraham Lincoln Encyclopedia.* New York: Da Capo, 1982, https://www.nps.gov/liho/learn/historyculture/peoriaspeech.htm

Lincoln, Abraham. 1855. Letter from Abraham Lincoln to Joshua Speed, August 24, 1855. From Roy P. Basler, ed., *Abraham Lincoln, 1809–1865.* New Brunswick, NJ: Rutgers University Press, 1953.

Magness, Philip W., and Sebastian N. Page. 2011. *Colonization after Emancipation: Lincoln and the Movement for Black Resettlement.* Columbia: University of Missouri Press.

Obama, Barack. 2005. "What I See in Lincoln's Eyes." CNN, Tuesday, June 28, http://www.cnn.com/2005/POLITICS/06/28/obama.lincoln.tm/.

Washington, John E. 2018. *They Knew Lincoln.* New York: Oxford University Press.

White, Ronald, C. 2010. *A. Lincoln: A Biography.* New York: Random House Trade Paperbacks.

Emancipation Era

President Abraham Lincoln attempted to legally end slavery when he issued the Emancipation Proclamation, which went into effect on January 1, 1863. The United States was in the midst of the American Civil War, so the number of slaves immediately set free is not exactly known. However, the proclamation targeted the entire slave population, at the time estimated to be between 2 million and 3 million. It was not until the Civil War ended on May 13, 1865, and then the Thirteenth Amendment to the U.S. Constitution was ratified on December 6, 1865, that slaves were fully legally emancipated. The vestiges of slavery, however, continued for decades. Although the federal government continued to pass laws guaranteeing such freedoms to blacks as voter equality, the problem was the lack of enforcement by the federal government and resistance from the states. Most presidents would not take aggressive stances on enforcement so as not to antagonize southern states and also because of the need to reunify the country to deal with a host of other domestic and international policy issues. They also contended with criticisms of the federal government intervening in issues that were deemed the right of states to manage their internal affairs.

As the federal government passed laws to support African Americans, southern states immediately began passing laws to prohibit equal rights for African Americans in practically every fashion. Laws prohibited voting, property ownership, free movement, and even marriage. Democratic legislatures in the South implemented Jim Crow laws that mandated racial segregation as well as legal inequality for blacks. These laws went into place in 1877, and some lasted until 1965. Along with these laws came social opposition to racial equality predominantly in the South, often accompanied by violence perpetuated by such groups as the Ku Klux Klan.

Presidents combated the issue of racial segregation and legal inequality for African Americans from the end of the Civil War through the 1960s. The most bitter legal and political battles occurred after the Civil War and during the first half of the 20th century. Presidents contended with the issue while at the same time trying to advance policies in other areas that required southern political support. These competing issues arose as the United States grew in territory and became more involved in international politics and diplomacy and as the population of the country became more diverse due to explosive immigration. Presidents also struggled with policies to fund federal programs for a country becoming more industrial based and as the agricultural industries were quickly replaced by technology. Still, full equal rights for African Americans remained a topic on the political agenda for all presidents during this time. Some presidents were very passive in taking actions, while others were more aggressive but still cautious.

An issue that plagued presidents during this period and for the next 100 years was the portrayal of the United States to the rest of the world. While the United States vehemently fought authoritarianism and communism in other parts of the world, presidents had to contend with the reputation of the United States when blacks were not afforded the same equality as whites. This dichotomy of the United States—wanting to be the leader of the free world while also serving as the example of a nation embroiled in racial segregation—was seen as hypocritical both at home and abroad.

Andrew Johnson

17th President of the United States
Presidential Term: April 15, 1865–March 4, 1869
Political Party: None (although Democratic until becoming vice president)
Vice President: None

Andrew Johnson was born on December 29, 1808, to a very poor family in Raleigh, North Carolina. He eventually moved to Greeneville, Tennessee, and became a tailor before entering local politics. He also owned at least half a dozen slaves in Tennessee. While serving in the U.S. Congress, Johnson did not support federal powers over the states, championed legislation supporting the poor, and believed in the rights of white citizens to own slaves as private property. However, he remained in the U.S. Senate when his home state of Tennessee seceded from the Union. As the only southern senator to remain loyal to the Union, Johnson gained northern support. He became vice president when President Abraham Lincoln won his second term in office. Since Johnson was a southern Democrat, he faced strong opposition from Radical Republicans in Congress to becoming vice president due to his proslavery views. Radical Republicans were a faction within the Republican Party who called for the complete eradication of slavery.

After the assassination of President Lincoln, Johnson succeeded to the presidency and supported the reconstruction of the southern states after the devastation of the American Civil War but did not take action to combat prewar laws against blacks being put in place by southern states. While Congress was in recess during the first eight months of Johnson's first term, he implemented his own reconstruction plan, which included issuing presidential pardons and amnesty to former southern rebels who would take an oath of allegiance to the United States. Part of that oath stated the following:

I, ----, declaring that I do, freely and forever, disclaim, and that I will never assert, right or title to slaves, and that I will never hereafter own a slave, or any interest therein, pursuant to the President's proclamation of date -- day of --, 1865, do solemnly swear (or affirm) in the presence of Almighty God that I will henceforth faithfully protect and defend the Constitution of the United States, and the union of the States thereunder.

I do further proclaim and declare that such persons as shall continue hostilities against the government of the United States, or give aid and comfort to insurgents and hostile persons after notice of this proclamation, or a reasonable time shall have elapsed within which notice must be presumed, will not be entitled to the pardon offered herein; and that all persons not hereinafter excepted, and who desire these benefits of the amnesty of the government, must within months from the date hereof comply with the terms and take the oath herein prescribed. (Library of Congress 2018)

As a result, many former Confederate leaders began to gain prominent positions in southern states such as Alexander Stephens, former vice president under Jefferson Davis, who was elected to the Senate in 1866 and to the U.S. House of Representatives in 1873 and then as governor of Georgia in 1882. Southern state legislatures began implementing Black Codes to limit the rights of blacks in such areas as voting and the types of jobs they could hold and public funds being provided for their education. Some states even had legal penalties that allowed blacks who violated codes to be sold into labor. The actions of President Johnson and southern legislatures upset Republicans not only because they wanted freedom for blacks but also because they wanted black votes to gain more political influence in the South. Radical Republicans initially refused to seat any congressional representative from the former Confederacy.

Johnson did not support legislation geared toward giving blacks equal rights. Under the Freedmen's Bureau bill, the Freedmen's Bureau was created under Lincoln's administration on March 3, 1865, to provide former slaves with education, food, housing, health care, and employment. Another version of the bill was introduced but was vetoed by Johnson on February 19, 1866. His veto stood, since Congress did not try to override it. However, Congress did pass the Civil Rights Act of 1866, establishing blacks as American citizens and forbidding discrimination against them. Johnson vetoed the legislation, calling it "another step, or rather a stride, toward centralization and the concentration of all legislative power in the national Government" (United States House of Representatives 2018). However, the president's veto was overwhelmingly overridden by Congress with a vote of 122 to 41 on April 9, 1866. This was the first time in history that Congress overrode a presidential veto on any major piece of legislation.

The first paragraph of the Civil Rights Act details how far-reaching the legislation was in granting rights to African Americans:

Be it enacted by the Senate and House of Representatives of the United States of America in Congress assembled, That all persons born in the United States and not subject to any foreign power, excluding Indians not taxed, are hereby declared to be citizens of the United States; and such citizens, of every race and color, without regard to any previous condition of slavery or involuntary servitude, except as a punishment for crime whereof the party shall have been duly convicted, shall have the same right, in every State and Territory in the United States, to make and enforce contracts, to sue, be parties, and give evidence, to inherit, purchase, lease, sell, hold, and convey real and personal property, and to full and equal benefit of all laws and proceedings for the security of person and property, as is enjoyed by white citizens, and shall be subject to like punishment, pains, and penalties, and to none other, any law, statute, ordinance, regulation, or custom, to the contrary notwithstanding.

The act also extended the authority of the Freedmen's Bureau and gave such additional freedoms to former slaves as the right to inherit, purchase, lease, sell, and hold personal property and to bear arms. Johnson made his views on this issue clear in his third State of the Union Address on December 3, 1867:

It is manifestly and avowedly the object of these laws to confer upon Negroes the privilege of voting and to disfranchise such a number of white citizens as will give the former a clear majority at all elections in the Southern States. This, to the minds of some persons, is so important that a violation of the Constitution is justified as a means of bringing it about. The morality is always false which excuses a wrong because it proposes to accomplish a desirable end. We are not permitted to do evil that good may come. But in this case the end itself is evil, as well as the means. The subjugation of the States to negro domination would be worse than the military despotism under which they are now suffering. It was believed beforehand that the people would endure any amount of military oppression for any length of time rather than degrade themselves by subjection to the negro race. Therefore they have been left without a choice. Negro suffrage was established by an act of Congress, and the military officers were commanded to superintend the process of clothing the negro race with the political privileges torn from white men. . . .

No independent government of any form has ever been successful in their hands. On the contrary, wherever they have been left to their own devices they have shown a constant tendency to relapse into barbarism. In the Southern States, however, Congress has undertaken to confer upon them the privilege of the ballot. Just released from slavery, it may be doubted whether as a class they know more than their ancestors how to organize and regulate civil society. Indeed, it is admitted that the blacks of the South are not only regardless of the rights of property, but so utterly ignorant of public affairs that their voting can consist in nothing more than carrying a ballot to the place where they are directed to deposit it. I need not remind you that the exercise of the elective franchise is the highest attribute of an American citizen, and that when guided by virtue, intelligence, patriotism, and a proper appreciation of our free institutions it constitutes the true basis of a democratic form of government, in which the sovereign power is lodged in the body of the people. A trust artificially created, not for its own sake, but solely as a means of promoting the general welfare, its influence for good must necessarily depend upon the elevated character and true allegiance of the elector. It ought, therefore, to be reposed in none except those who are fitted morally and mentally to administer it well; for if conferred upon persons who do not justly estimate its value and who are indifferent as to its results, it will only serve as a means of placing power in the hands of the unprincipled and ambitious, and must eventuate in the complete destruction of that liberty of which it should be the most powerful conservator. (Johnson 1867)

Congress passed the Fourteenth Amendment, adopted on July 9, 1868, which stated:

All persons born or naturalized in the United States and subject to the jurisdiction thereof, are citizens of the United States and of the State wherein they reside. No State shall make or enforce any law which shall abridge the privileges or immunities of citizens of the United States; nor shall any State deprive any person of life, liberty, or property, without due process of law; nor deny to any person within its jurisdiction the equal protection of the laws.

Johnson unsuccessfully tried to stop the amendment from passing by persuading southern states not to ratify it.

Johnson faced opposition from both Congress and citizens. He launched a speaking campaign in several cities to attempt to win support for his Reconstruction policies during the congressional elections of 1866. He faced hostile crowds while speaking in the Midwest, and Radical Republicans overwhelmingly won congressional elections. Ignoring the president, Congress enacted its own reconstruction plan and placed southern states under military control. In addition, Congress placed restrictions on President Johnson, which he violated, and this led to 11 charges being levied in impeachment proceedings against him in the U.S. House of Representatives on February 24, 1868. The most serious charge against him was removing federal officials without congressional approval, specifically Secretary of War Edwin M. Stanton, who was appointed under Lincoln and was loyal to Radical Republicans. Johnson attempted to test congressional laws by removing Stanton and replacing him first with Ulysses S. Grant and later with the very unpopular General Lorenzo Thomas. Stanton refused to be replaced and barricaded himself in his office. Johnson was acquitted after a three-month trial in the U.S. Senate on May 26, 1868, as a two-thirds vote could not be obtained against him (the vote was 35 against and 19 for impeachment).

President Johnson was not chosen by Democrats as their party's presidential nominee for the 1868 election. He did return to the Senate in 1875 after winning back his former seat representing Tennessee in an intensely contested election. He died a few months after returning to the Senate.

FURTHER READING

Gordon-Reed, Annette. 2011. *Andrew Johnson: The American Presidents Series; The 17th President, 1865–1869.* New York: Times Books.

Johnson, Andrew. 1867. "Third Annual Message, December 3, 1867." The American Presidency Project, http://www.presidency.ucsb.edu/ws/?pid=29508.

Library of Congress. 2018. "A Proclamation: Printed Ephemera Collection, Portfolio 235, Folder 26." Digital History, http://www.digitalhistory.uh.edu/exhibits/reconstruc tion/section4/section4_pardon1.html.

McKitrick, Eric L. 1960. *Andrew Johnson and Reconstruction.* New York: Oxford University Press.

Trefousse, Hans L. 1989. *Andrew Johnson: A Biography.* New York: Norton.

Trefousse, Hans L. 1999. *Impeachment of a President: Andrew Johnson, the Blacks, and Reconstruction.* New York: Fordham University Press.

United States House of Representatives. 2018. "The Civil Rights Bill of 1866." History, Art & Archives, http://history.house.gov/Historical-Highlights/1851–1900/The -Civil-Rights-Bill-of-1866/?sf24820132=1.

Ulysses Simpson Grant (born Hiram Ulysses Grant)

18th President of the United States
Presidential Term: March 4, 1869–March 4, 1877
Political Party: Republican
Vice President: Schuyler Colfax (1869–1873), Henry Wilson (1873–1875), None (1875–1877)

Ulysses Simpson Grant was born on April 27, 1822, in Point Pleasant, Ohio. He graduated from West Point and served in the Mexican-American War. Grant was commanding general of the Union Army during the American Civil War. He was appointed to the rank of brigadier general by President Abraham Lincoln in 1861. Robert E. Lee surrendered to Grant at Appomattox on April 9, 1865. Grant was the first U.S. four-star general, appointed at the recommendation of President Andrew Johnson. Grant was also the last U.S. president to own slaves. He had only one slave, William Jones, before the Civil War, and Grant gave Jones his freedom in 1859.

Grant assumed the presidency when the United States was still just beginning to develop policies and strategies associated with the end of slavery. As a hero from the Civil War, he was a leader in the Republican Party and reconstructionist efforts. The country was in many ways still struggling with how to rejoin a nation that was once divided literally, as the South had seceded from the Union. There were many factions in the South that were particularly resistant to supporting rights for blacks, even with federal laws being put into place. Even in the North racism and discrimination were common, as support for black freedom was not seen as giving blacks full racial equality with whites. President Grant supported giving rights to former slaves as part of the country's reconstruction but also wanted black support in the South to increase Republican leadership in those states. Because of a fraction in the Republican Party on the issue of rights for blacks, Grant was part of the Radical Republicans who supported black equality.

However, he did not personally seek to run for the presidency and relied on his popularity rather than political promises to win office.

Under Grant's presidency and with substantial influence from him personally, the Fifteenth Amendment was ratified and added to the U.S. Constitution on March 30, 1870. Grant called for the passing of this amendment during his inaugural address in stating, "The question of suffrage is one which is likely to agitate the public so long as a portion of the citizens of the nation are excluded from its privileges in any State. It seems to me very desirable that this question should be settled now, and I entertain the hope and express the desire that it may be by the ratification of the fifteenth article of amendment to the Constitution" (Grant 1869).

The Fifteenth Amendment guaranteed that "The right of citizens of the United States to vote shall not be denied or abridged by the United States, or by any State, on account of race,

During his presidency, Ulysses S. Grant signed the Civil Rights Bill of 1875 into law. The bill sought to guarantee blacks "full and equal enjoyment of the accommodations, advantages, facilities and privileges" of such public venues as inns, hotels, theaters, and public transportation. The bill was believed to be supported under the Thirteenth and Fourteenth Amendments, and it included criminal penalties for violations, including fines of as much as $500 and up to thirty days in jail. (Library of Congress)

color, or previous condition of servitude." As an example of his influence, Grant privately persuaded the governor of Nebraska to hold a special legislative session to push the state to a speedy ratification. Grant delivered a Special Message to the Senate and the House of Representatives on March 30, 1870, and called the amendment "a measure of grander importance than any other one act of the kind from the foundation of our free government to the present day" (Grant 1870). In that same message he stated the following:

Institutions like ours, in which all power is derived directly from the people, must depend mainly upon their intelligence, patriotism, and industry. I call the attention, therefore, of the newly enfranchised race to the importance of their striving in every honorable manner to make themselves worthy of their new privilege. To the race more favored heretofore by our laws I would say, Withhold no legal privilege of advancement to the new citizen. The framers of our Constitution firmly believed that a republican government could not endure without intelligence and education generally diffused among the people. The Father of his Country, in his Farewell Address, uses this language. (Grant 1870)

The Fifteenth Amendment alone did not stop efforts to attack the rights of blacks to vote, hold office, or serve on juries. This was particularly the case in southern states. Therefore, under President Grant, Congress passed a series of acts under the umbrella of what have been called the Enforcement Acts. The Enforcement Act of 1870, passed on May 31, implemented severe penalties for anyone who interfered with a citizen's right to vote, allowed federal judges to hear cases involving voting violations in congressional elections, and gave President Grant the power to use the military to protect civil rights. The Enforcement Act of 1871, passed on February 28, amended the first act and established federal supervision over congressional elections in areas with populations of more than 20,000 people. The Ku Klux Klan Act of 1871 was passed on April 20 due to Klan members murdering both blacks and whites who held office or voted. Some southern governors sympathized with the Klan and took little or no actions against it. This act therefore considered the actions of such racist groups to be terrorist acts, and thereby the president could suspend the writ of habeas corpus to violators as well as declare martial law against the organization. President Abraham Lincoln previously had suspended habeas corpus during the Civil War. President Grant decreed Klan members as insurgents in rebellion against the authority of the United States.

Grant used the Justice Department to attack the Klan, indict its leaders, and have them tried by predominantly black juries, dismantling the organization at least until the 1910s. He even sent troops into South Carolina in October 1871 and declared martial law in several counties in an attempt to push the Klan out of the state and restore order after hundreds of Klansmen terrorized the area. Grant was not always as aggressive in all southern states, as he always wanted southern states to support other policies. For example, he did not intervene in racial conflicts in Arkansas, Georgia, Louisiana, and Mississippi. Other issues reduced concern over rights for African Americans as the primary focus of the government, such as the Panic of 1873 that led to a global economic depression until 1879. As a result, the United States experienced widespread unemployment, business closures, and bankruptcies.

Grant continued his public insistence for equality for blacks, as evidenced on March 4, 1873, in his second inaugural address:

The effects of the late civil strife have been to free the slave and make him a citizen. Yet he is not possessed of the civil rights which citizenship should carry with it. This is wrong, and should be corrected. To this correction I stand committed, so far as Executive influence can avail.

Social equality is not a subject to be legislated upon, nor shall I ask that anything be done to advance the social status of the colored man, except to give him a fair chance to develop what there is good in him, give him access to the schools, and when he travels let him feel assured that his conduct will regulate the treatment and fare he will receive. (Grant 1873)

On March 1, 1875, Grant signed the Civil Rights Act of 1875. This was another legal attempt to ensure equality for African Americans in public accommodations and public transportation as well as allow blacks to serve on juries. Part of the law specifically stated "That all persons within the jurisdiction of the United States shall be entitled to the full and equal enjoyment of the accommodations, advantages, facilities, and privileges of inns, public conveyances on land or water, theaters, and other places of public amusement; subject only to the conditions and limitations established by law, and applicable alike to citizens of every race and color, regardless of any previous condition of servitude." The act was ineffective for several reasons. First, Grant in no way took actions to enforce the law. Second, states and even the federal courts considered the law unconstitutional. Finally, the law did not have public support. It was even criticized in the media. The law was eventually overturned by the U.S. Supreme Court in 1883, with the court finding that the federal government had no authority to regulate private organizations or individuals.

Grant did not seek a third term in office due to numerous scandals during his time in office. He also felt that his presidency was a failure due to his personal lack of knowledge and experience in politics and an economic depression that all took place under his administration. He lost support from the Republican Party for these reasons. Republican Rutherford Hayes (1822–1893), the governor of Ohio, won the presidency in 1876 in one of the most controversial elections in American history. Ulysses S. Grant died on July 23, 1885, in Wilton, New York.

FURTHER READING

Calhoun, Charles W. 2017. *The Presidency of Ulysses S. Grant.* Lawrence: University Press of Kansas.

Chernow, Ron. 2017. *Grant.* New York: Penguin.

Grant, Ulysses S. 1869. "Inaugural Address, March 4, 1869." The American Presidency Project, http://www.presidency.ucsb.edu/ws/index.php?pid=25820.

Grant, Ulysses S. 1870. "Special Message to the Senate and House of Representatives, March 30, 1870." National Park Service, https://www.nps.gov/ulsg/learn/history culture/grant-and-the-15th-amendment.htm.

Grant, Ulysses S. 1873. "Second Inaugural Address." Miller Center, https://millercenter .org/the-presidency/presidential-speeches/march-4-1873-second-inaugural -address.

Marszalek, John F., David S. Nolen, and Louie P. Gallo, eds. 2017. *The Personal Memoirs of Ulysses S. Grant.* Cambridge, MA: Harvard University Press.

Perret, Geoffrey. 1997. *Ulysses S. Grant: Soldier & President.* New York: Modern Library.

White, Ronald C. 2016. *American Ulysses: A Life of Ulysses S. Grant.* New York: Random House.

Post–Reconstruction Era

The end of Reconstruction was not based on equality for African Americans. Rather, it was marked by the end of federal efforts to continue to push policies for black equality. By the 1870s, the rights of blacks were suppressed by intimidation and violence in the South. The U.S. Supreme Court limited the effectiveness of federal laws and constitutional amendments in its rulings. This occurred when the federal government was marred by scandals and public mistrust as well as the country dealing with an economic depression.

The official end of Reconstruction came to be attributed to the Compromise of 1877. During the presidential election of 1876, Republican Rutherford B. Hayes from Ohio ran against Democrat Samuel B. Tilden, governor of New York. By midnight of election day Tilden appeared to be leading, with 184 of the 185 electoral votes needed to win. However, Republicans accused Democrats of using violence and intimidation to prevent blacks from voting in Florida, Louisiana, and South Carolina. The worst violation was in South Carolina, where armed whites and a black militia led to deaths on both sides. Moreover, South Carolina, Florida, and Louisiana submitted two results for the presidential election. Since there was no constitutional provision to deal with the issue of contested elections, the U.S. Congress appointed an electoral commission in January 1877 consisting of five members from the U.S. House of Representatives, five senators, and five Supreme Court justices. This membership consisted of eight Republicans and seven Democrats (after the Independent selection was replaced by a Republican).

While the commission was meeting, allies of Republican presidential candidate Hayes met in secret with southern Democrats to negotiate the election results at the Wormley Hotel in Washington, D.C. (which was owned by a black man, James Wormley) on February 26, 1877. In exchange for supporting Hayes as president in the contested election, Democrats were able to gain Republican agreement to withdraw federal troops from the South. Democrats in turn promised to support political and civil rights for blacks in the South. Before the compromise, Florida,

Louisiana, and South Carolina were the only southern states led by Reconstruction-era Republican governors. After the compromise these last three states were taken over by Democrats, thus officially ending the Reconstruction era. Republicans also promised that after Hayes was elected, he would support funding a railroad line to be built from Texas to California and appoint a southern conservative to his presidential cabinet.

During his acceptance of the Republican nomination for president, Hayes used the phrase "the blessings of honest and capable local self government," signaling his intention to limit the federal government's efforts to implement reconstruction policies. Southern states did not keep their promise to respect rights for southern blacks. In fact, stricter laws impeding equality for blacks were implemented as part of the Jim Crow era in the South. U.S. presidents for nearly the next 100 years had to deal with the negative effects of these laws.

The United States was moving from a majority agricultural economy to one based on technology and was expanding by gaining more western territory. This was one factor that ended the emphasis on slavery, which was based on economic support of the southern agricultural economy. However, racism and discrimination against African Americans was still a major issue, particularly in the southern states. Jim Crow laws forbade equality in voting, home ownership, employment, education, and practically all facets of social and political engagement.

Rutherford Birchard Hayes

19th President of the United States
Presidential Term: March 4, 1877–March 4, 1881
Political Party: Republican
Vice President: William A. Wheeler

Rutherford Birchard Hayes was born on October 4, 1822, in Delaware, Ohio. He earned a law degree from Harvard University before returning to Ohio to practice law. He opposed slavery and was active in the Republican Party. Hayes served as a Union soldier during the American Civil War and became a major in the 23rd Ohio Regiment. He had political support from blacks when he ran for the presidency, as did other Republican candidates at the time, due to the party's support for equality for blacks. For example, Frederick Douglass became the first black man to address a major political party convention when he spoke for racial equality at the 1876 Republican convention that nominated Hayes. Hayes lost the popular vote due to suppression of Republican votes in the South, particularly against black voters in Louisiana, South Carolina, and Florida. However, after he led in a very contentious Electoral College vote of 185 to 184, Hayes was declared the winner against his Democratic contender, Governor Samuel J. Tilden of New York.

President Hayes was the last president of the Reconstruction era. By the time he was elected president, Reconstruction in the South was all but over. Only Louisiana and South Carolina still implemented reconstructive policies, as by 1876 they were the only two states in the South that still had governors who were affiliated with the Republican Party. The focus of Hayes's administrative theory of government was meritrocratic, or the equal treatment of individuals without regard to political affiliation. For example, his cabinet selections included one member who was an ex-Confederate and Democrat and another who was a Liberal Republican in 1872 and opposed the election of Ulysses Grant as president.

Hayes did seek funding for education and voting rights for blacks and whites. Yet, he was clear that education for blacks should support training in manual labor. During his inaugural address, his views to repair the effects of the Civil War were apparent in such statements as the following:

Rutherford B. Hayes, the 19th president of the United States, became president as a result of a compromise between two political parties. The Republican Party ended Reconstruction and removed federal troops from southern states in exchange for victory in the disputed presidential election of 1876. (Library of Congress)

Let me assure my countrymen of the Southern States that it is my earnest desire to regard and promote their truest interest, the interests of the white and of the colored people both and equally and to put forth my best efforts in behalf of a civil policy which will forever wipe out in our political affairs the color line and the distinction between North and South, to the end that we may have not merely a united North or a united South, but a united country. (Hayes 1877)

Seeking to restore power to local and state governments in the South with good will, President Hayes withdrew federal troops in April 1877. This was due to the Compromise of 1877, which Republicans made to Democrats in the South in exchange for their support of Hayes running for president. Without federal troops, whites in southern states were free to continue violence and intimidation against blacks without being monitored. The withdrawal of troops was not only due to a promise to southern Democrats but was also because troops were primarily deployed to western states, and the Democratic-led House of Representatives would not support appropriation of any funds to the U.S. Army so long as troops were deployed in southern states. Even some Republican leaders were more concerned about economic problems such as falling prices and growing unemployment in northern states than violence against blacks in the South.

Hayes hoped that his show of support to the southern states would gain support for his policies and help build the Republican Party in the South. He also provided federal funds for infrastructure improvement projects in southern states. However, there was still southern opposition to supporting the party that implemented Reconstruction. For example, leading Democrats in Louisiana and South Carolina agreed to uphold voting laws, economic support, and civil rights for blacks if federal troops were withdrawn. After they were, brutality toward blacks increased substantially until no blacks were allowed to vote in those states for decades.

Hayes was challenged when Democrats won both houses of Congress in the congressional elections of 1878. Seeking to reverse policies supporting equal rights for blacks and to gain control of the White House in the next presidential election, they used the process of attaching riders to appropriation legislation. During this time in what has been termed the "Battle of the Riders," Hayes called the tactics of congressional Democrats unconstitutional and revolutionary. He vetoed bills that he disagreed with, and Congress failed to gain the two-thirds majority to override them. Hayes himself wrote messages to gain public opinion and Republican support for his actions. Although Republicans were more popular than Democrats, Hayes upheld his initial promise upon becoming president to not seek a second term in office. Rutherford B. Hayes died on January 17, 1893, in Fremont, Ohio.

FURTHER READING

Hayes, Rutherford B. 1877. "Inaugural Address, March 5, 1877." The American Presidency Project, http://www.presidency.ucsb.edu/ws/index.php?pid=25822.

Hoogenboom, Ari. 1988. *The Presidency of Rutherford B. Hayes.* Lawrence: University Press of Kansas.

Hoogenboom, Ari. 1995. *Rutherford B. Hayes: Warrior and President.* Lawrence: University Press of Kansas.

Levy, Debbie. 2007. *Rutherford B. Hayes (Presidential Leaders).* Minneapolis: Twenty-First Century Books.

Trefousse, Hans. 2002. *Rutherford B. Hayes.* New York: Times Books.

James Abram Garfield

20th President of the United States
Presidential Term: March 4, 1881–September 19, 1881
Political Party: Republican
Vice President: Chester A. Arthur

James Abram Garfield was born on November 19, 1831, in a log cabin in Orange, Ohio. After towing barges up the Ohio Canal as an occupation, he went to college and became an ordained Christian minister. He studied law on his own and passed the Ohio state bar. He was elected to the Ohio Senate in 1859. Garfield served as a lieutenant colonel in the Union Army during the American Civil War and then was elected to the U.S. House of Representatives.

By the time of the presidential election of 1880, the Republicans had adopted the term "GOP," for "Grand Old Party," and Democratic candidates openly campaigned in the South for a "white man's country" where white men ruled. The GOP acronym dates back to 1875. At that time, it meant "Gallant Old Party." The term was derived in the early days of the automobile and gained another popular although ultimately fleeting translation, "Get Out and Push." The term was used during the early days of automobiles when both political parties told their supporters to "Get Out and Push" as a means of motivating their voters.

Garfield won the election by one of the narrowest victories in the history of U.S. presidential elections, as he faced issues with Civil War reforms, tariffs, and government corruption. He swept the northern states in the election, while his opponent, Democrat Winfield Scott Hancock, took all the southern states. This would later be called the "Solid South," referencing a solid vote in southern states for a Democratic candidate.

Garfield had served as a major general in the Union Army during the Civil War. His term in office as president only lasted a few months (200 days), as he was assassinated the same year he took office. His short term in office was mostly unsuccessful due to infighting within the Republican Party and divisions between the factions of the Stalwarts and Half-Breeds. Garfield's agenda was mostly focused on civil service reform. The general belief and prevailing thought even among leading Radical Republicans was that Reconstruction was over. However, Garfield's support of black equal rights was evidenced during his inaugural address when he stated:

> The elevation of the negro race from slavery to the full rights of citizenship is the most important political change we have known since the adoption of the Constitution of 1787. No thoughtful man can fail to appreciate its beneficent effect upon our institutions and people. It has freed us from the perpetual danger of war and dissolution. It has added immensely to the moral and industrial forces of our people. It has liberated the master as well as the slave from a relation which wronged and enfeebled both. It has surrendered to their own guardianship the manhood of more than 5,000,000 people, and has opened to each one of them a career of freedom and usefulness. It has given new inspiration to the power of self-help in both races by making labor more honorable to the one and more necessary to the other. The influence of this force will grow greater and bear richer fruit with the coming years. (Garfield 1881)

Garfield appointed four black men to posts in his administration. Frederick Douglass was appointed recorder of deeds for the District of Columbia, Blanche K. Bruce was appointed registrar of the treasury, John Mercer Langston was named minister to Haiti and consul general to the Dominican Republic, and Henry Highland Garnet was appointed as minister to Liberia. Still, Garfield had the same policy focus as his predecessor, Rutherford B. Hayes, of seeking reconciliation with the South at the expense of black civil rights.

On July 2, 1881, President Garfield was shot while boarding a train in Washington, D.C., by a man seeking a federal government post based on personal patronage. This was a symbol of just how corrupt the federal government had become. Garfield died as a result of unsterilized tools used by the doctors to treat his bullet wound.

FURTHER READING

Feldman, Ruth Tenzer. 2005. *James A. Garfield.* Minneapolis: Lerner Publications.
Garfield James A. 1881. "Inaugural Address, March 4, 1881." The American Presidency Project, http://www.presidency.ucsb.edu/ws/index.php?pid=25823.
Garfield, James A. 2014. *Maxims of James Abram Garfield: General, Patriotic, Political.* Washington, DC: Westphalia.
Peskin, Allan. 1999. *Garfield: A Biography.* Kent, OH: Kent State University Press.
Rutkow, Ira. 2006. *James A. Garfield: The American Presidents Series; The 20th President, 1881.* New York: Times Books.

Chester Alan Arthur

21st President of the United States
Presidential Term: September 19, 1881–March 4, 1885
Political Party: Republican
Vice President: None

Chester Alan Arthur was born in Fairfield, Vermont, on October 5, 1829. He became a school teacher after graduating from college and studied law, practicing in New York City. As a lawyer, he represented a black woman who was denied a seat on a Manhattan streetcar. This case led to the desegregation of public transportation in New York City. Arthur served as quartermaster general of the State of New York during the American Civil War but never saw combat.

Arthur became president after the assassination of President James A. Garfield, having served only 200 days as vice president until Garfield was shot and later died. Arthur became vice president basically as part of the compromise within the Republican Party to appease nonsupporters of Garfield. Like his predecessor, President Arthur supported national reconciliation in the fight for equal rights for blacks. He aligned himself with Readjuster Democrats, who were independent of mainstream Democrats, in an effort to increase Republican control in southern states. The Readjuster Party, a split-off from the Democratic Party in Virginia, was a biracial group with a mix of Republicans and Democrats formed to wrench power away from the powerful and wealthy elites. They supported reducing Virginia's pre–Civil War debt.

The condition of blacks had not improved by the time President Arthur took office, even though the Civil War had ended almost two decades before. However, Reconstruction efforts had ended, and federal laws supporting African Americans had yet to be effective. The U.S. Supreme Court was unwilling to enforce those laws in court rulings, and the executive and legislative branches had been focused on comprise and conciliation. Writing in 1882, noted author and ex-slave Frederick Douglass stated the following:

Though slavery was abolished, the wrongs of my people were not ended. Though they were slaves, they were not yet quite free. No man can be truly free whose liberty is dependent upon the thoughts, feeling, and actions of others, and who has himself no means in his own hands for guarding, protecting, defending, and maintaining that liberty. Yet the Negro after his emancipation was precisely in this state of destitution. . . .

And yet the government had left the freedmen in a worse condition than either of these. It felt that it had done enough for him. It has made free, and henceforth he must make his own way in the world, or, as the slang phrase has it, "root, pig, or die." Yet he had none of the conditions for self-preservation or self-protection. He was free from the individual master but the slave of society. He had neither money, property, nor friends. He was free from the old plantation, but he had nothing but the dusty road under his feet. He was free from the old quarter that once gave him shelter, but a slave to the rains of summer and the frost of winter. He was in a word, literally tuned loose, naked, hungry, and destitute to the open sky. (Douglass 1882, 458)

Court cases continued, and a host of the most important took place during President Arthur's tenure in office. In the *Civil Rights Cases,* 109 U.S. 3 (1883), the Supreme Court heard a group of constitutional law cases filed by black plaintiffs against theaters, hotels, and transit companies that excluded them. The plaintiffs argued their protections guaranteed under the Civil Rights Act of 1875 entitled all citizens to equal civil and legal rights in public accommodations, public transportation, and jury service. The court ruled that the act was unconstitutional in terms of enforcing federal laws over public accommodations. After a ruling of 8 to 1, Justice Joseph Bradley gave the majority opinion:

When a man has emerged from slavery, and, by the aid of beneficent legislation, has shaken off the inseparable concomitants of that state, there must be some stage in the progress of his elevation when he takes the rank of a mere citizen and ceases to be the special favorite of the laws, and when his rights as a citizen or a man are to be protected in the ordinary modes by which other men's rights are protected. There were thousands of free colored people in this country before the abolition of slavery, enjoying all the essential rights of life, liberty and property the same as white citizens, yet no one at that time thought that it was any invasion of his personal status as a freeman because he was not admitted to all the privileges enjoyed by white citizens, or because he was subjected to discriminations in the enjoyment of accommodations in inns, public conveyances and places of amusement. Mere discriminations on account of race or color were not regarded as badges of slavery. If, since that time, the enjoyment of equal rights in all these respects has become established by constitutional enactment, it is not by force of the Thirteenth Amendment (which merely abolishes slavery), but by force of the Thirteenth and Fifteenth Amendments. (Cornell Law School 2018)

Arthur expressed disagreement with the high court's decision but offered little support to five different bills introduced by some congressional Republicans to replace the act. He also did not push Congress to pass new legislation.

Arthur was not generally considered a racist. He represented blacks when he was a lawyer in New York. In 1882 the Fisk Jubilee Singers from Nashville, Tennessee, performed for the president, becoming the first African American choir to perform at the White House. The group was organized in 1871 to tour and raise funds for college. Its early repertoire consisted mostly of traditional spirituals. The Fisk Jubilee Singers sang in some of the world's most acclaimed halls, cathedrals, and palaces. The group performed before such dignitaries as Queen Victoria, Mark Twain, Henry Wadsworth Longfellow, Ulysses S. Grant, the royal families of Germany and Holland, and the emperor of Japan. The performances spoke out loudly and boldly against racism in America and forced the issue onto the nation's headlines.

In 1883, the Pendleton Act was passed. This law's passage was primarily due to the shooting of former president James Garfield. It provided that government jobs would be obtained based on individual merit rather than political and personal merit. Since its passage, this act has benefited all government workers, including African Americans.

President Arthur was suffering from kidney disease from the time he became president. He was unable to run for reelection and died in 1886.

FURTHER READING

Douglass, Frederick. 1882. *Life and Times of Frederick Douglass.* Hartford, CT: Park Publishing.

Greenberger, Scott S. 2017. *The Unexpected President: The Life and Times of Chester A. Arthur.* New York: Da Capo.

Karabell, Zachary. 2004. *Chester Alan Arthur: The American Presidents Series; The 21st President, 1881–1885.* New York: Times Books.

Reeves, Thomas C. 1975. *Gentleman Boss: The Life of Chester Alan Arthur.* New York: Knopf.

Stephen Grover Cleveland

22nd and 24th President of the United States
First Presidential Term: March 4, 1885–March 4, 1889
Second Presidential Term: March 4, 1893–March 4, 1897
Political Party: Democratic
Vice President: Thomas A. Hendricks (March–November 1885),
None (1885–1889), Adlai E. Stevenson (1893–1897)

Stephen Grover Cleveland was born on March 18, 1837, in Caldwell, New Jersey. He started a law firm in 1862 and never served in the American Civil War after paying a Polish immigrant $300 to serve in his place. Cleveland served as sheriff of

Erie County, New York, before becoming mayor of Buffalo and then governor of New York.

Cleveland was the first Democrat to be elected president after the Civil War. The last Democrat before him was President James Buchannan, who served from 1857 until 1861. This was a major turning point for African Americans, given that Republicans were credited with ending slavery and instituting laws for African American equality against the staunch opposition of Democrats. During the Civil War, Cleveland served as assistant district attorney for Erie County, New York. Cleveland is also the only U.S. president to serve two nonconsecutive terms in office. He lost his first bid for reelection due to overwhelming opposition to his position on lowering foreign tariffs.

Blacks and Republicans were cautious and concerned about Cleveland's election, given that Reconstruction efforts were being challenged or reversed and southern states were still being controlled by Democrats and

Grover Cleveland served as president of the United States between the years 1885–1889 and 1893–1897. He refused to use federal power to enforce the Fifteenth Amendment of the U.S. Constitution, which guaranteed voting rights to African Americans. President Cleveland did not appoint any African Americans to patronage jobs, but did allow Frederick Douglass to continue in his job as recorder of deeds in Washington, D.C. (Library of Congress)

generally not supportive of equal rights for blacks. The Democrats were gaining influence partly due to infighting in the Republican Party. For example, Cleveland's Republican contender, James G. Blaine, had just as many enemies as supporters within the Republican Party. Cleveland also ran a campaign based on pointing out how corrupt politicians of the Republican Party were, and the nation wanted the government to end political and business corruption that had plagued the presidency since the term of Ulysses S. Grant. Republicans in general were losing power due to the disenfranchisement of black voting in the South. This was partly the reason that Cleveland was able to win a second term of office in 1892.

Cleveland was aware of the apprehension in having a Democratic president, particularly by blacks and those who supported their equality. In his inaugural address on March 4, 1885, he addressed this by stating the following:

> In the administration of a government pledged to do equal and exact justice to all men there should be no pretext for anxiety touching the protection of the freedmen in their rights or their security in the enjoyment of their privileges under the Constitution and its amendments. All discussion as to their fitness for the place accorded to them as American citizens is idle and unprofitable except as it suggests the necessity for their improvement. The fact that they are citizens entitles them to all the rights due to that relation and charges them with all its duties, obligations, and responsibilities. (Cleveland 1885)

During his second inaugural address on March 4, 1893, Cleveland affirmed his earlier statements:

> Loyalty to the principles upon which our Government rests positively demands that the equality before the law which it guarantees to every citizen should be justly and in good faith conceded in all parts of the land. The enjoyment of this right follows the badge of citizenship wherever found, and, unimpaired by race or color, it appeals for recognition to American manliness and fairness. (Cleveland 1893)

Still, Cleveland was not a supporter of equal rights for blacks in terms of laws or federal intervention with the states, even when black rights were being suppressed. He saw this as a social problem rather than a political one. He agreed with white southerners that blacks were inferior and therefore should not be given political or social equality. He did not support the Fifteenth Amendment, integrated schools in New York, or voting rights for blacks. During his tenure in office, hundreds of blacks were lynched in the South. Cleveland allowed Frederick Douglass to maintain his post as recorder of deeds for the District of Columbia but didn't appoint any other blacks to federal posts until Douglass resigned and Cleveland appointed another African American to replace him.

Cleveland did believe that blacks should obtain an education to improve their condition. He once stated to a black educator that "It seems to me of the utmost importance that if our colored boys are to exercise in their mature years the right of citizenship, they should be fitted to perform their duties intelligently and thoroughly" (*Alton Evening Telegraph* 1891, 2).

The Democratic Party gained control of both houses of Congress in 1892. They were then able to take action to dismantle laws put into effect as part of Reconstruction. Cleveland campaigned against the Lodge Bill of 1890, also called the Federal Elections Bill, that would allow federal circuit courts to appoint federal supervisors of congressional elections. The bill also would have made it a felony to interfere with voter registrations through such acts as violence, bribery, and stealing ballots. The bill narrowly passed in the House but was filibustered in the Senate. In 1894 Congress passed the Repeal Act, which repealed significant portions of the Enforcement Acts of 1870 and 1871 passed by Republicans as part of Reconstruction and ended federal control of elections. This led to the denial of black voters in states with laws or practices supporting this. Cleveland signed the repeal on February 8, 1894.

On March 17, 1886, the Carroll County Courthouse Massacre occurred in Mississippi. It resulted from two black brothers filing attempted murder charges against a white man who shot them for accidently spilling molasses on him. While blacks had the right to file such charges, whites were surprised and incensed that they did so. During the trial, a reported 50 to 100 armed men rode into the town on horses, ran into the courthouse, and shot at the two brothers and all black citizens attending the trial. While no whites were harmed, 10 blacks were killed onsite, and another 13 later died from their wounds. The event made national news and caused national outrage because no investigation was made by the court, the county, the governor of Mississippi, or its congressional senator. Former Mississippi Republican senator Blanche K. Bruce and former congressman John R. Lynch, both African Americans, met with President Cleveland on March 24 to request action by the federal government. However, Cleveland took no action.

The United States faced an economic depression that began with the Panic of 1893 and lasted until 1897. It began due to the collapse of two of the nation's largest employers, the Philadelphia and Reading Railroad and the National Cordage Company, causing the stock market to panic. The Pullman Palace Car Company, founded by George Pullman, producer of railroad cars, severely cut worker wages but did not decrease rents and other charges assessed on workers. This led workers to strike beginning on May 11, 1894. The Pullman company was one of the largest employers of African Americans during this period and is historically known as hiring blacks as Pullman Porters. Many credit Pullman with lifting African Americans into the middle class and giving blacks at the time a way to escape Jim Crow laws in the South with jobs working for the company.

Cleveland's administration reacted with federal troops being sent to quell the strike in its center of Chicago, and issued an injunction against the railroad union organizing strikers. An important point is that the union, the American Railway Union led by Eugene Victor Debs, banned African American workers from being members. Violence erupted in July 1894, and federal troops fired into a mob of workers. The strike eventually ended due to federal intervention and the loss of public support, as the strike impacted hundreds of thousands of workers across 27 states, leading to a national shutdown of railroads. The strike resulted in up to 30 deaths and hundreds of millions of dollars in property damage. As a result of the strike and due to recognition of the working class, Cleveland established Labor Day on June 28, 1894.

Cleveland established a close working relationship with Booker T. Washington in 1895. Washington gave a speech at the Cotton States and International Exposition on September 18, 1895, that later became the foundation for the Atlanta Compromise. This speech before a predominantly white audience led to this so-called compromise, which involved blacks submitting themselves to white political rule in exchange for whites providing them industrial education and due process of law. Washington called for blacks to start at the bottom of society and work their work up, as outlined in the following excerpt from his speech:

> Our greatest danger is that in the great leap from slavery to freedom we may overlook the fact that the masses of us are to live by the productions of our

hands, and fail to keep in mind that we shall prosper in proportion as we learn to dignify and glorify common labour, and put brains and skill into the common occupations of life; shall prosper in proportion as we learn to draw the line between the superficial and the substantial, the ornamental gewgaws of life and the useful. No race can prosper till it learns that there is as much dignity in tilling a field as in writing a poem. It is at the bottom of life we must begin, and not at the top. Nor should we permit our grievances to over-shadow our opportunities. (Washington 1901, 139)

Washington was invited to speak across the country and sent Cleveland a copy of his speech. Cleveland replied to Washington by letter on October 6, 1895:

I thank you with much enthusiasm for making the address. I have read it with intense interest, and I think the Exposition would be fully justified if it did not do more than furnish the opportunity for its delivery. Your words cannot fail to delight and encourage all who wish well for your race; and if our coloured fellow-citizens do not from your utterances gather new hope and form new determinations to gain every valuable advantage offered them by their citizenship, it will be strange indeed. (Harlan 1972, 83)

The two met in public and private several times afterward and developed a friend-ship. Washington's views were not shared by all other black leaders. Of notable contradiction were the views of W. E. B. Du Bois, leader of the Niagara Move-ment, who believed in equal rights for blacks, particularly in politics, and no com-promise to this effect.

The most damaging U.S. Supreme Court ruling against rights for African Americans occurred while President Cleveland was in office. In the case of *Plessy v. Ferguson,* 163 U.S. 537 (1896), the court ruled that racial segregation was con-stitutional as long as blacks were provided separate but equal facilities. The case originated when Homer Adolph Plessy sat in an all-white section of a train in Louisiana. The Supreme Court further held that state laws that mandated segrega-tion were "merely a legal distinction" and not in conflict with the Thirteenth or Fourteenth Amendments. The only Supreme Court justice to vote in the minority was John Marshall Harlan, who became known as the "Great Dissenter." Earlier in his life his family owned slaves, and Harlan opposed the Emancipation Procla-mation. He argued the U.S. Constitution was color blind, that all citizens were equal before the law, and that the white race was not the dominant race. He also argued against placing a large body of American citizens in a condition of legal inferiority. Restrictive laws based on race were expanded under the decision of the Supreme Court and were not overturned until the court's ruling in *Brown v. Board of Education of Topeka* in 1954. Cleveland was in full support of the court's ruling in the *Plessy* case. Three of the justices at the time had been appointed by Cleveland.

Booker T. Washington's relationship with Cleveland lasted after Cleveland left office. Washington held a fund-raiser in New York in 1903 to raise funds for Tuske-gee Institute. He invited Cleveland to speak. Feeling that he was supporting Wash-ington's case, Cleveland stated that freeing blacks from slavery had no more freed them "of their racial and slave-bred imperfections and deficiencies than it changed the color of their skin. I believe that among the nearly nine millions of negroes who have been intermixed with our citizenship there is still a grievous amount of ignorance, a sad amount of viciousness, and a tremendous amount of laziness and thriftlessness" (Cleveland 1903). Grover Cleveland died on June 24, 1908, in Princeton, New Jersey.

FURTHER READING

Alton Evening Telegraph. 1891. "Alton Evening Telegraph from Alton, Illinois, January 23, 1891." Newspapers.com, https://www.newspapers.com/newspage/16345463/.

Brodsky, Alyn. 2000. *Grover Cleveland: A Study in Character 1st Edition.* New York: St. Martin's.

Cleveland, Grover. 1885. "Inaugural Address, March 4, 1885." The American Presidency Project, http://www.presidency.ucsb.edu/ws/index.php?pid=25824.

Cleveland, Grover. 1893. "Inaugural Address, March 4, 1893." The American Presidency Project, http://www.presidency.ucsb.edu/ws/index.php?pid=25826.

Cleveland, Grover. 1903. "Responsibilities of the Races." *Florida Magazine* 5, no. 1 (January): 305–306.

Graff, Henry F. 2002. *Grover Cleveland (The American Presidents Series).* New York: Times Books.

Harlan, Louis R., ed. 1972. *The Booker T. Washington Papers,* Vol. 1, *The Autobiographical Writings.* Urbana: University of Illinois Press.

Jeffers, H. Paul. 2000. *An Honest President: The Life and Presidencies of Grover Cleveland.* New York: HarperCollins.

Nevins, Allan. 1987. *Grover Cleveland: A Study in Courage,* Vols. 1 and 2. Norwalk, CT: Easton.

Washington, Booker T. 1901. *Booker T. Washington's Own Story of His Life and Work.* Washington, DC: Library of Congress.

Benjamin Harrison

23rd President of the United States
Presidential Term: March 4, 1889–March 4, 1893
Political Party: Republican
Vice President: Levi P. Morton

Benjamin Harrison was born in North Bend, Ohio, on August 20, 1833, to a prominent Virginia family. He was named for his great-grandfather, who was one of the signers of the Declaration of Independence, and was the grandson of William Henry Harrison, the ninth president of the United States, who died from pneumonia only a month after he took office. The two have the distinction of being the only grandfather-grandson pair of presidents in the history of the United States. Benjamin Harrison practiced law in Indianapolis, Indiana, and was a Union Army colonel during most of the American Civil War, eventually rising to the rank of brigadier general. He was the last Civil War general to serve as president of the United Sates.

Like other Republicans, President Harrison supported free education, suffrage, and other legal rights for blacks. He also wanted to increase Republican political influence in the South by protecting the rights of blacks to vote and viewed this as a moral issue. Harrison supported the Lodge Bill of 1890, also called the Federal Elections Bill, that would allow federal circuit courts to appoint federal supervisors of congressional elections. It also would have made it a felony to interfere with voter registrations through such acts as violence or bribery and stealing ballots. The bill narrowly passed in the House but was filibustered in the Senate. Harrison addressed Congress's apathy to adopt the bill in his State of the Union Address given on December 1, 1890. During the address he stated the following:

> One cannot be justly charged with unfriendliness to any section or class who seeks only to restrain violations of law and of personal right. No community will find lawlessness profitable. No community can afford to have it known that the officers who are charged with the preservation of the public peace and the restraint of the criminal classes are themselves the product of fraud or violence. The magistrate is then without respect and the law without sanction. The floods of lawlessness can not be leveed and made to run in one channel. The killing of a United States marshal carrying a writ of arrest for an election offense is full of prompting and suggestion to men who are pursued by a city marshal for a crime against life or property.

> But it is said that this legislation will revive race animosities, and some have even suggested that when the peaceful methods of fraud are made impossible they may be supplanted by intimidation and violence. If the proposed law gives to any qualified elector by a hair's weight more than his equal influence or detracts by so much from any other qualified elector, it is fatally impeached. But if the law is equal and the animosities it is to evoke grow out of the fact that some electors have been accustomed to exercise the franchise for others as well as for themselves, then these animosities ought not to be confessed without shame, and can not be given any weight in the discussion without dishonor. No choice is left to me but to enforce with vigor all laws intended to secure to the citizen his constitutional rights and to recommend that the inadequacies of such laws be promptly remedied. If to promote with zeal and ready interest every project for the development of its material interests, its rivers, harbors, mines, and factories, and the intelligence, peace, and security under the law of its communities and its homes is not accepted as sufficient evidence of friendliness to any State or section, I can not add connivance at election practices that not only disturb local results, but rob the electors of other States and sections of their most priceless political rights. (Harrison 1890)

In the end, leading Republican congressmen agreed to let the bill die in exchange for southern support of two other bills they pushed, the Sherman Silver Purchase Act and the McKinley Tariff.

Harrison supported appointing blacks to positions in his administration. Frederick Douglass was appointed as U.S. resident minister and consul general to Haiti in 1889. A number of appointments were made to federal positions in different states, and this caused controversy by both whites and blacks. In 1891 Harrison appointed Minnie M. Cox as the first black female postmaster in the United States.

Cox was born in 1869 in Lexington, Mississippi, to former slaves William and Mary Geddings. She was the first postmaster in her community to have a telephone installed in her office. Some whites complained about blacks being appointed to any position, particularly in their state. For example, a black politician named Norris Wright Cuney from Texas was appointed collector of the Port of Customs at Galveston.

Northern blacks complained that too many positions were being given to southern blacks and that the black vote in the North was just as crucial as in the South. Some compromises were made to accommodate northern blacks by the president's staff and Republican state leaders. Douglass was even used to intervene in the dispute to ensure Republicans supported Harrison for his reelection bid.

Outraged at the continued violence against blacks, Harrison spoke against the increase in southern lynchings during his first annual message to Congress on December 3, 1889:

> But notwithstanding all this, in many parts of our country where the colored population is large the people of that race are by various devices deprived of any effective exercise of their political rights and of many of their civil rights. The wrong does not expend itself upon those whose votes are suppressed. Every constituency in the Union is wronged.

> It has been the hope of every patriot that a sense of justice and of respect for the law would work a gradual cure of these flagrant evils. Surely no one supposes that the present can be accepted as a permanent condition. If it is said that these communities must work out this problem for themselves, we have a right to ask whether they are at work upon it. Do they suggest any solution? When and under what conditions is the black man to have a free ballot? When is he in fact to have those full civil rights which have so long been his in law? When is that equality of influence which our form of government was intended to secure to the electors to be restored? This generation should courageously face these grave questions, and not leave them as a heritage of woe to the next. The consultation should proceed with candor, calmness, and great patience, upon the lines of justice and humanity, not of prejudice and cruelty. No question in our country can be at rest except upon the firm base of justice and of the law.

> I earnestly invoke the attention of Congress to the consideration of such measures within its well-defined constitutional powers as will secure to all our people a free exercise of the right of suffrage and every other civil right under the Constitution and laws of the United States. No evil, however deplorable, can justify the assumption either on the part of the Executive or of Congress of powers not granted, but both will be highly blamable if all the powers granted are not wisely but firmly used to correct these evils. The power to take the whole direction and control of the election of members of the House of Representatives is clearly given to the General Government. A partial and qualified supervision of these elections is now provided for by law, and in my opinion this law may be so strengthened and extended as to

secure on the whole better results than can be attained by a law taking all the processes of such election into Federal control. The colored man should be protected in all of his relations to the Federal Government, whether as litigant, juror, or witness in our courts, as an elector for members of Congress, or as a peaceful traveler upon our interstate railways. (Harrison 1889)

A delegation from the Virginia State Baptist Convention visited President Harrison in 1891 to request that he take a more aggressive stance against racial violence in the South. In a letter he responded, "I have endeavored to uphold the law as the single admissible rule of conduct for good citizens. I have appealed against race discrimination as to civil rights and immunities, and have asked that law abiding men of all creeds and colors should unite to discourage and suppress lawlessness. Lynchings are a reproach to any community" (Sinkler 1969, 209). However, he was also clear that the federal government would only get involved if federal laws were broken and that he would not use federal force to interfere with state authority. On December 6, 1892, Harrison again spoke on this issue during his annual message to Congress: "The frequent lynching of colored people accused of crime is without the excuse, which has sometimes been urged by mobs for a failure to pursue the appointed methods for the punishment of crime, that the accused have an undue influence over courts and juries. Such acts are a reproach to the community where they occur, and so far as they can be made the subject of Federal jurisdiction the strongest repressive legislation is demanded" (Harrison 1892).

Although Harrison supported some additional measures to support blacks, he failed to gain congressional support. A bill to grant federal funds to schools regardless of students' race and a constitutional amendment to overturn the 1883 U.S. Supreme Court rulings that declared Reconstruction civil rights acts unconstitutional both failed in Congress. The first bill, the Blair Education bill introduced by Henry W. Blair of New Hampshire, sought to reduce literacy through federal funding for eight years to public schools. It passed the Senate but remained in the House through 1888 and then was finally defeated in the Senate in 1890.

Harrison defeated Republican Grover Cleveland in the presidential election of 1888. When Harrison ran for reelection in 1892, he was defeated by Cleveland, making Cleveland the only president to serve two nonconsecutive terms in office. This was one of the most decisive elections in history, with Cleveland receiving 277 electoral votes compared to 145 for Harrison. Harrison lost mainly due to issues of high tariffs on foreign products, lack of support from his own political party, and opposition from political leaders due to his focus on civil service reforms. He died on March 13, 1901, in Indianapolis, Indiana.

FURTHER READING

Calhoun, Charles W. 2005. *Benjamin Harrison: The American Presidents Series; The 23rd President, 1889–1893.* New York: Times Books.

Harrison, Benjamin. 1889. "First Annual Message, December 3, 1889." The American Presidency Project, http://www.presidency.ucsb.edu/ws/index.php?pid=29530.

Harrison, Benjamin. 1890. "Second Annual Message, December 1, 1890." The American Presidency Project, http://www.presidency.ucsb.edu/ws/index.php?pid=29531.

Harrison, Benjamin. 1892. "Fourth Annual Message, December 6, 1892." The American Presidency Project, http://www.presidency.ucsb.edu/ws/index.php?pid=29533.

Moore, Anne Chiecko. 2006. *Benjamin Harrison: Centennial President.* New York: Nova Science.

Sievers, Harry J. 1996. *Benjamin Harrison: Hoosier President.* Newton, CT: American Political Biography.

Sinkler, George. 1969. "Benjamin Harrison and the Matter of Race." *Indiana Magazine of History* 65, no. 3 (September): 197–213.

Socolofsky, Homer E., and Spetter, Allan. 1987. *The Presidency of Benjamin Harrison.* Lawrence: University Press of Kansas.

William McKinley Jr.

25th President of the United States
Presidential Term: March 4, 1897–September 14, 1901
Political Party: Republican
Vice President: Garret Hobart (1897–1899), None (1899–1901),
Theodore Roosevelt (1901)

William McKinley Jr. was born on January 29, 1843, in Niles, Ohio. He won his first seat in Congress in 1876 and then served as governor of Ohio. McKinley was the last president to have served in the American Civil War and the only one who started the war as an enlisted soldier (a private) but later reached the rank of brevet major. As president he did not wish to alienate the South, so he took little action to deal with the increasing racial violence and legal exclusion of blacks. The U.S. Supreme Court's ruling in *Plessy v. Ferguson,* 163 U.S. 537 (1896) had greatly diminished equal rights for African Americans, with the court upholding the constitutionality of separate but equal facilities for whites and blacks, thus legalizing segregation. President McKinley did denounce lynchings in his inaugural address but did not

William McKinley Jr. was the 25th president of the United States. President McKinley was unwilling to alienate white southerners with his policies, and as a result, he did very little to address the disfranchisement of African Americans. McKinley's presidential initiatives in race relations were merely cosmetic. (Library of Congress)

take actions to deal with southern violence. In his first inaugural address on March 4, 1897, he stated:

> The great essential to our happiness and prosperity is that we adhere to the principles upon which the Government was established and insist upon their faithful observance. Equality of rights must prevail, and our laws be always and everywhere respected and obeyed. We may have failed in the discharge of our full duty as citizens of the great Republic, but it is consoling and encouraging to realize that free speech, a free press, free thought, free schools, the free and unmolested right of religious liberty and worship, and free and fair elections are dearer and more universally enjoyed to-day than ever before. These guaranties must be sacredly preserved and wisely strengthened. The constituted authorities must be cheerfully and vigorously upheld. Lynchings must not be tolerated in a great and civilized country like the United States; courts, not mobs, must execute the penalties of the law. The preservation of public order, the right of discussion, the integrity of courts, and the orderly administration of justice must continue forever the rock of safety upon which our Government securely rests. (McKinley 1897)

McKinley appointed 30 African Americans to positions of consequence predominantly as diplomats and record officers. For example, Walter L. Cohen from New Orleans was appointed as a customs inspector, and George B. Jackson, who was a former slave, was appointed as a customs collector in Presidio, Texas, on the Mexican border. These were regarded as low-level government positions and were fewer in number than had been appointed by previous Republican presidents.

The United States declared war on Spain in 1898. During the Spanish-American War, McKinley allowed for the recruitment and service of black soldiers in select states. He also required the War Department to commission black officers above the rank of lieutenant. Some states supported the war with segregated military units. Some blacks, particularly those who had served in the Civil War and lived in racist southern areas, saw this as a chance to serve their country and make positive strides toward equality. Blacks were also recruited because they were believed to be more attuned to combat in the tropical climate of the Cuban region. Booker T. Washington sent a letter to Secretary of the Navy John Davis Long on March 15, 1898, partly stating, "The climate of Cuba is peculiar and dangerus [*sic*] to the unaclimated [*sic*] white man. The Negro race in the South is accustomed to this climate. In the event of war, I would be responsible for placing at the service of the government at least ten thousand loyal, brave, strong black men in the South who crave an opportunity to show their loyalty to our land" (Harlan 1975, 389). Washington was also concerned about supporting blacks in Cuba:

> I believe all will agree that it is our duty to follow the work of destruction in Cuba with that of construction. One-half of the population of Cuba is composed of mulattoes or Negroes. All who have visited Cuba agree that they need to put them on their feet the strength that they can get by thorough intellectual, religious and industrial training, such as given at Hampton Institute and Tuskegee Institute. In the present depleted condition of the

island, industrial education for the young men and women is a matter of the first importance. It will do for them what it is doing for our people in the South. (Washington 1898)

Like other leading whites, McKinley supported the accommodationist views of Booker T. Washington and visited the Tuskegee Institute in 1898.

Supreme Court cases that diminished equality rights for African Americans continued under President McKinley as they had since the end of Reconstruction. In the case of *Williams v. Mississippi,* 170 U.S. 213 (1898), the Supreme Court upheld Mississippi's state constitution requirements for literacy tests and poll taxes as a prerequisite for voting for blacks only. The poll tax was applied retroactively from the time a person reached the age of 21. This impacted not only voting but also who could therefore serve on juries. The plaintiff in the case complained that he was convicted by an all-white jury for murder because blacks could not vote and therefore could not serve on juries. As a result, he argued that he was unable to receive an impartial trial and was deprived of his right to equal protection under the law. He was ultimately hanged after being found guilty. After the Supreme Court's ruling, other states enacted similar provisions; Mississippi's state constitution, for example, excluded most blacks and also poor whites from voting. This ruling further hampered McKinley's ability to implement actions to support blacks.

In 1898 white racist Democrats staged a successful coup on the local government of Wilmington, North Carolina, which at the time was predominantly black. Blacks in the city had gained professional status, owned leading businesses, and joined with progressive whites to attain leading positions in local government. While the North Carolina legislature was run by Democrats, the city of Wilmington remained under Republican control due to the black population. On November 10, 1898, led by former Confederate officer and white supremacist Alfred Moore Waddell, whites burned the black-owned newspaper and ousted blacks from the city, killing at least 14 black residents. McKinley was asked to provide federal support to the incident, known as the Wilmington Insurrection of 1898, the Wilmington Massacre of 1898, and the Wilmington Race Riot of 1898. He declined to provide any support. The following excerpt from an anonymous letter written by a black woman in Wilmington that was sent to McKinley on November 13, 1989, asking for federal help exemplified the condition:

Can we call on any other Nation for help? Why do you forsake the Negro? Who is not to blame for being here. This Grand and Noble Nation who flies to the help of suffering humanity of another Nation? And leave the Secessionists and born Rioters to slay us. Oh, that we had never seen the light of the world. When our parents belonged to them, why, the Negro was all right. Now, when they work and accumulate property they are all wrong. The Negroes that have been banished are all property owners to considerable extent, had they been worthless Negroes, we would not care. (Cott et al. 1996, 421)

Waddell became Wilmington's mayor after black councilmen and the black city mayor were forced to resign. Laws were then put in place to take away black rights, such as grandfather clauses requiring literacy tests and poll taxes for voting. Similar coups took place later in other cities, including Atlanta in 1906, Tulsa in 1921, and Rosewood in 1923. These can be partly attributed to the lack of action under President McKinley, hostility toward African Americans gaining prosperity, and the Compromise of 1877 that removed federal troops from the South.

President McKinley was assassinated. He was shot twice on September 6, 1901, by anarchist and former steel worker Leon Czologosz at the Pan-American Exposition in Buffalo, New York. McKinley would have been shot more than twice, but Czologosz was grabbed by James P. Parker, an African American. Parker was offered jobs and paid opportunities to have his photograph sold; however, he refused. He was clear that he did what he believed was his American duty and was quoted in a *Buffalo Commercial* article dated September 13, 1901: "I happened to be in a position where I could aid in the capture of the man. I do not think that the American people would like me to make capital out of the unfortunate circumstances. I am no freak anyway. I do not want to be exhibited in all kinds of shows. I am glad that I was able to be of service to the country" (Creighton 2016). Unfortunately, McKinley did not survive his injuries. He died from an infection from the wound on September 14, 1901.

FURTHER READING

Cott, Nancy F., Jeanne Boydston, Ann Braude, Lori Ginzberg, and Molly Ladd-Taylor, eds. 1996. *Root of Bitterness: Documents of the Social History of American Women.* 2nd ed. Lebanon, NH: Northeastern University Press.

Harlan, Louis R., ed. 1975. *The Booker T. Washington Papers,* Vol. 4, *1895–98.* Urbana: University of Illinois Press.

Merry, Robert W. 2017. *President McKinley: Architect of the American Century.* New York: Simon and Schuster.

Morgan, H. Wayne. 2003. *William McKinley and His America.* 2nd ed. Kent, OH: Kent State University Press.

Phillips, Kevin. 2003. *William McKinley: The American Presidents Series; The 25th President, 1897–1901.* New York: Times Books.

Snow, Jane Elliot. 1908. *The Life of William McKinley: Twenty-Fifth President of the United States.* Cleveland, OH: Gardner Printing.

Theodore Roosevelt Jr.

26th President of the United States
Presidential Term: September 14, 1901–March 4, 1909
Political Party: Republican, also Progressive Party or Bull Moose Party
Vice President: None (1901–1905), Charles W. Fairbanks (1905–1909)

Theodore Roosevelt Jr. was born to a wealthy family in New York City on October 27, 1858. He faced several personal calamities, first being a sickly child and then his wife and mother dying on the same day in 1884. After losing a bid for mayor of New York City in 1886, he was later appointed to the U.S. Civil Service Commission by President Benjamin Harrison. Roosevelt became assistant secretary of the U.S. Navy under President William McKinley in 1897. Roosevelt also served as the 33rd governor of New York from 1899 to 1900 and the 25th vice president of the United States from March to September 1901 under McKinley.

Roosevelt assumed the presidency after an assassin killed McKinley in 1901. Roosevelt became the country's youngest president at the time at age 43. President Roosevelt believed that blacks as a race were inferior to whites but also felt that some individual blacks were better than some individual white people. For example, he admired Booker T. Washington so much that he invited Washington to the White House on October 16, 1901, for dinner. Washington holds the distinction of being the first African American invited to dine at the White House. Roosevelt received extreme political backlash from the southern press and whites in both the North and the South due to this meeting, as eating together with a black man was seen as a sign of "social equality." A newspaper in Tennessee wrote that the event was "the most damnable outrage that has ever been perpetrated by any citizen of the United States" (Booker 2000, 125). Roosevelt commented on the entire event in a letter to Alboin W. Tourgee, the U.S. consul at Bordeaux, France on November 8, 1901:

When I asked Booker T. Washington to dinner I did not devote very much thought to the matter one way or the other. I respect him greatly and believe in the work he has done. I have consulted so much with him it seemed to me that it was natural to ask him to dinner to talk over this work, and the very fact that I felt a moment's qualm on inviting him because of his color made me ashamed of myself and made me hasten to send the invitation. I did not think of its bearing one way or the other, either on my own future or on anything else. As things have turned out, I am very glad that I asked him, for the clamor aroused by the act makes me feel as if the act was necessary.

I have not been able to think out any solution of the terrible problem offered by the presence of the negro on this continent, but of one thing I am sure, and that is that inasmuch as he is here and can neither be killed nor driven away, the only wise and honorable and Christian thing to do is to treat each black man and each white man strictly on his merits as a man, giving him no more and no less than he shows himself worthy to have. I say I am "sure" that this is the right solution. Of course I know that we see through a glass dimly, and, after all, it may be that I am wrong; but if I am, then all my thoughts and beliefs are wrong, and my whole way of looking at life is wrong. At any rate, while I am in public life, however short a time that may be, I am in honor bound to act up to my beliefs and convictions. I do not intend to offend the prejudices of anyone else, but neither do I intend to allow their prejudices to make me false to my principles. (Bishop 1920)

Roosevelt did not publicly apologize for his decision. However, he did not invite Washington or any other blacks to the White House again and also did not fight to support blacks in government positions in the South, which was the nature of the meeting he was having with Washington. Washington continued to give Roosevelt advice through other means, but Roosevelt lost support from many southern congressmen because of the visit.

Roosevelt did support Minnie M. Cox, the first female black postmaster appointed in the United States. She was originally appointed by President Benjamin Harrison to Indianola, Mississippi, but was removed and replaced by a white woman by President Grover Cleveland in 1892 and then reappointed by President McKinley in 1897. President Roosevelt appointed her for another term. White people in the area were upset by her appointment, and the white supremacist editor of the *Greenwood Commonwealth,* James Vardaman, made her appointment a major issue. He and other whites demanded that she step down, but she refused. Roosevelt would not accept her resignation or send troops to protect her but instead closed the Indianola post office until the whites accepted her. When they would not, he kept it closed until Cox's term expired on January 1, 1904. Cox continued to receive her full salary for the period during which the post office was closed. When Cox's post expired in 1904, Roosevelt then appointed a friend of Cox's, William Martin, to the post. Cox and her husband left the area out of fear for their safety but returned in 1904 to open the Delta Penny Savings Bank. Cox's bank assisted both black and white customers.

Roosevelt angered blacks with his comments on the lynchings that continued in the South in a letter he wrote in August 1903. Although he condemned lynchings based on race alone, he gave support to the practice based on the alleged crime of the lynching victim in which no sympathy is warranted:

> In a certain proportion of these cases the man lynched has been guilty of a crime horrible beyond description; a crime so horrible that as far as he himself is concerned he has forfeited the right to any kind of sympathy whatsoever. The feeling of all good citizens that such a hideous crime shall not be hideously punished by mob violence is due not in the least to sympathy for the criminal, but to a very lively sense of the train of dreadful consequences which follows the course taken by the mob in exacting inhuman vengeance for an inhuman wrong. In such cases, moreover, it is well to remember that the criminal not merely sins against humanity in inexpiable and unpardonable fashion, but sins particularly against his own race, and does them a wrong far greater than any white man can possibly do them. (Miller 1904)

Given the plight of African Americans at the time, the origins of the most progressive black organization began under the presidency of Roosevelt. The Niagara Movement originated in 1905 to demand full equality for blacks and in opposition to Booker T. Washington's philosophy of accommodationism. Led by W. E. B. Du Bois and William Monroe Trotter, the group met annually until 1908 and eventually led to the founding of the National Association for the Advancement of Colored People (NAACP) in 1909. One of the first actions the group took after its founding in 1909 was to write a letter to Roosevelt in condemnation of the Brownsville Incident in 1906.

In 1906, a small group of black soldiers were accused of engaging in a shooting spree in Brownsville, Texas. One white man, a bartender, was killed, and another, a police officer, was wounded. There were conflicting details on what actually occurred as well as a lack of any physical evidence that the black soldiers committed any crime. What was known was that there was resentment of the Buffalo Soldiers, black soldiers serving in a segregated unit at nearby Fort Brown in Cameron County, Texas. Regardless of the lack of evidence and their white commanders reporting that the men were in their barracks the night of the shooting, they were assumed guilty by the U.S. Army and the War Department inspector general, and President Roosevelt ordered the dishonorable discharge of 167 black soldiers from three companies without holding a military trial. As a result of the discharge, all the men lost their pensions. This was after a Texas court had cleared the men of any wrongdoing, and there was evidence that white citizens had planted shells and other items to frame the soldiers. Some of the African American soldiers had received the Medal of Honor, and some officers and clergymen in the community spoke about their high character. To the anger of many, Roosevelt waited until after the November elections and after blacks had cast their votes in support of him and other Republican candidates. This event turned black support away from Roosevelt, and even white members of Congress and some across the country were upset at his decision. The black soldiers were not exonerated of crimes until the 1970s.

In 1902, Roosevelt took a controversial position when he began espousing his concern over the "race suicide" of white America. On October 18, 1902, he wrote a letter to writer Marie Van Horst commenting on his appreciation for her article "The Woman Who Toils" famously known as "Roosevelt's Famous Race Suicide Letter." In one excerpt from this letter he stated the following:

> If a man or woman, through no fault of his or hers, goes throughout life denied those highest of all joys which spring only from home life, from the having and bringing up of many healthy children, I feel for them deep and respectful sympathy—the sympathy one extends to the gallant fellow killed at the beginning of a campaign, or the man who toils hard and is brought to ruin by the fault of others. But the man or woman who deliberately avoids marriage, and has a heart so cold as to know no passion and a brain so shallow and selfish as to dislike having children, is in effect a criminal against the race, and should be an object of contemptuous abhorrence by all healthy people. (Cheney 1919, 132)

Because of increased immigration, Roosevelt called on white women to exercise their patriotic duty to have more children. In his sixth annual message to Congress delivered on December 3, 1906, he stated:

> When home ties are loosened; when men and women cease to regard a worthy family life, with all its duties fully performed, and all its responsibilities lived up to, as the life best worth living; then evil days for the commonwealth are at hand. There are regions in our land, and classes of our population, where the birth rate has sunk below the death rate. Surely it should need no demonstration to show that wilful sterility is, from the standpoint of the nation, from the standpoint of the human race, the one sin for which the

penalty is national death, race death; a sin for which there is no atonement; a sin which is the more dreadful exactly in proportion as the men and women guilty thereof are in other respects, in character, and bodily and mental powers, those whom for the sake of the state it would be well to see the fathers and mothers of many healthy children, well brought up in homes made happy by their presence. No man, no woman, can shirk the primary duties of life, whether for love of ease and pleasure, or for any other cause, and retain his or her self-respect. (Roosevelt 1906)

Roosevelt spoke on race relations during a speech to the New York Republican Club on February 13, 1905. There was continued racial tension toward blacks, which was exacerbated by an increase in Asian immigrants. During his address, titled "Lincoln and the Race Problem," he outlined the need for slow actions to address social and economic equality for blacks and the need for training for blacks by whites, which he referred to as the "forward race":

If in any community the level of intelligence, morality and thrift among the colored men can be raised, it is, humanly speaking, sure that the same level among the whites will be raised to an even higher degree, and it is no less sure that the debasement of the blacks will in the end carry with it an attendant debasement of the whites. The problem is so to adjust the relations between two races of different ethnic type that the rights of neither be abridged nor jeoparded; that the backward race be trained so that it may enter into the possession of true freedom—not false freedom—true freedom, while the forward race is enabled to preserve unharmed the high civilization wrought out by its forefathers. The working out of this problem must necessarily be slow; it is not possible in off-hand fashion to obtain or to confer the priceless boons of freedom, industrial efficiency, political capacity and domestic morality. (Lewis and Roosevelt 2010)

Roosevelt kept a promise he had made in 1904 and did not seek reelection for a third term in office. He died on January 6, 1919.

FURTHER READING

Auchincloss, Louis. 2002. *Theodore Roosevelt: The American Presidents Series; The 26th President, 1901–1909.* New York: Times Books.

Bishop, Joseph Bucklin. 1920. *Theodore Roosevelt and His Time: Shown in His Own Letters.* New York: Scribner.

Booker, Christopher B. 2000. *"I Will Wear No Chain": A Social History of African American Males.* Westport, CT: Praeger.

Cheney, Albert Loren. 1919. *Personal Memoirs of the Home Life of the Late Theodore Roosevelt as Soldier, Governor, Vice President, and President, in Relation to Oyster Bay.* Washington, DC: Cheney Publishing.

Gould, Lewis L. 2012. *Theodore Roosevelt.* New York: Oxford University Press.

Lewis, Alfred Henry, and Theodore Roosevelt. 2010. *A Compilation of the Messages and Speeches of Theodore Roosevelt, 1901–1905.* Washington, DC: Bureau of National Literature and Art.

Morris, Edmund. 1979. *The Rise of Theodore Roosevelt*. New York: Random House.
Roosevelt, Theodore. 1906. "Sixth Annual Message, December 3, 1906." The American Presidency Project, http://www.presidency.ucsb.edu/ws/?pid=29547.
Roosevelt, Theodore. 1920. *Theodore Roosevelt: An Autobiography*. New York: Scribner.
Roosevelt, Theodore. 2004. *Theodore Roosevelt: Letters and Speeches*. New York: Library of America.

William Howard Taft

27th President of the United States
Presidential Term: March 4, 1909–March 4, 1913
Political Party: Republican
Vice President: James S. Sherman (1909–1912), None (1912–1913)

William Howard Taft was born on September 15, 1857, in Cincinnati, Ohio. His father, Alphonso Taft, was a Republican attorney who served as secretary of war and attorney general under President Ulysses S. Grant. The senior Taft later served as ambassador to Austria-Hungary and Russia under President Chester A. Arthur.

The junior Taft holds the distinction of being the only person to have served as president of the United States and chief justice of the U.S. Supreme Court, serving in the latter position from 1921 through 1930. He served as secretary of war under President Theodore Roosevelt, and Roosevelt personally chose Taft as his presidential successor. Roosevelt kept a campaign promise he made in 1904 upon winning his second term in office that he would not run for a third.

President Taft took office when African Americans were facing greater discrimination in the South. Jim Crow laws had been expanded to include such prohibitions as interracial marriage. The Ku Klux Klan was again gaining power in the South and reached its peak membership by 1920. Yet Taft touted the rights of blacks and extensively discussed their status during this inaugural address on Thursday, March 4, 1909:

William Howard Taft was the 27th president of the United States. President Taft met with African American leader and educator Booker T. Washington, co-founder of the Tuskegee Institute. He endorsed Washington's self-reliance courses for African Americans, which focused on building practical, employable skills. (Library of Congress)

There was a time when Northerners who sympathized with the negro in his necessary struggle for better conditions sought to give him the suffrage as a protection to enforce its exercise against the prevailing sentiment of the South. The movement proved to be a failure. What remains is the fifteenth amendment to the Constitution and the right to have statutes of States specifying qualifications for electors subjected to the test of compliance with that amendment. This is a great protection to the negro. It never will be repealed, and it never ought to be repealed. If it had not passed, it might be difficult now to adopt it; but with it in our fundamental law, the policy of Southern legislation must and will tend to obey it, and so long as the statutes of the States meet the test of this amendment and are not otherwise in conflict with the Constitution and laws of the United States, it is not the disposition or within the province of the Federal Government to interfere with the regulation by Southern States of their domestic affairs. There is in the South a stronger feeling than ever among the intelligent well-to-do, an influential element in favor of the industrial education of the negro and the encouragement of the race to make themselves useful members of the community. The progress which the negro has made in the last fifty years, from slavery, when its statistics are reviewed, is marvelous, and it furnishes every reason to hope that in the next twenty-five years a still greater improvement in his condition as a productive member of society, on the farm, and in the shop, and in other occupations may come.

The negroes are now Americans. Their ancestors came here years ago against their will, and this is their only country and their only flag. They have shown themselves anxious to live for it and to die for it. Encountering the race feeling against them, subjected at times to cruel injustice growing out of it, they may well have our profound sympathy and aid in the struggle they are making. We are charged with the sacred duty of making their path as smooth and easy as we can. Any recognition of their distinguished men, any appointment to office from among their number, is properly taken as an encouragement and an appreciation of their progress, and this just policy should be pursued when suitable occasion offers.

But it may well admit of doubt whether, in the case of any race, an appointment of one of their number to a local office in a community in which the race feeling is so widespread and acute as to interfere with the ease and facility with which the local government business can be done by the appointee is of sufficient benefit by way of encouragement to the race to outweigh the recurrence and increase of race feeling which such an appointment is likely to engender. Therefore the Executive, in recognizing the negro race by appointments, must exercise a careful discretion not thereby to do it more harm than good. On the other hand, we must be careful not to encourage the mere pretense of race feeling manufactured in the interest of individual political ambition.

Personally, I have not the slightest race prejudice or feeling, and recognition of its existence only awakens in my heart a deeper sympathy for those who have to bear it or suffer from it, and I question the wisdom of a policy which is likely to increase it. Meantime, if nothing is done to prevent it, a better feeling between the negroes and the whites in the South will continue to grow, and more and more of the white people will come to realize that the future of the South is to be much benefited by the industrial and intellectual progress of the negro. The exercise of political franchises by those of this race who are intelligent and well to do will be acquiesced in, and the right to vote will be withheld only from the ignorant and irresponsible of both races. (Taft 1909)

Taft's view on blacks was evidenced when he told African American college graduates in North Carolina in 1909, "Your race is meant to be a race of farmers, first, last and for all times" (Katz 1995, 350). In a speech to the graduating class of Howard University on May 26, 1909, he stated:

In all the growing communities of the South—I mean where there is a touch of the modern and a touch of progress and a touch of civilization—the white men of progress are beginning to appreciate the advantage of having a class like the colored men that they have there. They are anxious that they have an industrial education. They are anxious that they should make their way in the world and show their usefulness in the community. The truth is that the greatest hope that the Negro has, because he lives chiefly in the South, is the friendship and the sympathy of the white men with whom he lives in that neighbourhood. I know it is not the habit to think so, but it is growing and one of the things that misleads us most is the desperate, the extreme statements of white men from the South on the subject, but really they don't mean what they say. They have a theory that it may give them sometimes a little boost politically to talk in extremes and superlatives, but I have heard expressions from leading Negroes in various cities that confirm my judgment that the situation is growing better and better. (Taft 1910, 114–115)

Under his so-called Southern Policy, he would not appoint any blacks to government positions where he felt it would cause racial friction, particularly in southern states. On February 23, 1909, he wrote to a correspondent in Missouri and outlined that "I am going to take a decided step in respect to Southern Negro appointments. I am not going to put in places of such prominence in the South where the race feeling is strong; but I shall look about and make appointments in the North and recognize the Negro as often as I can." Further, "There is no constitutional right in anyone to hold office. The question is one of fitness. A one-legged man would hardly be selected for a mail carrier, and although we would deplore his misfortune, nevertheless we would not seek to neutralize it by giving him a place he could not fill" (Pringle 1986). Taft even went so far as to remove existing black officeholders from their positions, especially in southern states.

Taft did meet with Booker T. Washington on several occasions and took advice from him, and Taft supported blacks being uplifted through education and entrepreneurship, as Washington espoused. However, Taft did not support blacks getting involved in politics.

Taft made a historical appointment when he named William Henry Lewis of Massachusetts as assistant attorney general of the United States in 1911. This appointment seemed in contradiction to the president's prior stance. It also sparked national controversy and staunch southern opposition, as this was the highest honor given to any black person in the federal government in the history of the United States at the time. After a heated confirmation hearing led by southern Democrats, Lewis was confirmed by the Senate on June 14, 1911, and went to the White House to personally thank Taft. Lewis was also the first African American admitted to the American Bar Association (ABA). The ABA Executive Committee voted to oust him in 1912 due to his race after finding out for the first time that he was black when he entered the ABA's convention hall. Lewis did not disclose his race when he applied because he wasn't asked to. The ABA retained Lewis, however, after U.S. attorney general George W. Wickersham sent a letter to all 4,700 members of the ABA condemning the decision to oust Lewis and threatening to resign himself.

President Taft lost his bid for reelection to a second term because he did not continue the policies of his predecessor, Theodore Roosevelt. Roosevelt created a third party, the Progressive Party, to run against Taft. This split in the Republican Party led to the victory of Democrat Woodrow Wilson, with Taft coming in third in the polls after only winning two states. William Howard Taft died on March 8, 1930, in Washington, D.C.

FURTHER READING

Anderson, Judith Icke. 1981. *William Howard Taft: An Intimate History.* New York: Norton.

Katz, William Loren. 1995. *Eyewitness: A Living Documentary of the African American Contribution to American History.* New York: Simon and Schuster.

Pringle, Henry F. 1986. *The Life and Times of William Howard Taft: A Biography.* 2 vols. Norwalk, CT: Easton.

Rosen, Jeffrey. 2018. *William Howard Taft: The American Presidents Series; The 27th President, 1909–1913.* New York: Times Books.

Taft, William Howard. 1909. "Inaugural Address, March 4, 1909." The American Presidency Project, http://www.presidency.ucsb.edu/ws/index.php?pid=25830.

Taft, William Howard. 1910. *Presidential Addresses and State Papers of William Howard Taft from March 4, 1909, to March 4, 1910,* Vol. 1. New York: Doubleday, Page.

Taft, William Howard. 2002. *The Collected Works of William Howard Taft,* Vol. 3, *Presidential Addresses and State Papers.* Athens: Ohio University Press.

Woodrow Wilson (born Thomas Woodrow Wilson)

28th President of the United States
Presidential Term: March 4, 1913–March 4, 1921
Political Party: Democratic
Vice President: Thomas R. Marshall

Woodrow Wilson was born Thomas Woodrow Wilson in Staunton, Virginia, on December 28, 1856. His father was a Presbyterian minister, and his mother was the daughter of a minister. Wilson grew up in Augusta, Georgia, and Columbia,

South Carolina, where his father served as a chaplain in the Confederate Army. Wilson went to law school at the University of Virginia and served as president of Princeton from 1902 to 1910 before becoming governor of New Jersey.

President Wilson implemented policies and engaged in practices that clearly exhibited his racist views of blacks. He was progressive in other areas to the point of earning the title "Father of Public Administration" for his academic writings and development of policies that reshaped federal governance. The School of Public and International Affairs at Princeton University is named after Woodrow Wilson. He was the first southern-born president elected since Zachary Taylor in 1848, and southerners were given leading political roles under his administration. Black voters switched from the Republican Party to support Wilson, as they were disappointed at the stances taken previously by Presidents Theodore Roosevelt and William Howard Taft. On October 21, 1912, as part of his campaign promises, Wilson pledged the following to African Americans in a letter to Alexander Walters, head of the National Colored Democratic League:

> My earnest wish [is] to see justice done them in every matter, and not mere grudging justice, but justice executed with liberality and cordial good feeling. . . . My sympathy with them is of long standing, and I want to assure them through you that should I become President of the United States they may count upon me for absolute fair dealing and for everything by which I could assist in advancing the interest of their race in the United States. (Walsh 2014, 73)

The letter was published in African American newspapers and magazines, and Wilson sought and gained support from Oswald Garrison Villard, vice president of the National Association for the Advancement of Colored People (NAACP), and director of publicity and research W. E. B. Du Bois as well as Monroe Trotter, founder of the National Equal Rights League. Du Bois went so far as to endorse Wilson in the NAACP's *The Crisis* by writing, "We sincerely believe that even in the face of promises disconcertingly vague, and in the face of the solid cast-ridden South, it is better to elect Woodrow Wilson president of the United States and prove once for all if the Democratic Party dares to be democratic when it comes to black men. It has proven that it can be in many Northern states and cities. Can it be in the nation? We hope so, and we are willing to risk a trial" (Du Bois 1912, 29). Du Bois later reflected on Wilson by stating, "In 1912, I wanted to support Theodore Roosevelt, but his Bull Moose convention dodged the Negro problem, and I tried to help elect Wilson as a liberal Southerner. Under Wilson came the worst attempt at Jim Crow legislation and discrimination in civil service that we had experienced since the Civil War" (Du Bois 1956).

Although blacks supported Wilson when he ran for office due to his progressive platform based on social justice and opportunities for all, they quickly opposed his presidency when he appointed segregationist cabinet members. At the time Washington, D.C., was predominantly segregated, but the federal government was integrated, with blacks and white working together in federal agencies. When Wilson took office, blacks had risen to represent 5 percent of the federal workforce nationwide (Rothstein 2016). Wilson's administration quickly changed this by segregating the federal workplace. This segregation included work areas, rest-rooms, and cafeterias as well as demoting blacks from supervisory positions so none would be in charge of whites. Cabinet members Treasury Secretary William G. McAdoo (Wilson's son-in-law) and Postmaster General Albert S. Burleson were the most aggressive in segregating employees in their departments, with no objection from Wilson. In some offices, screens were used to separate workers by race and also so that customers could not see black workers. Under Wilson's administration, federal departments were segregated, which was consistent with his personal views that integration would create tension between blacks and whites. Wilson told a group of protesting black professionals against segregation in federal buildings that "segregation is not a humiliation but a benefit, and ought to be so regarded by you gentlemen" (Norton et al. 2015, 558).

Under President Wilson, officials in the U.S. Postal Service and the Treasury Department were allowed to discharge black workers around the country. For example, 35 blacks were fired from their jobs in Atlanta, Georgia, in 1913. The Collector of Internal Revenue for Georgia explained that these firings were because "there are no government positions for Negros in the South. A Negro's place is in the corn field" (Gossett 1997, 279). In 1914, a new policy was put in place to require a photograph on all civil service job applications. This ensured that potential black workers could be easily identified and that more could not be hired. This practice did not end until 1940.

The segregation under President Wilson was protested by the NAACP, the National Independent Political League, black and white citizens as well as some members of Congress. Wilson's position was that

> It is true that the segregation of the colored employees in the several depart-ments was begun upon the initiative and at the suggestion of several of the heads of the departments, but as much in the interest of the Negroes as for any other reason, with the approval of some of the most influential Negroes I know, and with the idea that the friction, or rather the discontent and uneasi-ness, which had prevailed in many of the departments would thereby be removed. (McInerney and Israel 2013, 191)

In letters to NAACP board chairman Oswald Garrison Villard, Wilson argued that segregation helped blacks because "We are rendering them more safe in their possession of the office and less likely to be discriminated against" (Newton 1951). Even Booker T. Washington, an advocate for cooperation rather than con-frontation, stated that he "had never seen the colored people so discouraged and bitter as they are at the present time" after a visit to Washington, D.C., in 1913 (Ginzberg and Eichner 1993, 275).

Even positions that had previously been reserved for blacks were given to whites under President Wilson. This even included the long-held tradition under previous administrations of appointing a black ambassador to Haiti. A black per-son had held the position of registrar of the treasury on five previous occasions. However, southern racist congressmen were successful in blocking the appoint-ment of Edward Patterson. Wilson did not confront the congressmen and allowed Patterson to withdraw his name. Patterson stated, "I refuse to embarrass your administration, Mr. President, by insisting upon my confirmation, and I also believe it is best for my race that I withdraw my name from further consideration" (Wilson 1978, 98).

On November 12, 1914, Wilson met with a group led by civil rights leader William Monroe Trotter to discuss cases of racial segregation across federal departments. Trotter was one of the founders of the Niagara Movement in 1905, which eventually led to the establishment of the NAACP. At one point in the meeting Trotter stated,

> Only two years ago you were heralded as perhaps the second Lincoln, and now the Afro-American leaders who supported you are hounded as false leaders and traitors to their race. . . . Have you a "New Freedom" for white Americans and a new slavery for your Afro-American fellow citizens? God forbid! . . . We are sorely disappointed that you take the position that the separation itself is not wrong, is not injurious, is not rightly offensive to you. (Lehr 2015)

As the exchange became more heated, Wilson retorted, "If you think that you gentlemen, as an organization, and all other Negro citizens of this country, that you are being humiliated, you will believe it. If you take it as a humiliation, which it is not intended as, and sow the seed of that impression all over the country, why the consequence will be very serious." Wilson stated, "You have spoiled the whole cause for which you came" before ending the meeting (Cooper 2009, 270–227).

On March 21, 1915, Wilson held a White House screening of the silent film *Birth of a Nation* for members of his cabinet and their families. The film was based on the novel *The Clansman,* which was written by Wilson's friend, political supporter, and former classmate from John Hopkins University Thomas Dixon. The film criticized Reconstruction as a period of blacks gaining power and sexually forcing themselves on white woman. The Ku Klux Klan was hailed as the savior of the South. The film included quotes from President Wilson including "Adventurers swarmed out of the North, as much the enemies of one race as of the other, to cozen, beguile and use the Negroes. The white men were aroused by a mere instinct of self-preservation—until at last there sprung into existence a great Ku Klux Klan, a veritable empire of the South, to protect the Southern country" (Stockbridge 1921, 21). Wilson's comments about the film included the statement "It is like writing history with lightning, and my only regret is that it is all so terribly true." The president's wife also encouraged segregation so that white women would not be subjected to the sexuality and diseases of black men. Addressing the issue in the NAACP's *The Crisis,* Du Bois wrote, "The federal government has set the colored apart as if mere contact with them were contamination. Behind screens and closed doors they now sit as though leprous. How long will it be before the hateful epithets of 'n----r' and 'Jim Crow' are openly applied?" (Wormser 1933).

The United States entered World War I in 1917 with a segregated military. Many blacks fought in the war due to Wilson's declaration that the United States was entering the war because "The world must be made safe for democracy." Blacks felt that supporting the war would help the plight of inequality for blacks in the United States. For example, an article in Baltimore's *Afro-American* stated,

"Let us have a real democracy for the United States and then we can advise a house cleaning over on the other side of the water" (Williams 2010, 24). When a draft was issued by the government under the Selective Service Act passed on May 18, 1917, over 1 million black men responded, and approximately 370,000 black men were inducted into the army predominantly into support troops. Blacks comprised only 10 percent of the U.S. population but 13 percent of the U.S. Army's wartime population.

Blacks were allowed to join partly because the United States did not have enough white soldiers to successfully fight in the war. Although there had been blacks who had died in combat since the American Revolutionary War, prior to World War I blacks were routinely denied access to military service. Even as a result of the draft, blacks were not allowed to serve in the U.S. Marine Corps and could only serve in limited positions in the U.S. Navy and the Coast Guard. Both at home and overseas, blacks were not allowed to fight alongside white soldiers. Some were given lower-standard quarters, uniforms, and food. Blacks were restricted from serving in combat until 1917, when the army created the 92nd and 93rd Divisions. These two units consisted of 40,000 African American men. Although they were opposed by American white commanders, they were revered by French officials. A delegation of black soldiers protested discrimination instituted by the government.

A positive aspect of the war was the Great Migration of blacks from the South to northern states from 1914 through 1920. Approximately 500,000 blacks from southern states moved to such cities as New York, Chicago, Cleveland, Detroit, and Pittsburgh. Many benefited from the factories producing products in support of the war, in addition to the absence of Jim Crow laws forbidding such actions as voting. Along with economic growth, blacks created an explosion of artistic and cultural centers.

However, during and after the war there were race riots across the country as the competition for jobs and housing increased racial tension. White factory workers were also angered at losing jobs to blacks as well as factory owners using blacks to combat striking white workers and attempts to unionize. Blacks were killed at the hands of white mobs in many instances. One of the worst conflicts occurred in East St. Louis, Illinois, on July 2, 1917, and resulted in 30 blacks and 9 whites being killed as well as hundreds being wounded. Approximately 6,000 blacks were forced to flee their homes. The NAACP organized the largest civil rights march up to that time in response to this event as well as mob violence and lynchings across the country, with 10,000 blacks walking silently down Fifth Avenue in New York City on July 28, 1917. The event was called the NAACP Silent Protest Parade. In addition to the events in East St. Louis, thousands of white men were involved in the killing of Ell Persons, a single black man, in Memphis, Tennessee, in 1915. A mob of 10,000 white men had attended a lynching of a black man, Jesse Washington, in Waco, Texas, in 1916.

In August 1917, representatives of the NAACP Silent Protest Parade petitioned President Wilson and Congress to take action. In their petition they stated that in the "last thirty-one years 2,867 colored men and women have been lynched by mobs without trial. . . . We believe that this spirit of lawlessness is doing untold injury to our country and we submit that the record proves that the States are either unwilling or unable to put down lynching and mob violence" (Jones 1919, 21). Wilson took no action to support ending the conflicts.

When the war ended, leading nations met in Versailles, France for peace talks. In addition to the goal of signing a peace treaty was the establishment of the League of Nations. Wilson was a leader in blocking a proposal from Japan to include racial equality as a founding principle of the League of Nations. The United States never joined the league, although Wilson was awarded the Nobel Peace Prize in 1919 based on its creation.

World War I ended on November 11, 1918. When black soldiers returned to the United States, they led community efforts to gain equality. The summer of 1919 became known as Red Summer, as assaults against blacks skyrocketed and the number of lynchings spiked. Race riots also occurred, particularly in Chicago and Washington, D.C. However, due to the Great Migration and blacks returning from serving in the war, blacks were more aggressive in resisting oppression. Instead, the "New Negro" demanded racial justice throughout the country. Black membership surged in the NAACP and in the more militant United Negro Improvement Association, led by Marcus Garvey.

After Wilson left the White House, he became president of Princeton University. His segregationist views did not change, as he refused to admit African American students into Princeton University. Due to the policies that he put into place while president of the United States, initiatives against African Americans still continued after he left office, even those supported by the federal government. For example, the federal government built a hospital in Tuskegee, Alabama, in 1923 for African American veterans of World War I. However, the hospital's policy was that no African Americans would be hired as doctors, nurses, or staff members. Woodrow Wilson passed away on February 3, 1924, in Washington, D.C.

FURTHER READING

Brands, H. W. 2003. *Woodrow Wilson: The American Presidents Series; The 28th President, 1913–1921.* New York: Times Books.

Cooper, John Milton, Jr. 2009. *Woodrow Wilson: A Biography.* New York: Vintage Books.

Du Bois, W. E. B. 1912. "Editorial." *The Crisis* 5, no. 1 (November 1912): 29–30.

Du Bois, W. E. B. 1956. "Why I Won't Vote." *The Nation,* October 20, http://www.hartford-hwp.com/archives/45a/298.html.

Ginzberg, Eli, and Alfred S. Eichner. 1993. *Troublesome Presence: Democracy and Black Americans.* Piscataway, NJ: Transaction Publishers.

Gossett, Thomas. 1997. *Race: The History of an Idea in America.* New York: Oxford University Press.

Jones, Jenkin Lloyd, ed. 1919. *Unity* 84, no. 5 (October 2): 21.

Journal of Executive Proceedings of the Senate of the United States of America, Vols. 25–27, From March 1837 to September 13, 1841, Vol. V. 1887. Washington, DC: U.S. Government Printing Office.

Lehr, Dick. 2015. *The Birth of a Movement: How Birth of a Nation Ignited the Battle for Civil Rights.* New York: PublicAffairs.

Maynard, William Barksdale. 2008. *Woodrow Wilson: Princeton to the Presidency.* New Haven, CT: Yale University Press.

McInerney, Thomas J., and Fred L. Israel, eds. 2013. *Presidential Documents: Words That Shaped a Nation from Washington to Obama.* 2nd ed. New York: Routledge.

Newton, Michael. 1951. *White Robes and Burning Crosses: A History of the Ku Klux Klan from 1866.* Jefferson, NC: McFarland.

Norton, Mary Beth, James Kamensky, Carol Sheriff, David W. Blight, Howard P. Chudacoff, Fredrik Logevall, and Beth Bailey. 2015. *A People and a Nation,* Vol. 2, *Since 1865.* Stamford, CT: Cengage Learning.

Patler, Nicholas. 2004. *Jim Crow and the Wilson Administration: Protesting Federal Segregation in the Early Twentieth Century.* Boulder: University Press of Colorado.

Rothstein, Richard. 2016. "Judge Woodrow Wilson's Racism by the Standards of His Time." *Newsweek,* May 8, http://www.newsweek.com/judge-woodrow-wilson-racism-standards-his-time-456232.

Stockbridge, Frank Parker. 1921. "The Ku Klux Klan Revival." *Current History: A Monthly Magazine of the New York Times* 12 (April–September): 19–25.

Walsh, Kenneth T. 2014. *Family of Freedom: Presidents and African Americans in the White House.* New York: Routledge.

Williams, Chad Louis. 2010. *Torchbearers of Democracy: African American Soldiers in the World War I Era.* Chapel Hill: University of North Carolina Press.

Wilson, Woodrow. 1978. *The Papers of Woodrow Wilson.* Princeton, NJ: Princeton University Press.

Wormser, Richard. 1933. *The Rise and Fall of Jim Crow.* New York: St. Martin's.

Yellin, Eric S. 2013. *Racism in the Nation's Service: Government Workers and the Color Line in Woodrow Wilson's America.* Chapel Hill: University of North Carolina Press.

Warren Gamaliel Harding

29th President of the United States
Presidential Term: March 4, 1921–August 2, 1923
Political Party: Republican
Vice President: Calvin Coolidge

Warren Gamaliel Harding was born on November 2, 1865, in Corsica, Ohio (today called Blooming Grove). Harding is considered one of the worst presidents in U.S. history due to sexual and corruption scandals that occurred during his presidency. Besides his affairs with very young women and drinking in the White House, his cabinet and top posts were held by men known as the "Ohio Gang" who used the system for their personal gain. Most of the scandals that occurred during his administration were not uncovered until after his death. For example, the Teapot Dome Scandal involved Secretary of the Interior Albert Fall taking gifts and personal loans in exchange for public land that was being rented to oil companies. Eventually, many in Harding's administration were charged with defrauding the government, but few ever actually served any jail time.

President Harding was never charged with crimes or considered part of the monetary scandals of others in his administration. He became president when the nation was still recovering from World War I, and the debate over the League of Nations was still raging. While he did not support immigration, he was generally considered one of the most vocal presidents to advocate for the rights of African Americans.

Blacks supported Harding after suffering under the segregationist administration of President Woodrow Wilson. Domestically, discrimination against African Americans continued in the South under Jim Crows laws. However, the Great Migration that began in 1916 was steadily increasing the number of blacks living in northern cities. Harding criticized the Great Migration as the cause of increased racial tensions between blacks and whites.

Harding openly criticized the unfair treatment of African Americans. He supported the passage of the Dyer antilynching bill that would have provided penalties and federal prosecutions for those charged. The bill had been introduced in the House of Representatives in 1918 and would have punished state and local officials who did not protect individuals from mobs, allowed for federal prosecution of those who perpetrated lynchings, and required com-

Warren Harding served as president of the United States from 1921 until 1923. President Harding delivered a speech in Alabama in which he condemned lynchings committed primarily by white supremacists against African Americans in the Deep South. Harding died less than three years into his term. (Library of Congress)

pensation of $10,000 to the family of any person who was lynched. The act passed in the House of Representatives on January 26, 1922. However, southern Democrats in Congress rigorously fought against the bill's passage into law and were successful in defeating it in December 1922 through a filibuster in the Senate.

Harding gave his "Address to a Joint Session of Congress on Urgent National Problems" on April 12, 1921. He was clear on his opposition to lynchings and his support of improved race relations:

Somewhat related to the foregoing human problems is the race question. Congress ought to wipe the stain of barbaric lynching from the banners of a free and orderly, representative democracy. We face the fact that many millions of people of African descent are numbered among our population, and that in a number of states they constitute a very large proportion of the total population. It is unnecessary to recount the difficulties incident to this condition, nor to emphasize the fact that it is a condition which cannot be removed. There has been suggestion, however, that some of its difficulties might be ameliorated by a humane and enlightened consideration of it, a study of its many aspects, and an effort to formulate, if not a policy, at least a national attitude of mind calculated to bring about the most satisfactory possible adjustment of relations between the races, and of each race to the national life. One proposal is the creation of a commission embracing representatives of both races, to study and report on the entire subject. The proposal has real merit. I am convinced that in mutual tolerance, understanding, charity, recognition of the interdependence of the races, and the maintenance of the rights of citizenship lies the road to righteous adjustment. (Harding 1921)

On October 26, 1921, Harding spoke before an integrated crowd of thousands in Birmingham, Alabama, in commemoration of the city's 50th anniversary. He surprised the audience by speaking against lynchings and supporting the voting rights of African Americans in a city known for segregation, racial violence, and discrimination. It many respects, the city was one of the centers of Jim Crow laws. Harding's speech was given when membership in the Ku Klux Klan reached its peak. In his speech, he stated the following:

Politically and economically there need be no occasion for great and permanent differentiation, for limitations of the individual's opportunity, provided that on both sides there shall be recognition of the absolute divergence in things social and racial. Men of both races may well stand uncompromisingly against every suggestion of social equality. Indeed, it would be helpful to have that word "equality" eliminated from this consideration; to have it accepted on both sides that this is not a question of social equality, but a question of recognizing a fundamental, eternal and inescapable difference. We shall have made real progress when we develop an attitude in the public and community thought of both races which recognizes this difference. Take the political aspect. I would say let the black man vote when he is fit to vote: prohibit the white man voting when he is unfit to vote. Especially would I appeal to the self-respect of the colored race. I would inculcate in it the wish to improve itself as a distinct race, with a heredity, a set of traditions, an array of aspirations all its own. Out of such racial ambitions and pride will come natural segregations, without narrowing and rights, such as are proceeding in both rural and urban communities now in Southern States, satisfying natural inclinations and adding notably to happiness and contentment. On the other hand I would insist upon equal educational opportunity for both. This does not mean that both would become equally educated within a generation or two generations or ten generations. Even men of the same race do not accomplish such an equality as that. There must be such education among the colored people as will enable them to develop their own leader, capable of understanding and sympathizing with such a differentiation between the two races as I have suggested—leaders who will inspire the race with proper ideals of race pride, of national pride, of an honorable destiny; and important participation in the universal effort for advancement of humanity as a whole. Racial amalgamation there cannot be. (Wheeler and Crane 1921, 706)

One of the most profound statements from his speech was "Whether you like it or not, unless our democracy is a lie, you must stand for that equality." The whites in attendance were shocked and silent, including the governor of Alabama, Thomas Kilby, and state legislators of Alabama seated behind Harding. Blacks cheered the president. W. E. B. Du Bois commented on the president's speech in the National Association for the Advancement of Colored People's *The Crisis* by stating, "For fifty years we who, pro and con, have discussed the Negro Problem, have been skulking behind a phrase—'Social Equality.' Today President Harding's speech, like sudden thunder in blue skies, ends the hiding and drives us all into the clear light of truth" (Harris and Tichenor 2010, 178).

Harding appointed some African Americans to federal positions, such as Walter L. Cohen to comptroller of customs. Harding wanted to establish an international commission to improve race relations, but this was blocked by southern Democrats.

President Harding died suddenly of a suspected heart attack in San Francisco, California, on August 2, 1923. Rumors that he had black ancestry persisted during most of his life and have continued since his death. They originated, however, when he was running for president. No physical proof has surfaced to substantiate these rumors.

FURTHER READING

Dean, John W. 2004. *Warren G. Harding: The American Presidents Series; The 29th President, 1921–1923.* New York: Times Books.

Harding, William G. 1921. "Address to a Joint Session of Congress on Urgent National Problems, April 12, 1921." The American Presidency Project, http://www.presidency.ucsb.edu/ws/index.php?pid=126413.

Harris, Richard A., and Daniel J. Tichenor, eds. 2010. *A History of the U.S. Political System: Ideas, Interests, and Institutions.* Santa Barbara, CA: ABC-CLIO.

Landau, Elaine. 2005. *Warren G. Harding.* Minneapolis: Lerner Publishing.

Mee, Charles L., Jr. 2014. *The Ohio Gang: The World of Warren G. Harding.* Lanham, MD: Rowman and Littlefield.

Trani, Eugene P., and Wilson, David L. 1977. *The Presidency of Warren G. Harding.* Lawrence: University Press of Kansas.

Wheeler, Edward J., and Frank Crane. 1921. "President Harding Discourses on the Color Line." *Current Opinion* 71, no. 1 (July–December): 704–706.

Calvin Coolidge (born John Calvin Coolidge Jr.)

30th President of the United States
Presidential Term: August 2, 1923–March 4, 1929
Political Party: Republican
Vice President: Charles G. Dawes

Calvin Coolidge (the only U.S. president born on July 4) was born John Calvin Coolidge Jr. in 1872 in Plymouth Notch, Vermont, and took office after the death of President William G. Harding, as Coolidge was his vice president. Coolidge had a primary task of restoring respect to the office of the president after the many personal and administrative scandals of Harding's administration. A succinct and even-tempered man, Coolidge was very quiet in social settings, particularly parties, earning him the nickname "Silent Cal."

President Coolidge was a clear supporter of equal rights for African Americans. During his first State of the Union Address, delivered on December 6, 1923, he outlined his support for Negro rights as well as federal funding for medical training at Howard University:

> Numbered among our population are some 12,000,000 colored people. Under our Constitution their rights are just as sacred as those of any other citizen. It is both a public and a private duty to protect those rights. The Congress ought to exercise all its powers of prevention and punishment against the hideous crime of lynching, of which the Negroes are by no means the sole sufferers, but for which they furnish a majority of the victims.

> Already a considerable sum is appropriated to give the Negroes vocational training in agriculture. About half a million dollars is recommended for medical courses at Howard University to help contribute to the education of 500 colored doctors needed each year. On account of the integration of large numbers into industrial centers, it has been proposed that a commission be created, composed of members from both races, to formulate a better policy for mutual understanding and confidence. Such an effort is to be commended. Everyone would rejoice in the accomplishment of the results which it seeks. But it is well to recognize that these difficulties are to a large extent local problems which must be worked out by the mutual forbearance and human kindness of each community. Such a method gives much more promise of a real remedy than outside interference. (Coolidge 1923)

During his commencement address at Howard University on June 6, 1924, Coolidge praised the progress that blacks had made in the United States:

> The accomplishments of the colored people in the United States, in the brief historic period since they were brought here from the restrictions of their native continent, cannot but make us realize that there is something essential in our civilization which gives it a special power. I think we shall be able to agree that this particular element is the Christian religion, whose influence always and everywhere has been a force for the illumination and advancement of the peoples who have come under its sway.

> The progress of the colored people on this continent is one of the marvels of modern history. We are perhaps even yet too near to this phenomenon to be able fully to appreciate its significance. That can be impressed on us only as we study and contrast the rapid advancement of the colored people in America with the slow and painful upward movement of humanity as a whole throughout the long human story. (Coolidge 1926, 31)

President Coolidge was vocal in his disdain for racism in public appointments. In 1924, U.S. Army sergeant Charles Gardner wrote to Coolidge protesting the

Republicans' nomination of a black dentist to New York's 21st Congressional District in Harlem. Coolidge responded with the following in a letter dated August 9, 1924:

> My dear Sir: Your letter is received, accompanied by a newspaper clipping which discusses the possibility that a colored man may be the Republican nominee for Congress from one of the New York districts . . . you say:
>
> "It is of some concern whether a Negro is allowed to run for Congress anywhere, at any time, in any party, in this, a white man's country."
>
> I was amazed to receive such a letter. During the war 500,000 colored men and boys were called up under the draft, not one of whom sought to evade it. [As president, I am] one who feels a responsibility for living up to the traditions and maintaining the principles of the Republican Party. Our Constitution guarantees equal rights to all our citizens, without discrimination on account of race or color. I have taken my oath to support that Constitution.
>
> Yours very truly, etc.
>
> Calvin Coolidge.
(Bean 2009, 148)

Coolidge welcomed many distinguished blacks to the White House. In September 1923, he met with officials of the Negro National Educational Congress to hear their concerns on segregation and discrimination in the federal government. In October of that same year, he gave an interview to a group sponsored by African American spokesperson and editor William Monroe Trotter. In that same month, Coolidge met with Tuskegee Institute principal Robert Russa Moton to discuss the state of political issues impacting the southern Republican Party. Moton, Emmett Jay Scott, and William H. Lewis (all from Tuskegee) were primary advisers to the president on race issues during his administration.

Coolidge also supported antilynching legislation, although he took no aggressive action to make Congress take action on the issue. It must be noted that the number of lynchings in the country still significantly dropped during his administration from the highs of the early 1920s. While he opposed the Ku Klux Klan, he was also nonconfrontational on the issue. Coolidge is historically known as a soft-spoken president who avoided some controversial topics. As a result, there were critics on some issues, such as his response to the 1927 Mississippi flood that killed hundreds and left some 200,000 African Americans displaced. While most white communities were saved, black communities were flooded to reduce pressure on the levees. Some migrated to the North, while many of those who remained were treated poorly in refugee camps. Thousands of blacks were forced to work for rations under armed oversight by the National Guard and local white planters. Coolidge declined demands to visit the devastated area because he felt that doing so would lead to requests for greater federal intervention, and he would not speak on the radio to appeal for private support. He wanted the state to handle the issue and also did not want to jeopardize federal budget surpluses.

In response to broken promises by President Coolidge, W. E. B. Du Bois was among his critics. In the July 1927 issue of *The Crisis,* Du Bois characterized the refugees as being concentrated into "slave camps" overseen by "big planters of Mississippi and Louisiana and the lynchers of Arkansas." In regard to the president, Du Bois stated that "Mr. Hoover is too busy having his picture taken and Mr. Coolidge, when an Arkansas mob burns the body of an imbecile, feeding the bonfire with lumber torn from a Negro church, while the mayor of the city keeps the Negro leaders imprisoned in their own business block—Mr. Coolidge tells the world of the privileges of American civilization" (Lewis 2000, 244). This was a stark difference from Du Bois's remarks that Coolidge deserved the 1 million votes he received from the black community in 1924. Then Secretary of Commerce Herbert Hoover went to the region to improve relief efforts. He wanted the Republican nomination for president in the next presidential election and knew that he needed the black vote. He asked African American leaders to tell blacks to vote for him and said that he would champion their causes if he became president.

On November 18, 1927, Coolidge signed the order to release Marcus Garvey from prison and deport him from New Orleans to Jamaica. Garvey was imprisoned for championing racial independence for African Americans and was thus targeted by the Justice Department as a radical. He was convicted on mail fraud and conspiracy, since he used the mail to send information about his cause, and was given the maximum punishment of five years in prison on June 18, 1923. Attorney General John G. Sargent recommended that Coolidge commute Garvey's sentence, since two years had been served and keeping him in prison would have negative impact from Garvey's followers, "who comprise a considerable portion of the Negro population of the United States" (Muhammad 1987).

On March 4, 1929, Coolidge signed Public Resolution 107, which authorized a National Memorial Commission to design and construct a national monument that would stand as a "tribute to the Negro's contributions to the achievements of America" (United States Congress 2003, 26). The memorial building would be used for public meetings, events, and exhibitions celebrating African Americans. Due to resistance from southern Democrats, the legislation was signed without any supporting funding. Coolidge's dream was revived in December 2001, when President George W. Bush signed Public Law 107-106 authorizing a presidential commission. This led to the eventual construction and opening of the National Museum of African American History and Culture as part of the Smithsonian in Washington, D.C. The museum officially opened on September 24, 2016.

President Coolidge chose not to run for reelection in 1928. To announce his decision, he simply handed handwritten strips of paper to reporters traveling with him on his summer vacation in 1927 containing the statement "I do not choose to run for President in 1928." There remains speculation about his decision. One explanation is that he believed that the president should only serve two terms. Some say it was because he predicted the market crash of 1929 that would usher in the Great Depression. However, he publicly stated that he declined to run due to the mental toll of holding the office of the presidency. Other historians point out that he was still mourning the death of his son in 1924 from a blister he developed while playing tennis. At the time penicillin had not been invented, and Coolidge later stated about his son's death that "the power and the glory of the presidency went with him" (Gould 2001, 266). Calvin Coolidge died on January 5, 1933, in Northampton, Massachusetts.

FURTHER READING

Bean, Jonathan, ed. 2009. *Race and Liberty in America: The Essential Reader.* Louisville: University Press of Kentucky.

Coolidge, Calvin. 1923. "First Annual Message, December 6, 1923." The American Presidency Project, http://www.presidency.ucsb.edu/ws/index.php?pid=29564.

Coolidge, Calvin. 2017. *The Autobiography of Calvin Coolidge.* New York: Andesite.

Gould, Lewis L., ed. 2001. *American First Ladies: Their Lives and Their Legacy.* 2nd ed. New York: Routledge.

Greenberg, David. 2006. *Calvin Coolidge.* New York: Times Books.

Lewis, David L. 2000. *W. E. B. Du Bois: The Fight for Equality and the American Century, 1919–1963.* New York: Henry Holt.

Muhammad, Askia. 1987. "A Mistreated Black Pioneer." *Washington Post,* August 16, https://www.washingtonpost.com/archive/opinions/1987/08/16/a-mistreated-black-pioneer/f32d2785-446b-4e89-a88a-68cd76668811/?utm_term=.c8952c3cadeb.

Shlaes, Amity. 2013. *Coolidge.* New York: HarperCollins.

Sobel, Robert. 1998. *Coolidge: An American Enigma.* Washington, DC: Regnery.

United States Congress. 2003. *H.R. 2205, Legislation to Establish within the Smithsonian Institution a National Museum of African-American History and Culture: Hearing before the Committee on House Administration, House of Representatives, One Hundred Eighth Congress, First Session, Hearing Held in Washington, Dc, July 9, 2003,* Vols. 81–83. Washington, DC: U.S. Government Printing Office.

Herbert Clark Hoover

31st President of the United States
Presidential Term: March 4, 1929–March 4, 1933
Political Party: Republican
Vice President: Charles Curtis

Herbert Clark Hoover was born in West Branch, Iowa, on August 10, 1874, the second of three children in a Quaker family. He was one of the first attendees at the new Stanford University when it opened in 1891. Hoover served as secretary of commerce under President Calvin Coolidge. While in this post, Hoover integrated the Census Bureau. He was the first Republican candidate for president to win Deep South states, including Virginia, North Carolina, Florida, Texas, and Tennessee. He achieved this by appealing to white voters and making it clear that he wanted to purge blacks from the Republican Party, exchanging his promises for support from business-oriented southern whites. George F. Garcia summarized the general perception of President Hoover among African Americans:

Herbert Hoover was considered a racist by many of his black contemporaries. W. E. B. Du Bois, the great civil rights leader, charged Hoover with

Herbert Hoover was the 31st president of the United States. In the election of 1928, to gain Republican votes in southern states, Hoover used a "Southern strategy," in which he appealed to white voters and used the support of the Ku Klux Klan against his Catholic opponent. He won victories in Tennessee, North Carolina, Florida, Virginia, and Texas. (Library of Congress)

being an undemocratic racist who saw blacks as a species of "sub-men." Walter White, the Executive Director of the National Association for the Advancement of Colored People (NAACP) during Hoover's presidency, contemptuously referred to Hoover as "the man in the lily-White House." Even Robert R. Moton, the conservative successor to Booker T. Washington as political advisor to Republican presidents on the "race question," came to believe that by his actions as president. Hoover had shown his contempt for blacks. (Garcia 1979, 507)

W. E. B. Du Bois characterized Hoover as a sinister enemy of the black race in a November 1928 issue of *The Crisis,* writing, "No one in our day has helped disenfranchisement and race hatred more than Herbert Hoover by his 'Lily White' policy, his appointments to office, and his failure to recognize and appreciate the plight of the Forgotten Black Man" (Lisio 1985, 270). In a 1932 issue of *The Crisis,* Du Bois stated the following in assessing Hoover's record in supporting African Americans for federal appointments:

> Herbert Hoover practically promised in his 1928 campaign speech at Elizabethton, Tenn., that he would appoint to office no persons to whom white Southerners objected. He has more than carried out this promise and has made fewer first-class appointments of Negroes to office than any President since Andrew Jackson. His few minor appointments have been mediocre and political. Particularly, in cases like Haiti and Ethiopia, where logic and courtesy gave him unusual opportunity to recognize Negroes, he flatly ignored them. In the Civil Service, he has allowed eligible Negroes systematically to be refused appointment, and colored appointees to be dismissed from their positions; while in the diplomatic and consular service, he has reduced the number of incumbents and made few new appointments. (Du Bois 1932, 362)

As far as black appointments, Garcia points out that Hoover

> raised the total number of black employees in the federal service to a figure
> of 54,684 and had considerably increased the number of black appointments
> to such posts as business specialist, education advisor, assistant solicitor, and
> assistant district attorney. A later black publication would concede that
> Hoover did make as many "first-class" black appointments as Harding and
> Coolidge combined, but during his presidency blacks found this exceedingly
> difficult to believe. (Garcia 1980, 472)

Understandably, the Great Depression consumed Hoover's presidency. Although
the laissez-faire policies of President Coolidge have been credited to leading to the
Great Depression, President Hoover was personally blamed. Shanty towns constructed across the country by the unemployed who became homeless were named
"Hoover Towns." His policies were seen as unsuccessful to the point that his train
was pelted with eggs and rotten meat when he campaigned for reelection in 1932.
Many accused him of being indifferent to the suffering of millions across the
country. There were even attempts to kill him while campaigning.

African Americans were particularly disheartened, given that they were hardest hit by the Great Depression. By 1932, more than half of the blacks living in the
South were unemployed. More blacks moved to urban areas from the southern
agricultural areas but encountered problems in cities as well. Jobs that were traditionally given to blacks were being given to struggling whites. According to the
1930 census, "56% of the total Negro population lived in rural areas," while "97%
lived in the South and 80% of those who resided in the South were at the bottom
of the agricultural stratum as wage hands, sharecroppers, share tenants and cash
tenants" (Wolters 1970, 18).

Hoover faced political opposition from organized African American groups.
On March 21, 1930, the president nominated John J. Parker to the U.S. Supreme
Court. The NAACP aggressively fought Parker's confirmation due to negative
comments he had made about blacks during his run for governor of North Carolina. Parker had supported disenfranchising the black vote. NAACP president
Walter White testified against Parker before the Senate and also had members of
the organization telegraph their senators and threaten to vote against them in the
next elections if Parker was confirmed. Parker's nomination was defeated by a
Senate vote of 41 to 39. Parker's confirmation was also contested by the American
Civil Liberties Union (ACLU) and the labor unions because of his support of "yel-
low dog" contracts, in which employees would take a job under the condition that
they agreed not to join unions.

During Hoover's administration, Illinois voters elected Oscar DePriest, the first
black Republican to the House of Representatives since Reconstruction in 1929.
First Lady Lou Hoover broke with custom and invited DePriest's wife, Jessie, to
the White House for a traditional tea visit for congressional wives on June 12,
1929. This was the first time an African American had visited the White House
since Booker T. Washington dined with President Theodore Roosevelt in 1901.
There were protests by southern racists in response to the First Lady meeting with
Jessie DePriest. In response, President Hoover invited Robert R. Moton, president
of Tuskegee University, to the White House.

President Hoover supported education and training for African Americans. For example, on April 1, 1930, he sent a letter to Eugene Kinckle Jones, executive secretary of the National Urban League, commending the league on its job training efforts for blacks:

Dear Mr. Jones:

The first step toward being a good citizen is to achieve economic independence. It is the soil in which self respect takes root, and from which may then grow all the moral and spiritual enrichments of life. The work of the National Urban League to train Negroes in the city to find new lines of occupation is fundamental to the progress of the race. I wish you success in this undertaking.

Yours faithfully,

> HERBERT HOOVER
> (Hoover 1930a)

Hoover was open in his opposition to lynchings. In a letter dated August 13, 1930, to a correspondent, he replied the following:

Dear Sir:

I have your letter of August 9th.

The question you raise is hardly appropriate for the governors' conference which is dealing with a special subject. Every decent citizen must condemn the lynching evil as an undermining of the very essence of justice and democracy.

Yours faithfully,

> HERBERT HOOVER
> (Hoover 1930b)

The conference he was referring to was a White House Conference on Drought Relief, attended by governors of the drought states that were hit hardest by the issue in 1930. Hoover, however, never supported federal legislation criminalizing lynching. Interestingly, the first prison sentence he pardoned under his executive authority was a black man convicted of murdering a white women because there was no eyewitness to the crime, and the verdict was based on a forced confession by the man.

Also in 1930, Hoover was personally criticized along with the War Department for providing segregated accommodations for mothers traveling to Europe to visit the graves of their sons and husbands. President Coolidge signed a law in March 1929 authorizing and funding Gold Star Mothers, who were mothers and widows of soldiers whose remains could not be returned to the United States from Europe for whatever reason. Five million dollars were appropriated to cover two-week all-expense-paid trips for these mothers to travel to Europe, which supported 17,389 women, of which 624 were African Americans. In 1930 while white women were allowed to travel on luxury liners to France, the black women were segregated and provided accommodations on commercial freight ships, which some referred to as "cattle boats." The NAACP led the protest against the segregation, and some black women refused to travel on the freight ships. The black Chicago newspaper *Metropolitan News* ran a front-page article on the issue with the headline "Gold Star Black Mothers: STAY OUT OF FRANCE If Forced to Sail on Jim Crow Ships!" William Monroe Trotter warned Hoover that the use of segregated ships was seen as his "deference to the prejudice of Southern white women" (Lisio 1985, 236). Hoover would not respond to questions and referred the issue to the War Department, since as he saw it the department had sole authority to run the program. The War Department resisted claims that it was wrong. In response to one letter, Assistant Secretary of War F. H. Payne responded,

> After thorough study, the conclusion was reached that the formation of white and colored groups of mothers and widows would best assure the contentment and comfort of the pilgrims themselves. No discrimination as between the various groups is contemplated. All groups will receive like accommodations at hotels and on steamships, and the representatives of the War Department will, at all times, be as solicitous of the welfare of the colored mothers and widows as they will be of the welfare of those of the white race. . . . It would seem natural to assume that these mothers and widows would prefer to seek solace in their grief from companions of their own race. (Potter 1999)

Between 1930 and 1933, 6,693 Gold Star Mothers traveled to Europe, of which 168 were black.

Another issue that occurred with the War Department stemmed from efforts to reduce the size of the U.S. Army beginning in 1931. The reduction of the Tenth Cavalry, a black unit, saw cuts that were much greater than for white units. In addition, promotions in the unit were cancelled, and a ceiling was placed on the number of black officers allowed. Black leaders such as Robert R. Moton were vocal on the issue, leading Hoover to ask for an investigation. After acting secretary of war F. H. Payne reported that this action was based on efficiency versus racism, Hoover took no further action.

President Herbert Hoover is credited with turning blacks from the Republican Party, leading to blacks voting predominantly Democrat starting in the mid-20th century. He was nationally unpopular because of the Great Depression when he ran for reelection in 1932. He was soundly defeated by Franklin Delano Roosevelt, with Roosevelt winning 472 electoral votes compared to only 59 for Hoover. Democrats also won both houses of Congress.

FURTHER READING

Du Bois, W. E. B. 1932. "Herbert Hoover." *The Crisis* 39, no. 11 (November): 362.
Garcia, George F. 1979. "Herbert Hoover and the Issue of Race." *Annals of Iowa* 44, no. 7 (Winter): 507–515.

Garcia, George F. 1980. "Black Disaffection from the Republican Party during the Presidency of Herbert Hoover, 1928–1932." *Annals of Iowa* 45, no. 6: 462–477, https://ir.uiowa.edu/cgi/viewcontent.cgi?article=8734&context=annals-of-iowa.

Hoover, Herbert. 1930a. "Message Commending the National Urban League on Its Job Training Efforts for Negroes, March 13, 1930." The American Presidency Project, http://www.presidency.ucsb.edu/ws/index.php?pid=22548.

Hoover Herbert. 1930b. "Message Condemning Lynching, September 23, 1930." The American Presidency Project, http://www.presidency.ucsb.edu/ws/index.php?pid=22360.

Hoover, Herbert. 2016. *American Individualism.* Stanford, CA: Hoover Institution Press.

Jeansonne, Glen. 2016. *Herbert Hoover: A Life.* New York: New American Library.

Leuchtenburg, William E. 2009. *Herbert Hoover: The American Presidents Series; The 31st President, 1929–1933.* New York: Times Books.

Lisio, Donald J. 1985. *Hoover, Blacks, and Lily-Whites: A Study of Southern Strategies.* Chapel Hill: University of North Carolina Press.

Rappleye, Charles. 2017. *Herbert Hoover in the White House: The Ordeal of the Presidency.* New York: Simon and Schuster.

Whyte, Kenneth. 2017. *Hoover: An Extraordinary Life in Extraordinary Times.* New York: Knopf.

Wolters, Raymond. 1970. *Negroes and the Great Depression: The Problem of Economic Recovery,* Vol. 6. Westport, CT: Greenwood.

Franklin Delano Roosevelt Sr.

32nd President of the United States
Presidential Term: March 4, 1933–April 12, 1945
Political Party: Democratic
Vice President: John Nance Garner (1933–1941), Henry A. Wallace (1941–1945), Harry S. Truman (1945)

Franklin Delano Roosevelt Sr. (widely known by his initials FDR) was born to a wealthy family in Hyde Park, New York, on January 30, 1882. He attended such elite schools as Groton and Harvard after being educated by private tutors. Roosevelt married Anna Eleanor Roosevelt, his distant cousin and the niece of former president Theodore Roosevelt, in 1905. Franklin Roosevelt obtained a law degree from Columbia and then practiced law on Wall Street before being appointed assistant secretary of the navy by President Woodrow Wilson.

President Roosevelt served a record four presidential terms in office. He won the presidency in 1932 due to his plan to deal with the Great Depression. President Herbert Hoover still won the majority of the black vote, but Roosevelt is credited with turning the black vote to Democrats due to policies benefiting African Americans during his term. African Americans were disappointed in the performance and policies of Hoover; they had given up support to the Republican Party as well. In the election of 1936, Roosevelt overwhelmingly won the black vote. The initial years of his presidency were consumed by the Great Depression, and he instituted new policies under his New Deal program that included a range of economic stimulus programs, from public works projects to regulatory reforms to the establishment of new federal agencies. These policies were not directly designed to support African Americans, but they benefited black along with white Americans. For example, by 1935 the Federal Emergency Relief Administration was supporting 30 percent of the black population. Blacks also benefited from wage laws and unionization (Giorgio 2015).

The presidency of Franklin Roosevelt is viewed as the first time that civil rights was thrust to the forefront of American public policy and seen as a relevant political issue. Although Roosevelt was cautious to not offend southern whites, both he and his wife Eleanor were open to hearing grievances from the black community and taking them seriously. As noted by Harvard Sitkoff,

> Perhaps most importantly, blacks in the thirties lauded the manifold ways in which the New Deal reform spirit ushered in a new political climate in which Afro-Americans and their allies could begin to struggle with expectation of success. They took heart from the expanding authority of the federal government and the changing balance of power in the Democratic Party, as well as from the overt sympathy for the underprivileged shown by the Roosevelt administration; and they made common cause with fellow sufferers in pressing the New Deal to become even more of an instrument for humane, liberal reform. (Sitkoff 2010, 39–40)

Eleanor Roosevelt wanted her husband to appoint an African American to a high position in his administration to advise him on policy issues impacting blacks. On November 22, 1941, she wrote a letter to him: "I have been asked to call your attention to the importance of having a Negro in a position who can actually confer with the president occasionally on problems that are pertinent to Negroes, and who can have a very close affiliation with the Under-Secretaries of the President as to the Negro's cause." The president replied to her note by writing, "No—any more than I can put in a Jew as such or a Spiritualist as such—FDR" (Franklin D. Roosevelt Presidential Library and Museum 2018a).

The president and his wife eventually relied on a group of African Americans as trusted advisers. The Black Cabinet (also known as the "Federal Council of Negro Affairs" and the "Black Brain Trust") was made up of 45 African Americans who advised the administration from 1933 through 1945. The group got its name from Mary McLeod Bethune in 1936, who herself served as an adviser. She, like other blacks, switched from the Republican Party to become a Democrat. Known as "The First Lady of the Struggle," she was a stateswoman, philanthropist, and civil rights leader and is best known for founding the private Bethune-Cookman University in Daytona Beach, Florida, to educate blacks in 1904. The school was originally named the Daytona Educational and Industrial Training School but merged with Cookman Institute of Jacksonville, Florida, in 1923 to become coeducational. The Black Cabinet worked toward such causes as ensuring that blacks received 10 percent of welfare funds, since blacks comprised 10 percent of the population, and equal pay and adequate working conditions for blacks and whites. Its members worked in various federal departments and agencies, as outlined in the following list of members in 1938:

- Mary McLeod Bethune, National Youth Administration
- Edgar G. Brown, Civilian Conservation Corps
- Dr. Roscoe C. Brown, Public Health Service
- Dr. Ambrose Caliver, Department of the Interior
- Joseph H. Evans, Farm Security Administration
- Charles E. Hall, Department of Commerce
- Joseph R. Houchins, Department of Commerce
- William J. Houston, Department of Justice
- Henry A. Hunt, Farm Credit Administration
- Dewey R. Jones, Department of the Interior
- Edward H. Lawson Jr., Works Projects Administration
- Ralph E. Mizelle, U.S. Postal Service
- Lawrence A. Oxley, Department of Labor
- J. Parker Prescott, Housing Authority
- Alfred Edgar Smith, Works Projects Administration
- Dr. William J. Thomkins, Recorder of Deeds
- Dr. Robert C. Weaver, Federal Housing Authority
- Arthur Weiseger, Department of Labor
- John W. Whitten, Works Projects Administration

Roosevelt also made notable black appointments. In 1937 he appointed the first African American federal judge, William Henry Hastie Jr., who served for the U.S. District Court for the Virgin Islands. He later became the first African American appellate judge under President Harry S. Truman on October 21, 1949, and served as the first African American governor of the Virgin Islands from 1946 through 1949. Roosevelt also promoted the first African American general in the U.S. military, U.S. Army Brigadier General Benjamin Oliver Davis Sr., on October 25, 1940. His son, Benjamin Oliver Davis Jr., later became the first African American general in the U.S. Air Force on December 9, 1998, and went on to advance to four-star general under President Bill Clinton.

First Lady Eleanor Roosevelt was supportive of rights for African Americans. She not only attempted to sway the president's decisions on issues but also took action herself. For example, in 1938 she attended an event in Birmingham, Alabama, where ordinances segregated blacks and whites. Mrs. Roosevelt could not sit with Mary McLeod Bethune and her other black friends. The First Lady then placed her chair in the center aisle between the black and white sections. In one of the most historical examples in 1939, Howard University petitioned the Daughters of the American Revolution to use Constitution Hall in Washington, D.C., for a concert featuring renowned African American opera singer Marian Anderson. Because the venue was segregated, the request was denied. Mrs. Roosevelt intervened by first resigning from the organization on February 26, 1939, declaring it "set an example which seems to me unfortunate." Further, she wrote, "To remain as a member implies approval of that action, and therefore, I am resigning" (Franklin D. Roosevelt Presidential Library and Museum 2018b). Working with the National Association for the Advancement of Colored People (NAACP) and the Department of Interior, whose secretary Harold Ickes was African American and a former president of the Chicago NAACP, they gained the president's approval and held an outdoor concert featuring Anderson at the Lincoln Memorial on April 9, Easter Day. The event was attended by an integrated crowd of 75,000 people, including citizens and dignitaries. The event was also broadcast over the radio. Later that year Anderson performed at the White House as part of the entertainment during a state visit by King George VI and Queen Elizabeth of England. Anderson's first performance in the White House was earlier in 1936. Notably, she also sang at the inauguration of President John F. Kennedy on January 20, 1961, and performed for Kennedy and dignitaries in the East Room of the White House in 1962. During her time as First Lady, Mrs. Roosevelt invited hundreds of blacks to the White House and was pictured with them and also held fundraisers for many black causes.

African Americans still faced discrimination, particularly in the South. In the North, they suffered worse from the Great Depression and faced severe economic, housing, and social disparities. Still, African Americans greatly benefited from programs under President Roosevelt's administration, as outlined by the Roosevelt Institute:

> With respect to the critical issue of employment, for example, we know that by 1935, the Works Progress Administration (WPA) was employing approximately 350,000 African Americans annually, about 15% of its total workforce. In the Civilian Conservation Corps, the percentage of blacks who took part climbed from roughly 3% at its outset in 1933 to over 11% by the close of 1938 with a total of more than 350,000 having been enrolled in the CCC by the time the program was shut down in 1942. The National Youth Administration, under the direction of Aubrey Williams, hired more black administrators than any other New Deal agency; employed African American supervisors to oversee the work the agency was doing on behalf of black youth for each state in the south; and assisted more than 300,000 Africa American youth during the Depression. In 1934, the Public Works Administration (PWA) inserted a clause in all government construction contracts that established a quota for the hiring of black laborers based on the 1930 labor census and as a consequence a significant number of blacks received skilled employment on PWA projects. ("African Americans and the New Deal" 2010)

There are contrary views on the benefits of President Roosevelt's New Deal policies, and some feel that blacks were actually harmed. For example, Jim Powell of the Cato Institute reports many negative impacts to blacks, to include the following:

> The flagship of the New Deal was the National Industrial Recovery Act, passed in June 1933. It authorized the president to issue executive orders establishing some 700 industrial cartels, which restricted output and forced

wages and prices above market levels. The minimum wage regulations made it illegal for employers to hire people who weren't worth the minimum because they lacked skills. As a result, some 500,000 blacks, particularly in the South, were estimated to have lost their jobs.

Marginal workers, such as unskilled blacks, desperately needed an expanding economy to create more jobs. Yet New Deal policies made it harder for employers to hire people. Roosevelt tripled federal taxes between 1933 and 1940. Social security excise taxes on payrolls discouraged employers from hiring. New Deal securities laws made it harder for employers to raise capital. New Deal antitrust lawsuits harassed some 150 employers and whole industries. Whatever the merits of such policies might have been, it was bizarre to disrupt private-sector employment when the median unemployment rate was 17 percent.

The Agricultural Adjustment Act (1933) aimed to help farmers by cutting farm production and forcing up food prices. Less production meant less work for thousands of poor black sharecroppers. In addition, blacks were among the 100 million consumers forced to pay higher food prices because of the act.

The Wagner Act (1935) harmed blacks by making labor union monopolies legal. Economists Thomas E. Hall and J. David Ferguson explained: "By encouraging unionization, the Wagner Act raised the number of insiders (those with jobs) who had the incentive and ability to exclude outsiders (those without jobs). Once high wages have been negotiated, employers are less likely to hire outsiders, and thus the insiders could protect their own interest." (Powell 2003)

The Agricultural Adjustment Administration provided subsidies to farmers to not plant crops. This raised crop prices and also reduced market surpluses. This hurt blacks, as first, they found it more difficult to buy food, and second, those who were sharecroppers in the South lost their source of income because the subsidies only went to landowners, who were predominantly white. Roosevelt also increased business regulations, which led to job losses for unskilled workers, which included many blacks. He tripled federal taxes between 1933 and 1940, and this discouraged some hiring.

There were cases in which black lives improved but not at the same level as whites. For example, blacks were paid less than whites under the new WPA. Mrs. Roosevelt was very vocal on this issue. She saw the discrimination firsthand after visiting project locations and wrote, "It is all wrong to discriminate between white and black men!" (Goodwin 1994, 163). As a result in 1935, President Roosevelt signed an executive order barring discrimination in the administration of WPA programs. Still, the Federal Housing Authority did not support blacks buying homes in white neighborhoods, and black jobs were not covered under the Social Security Act. Roosevelt would not push New Deal legislation directly supporting African Americans, as he was concerned with upsetting southern Democrats. However, some members of his administration did support civil rights. For example, Harry L. Hopkins, one of the architects of the New Deal and relief programs under the WPA, sent a letter to White House press secretary Stephen Early on June 17, 1935, urging the president to use antidiscrimination language in a presentation.

Among the talking points recommended by Hopkins was "It is essential that there be no discrimination in this work because of race, religion or politics, with particular emphasis on the latter. The real objective is to take three and a half million unemployed from the relief rolls and put them to work on useful projects" (Hopkins 1935).

The president was also criticized for not pushing antilynching legislation in 1934, particularly as the number of lynchings in the South increased during the Great Depression, with few prosecutions by state and local officials. However, President Roosevelt was realistic in terms of the executive powers he held. Referring to his powers in comparison to those of Congress, he explained to NAACP Executive Secretary Walter White, who was pressing the president to support the Costigan-Wagner bill allowing the federal government to prosecute offenders, that

> I did not choose the tools with which I must work. Had I been permitted to choose them I would have selected quite different ones. But I've got to get legislation passed to save America. The Southerners by reason of the seniority in Congress, are chairmen or occupy strategic places on most of the Senate and House Committees. If I come out for the anti-lynching bill now, they will block every bill I ask Congress to pass to keep America from collapsing. (Goodwin 1994, 163)

Mrs. Roosevelt even arranged a meeting between herself, White, and the president on May 7, 1934, over tea. The president expressed his private support for the bill but declined to take any action to block an expected Senate filibuster. President Roosevelt knew that Congress would fight his New Deal policies if he pushed for the antilynching law, which would then have a negative impact on the entire country. This was particularly the case given that Democrats later lost their majority in Congress, and southern legislators were gaining power. In 1935, the antilynching legislation did not pass; however, Congress approved the New Deal program's Social Security Act and National Labor Relations Act. Roosevelt knew that he also would need congressional support for war policies, given the growing threat of Germany under a Nazi regime and request for support from Europe coupled with a U.S. policy still based on isolationism after World War I. Conversely, Mrs. Roosevelt supported the antilynching legislation to the point of accepting White's invitation to attend an NAACP art exhibit, "A Commentary on Lynching."

Joining unions was a contentious topic during President Roosevelt's administration and particularly during his implementation of New Deal policies. African American workers joined unions to increase securing employment rights. During Reconstruction and many decades that followed, they were not allowed to join unions. For example, in 1925 the Brotherhood of Sleeping Car Porters (BSCP) was the first black union to be allowed into the American Federation of Labor. The BSCP pushed the makers and operators of Pullman passenger cars to engage in negotiations in 1935. The BSCP was founded by A. Philip Randolph and Cottrell Laurence "C. L." Dellums. Their bargaining power was aided by laws passed under Roosevelt, such as the National Industrial Recovery Act of 1933 and the National Labor Relations Act of 1935 (also known as the Wagner Act). The former was ruled unconstitutional by the U.S. Supreme Court in 1935, so the latter was passed to establish "the right to self-organization, to form, join, or assist labor organizations, to bargain collectively through representatives of their own choosing, and to engage in concerted activities for the purpose of collective bargaining or other mutual aid and protection" (National Labor Relations Review Board 2018). The Supreme Court upheld the constitutionality of the 1935 act in *National Labor Relations Board v. Jones & Laughlin Steel Corporation,* 301 U.S. 1 (1937).

When Roosevelt ran for reelection in 1936, he had the overwhelming support of African Americans. Over 70 percent of blacks voted for him in the election, and that rate held in his next two runs for president in 1940 and 1944. Most blacks still identified as Republican, and they didn't officially change their political party affiliation until after the passage of the Civil Rights Act in 1964 and then the Voting Rights Act of 1965, and Lyndon Johnson ran for president in 1968.

In 1937, Roosevelt's nomination of Hugo L. Black to serve as an associate justice on the Supreme Court was confirmed by the Senate. This was a controversial appointment, given that Black had once been a member of the Ku Klux Klan. He did specify that he resigned from the Klan in 1925 and stated the following during a radio address on October 1, 1937, with an audience of over 50 million people listening:

> The insinuations of racial and religious intolerance made concerning me are based on the fact that I joined the Ku Klux Klan about 15 years ago. I did join the Klan. I later resigned. I never rejoined. What appeared then, or what appears now, on the records of that organization I do not know.
>
> I never had considered and I do not now consider the unsolicited card given to me shortly after my nomination to the Senate [in 1926] as a membership of any kind in the Ku Klux Klan. I never used it. I did not even keep it.
>
> Before becoming a Senator I dropped the Klan. I have had nothing to do with it since that time. I abandoned it. I completely discontinued any association with the organization. I have never resumed it and never expect to do so. (Ball 1996)

After a series of articles on the topic were published in the *Pittsburgh Post-Gazette* by Ray Springle, Roosevelt was asked on a few occasions whether he was aware of Black's affiliation with the Klan before he made the appointment during a press conference in 1937. Roosevelt responded,

> Anticipating what you are going to ask and in order to save time (laughter), I know approximately what is on your minds and I want to be helpful if I can. Therefore I am going to give you this statement for direct quotation. Get out your pencils. (Reading) "I know only what I have read in the newspapers. I know that the stories are appearing 'serially'—not seriously, I said 'serially'— and their publication is not complete." Mr. Justice Black is in Europe where, undoubtedly, he cannot get the full text of these articles. Until such time as he returns, there is no further comment to be made. (Roosevelt 1937)

As far as his record while serving on the Supreme Court, Black voted in favor of racial segregation in *Brown v. Board of Education of Topeka, Kansas* in 1954 and also in favor of the 18 Klan members being sent to trial in connection with the deaths of James Chaney, Andrew Goodman, and Michael Schwerner in the case *United States v. Price,* 383 U.S. 787 (1966).

President Roosevelt resisted efforts to end discrimination by the military. Mrs. Roosevelt arranged a meeting with the president on September 27, 1940, to include civil rights leaders A. Philip Randolph of the BSCP, Walter White of the NAACP, and Arnold Hill of the Urban League. Also in attendance were Navy Secretary Frank Knox and Assistant Secretary of War Robert Patterson. The black leaders thought the president would support their concerns after leaving the meeting but were disappointed when later only minor changes would be made, but overall policies would remain basically the same.

The Army Air Corps eventually ended its ban on black pilots. Nearly 1,000 black pilots received training at Moton Field (Tuskegee's Army Air Field) and Alabama's Tuskegee Institute and became part of the infamous Tuskegee Airmen, officially the 332nd Fighter Group and the 477th Bombardment Group. The unit included 15,000 ground personnel. The program gained national attention when Mrs. Roosevelt visited the flight program in March 1941 and flew with African America chief civilian instructor C. Alfred "Chief" Anderson. The airmen flew approximately 15,500 combat missions during World War II in North Africa, Italy, and Germany and earned over 150 Distinguished Flying Crosses.

In 1941, A. Philip Randolph threatened President Roosevelt that there would be a 100,000-person march on Washington, D.C., if actions were not taken to end discrimination in the military and defense industries. Dr. Martin Luther King, Jr. would use this as a model in the March on Washington for Jobs and Freedom in 1963. At first, the president sent a memo to William Knudsen and Sidney Hillman at the agency overseeing the defense industry, the Office of Production Management, on May 27, 1941, asking them to consider hiring more blacks. Knudsen replied the next day that actions would be taken to "quietly" increase the number of blacks. Rudolph was dissatisfied with this quiet strategy and continued to threaten a march on July 1, with the goal of 100,000 black participants. As a result, on June 25, 1941, Roosevelt issued Executive Order 8802, which created the Fair Employment Practice Committee (FEPC) to oversee the order and outlined that

> there shall be no discrimination in the employment of workers in defense industries or government because of race, creed, color, or national origin, and I hereby declare that it is the duty of employers and of labor organizations, in furtherance of said policy and of this order, to provide for the full and equitable participation of all workers in defense industries, with discrimination because of race, creed, color, or national origin. (Equal Employment Opportunity Commission 2018)

The order also established the FEPC to investigate and remedy any cases of discriminatory practices. Black leaders such as trade unionist A. Philip Randolph, Walter White of the NAACP, and T. Arnold Hill of the Urban League were instrumental in having the president issue this order. While the U.S. Navy and the U.S. Marine Corps found ways to circumvent the order at first, it did lead to the military being fully integrated under President Harry S. Truman in 1951.

President Roosevelt also sent a memorandum to all heads of government departments and agencies on September 3, 1941, urging them to implement fair practices:

> It has come to my attention that there is in the Federal establishment a lack of uniformity and possibly some lack of sympathetic attitude toward the problems of minority groups, particularly those relating to the employment and assignment of Negroes in the Federal Civil Service.
>
> With a view to improving the situation, it is my desire that all departments and independent establishments in the Federal Government make a thorough examination of their personnel policies and practices to the end that they may be able to assure me that in the Federal Service that doors of employment are open to all loyal and qualified workers regardless of creed, race, or national origin.
>
> It is imperative that we deal with this problem speedily and effectively. I shall look for immediate steps to be taken by all departments and independent establishments of the Government to facilitate and put into effect this policy of non-discrimination in Federal employment. (Henderson 1943, 119)

The United States officially entered World War II as a result of the Japanese attack on Pearl Harbor on December 7, 1941. The need to support the war with increased production was the impetus that ended the Great Depression. The war led to increased jobs, and blacks benefited. However, there was tension particularly in urban cities as the black population increased with the continued Great Migration. For example, in 1943 race riots occurred in Detroit, Michigan; Beaumont, Texas; and Harlem, New York. Later there were riots in Los Angeles, California, and Mobile, Alabama.

In Detroit, the automotive industry was converted to factories supporting the war. By 1943, 150,000 blacks had moved to the city within just two years, along with 100,000 others. The Detroit riots started with a fight among youths in a public park known as Belle Isle but grew into fights among workers, local sailors, and finally mobs of both white and black citizens. It was fueled by rumors of racial killings by both whites and blacks. The riot lasted from June 20 through June 22, leaving 34 killed (of whom 25 were black) and 1,000 injured (of whom 75 percent were black). The riots ended after 3,800 federal troops were sent in by Roosevelt at the request of the mayor and governor for assistance. Local police and the federal troops were responsible for the killing and wounding of most of the blacks. In Beaumont, after rumors spread of a white woman being raped by a black man, tension arose between whites and blacks working at the shipyard.

After World War II, discriminatory practices against African Americans reached a new forefront in terms of the American political agenda. This was especially the case given that the United States had fought against German tyranny, based largely on racial policies and antidemocracy. African Americans adopted the Double V campaign in demanding victory overseas as well as victory in the United States over white supremacy. This discontent and the organization of blacks into formal groups was the impetus for the Civil Rights Movement. Beyond the NAACP, another group that was instrumental in starting the Civil Rights Movement was founded while Roosevelt was in office. The Congress of Racial Equality (CORE) was founded in Chicago, Illinois, in 1942 on the campus of the University of Chicago. The organization gained national attention in the 1960s.

President Roosevelt died from a cerebral hemorrhage on April 12, 1945. His death shocked the country and the world because his illness (polio) had been hidden from the public. Hundreds of thousands of people lined the train route carrying his body from Warm Springs, Georgia, to Washington, D.C., and finally to Hyde Park, New York.

FURTHER READING

"African Americans and the New Deal: A Look Back in History." 2010. Roosevelt Institute, February 5, http://rooseveltinstitute.org/african-americans-and-new-deal-look-back-history/.

Ball, Howard. 1996. *Hugo L. Black: Cold Steel Warrior.* New York: Oxford University Press.

Black, Conrad. 2003. *Franklin Delano Roosevelt: Champion of Freedom.* New York: PublicAffairs.

Blanchet, Benjamin. 2017. "Pride and Shame: Millard Fillmore's Controversial Legacy at UB," The Spectrum, May 8, http://www.ubspectrum.com/article/2017/05/millard-fillmore-controversial-legacy-at-ub.

Brands, H. W. 2009. *Traitor to His Class: The Privileged Life and Radical Presidency of Franklin Delano Roosevelt.* New York: Anchor Books.

Brinkley, Alan. 2010. *Franklin Delano Roosevelt.* New York: Oxford University Press.

Dallek, Robert. 2017. *Franklin D. Roosevelt: A Political Life.* New York: Viking.

Giorgio, Papa. 2015. "Herbert Hoover and the Changing Demographic of Black Voters." Religio-Political Talk, May 30, http://religiopoliticaltalk.com/herbert-hoover-and-the-changing-demographic-of-black-voters/.

Goodwin, Doris Kearns. 1994. *No Ordinary Time: Franklin & Eleanor Roosevelt; The Home Front in World War II.* New York: Simon and Schuster.

Hall, Thomas E., and J. David Ferguson. 1998. *The Great Depression: An International Disaster of Perverse Economic Policies.* Ann Arbor: University of Michigan Press.

Henderson, Elmer W. 1943. "Negroes in Government Employment." *Opportunity Journal of Negro Life* (July): 118–132.

Hopkins, Harry L. 1935. *Letter to the Honorable Stephen Early, Secretary to the President, June 17, 1935,* http://fdranewdealerinhope.weebly.com/racial-discrimination.html.

Jenkins, Roy. 2003. *Franklin Delano Roosevelt: The American Presidents Series; The 32nd President, 1933–1945.* New York: Times Books.

Powell, Jim. 2003. "Why Did FDR's New Deal Harm Blacks?" Cato Institute, December 3, https://www.cato.org/publications/commentary/why-did-fdrs-new-deal-harm-blacks.

Roosevelt, Franklin D. 1937. "Excerpts from the Press Conference, September 14, 1937." The American Presidency Project, http://www.presidency.ucsb.edu/ws/index.php?pid=15455.

Smith, Jean Edward. 2007. *FDR.* New York: Random House.

Wicker, Christine. 2017. *The Simple Faith of Franklin Delano Roosevelt: Religion's Role in the FDR Presidency.* Washington, DC: Smithsonian Books.

Civil Rights Era

The Civil Rights Movement began in the 1950s and intensified in the 1960s. Along with the social and legal gains African Americans were struggling to finally achieve, this era was also marked by aggressive resistance by segregationists. What is most troubling was the violence perpetrated by law enforcement officials with the support of political leaders, particularly in the South.

Basically, all U.S. presidents during this time were initially resistant to taking a stance on civil rights. They felt that the advancement of civil rights for black people was being implemented too quickly, and they were not ready to enact federal laws for several reasons. Southern state governments hindered progressive changes and had been a thorn for most U.S. presidents. First, most of the presidents needed southern political support for other issues on the national agenda. This era occurred during the height of the Cold War, and the country was also dealing with such domestic issues as poverty and infrastructure growth. Southern support was also needed to become elected, and most did not want to risk politically alienating themselves from half of the country over the issue of civil rights. Second, some U.S. presidents were from the South and had to placate southern constituents to gain support, and those who were not from the South were not fully aware of the conditions that African Americans were facing. Finally, many presidents felt pressured into taking action when they were not politically ready.

The advent of television is one of the phenomena that can be attributed to forcing U.S. presidents to take action in dealing with racial issues in the United States. In 1950, there were only about 3.8 million U.S. households with a television. By the 1960s, this number grew to over 50 million. In percentages, only 9 percent of households owned a television in 1950 compared to over 90 percent in the 1960s. The images of African Americans being beaten by police, sprayed with fire hoses, and bitten by police dogs and news reports of racially motivated murders were broadcast into the homes of people around the world. The sheer shock of how blacks were being treated and the calls of civil rights leaders blaming presidents for lack of action forced presidents during this era to take aggressive stances.

Another factor that forced presidents during this era to act was organized African American groups. The Southern Christian Leadership Conference, the Congress of Racial Equality, and even the Black Panthers and the Nation of Islam all forced the federal government to take action to address civil rights. The latter two used strategies and rhetoric based on aggressive stances to take freedoms that were guaranteed African Americans by law through force and even violence. However, the former two based their strategies on nonviolence. Two basic strategies were used by civil rights leaders and organizations during the Civil Rights Movement. The first strategy was to test how the courts would rule on civil rights violations based on defenses of protections guaranteed in the U.S. Constitution. The second strategy was to test how presidents would respond when the nation and even the world were forced to recognize the treatment of African Americans, particularly in the still segregated South. As a result, by the end of the civil rights era sweeping legislation was passed that not only guaranteed equal rights for African Americans but also provided the federal government with enforcement capabilities to ensure compliance by state and local governments as well as private groups and individuals.

Harry S. Truman

33rd President of the United States
Presidential Term: April 12, 1945–January 20, 1953
Political Party: Democratic
Vice President: None (1945–1949), Alben W. Barkley (1949–1953)

Harry S. Truman was born on May 8, 1884, in Lamar, Missouri. He was not given a middle name. The "S" was given to honor both of his grandfathers, Anderson Shipp Truman and Solomon Young. Harry Truman served in World War I as part of the National Guard and ultimately became a U.S. senator in 1934. He was best known for chairing a committee to investigate fraud in defense contracting.

Truman assumed the presidency after the death of Franklin Delano Roosevelt on April 12, 1945. Truman had only been vice president since January 20 of that year and had hardly seen President Roosevelt. Truman had not even been briefed on the development of the atomic bomb, which was being developed to end World War II. He told reporters, "I felt like the moon, the stars, and all the planets had fallen on me." He was very concerned about First Lady Eleanor Roosevelt and asked her "Is there anything we can do for you? For you are the one in trouble now!" (Goethals 2015, 166)

Demands for civil rights by African Americans were then at the forefront of American politics and the nation's social and cultural framework. Roosevelt and Eleanor had supported civil rights for blacks more than any former administration since Abraham Lincoln. Black veterans returning home from World War II were active in demanding equal rights, and this included significantly increasing the membership of the National Association for the Advancement of Colored People

(NAACP) and the Congress of Racial Equality (CORE). They had learned valuable skills while serving in the military, including the use of weapons, and were able to pursue their education using the G.I. Bill (officially the Servicemen's Readjustment Act of 1944), signed into law by Roosevelt on June 22, 1944. This latter was of particular concern to southern white supremacists who had historically used violence as a means to intimidate blacks. For example, on July 2, 1946, Medgar Evers, his brother Charles, and four other black veterans were the first blacks who attempted to register to vote at the courthouse in Decatur, Mississippi. They were met by armed white men, so they went back to their homes to get their guns. Although they were unsuccessful that day and didn't resort to using violence, Evers

Harry S. Truman was the 33rd president of the United States. President Truman did not start out as a champion of African Americans; he evolved from being a farm boy raised by Confederate sympathizers to the president who signed the order to desegregate the armed forces in 1948. (Library of Congress)

became active in supporting the Student Nonviolent Coordinating Committee and CORE before he was assassinated in 1963.

Truman aggressively supported equal rights for African Americans during his administration. To some this was a surprise, given that he grew up in a segregated town in Missouri. He was also a former member of a Missouri chapter of the Ku Klux Klan between 1920 and 1922 and was known to use ethnic slurs in referring to Jews and Italians. However, Truman was shocked by the discriminatory treatment of African Americans. For example, in 1946 he learned that a mob in Georgia shot and killed two black men and their wives, yet no one stood trial for the incident. In South Carolina, the police pulled an African American soldier from a bus and beat him so severely that he was blinded. Truman espoused the need for fairness and deeply believed in the tenets of the U.S. Constitution and the Declaration of Independence. At a political rally in 1940, he made the statement "I believe in the brotherhood of man, not merely the brotherhood of white men, but the brotherhood of all men before law. I believe in the Constitution and the Declaration of Independence. In giving the Negroes the rights which are theirs, we are only acting in accord with our own ideals of a true democracy" (Helm 1947, 137).

On June 29, 1947, Truman was the first president to address the NAACP. During the NAACP's 38th Annual Convention and from the steps of the Lincoln

Memorial before a crowd of 10,000, the president outlined the guaranteed rights of all Americans. As part of his speech he stated the following:

> There is no justifiable reason for discrimination because of ancestry, or religion, or race, or color. We must not tolerate such limitations on the freedom of any of our people and on their enjoyment of basic rights which every citizen in a truly democratic society must possess. Every man should have the right to a decent home, the right to an education, the right to adequate medical care, the right to a worthwhile job, the right to an equal share in making the public decisions through the ballot, and the right to a fair trial in a fair court. We must insure that these rights—on equal terms—are enjoyed by every citizen. To these principles I pledge my full and continued support. (Truman 1947)

Roosevelt had issued Executive Order 8802 to combat discrimination in defense industries and thereby created the Fair Employment Practice Committee. However, this committee was abolished by Congress in 1946. In response, on December 5, 1946, Truman signed Executive Order 9808, which created the President's Committee on Civil Rights to investigate the status of civil rights in the United States and propose strategies to both strengthen and protect these rights. In December 1947, the committee submitted a 178-page report titled *To Secure These Rights: The Report of the President's Committee on Civil Rights.* The report outlined a 10-point agenda of civil rights reform. Among the recommendations were the reorganization of the Department of Justice's Civil Rights Section and the forming of a special unit of civil rights investigators in the Federal Bureau of Investigation, a permanent Commission on Civil Rights in the Executive Office of the president along with a joint Standing Committee on Civil Rights in Congress, and civil rights commissions in the states. The following are additional recommendations:

1. Action by the states or Congress to end poll taxes as a voting prerequisite.

2. The enactment by Congress of a statute protecting the right of qualified persons to participate in federal primaries and elections against interference by public officers and private persons.

3. The enactment by Congress of a statute protecting the right to qualify for, or participate in, federal or state primaries or elections against discriminatory action by state officers based on race or color, or depending on any other unreasonable classification of persons for voting purposes.

4. The enactment by Congress of legislation establishing local self government for the District of Columbia; and the amendment of the Constitution to extend suffrage in presidential elections, and representation in Congress to District residents.

5. The granting of suffrage by the States of New Mexico and Arizona to their Indian citizens.

6. The modification of the federal naturalization laws to permit the granting of citizenship without regard to the race, color, or national origin of applicants.

7. The repeal by the states of laws discriminating against aliens who are ineligible for citizenship because of race, color, or national origin.

8. The enactment by Congress of legislation granting citizenship to the people of Guam and American Samoa.

9. The enactment by Congress of legislation, followed by appropriate administrative action, to end immediately all discrimination and segregation based on race, color, creed, or national origin, in the organization and activities of all branches of the Armed Services.

10. The enactment by Congress of legislation providing that no member of the armed forces shall be subject to discrimination of any kind by any public authority or place of public accommodation, recreation, transportation, or other service or business.

The committee was disbanded in December 1947, and Truman advanced its recommendations by two additional executive orders. Executive Order 9980, signed on July 26, 1948, desegregated the federal workforce by ordering, "All personnel actions taken by Federal appointing officers shall be based solely on merit and fitness; and such officers are authorized and directed to take appropriate steps to ensure that in all such actions there shall be no discrimination because of race, color, religion, or national origin." The order also established

in the Civil Service Commission a Fair Employment Board (hereinafter referred to as the Board) of not less than seven persons, the members of which shall be officers or employees of the Commission. The Board shall—

(a) Have authority to review decisions made by the head of any department which are appealed pursuant to the provisions of this order, or referred to the Board by the head of the department for advice, and to make recommendations to such head. In any instance in which the recommendation of the Board is not promptly and fully carried out the case shall be reported by the Board to the President, for such action as he finds necessary.

(b) Make rules and regulations, in consultation with the Civil Service Commission, deemed necessary to carry out the Board's duties and responsibilities under this order.

(c) Advise all departments on problems and policies relating to fair employment.

(d) Disseminate information pertinent to fair-employment programs.

(e) Coordinate the fair-employment policies and procedures of the several departments.

(f) Make reports and submit recommendations to the Civil Service Commission for transmittal to the President from time to time, as may be necessary to the maintenance of the fair-employment program.

Executive Order 9981, signed on July 26, 1948, desegregated the U.S. armed services. Truman was appalled at the treatment of some African American veterans when they returned home from the war. In 1948 he stated, "My stomach turned over when I learned that Negro soldiers, just back from overseas, were being dumped out of army trucks in Mississippi and beaten. Whatever my inclinations as a native of Missouri might have been, as President I know this is bad. I shall fight to end evils like this" (Nielsen 2009, 167). The order stated, "It is hereby declared to be the policy of the President that there shall be equality of treatment and opportunity for all persons in the armed services without regard to race, color, religion or national origin. This policy shall be put into effect as rapidly as possible, having due regard to the time required to effectuate any necessary changes without impairing efficiency or morale." Further, "There shall be created in the National Military Establishment an advisory committee to be known as the President's Committee on Equality of Treatment and Opportunity in the Armed Services, which shall be composed of seven members to be designated by the President."

The president didn't issue the order without pressure from African American leaders. In November 1947, A. Philip Randolph and Grant Reynolds organized the Committee against Jim Crow in Military Service and Training, and Randolph testified before the Senate Armed Services Committee that African Americans would refuse to serve in the military if a proposed new draft law did not forbid segregation. Twenty African American organizations met in New York City on March 27, 1948, and issued the "Declaration of Negro Voters" through the Press Service of the NAACP. The declaration opened by stating the following:

> Meeting as Negro Americans but also as citizens of the United States, we reaffirm our devotion to the principles of democracy and our support of candidates who and measures which advance the cause of democracy. We call upon Negro voters to utilize in the coming primaries and national elections the balance of power they hold in at least seventeen states with 295 electoral votes to the end that the best possible President, Vice President and Congress shall be chosen to guide America during the troubled years ahead. We warn Negro men and women to avoid hasty emotional and sentimental political decisions and commitments. We urge meticulous scrutiny of not only the statements but of the voting and public records of every candidate, irrespective of party, whether he aspire to the Presidency or to Congress, or other state or local office. (NAACP 1948)

The declaration was clear on demands to integrate the military:

> As an all-important immediate step, we insist that every vestige of segregation and discrimination in the armed services be forthwith abolished and that any public official, however high his rank, who fails to act against these evils be removed from office. Beyond the abolition of segregation and discrimination in the regular military establishment and its reserve components, we will insist that state political organizations and candidates for state office commit themselves to the abolition of segregation and discrimination in all National Guard units.

On April 26, 1948, 16 African American leaders informed Secretary of Defense James V. Forrestal that African Americans would react strongly if the armed services were not integrated, and on June 26, 1948, Randolph announced the formation of the League for Non-Violent Civil Disobedience against Military Segregation. He informed the president that black youths would resist the draft law unless an executive order was issued ending segregation in the military. In July 1948, this was a hot topic at the Democratic National Convention. The convention rejected a recommendation from Mayor Hubert H. Humphrey of Minneapolis, Minnesota, to end segregation in the armed services, and Truman and his advisers supported a moderate platform plank for civil rights that would appease southern Democrats. However, the delegates overturned the platform committee in favor of a more aggressive stance on civil rights that included desegregating the armed forces. The Truman administration immediately began drafting Executive Order 9981.

Per the executive order, the Committee on Equality of Treatment and Opportunity in the Armed Services, better known as the Fahy Committee and named after chairman Charles H. Fahy, was established to review any issues with desegregating the military and report back to President Truman. Fahy had served as the 26th solicitor general of the United States under President Franklin D. Roosevelt. The five-member committee included two African Americans. They met with leaders of the armed forces in 1949. The leaders of the U.S. Army and the U.S. Marine Corps defended their segregation policies, while the U.S. Navy and the newly formed U.S. Air Force announced that they would comply with the order. The army was adamant in retaining its 10 percent recruitment quota for enlistment of African Americans and maintained this quota until 1950. During hearings, the Marine Corps admitted that only 1 of its 8,200 officers was African American, and the navy admitted it only had five African Americans among its 45,000. The commission was abolished on July 6, 1950, after Truman found their review successful. Fahy later became a judge with the U.S. Court of Appeals for the District of Columbia Circuit, serving from 1950 until 1967.

Truman sent a Special Message to Congress on Civil Rights on February 2, 1948, that requested legislation to enact recommendations from the President's Committee on Civil Rights. The message specifically asked Congress to enact legislation for the following:

1. Establishing a permanent Commission on Civil Rights, a Joint Congressional Committee on Civil Rights, and a Civil Rights Division in the Department of Justice.
2. Strengthening existing civil rights statutes.
3. Providing Federal protection against lynching.
4. Protecting more adequately the right to vote.
5. Establishing a Fair Employment Practice Commission to prevent unfair discrimination in employment.
6. Prohibiting discrimination in interstate transportation facilities.
7. Providing home-rule and suffrage in Presidential elections for the residents of the District of Columbia.
8. Providing Statehood for Hawaii and Alaska and a greater measure of self-government for our island possessions.
9. Equalizing the opportunities for residents of the United States to become naturalized citizens.
10. Settling the evacuation claims of Japanese-Americans. (Truman 1948)

When Truman ran for reelection in 1948, a fracture developed in the Democratic Party because of the president's stance on equal rights. Southern white democrats who were particularly angered formed the States' Rights Democratic Party, also known as the Dixiecrat Party. This short-lived political party was an alternative to the Democratic Party in the South in 1948. The States' Rights Democratic Party nominated Strom Thurmond from South Carolina as its Democratic presidential candidate. African Americans were very pleased with the president, and he gained 77 percent of the black vote. Truman won 303 electoral votes, compared to 16 for Republican challenger Thomas E. Dewey and only 39 for Thurmond. Thurmond won the states of South Carolina, Louisiana, Mississippi, and Alabama.

The United States fought in the Korean War during Truman's administration. The president described U.S. participation as "police action" rather than war, perhaps since there was lack of support for U.S. involvement before, during, and even after the war. As with every other American conflict, African Americans served their country. The war lasted from June 25, 1950, to July 27, 1953. When the war began, African Americans comprised approximately 8 percent of the U.S. military, or 100,000. By the end of the war, over 600,000 had served in the military. Although Truman's executive order was signed in 1948, resistance to allowing African Americans to serve in integrated units continued for years across the armed services. Full segregation did not end until October 1951, when the all-black 24th Infantry Regiment that had been established in 1869 was disbanded. The regiment had served in the Spanish-American War, World War I, World War II, and the beginning of the Korean War. It was among more than 100 black units that served in Korea but the largest and only unit of regiment size. The unit was given the least training and subjected to the most dismal conditions:

> In late September 1950, two months after the beginning of the Korean War, the commander of the 25th Infantry Division, Maj. Gen. William B. Kean, requested that the Eighth Army disband the all-black 24th Infantry Regiment because it had shown itself "untrustworthy and incapable of carrying out missions expected of an infantry regiment." Thus began a controversy that has continued to this day. Critics of the racially segregated regiment have charged that the 24th was a dismal failure in combat. The African-American veterans of the organization and others have responded that the unit did far better than its antagonists would concede and that its main problem was the racial prejudice endemic to the Army of that day. (Bowers, Hammond, and MacGarrigle 1996, xi)

There were other acts of discrimination against black soldiers serving in Korea. General Douglas MacArthur, commander of U.S. forces, was accused of supporting segregation and racial discrimination. Incidentally, he was relieved of command by Truman in April 1951 after disagreements about the military strategy being used in the conflict. The NAACP sent then attorney Thurgood Marshall to the area to investigate the court-martial of 39 black soldiers in Korea and Japan. Marshall would later become the first African American to be appointed to the U.S. Supreme Court. He arrived in Korea on January 14, 1951, and was able to get most of the soldiers cleared of charges. Marshall was later interviewed about his findings:

Marshall: There were records of trials, so-called trials, in the middle of the night where the men were sentenced to life imprisonment in hearings that lasted less than ten minutes. They were the old well-known drumhead court-martials, done in the heat of passion and in the heat of war.

There were fifty or sixty involved. One death penalty case. I remember in particular: the record showed that this man was charged with being absent in the presence of the enemy. Instead of being charged with AWOL (Absent Without Leave), he was charged with cowardice in the presence of the enemy. And fortunately for him, he produced two witnesses: a major in the Medical Corps and a lieutenant in the Nurse Corps, both of whom testified that he was in a base hospital the very day that he was supposed to be AWOL. And despite their testimony, he was convicted and given life imprisonment.

Just prior to that, I was given an audience with General MacArthur, and I found it very interesting. I questioned him about the continuation of segregation in the Army and he said he was working on it. And I asked him how many years he'd been working on it, and he didn't really remember how many.

I reminded him that at the very time we were talking, the Air Force was completely integrated, and the Navy was quite integrated, and the only group not integrated was the Army. He said that he didn't find the Negroes qualified, and when he found them qualified, they would be integrated.

Interviewer: Do you have any further impressions of General MacArthur? Do you feel he was definitely biased or just opinionated?

Marshall: He was as biased as any person I've run across.

Interviewer: In other words, he felt basically that blacks were inferior?

Marshall: Inferior. No question about it. No question about it. I told him about all these instances. I said, "Well look, General—you've got all those guards out there with all this spit and polish and there's not one Negro in the whole group."

He said, "There's none qualified."

I said, "Well, what's qualification?"

He said, "In field battle, et cetera, et cetera, et cetera."

I said, "Well, I just talked to a Negro yesterday, a sergeant, who has killed more people with a rifle than anybody in history. And he's not qualified?"

And he said, "No."

I said, "Well, now, General, remember yesterday you had the big band playing at the ceremony over there?"

He said, "Yes, wasn't it wonderful?"

I said, "Yeah. The Headquarters Band, it's beautiful." I said, "Now General, just between you and me, g—damn it, don't you tell me that there's no Negro who can play a horn!"

That's when he said for me to go.

There's gotta be prejudice. That's all it is.

Best proof of it was—General [Matthew] Ridgeway took over after him, and desegregated in about three weeks. Desegregated the whole thing. And the only opposition he found was among the Negroes [laughter]. They didn't want to be integrated. No, that man was something. ("Korean War Courts Martial" 1951)

U.S. forces were badly beaten by the North Korean People's Army during the early part of the war. As U.S. military losses mounted in white units, commanders began to accept blacks to replace fallen soldiers. This led to integrated units, and the army formally announced its plan for full desegregation on July 26, 1951, three years after Truman issued Executive Order 9981.

On December 3, 1951, Truman signed Executive Order 10308, titled "Improving the Means for Obtaining Compliance with the Nondiscrimination Provisions of Federal Contracts." It required federal contracting agencies to include provisions in all contracts obligating contractors "not to discriminate against any employee or applicant for employment because of race, color, creed, or national origin."

One action that did not help African Americans was the Housing Act of 1949. Truman wanted to improve public housing and foster urban renewal, and this was part of his domestic policy program called the Fair Deal. Many blacks lived in the slums and ghettos of urban cities, and the plan was widely criticized by African Americans as "Negro removal." The program suffered from poor planning, corruption, lack of support from home builders, the continuation of public housing, and a continued decline in slum neighborhoods. More homes for blacks were demolished than were newly constructed. Through the 1950s and 1960s, 300,000 families actually lost their homes, of which half were black. Some areas that were previously predominantly occupied by minorities were replaced with expensive housing that poor minorities could not afford or were forced out of due to housing discrimination.

During his address at the National Convention Banquet of the Americans for Democratic Action (ADA) on May 17, 1952, Truman stated the following:

There is another thing we must stand firm on. That is our pledge on the issue of civil rights. No citizen of this great country ought to be discriminated against because of his race, religion, or national origin. That is the essence of the American ideal and the American Constitution. I made that statement verbatim in the speech on March 29th, in which I said I would not run for President, and I hope that speech, and this, will be the fundamental basis of the platform of the Democratic Party in Chicago.

We have made good progress on civil rights since 1948, in the Federal Government, in the Armed forces, and in the States. But we still need the legislation which I recommended to the Congress over 4 years ago. We must go ahead to secure for all our citizens—east, west, north, and south—the right of equal opportunity in our economic and political life, and the right to equal protection under the law. That is real, true, 100 percent Americanism.

This is very important to us abroad as well as at home. The vision of equal rights is the greatest inspiration of human beings throughout the world. There is one member of this ADA who can tell us from her own experience how important it is for the world to know that we share this vision. She has been our spokesman on this subject in the councils of the United Nations and she has done a wonderful job—and that is Mrs. Roosevelt. (Truman 1952)

President Truman did not run for a third term in office. It is widely believed that the tolls of the Korean War, allegations of corruption within his administration, and battles over communism under McCarthyism were among the reasons he did not seek reelection.

FURTHER READING

American RadioWorks. 1951. Korean War Courts Martial: Interview with Thurgood Marshall, http://americanradioworks.publicradio.org/features/marshall/korea.html.

Baime, A. J. 2017. *The Accidental President: Harry S. Truman and the Four Months That Changed the World.* New York: Houghton Mifflin Harcourt.

Dallek, Robert. 2008. *Harry S. Truman: The American Presidents Series; The 33rd President, 1945–1953.* New York: Times Books.

Gardner, Michael. 2002. *Harry Truman and Civil Rights: Moral Courage and Political Risks.* Carbondale: Southern Illinois University Press.

Goethals, George R. 2015. *Presidential Leadership and African Americans: "An American Dilemma" from Slavery to the White House.* New York: Routledge.

Hammond, Scott J., Kevin R. Hardwick, and Howard L. Lubert, eds. 2007. *Classics of American Political and Constitutional Thought,* Vol. 2, *Reconstruction to the Present.* Indianapolis: Hackett Publishing.

Helm, William Picket. 1947. *Harry Truman: A Political Biography.* New York: Duell, Sloan, and Pearce.

NAACP. 1948. "Declaration of Negro Voters." Harry S. Truman Library and Museum, https://www.trumanlibrary.org/whistlestop/study_collections/trumancivilrights/documents/pdfs/9-2.pdf.

Nielsen, Niels C. 2009. *God in the Obama Era: Presidents' Religion and Ethics from George Washington to Barack Obama.* New York: Morgan James Publishing.

Truman, Harry S. 1952. "Address at the National Convention Banquet of the Americans for Democratic Action, May 17, 1952." Harry S. Truman Presidential Library and Museum, https://www.trumanlibrary.org/publicpapers/index.php?pid=1296.

Truman, Harry S. 1955. *Memoirs by Harry S. Truman.* 2 vols. New York: Doubleday.

Truman, Harry S. 1989. *Where the Buck Stops: The Personal and Private Writings of Harry S. Truman.* New York: Warner Books.

Truman, Harry S. 2002. *The Autobiography of Harry S. Truman.* Columbia: University of Missouri Press.

Dwight David "Ike" Eisenhower

34th President of the United States
Presidential Term: January 20, 1953–January 20, 1961
Political Party: Republican
Vice President: Richard Nixon

Dwight David Eisenhower (later nicknamed Ike) was born in Denison, Texas, on October 14, 1890, to a poor family and later joined the U.S. Military Academy at West Point. He served as a five-star general during World War II. Eisenhower was the first Republican president since 1928, and his administration was primarily focused on the Cold War. His most notable action supporting African Americans was his signing of the Civil Rights Act of 1957 and sending troops to enforce the court order to integrate schools in Little Rock, Arkansas. Still, Eisenhower was slow in supporting full civil rights. He favored a moderate and slow approach and was sympathetic to white southerners who complained about the drastic changes to their lives. The president resisted calls by civil rights leaders such as Dr. Martin Luther King, Jr. for more action by the federal government. Many civil rights issues intensified under Eisenhower, since the legislation passed only dealt with voting rights, leading to the more heated civil rights struggle that culminated in the 1960s. However, it must be recognized that Eisenhower also favored a more constitutional approach to deal with civil rights based on the powers that were granted to the states and the federal government. Because he did pass the Civil Rights Act of 1957 and met with African American leaders, he was able to garner 23–25 percent of the black vote in 1952 and 39–40 percent of the black vote in 1956 when most blacks at the time identified themselves as affiliated with the Democratic Party.

In his first State of the Union Address to Congress on February 2, 1953, President Eisenhower vowed to continue desegregation of the military as begun by his predecessor, President Harry S. Truman. Although Truman issued Executive Order 9981 on July 26, 1948, it was really Eisenhower who was more instrumental in its implementation due to resistance from the military services during the first few years of the order. He stated, "I propose to use whatever authority exists in the office of the President to end segregation in the District of Columbia, including the Federal Government, and any segregation in the Armed Forces" (Eisenhower 1953a). To force the military services to comply, he threatened their military spending. During the president's news conference on March 19, 1953, he made this clear:

> I will say this—I repeat it, I have said it again and again: wherever Federal funds are expended for anything, I do not see how any American can justify—legally, or logically, or morally—a discrimination in the expenditure of those funds as among our citizens. All are taxed to provide those funds. If there is any benefit to be derived from them, I think they must all share, regardless of such inconsequential factors as race and religion. (Eisenhower 1953b)

On August 13, 1953, Eisenhower signed Executive Order 10479, which created the Government Contracts Committee. The order charged all "government contracting agencies to include in their contracts a provision obligating the government contractor not to discriminate against any employee or applicant for employment because of race, creed, color, or national origin and obligating the government contractor to include a similar provision in all subcontracts."

Eisenhower appointed Vice President Richard Nixon to serve as its chairman. The purpose of the committee was to end discrimination in companies receiving contracts from the federal government. The committee was hampered by a small budget and limited staff and was also instructed to only end contracts when absolutely necessary.

In 1954, the U.S. Supreme Court legally ended segregation in its historic ruling in *Brown v. Board of Education of Topeka, Kansas,* 347 U.S. 483 (1954). The plaintiffs were represented by lead attorney Thurgood Marshall, who would later become the first African American solicitor general and Supreme Court justice. In the case, the court ruled that state laws establishing separate public schools for black and white students were unconstitutional and thus overturned the Supreme Court's ruling in *Plessy v. Ferguson,* 163 U.S. 537 (1896), that separate but equal facilities were constitutional. The chief justice of the Supreme Court at the time, Earl Warren, had been nominated to the court by Eisenhower and served from 1953 until 1969. During the time Warren served as chief justice, the Supreme Court was referred to as the Warren Court. During that time, the liberal stances of the court led to landmark rulings supporting civil rights, civil liberties, and judicial power.

Eisenhower never publicly endorsed the Supreme Court's decision. While the case was being heard, he invited Chief Justice Warren and some plaintiffs of the southern states to a White House dinner. During that event, the president did give his views on southern whites in terms of segregation by stating, "These are not bad people. All they are concerned about is to see that their sweet little girls are not required to sit in school alongside some big overgrown Negroes" (Bloom 1987, 106).

After the Supreme Court's ruling, southern states passed the Southern Manifesto in 1956 to oppose racial integration in public places. The document was signed by 99 southern Democrats and two southern Republicans representing the states of Alabama, Arkansas, Florida, Georgia, Louisiana, Mississippi, North Carolina, South Carolina, Tennessee, Texas, and Virginia. The signers argued that the Supreme Court overstepped its powers per the Tenth Amendment of the U.S. Constitution, and the states would use all lawful means possible to reverse the high court's decision. The states also pledged to resist the chaos and confusion that would result from schools being desegregated. Across the South, states established private "academies" for white children only, while some localities completely closed public schools.

Eisenhower took actions to enforce the Supreme Court's ruling. Arkansas governor Orval Faubus used the state's National Guard to block the doors of Central High School in Little Rock, Arkansas, in 1957 to stop nine African American students (known as the Little Rock Nine) from attending the school. The National Association for the Advancement of Colored People (NAACP) attempted to register black students in all-white schools across the South, including Little Rock, to test the enforcement of the Supreme Court's ruling in the *Brown* case. Eisenhower sent several communications to Faubus trying to obtain his agreement to comply. When Faubus did not, the president determined this to be an obstruction of justice. Eisenhower sent federal troops to force the governor and the school system to comply. He ordered the 101st Airborne Division of the U.S. Army to the school on September 24, 1957, but without its black soldiers. He also placed the entire 10,000 Arkansas National Guard under federal control, no longer allowing Governor Faubus to order them. This was all part of Executive Order 10730, which the president began by stating:

> Whereas certain persons in the State of Arkansas, individually and in unlawful assemblages, combinations, and conspiracies, have willfully obstructed the enforcement of orders of the United States District Court for the Eastern District of Arkansas with respect to matters relating to the enrollment and attendance at public schools, particularly at Central High School, located in Little Rock School District, Little Rock, Arkansas, and

> Whereas such willful obstruction of justice hinders the execution of the laws of that state and of the United States, and makes it impracticable to enforce such laws by the ordinary course of judicial proceedings; and

> Whereas such obstruction of justice constitutes a denial of the equal protection of the laws secured by the Constitution of the United States and impedes the course of justice under those laws;

> Now, therefore, I, Dwight D. Eisenhower, President of the United States, under and by virtue of the authority vested in me by the Constitution and statutes of the United States, including Chapter 15 of the United States Code, particularly sections 332, 333 and 334, thereof, do command all persons engaged in such obstruction of justice to cease and desist therefrom, and to disperse forthwith.

The troops remained there throughout the entire school year, and the president was given situation reports throughout the year. It was a difficult year in which the students were taunted, spat upon, and called names, and one even had acid thrown into her eyes. The Little Rock Nine included Ernest Green, Elizabeth Eckford, Jefferson Thomas, Terrence Roberts, Carlotta Walls LaNier, Minnijean Brown, Gloria Ray Karlmark, Thelma Mothershed, and Melba Pattillo Beals. Green was the first African American to graduate from Central High School. During the summer of 1958, Faubus was successful in convincing voters to support a referendum to close all public schools for the entire upcoming school year rather than allow desegregation. This was known as "The Lost Year."

Eisenhower caused ire in many blacks when he said before the black National Newspaper Publishers Association in 1957 that "No one is more anxious than I am to see Negroes receive first-class citizenship in this country . . . but you must be patient" (Borstelmann 2001, 92). During that time he was contacted by many for and against his actions. For example, he received a letter from Jackie Robinson, who in 1947 became the first African American to play in major league baseball, on May 13, 1958, condemning the president's comments that blacks should be patient but recognizing the federal intervention at Little Rock:

> As the chief executive of our nation, I respectfully suggest that you unwittingly crush the spirit of freedom in Negros by constantly urging forbearance and give hope to those pro-segregation leaders like Governor Faubus who would take from us even those freedoms we now enjoy. Your own experience with Governor Faubus is proof enough that forbearance and not eventual integration is the goal the pro-segregation leaders seek.

> In my view, an unequivocal statement backed up by action such as you demonstrated you could take last fall in dealing with Governor Faubus if it became necessary, would let it be known that America is determined to provide—in the near future—for Negroes—the freedoms we are entitled to under the constitution. (Long 2008, 57)

Eisenhower responded to Robinson on June 4, 1958:

> Thank you very much for taking the time to write me some of the thoughts you had after the meeting of the Negro leaders here in Washington. While I understand the points you make about the use of patience and forbearance, I have never urged them as substitutes for constructive action or progress.

> If you will review my talk made at the meeting, you will see that at no point did I advocate a cessation of effort on the part of individuals, organizations, or government, to bring to fruition for all Americans, the enjoyment of all the privileges of citizenship spelled out in our Constitution.

> I am firmly on record as believing that every citizen—of every race and creed—deserves to enjoy equal civil rights and liberties, for there can be no such citizen in a democracy as a half-free citizen.

> I should say here that we have much reason to be proud of the progress our people are making in mutual understanding—the chief buttress of human and civil rights. Steadily we are moving closer to the goal of fair and equal treatment of citizens without regard to race or color.

> This progress, I am confident, will continue. And it is gifted persons such as yourself, born out of the crucible of the struggle for personal dignity and achievement, who will help lead the way towards the goals we seek. (Long 2008, 57)

Another turning point in the Civil Rights Movement that brought national attention to the treatment of African Americans in the South was the murder of Emmett Till. In August 1955, the 14-year-old boy from Chicago, Illinois, was visiting relatives in Money, Mississippi. After being what was described as "too friendly" with a local white girl, the young Till was kidnapped during the night at gunpoint by two white men, beaten almost beyond recognition, and then shot to death. His mother insisted on an open casket, and the pictures of the young boy's body shocked people around the world. An all-white jury did not convict the men. The

Chicago Defender sent a telegram to the president on September 1, 1955, stating the following: "A Chicago boy, Emmett Louis Till 14 was kidnapped and lynched in Mississippi this week, would you let us know if your office has plans to take any action with reference to this shocking act of lawlessness." On September 2, 1955, J. William Barba, assistant to the special counsel to the president, replied:

> The President has asked me to write you in connection with your wire of September first concerning the shocking death of Emmett Louis Till in Mississippi.
>
> We are advised that the Department of Justice has been in close contact with the development of this case, but so far their inquiry has failed to reveal any facts which provide a basis for Federal jurisdiction or action. It appears, therefore, that at the present time, the matter is solely within the jurisdiction of the State of Mississippi. In the event any basis for Federal jurisdiction does develop, you may be sure that appropriate action will be taken.

J. Edgar Hoover was then director of the Federal Bureau of Investigation (FBI). He considered the matter an attempt by the Communist Party to pressure the federal government. He sent the following letter to Dillon Anderson, special assistant to the president, on November 22, 1955:

> Reference is made to my previous communications calling to your attention agitational activity in connection with the death of Emmett Louis Till, fourteen-year-old Negro Chicago boy who was allegedly murdered in Mississippi.
>
> I thought you and the President would be interested in the attached copy of a letter dated September 29, 1955, directed to all Communist Party districts from the headquarters of the Communist Party, USA, which sets forth the proposals of the Communist Party's campaign to exert pressures against the Eisenhower Administration and Attorney General Brownell to intervene in the Emmett Louis Till lynching.
>
> This information has been made available to the Attorney General and the intelligence agencies of the Armed Forces.
>
> As additional pertinent information is received in this regard it will be furnished to you promptly. ("Civil Rights" 2018)

This drive to combat communism would continue to impact African Americans and other groups in particular due to the efforts of Hoover and the McCarthyist movement. Civil rights leaders and organizations were investigated as communist members or sympathizers for decades.

In 1955, Eisenhower appointed the first black to serve in an executive position in the White House. E. Fredrick Morrow became administrative officer for special projects and served in that position until 1961. Previously, he was a field secretary for the NAACP before World War II. During the war, he joined the Field Artillery branch of the U.S. Army and was promoted from a private when he enlisted in 1942 to a major before he left the service in 1946. He served on President

Eisenhower's campaign as a personal adviser and administrative assistant and then became an executive in the Commerce Department in 1955. While in the position, Morrow faced challenges in the White House; for example, some staff refused to serve under him, and white women came to his office in pairs rather than alone. He gave hundreds of speeches before black audiences on behalf of the administration and even addressed the 1960 Republican National Convention. Morrow later wrote that he was disappointed that Eisenhower didn't take a more aggressive stance on civil rights.

On December 1, 1955, Rosa Parks refused to sit at the back of a bus in Montgomery, Alabama. Led by Dr. Martin Luther King, Jr., blacks in the city boycotted riding all buses through December 20, 1956. The Montgomery Bus Boycott brought the subject of racial segregation to the forefront of American politics. The bus boycott lasted 381 days. The city's law on bus segregation was ruled in violation of the Fourteenth Amendment in *Browder v. Gayle,* 142 F. Supp. 707 (1956), by a three-judge panel of the U.S. District Court for the Middle District of Alabama. The Supreme Court affirmed the lower court's decision on November 13, 1956. The NAACP was the plaintiff, and the case was argued by Thurgood Marshall. The event brought Dr. King national attention due to his charismatic nature and ability to stir emotions with his speaking.

Eisenhower was not in support of the protest or the attention it gained. On March 21, 1956, Robert G. Spivack of the *New York Post* asked the president, "With regard to the situation in Alabama, Mr. President, how do you feel about Negroes being brought to trial for refusing to ride the Montgomery buses?" (Eisenhower 1956, 335). President Eisenhower responded with the following:

Well, you are asking me, I think, to be more of a lawyer than I certainly am. But, as I understand it, there is a State law about boycotts, and it is under that kind of thing that these people are being brought to trial.

I think that the statement I made last week on this whole subject represents all the views that I now have to make; and I do believe that it is incumbent on all the South to show some progress. That is what the Supreme Court asked for. And they turned it over to local district courts.

I believe that we should not stagnate; but again I plead for understanding, for really sympathetic consideration of a problem that is far larger both in its emotional and even in its physical aspects than most of us realize. (Eisenhower 1956)

On September 9, 1957, Eisenhower signed the first piece of civil rights legislation since Reconstruction, the Civil Rights Act of 1957. Up until the time of this law, only approximately 20 percent of African Americans were registered to vote due to disenfranchisement and laws in some states that required poll taxes, literacy tests, and other impediments that ensured blacks were not allowed to register. The initial bill was watered down due to opposition by southern Democrats mostly in the Senate but was supported by Senate majority leader and future president Lyndon Johnson. Senator Strom Thurmond from South Carolina sustained the longest filibuster in history to attempt to stop a vote on the bill. He spoke for 24 hours and 18 minutes; the speech included the Declaration of Independence, the Bill of Rights, every state's election laws, George Washington's Farewell Address, and Thurmond's grandmother's biscuit recipe. Still, the administration held steadfast to passing some legislation. During the fight, Vice President Richard Nixon asked to keep the bill alive and said that he had a sworn duty to "support legislation which will guarantee the right of all of our citizens to vote, regardless of their race, creed or color" (Movroydis 2017).

The final version of the law established the six-member U.S. Commission on Civil Rights to investigate allegations of voter infringement and authorized the Civil Rights Division in the Department of Justice to seek federal injunctions to protect African American voting rights. Because the legislation was mostly ineffective, African Americans didn't see much benefit from the new law. One of its provisions was a jury trial for anyone found obstructing voting rights. This was ineffective in southern states, where blacks were predominantly excluded from serving on juries due to existing Jim Crow laws. The original provision giving the attorney general the power to file lawsuits to protect broad constitutional rights of all Americans, to include school desegregation, was also taken out of the final law. However, the new law did serve as a symbol that the federal government was willing to take up the cause of supporting African American rights and that this was perhaps a precursor for stronger laws in the future. For example, Dr. King sent a letter to Nixon dated August 30, 1957, stating the new law was better than nothing at all:

> Since our meeting together many significant things have happened in the life of our nation, particularly in the realm of civil rights. Just this morning our local paper revealed that the compromised Civil Rights Bill was finally passed by the Senate. After considering all angles I have come to the conclusion that the present bill is far better than no bill at all. This limited bill still provides district judges with power to maintain order and to insist upon compliance with their orders. This could be a powerful incentive in changes in behaviour and attitude. I realize that many sincere leaders, both Negro and white, feel that no bill is better than the present bill, and that since we have waited this long for civil rights legislation we can afford to wait an additional year to get stronger legislation in this area. While I sympathize with this point of view, I feel that civil rights legislation is urgent now, and the present limited bill will go a long way to insure it. So it is my hope that the President will not veto the bill. (King 1957)

Also on August 30, Adam Clayton Powell Jr., member of the House of Representatives and one of only three African American members of Congress at that time, sent a press release. The following is an excerpt from that release, cabled from Berchtesgaden, Germany:

> This completely vindicates my support of President Eisenhower regardless of what may happen to me. Personally, I am proud to have campaigned for one who has kept every word to me. After 80 years of political slavery, this is the second emancipation.

On October 11, 1956, President Eisenhower promised me, first, he would call for this bill in his State of the Union message; second, he would spell it out specifically; third, his Attorney General would press for early consideration of the bill; fourth, his Congressional leaders would fight for early passage. (Powell 1957)

On June 23, 1958, Eisenhower met with civil rights leaders Dr. Martin Luther King, Jr., president of the Southern Christian Leadership Conference; A. Philip Randolph, president of the Brotherhood of Sleeping Car Porters; Roy Wilkins, president of the NAACP; and Lester B. Grander, executive secretary to the National Urban League. After commending the president on actions taken in Little Rock and his leadership, the civil rights leaders made a request of the president to take action on nine objectives:

1. The President of the United States should declare in a nationwide pronouncement, prior to September, that the law [Civil Rights Act of 1957] will be vigorously upheld with the total resources at his command.

2. Much emphasis has been laid on the need for restoring communication between white and colored Southerners who are troubled by a common fear of reaction. The President can well set the example in this matter by convoking a White House Conference of constructive leadership to discuss ways and means of complying peaceably with the Court's rulings.

3. Information, resources and advice of the appropriate government agencies addressed to the problems of integration should be made available to all officials and community groups seeking to work out a program of education and action.

4. The President should request both parties to lay aside partisanship so that the Congress can enact a civil rights bill which will include Part III originally in the 1957 bill, in order that constitutional rights other than voting rights may be enforced by the United States Attorney General. Lack of adequate and clear statutory authority has made the Federal Government a mere spectator in the disgraceful maneuverings at Little Rock.

5. We urge the President to direct the Department of Justice to give all legal assistance possible under the law, including the filing of a brief as a friend of the court and appearance of counsel, in the appeal from the Lemly decision in the Little Rock case [Harry Jacob Lemly served on the U.S. District Courts for the Eastern District of Arkansas and the Western District of Arkansas and granted the Little Rock school board a two-year delay in implementing the desegregation order in 1957].

6. The President of the United States should direct the Department of Justice to act now to protect the right of citizens to register and vote. In the nine months since the enactment of the 1957 Civil Rights Act, overt acts have been committed against prospective Negro registrants in some areas and numerous complaints have been submitted to the Department, but, to date, not a single case has reached a court of law. Unless immediate action is undertaken, thousands of Negro citizens will be denied the right to cast a ballot in the 1958 elections.

7. The President should direct the Department of Justice to act under existing statutes in the wave of bombings in churches, synagogues, homes and community centers; also in the murderous brutality directed against Negro citizens in Dawson, Georgia, and other communities.

8. In order to counteract the deliberate hamstringing of the new Civil Rights Commission, the President should recommend to the Congress the extension of its life for at least a full year beyond its present expiration date.

9. The President should make it clear both in statement and in act that he believes in the principle that federal money should not be used to underwrite segregation in violation of the federal constitutional rights of millions of Negro citizens; and that this principle should be applied whether in matters of federal aid to education, hospitals, housing, or any other grants-in-aid to state and local governments. In support of national policy, the Federal Government should finance continuation of public schools where state funds are withdrawn because of integration. (Carson 2000)

Eisenhower first spoke of his disappointment to hear that African Americans were so bitter after five and a half years of effort and action to support them by his administration. The leaders responded that the bitterness was not directed at the president or his administration but at the slow progress being made in their communities. The president spoke to the need for diligent but careful action and said that he would consider the nine objectives and establish a committee.

On February 5, 1959, Eisenhower sent a Special Message to Congress on Civil Rights. In it he called for legislation to achieve "the goal of full equality under law for all people" (The White House 1958). To that end, he asked for legislation to address seven areas:

First, I recommend legislation to strengthen the law dealing with obstructions of justice so as to provide expressly that the use of force or threats of force to obstruct Court orders in school desegregation cases shall be a Federal offense. . . .

Second, I recommend legislation to confer additional investigative authority on the FBI in the case of crimes involving the destruction or attempted destruction of schools or churches, by making flight from one State to another to avoid detention or prosecution for such a crime a Federal offense. . . .

Third, I recommend legislation to give the Attorney General power to inspect Federal election records, and to require that such records be preserved for a reasonable period of time so as to permit such inspection. . . .

Fourth, I recommend legislation to provide a temporary program of financial and technical aid to State and local agencies to assist them in making the necessary adjustments required by school desegregation decisions. . . .

Fifth, I recommend legislation to authorize, on a temporary basis, provision for the education of children of members of the Armed Forces when State-administered public schools have been closed because of desegregation decisions or orders.

Sixth, I recommend that Congress give consideration to the establishing of a statutory Commission on Equal Job Opportunity under Government Contracts. . . .

Seventh, I recommend legislation to extend the life of the Civil Rights Commission for an additional two years. (The White House 1958)

While Congress mulled over the president's legislative request, civil rights demonstrations intensified under Eisenhower's administration. On February 1, 1960, four black college students staged a sit-in at the lunch counter of Woolworth's in Greensboro, North Carolina. Ezell A. Blair (now Jibreel Khazan), Franklin McClain, Joseph A. McNeil, and David L. Richmond, students at historic black North Carolina A&T University, were forbidden from eating at the lunch counter and were asked to leave. They refused, and subsequent sit-ins grew to over 50 students. This sparked similar protests across the South involving 65 students in 12 states.

To achieve these goals established in Eisenhower's request to Congress, a bill was introduced in the House on March 10, 1960. After compromises and attempts by southern Democrats to stop the bill, it was finally passed by Congress, and on May 6, 1960, Eisenhower signed the Civil Rights Act of 1960. It was meant to strengthen some elements of the watered-down Civil Rights Act of 1957. It extended the two-year life of the Civil Rights Commission and put in place federal inspection of local voter registration polls. Additionally, any person who obstructed another's right to register to vote would face fines and possible imprisonment. The president made a statement on signing the act on May 6, outlining what would be achieved by the new law but also his disappointment at two areas that were taken out during congressional compromise:

I have today signed into law the Civil Rights Act of 1960. It is only the second civil rights measure to pass the Congress in 85 years. As was the case with the Act of 1957, recommendations of this Administration underlie the features of the Civil Rights Act of 1960.

The new Act is concerned with a range of civil rights problems. One title makes it a crime to obstruct rights or duties under Federal court orders by force or threat of force. That provision will be an important deterrent to such obstruction which interferes with the execution of Federal court orders, including those involving school desegregation. Provision is also made to assure free public education to all children of Armed Forces personnel in the United States where local public school facilities are unavailable. By authorizing the FBI to investigate certain bombings or attempted bombings of schools, churches and other structures, the Act will deter such heinous acts of lawlessness.

The new Act also deals significantly with that key constitutional right of every American, the right to vote without discrimination on account of race or color. One provision, which requires the retention of voting records, will be of invaluable aid in the successful enforcement of existing voting rights statutes. Another provision authorizes the use by federal courts of voting referees. It holds great promise of making the Fifteenth Amendment of the Constitution fully meaningful.

While I regret that Congress saw fit to eliminate two of my recommendations, I believe the Act is an historic step forward in the field of civil rights. With continuing help from all responsible persons, the new law will play an important role in the days ahead in attaining our goal of equality under law in all areas of our country for all Americans. (Eisenhower 1960)

President Eisenhower could not run for a third term in office. On February 27, 1957, the Twenty-Second Amendment was added to the Constitution, limiting terms in office to two for the president of the United States. Dwight D. Eisenhower passed away on March 28, 1969, in Washington, D.C.

FURTHER READING

Bloom, Jack M. 1987. *Class, Race, and the Civil Rights Movement.* Bloomington: Indiana University Press.

Borstelmann, Thomas. 2001. *The Cold War and the Color Line: American Race Relations in the Global Arena.* Cambridge, MA: Harvard University Press.

"Civil Rights: Emmett Till Case." 2018. Dwight D. Eisenhower Presidential Library and Museum, https://www.dwightdeisenhower.com/387/Civil-Rights-Emmett-Till -Case.

Darby, Jean. 2004. *Dwight D. Eisenhower.* Minneapolis: Lerner Publications.

Eisenhower, Dwight D. 1953a. "Annual Message to the Congress on the State of the Union, February 2, 1953." The American Presidency Project, http://www.presi dency.ucsb.edu/ws/?pid=9829.

Eisenhower, Dwight D. 1953b. "The President's News Conference, March 19, 1953." The American Presidency Project, http://www.presidency.ucsb.edu/ws/index.php?pid =9798.

Eisenhower, Dwight D. 1956. "The President's News Conference, March 21, 1956." The American Presidency Project, http://www.presidency.ucsb.edu/ws/index.php?pid =10759.

Eisenhower, Dwight D. 1960. "Statement by the President upon Signing the Civil Rights Act of 1960, May 6, 1960." The American Presidency Project, http://www.presi dency.ucsb.edu/ws/?pid=11771.

Hitchcock, William I. 2018. *The Age of Eisenhower: America and the World in the 1950s.* New York: Simon and Schuster.

Johnson, Paul. 2015. *Eisenhower: A Life.* New York: Penguin Books.

King, Martin Luther, Jr. 1957. "Letter to Richard M. Nixon, on Civil Rights Act of 1957, Voter Registration." The Martin Luther King, Jr. Research and Education Institute, Stanford University, https://kinginstitute.stanford.edu/king-papers/documents /richard-m-nixon-1.

Long, Michael G., ed. 2008. *First Class Citizenship: The Civil Rights Letters of Jackie Robinson.* New York: Times Books.

Movroydis, Jonathan. 2017. "RN, MLK, and the Civil Rights Act of 1957." Richard Nixon Foundation, Library and Museum, https://www.nixonfoundation.org/2017/01/rn -mlk-and-the-civil-rights-act-of-1957/.

Powell, Adam Clayton, Jr. 1957. "Message from Berchtesgaden, Germany on August 30, 1957." Dwight D. Eisenhower Presidential Library, Museum and Boyhood Home, https://www.eisenhower.archives.gov/research/online_documents/civil_rights _act/1957_08_30_Press_Release_Powell.pdf.

Smith, Jean Edward. 2013. *Eisenhower in War and Peace.* New York: Random House.

The White House. 1958. "Meeting of Negro Leaders with the President—June 23, 1958." Dwight D. Eisenhower Presidential Library, Museum and Boyhood Home, https:// www.eisenhower.archives.gov/research/online_documents/civil_rights_eisen hower_administration/1958_06_23_Meeting_of_Negro_Leaders.pdf.

Wicker Tom. 2002. *Dwight D. Eisenhower: The American Presidents Series; The 34th President.* New York: Times Books.

John Fitzgerald "Jack" Kennedy

35th President of the United States
Presidential Term: January 20, 1961–November 22, 1963
Political Party: Democratic
Vice President: Lyndon B. Johnson

John Fitzgerald Kennedy (nicknamed Jack) was born into the wealthy Kennedy family in Brookline, Massachusetts, on May 29, 1917. His father, Joseph Patrick Kennedy Sr., was active in national politics and was appointed by President Franklin D. Roosevelt as the first chairman of the U.S. Securities and Exchange Commission. Joseph Kennedy later directed the Maritime Commission and served as the U.S. ambassador to the United Kingdom from 1938 until late 1940.

John F. Kennedy had health issues throughout his childhood due to Addison's disease, which impacts the adrenal glands. He graduated from Harvard, joined the U.S. Navy, and served in World War II. When he came home, he was elected to Congress, first to the U.S. House of Representatives and then to the Senate.

John F. Kennedy was the 35th president of the United States. Elected in November 1960, President Kennedy was cautious about getting involved in the issue of civil rights for African Americans. However, in a 1963 speech he proposed legislation that would become the Civil Rights Act of 1964. (John F. Kennedy Presidential Library)

Kennedy won the 1960 election by one the closest margins in history, with 49.7 percent of the popular vote compared to 49.5 percent for Republican contender and former vice president Richard M. Nixon. Kennedy faced opposition because he was Catholic, lacked experience, and was from a wealthy northern family. He selected Senator Lyndon B. Johnson as his vice presidential running mate. Kennedy received only 68 percent of the black vote. While on the campaign trail, he began gaining support from blacks after he called Georgia governor Ernest Vandiver to personally arrange the release of Dr. Martin Luther King, Jr. from jail after a sit-in at the segregated Rich's department store lunch counter. Kennedy also called Coretta Scott King. He was persuaded to take these actions by his brother-in-law Sargent Shriver, who was also serving as head of the campaign's civil rights section, and White House aide Harris Wofford, who was a longtime friend of the King family. Robert "Bobby" Kennedy, John Kennedy's brother, served as the U.S. attorney general. John Kennedy was at first reluctant about the call for fear of alienating white southern Democrats. Bobby Kennedy was upset the call was made, as he feared that it would damage his brother's chance at winning the presidency. However, the call and public recognition by Dr. King upon his release caused a wave of support for Kennedy from African Americans, which very well may have led to him winning the election. Richard Nixon chose to remain silent on the issue even after being visited by baseball hero and civil rights activist Jackie Robinson. After his release, Dr. King made it public that he had not heard from Nixon or any Republican while in jail. Dr. King did not publicly endorse Kennedy, but the news of the phone call spread throughout the African American community and energized black voters in the close election. Reverend Martin Luther King Sr. reportedly stated, "I had expected to vote against Senator Kennedy because of his religion. Now he can be my president, Catholic or whatever he is" (O'Brien 2005).

President Kennedy took office at the height of the Cold War and when the Civil Rights Movement had reached its height in the United States. Jim Crow laws were still in place across the South, and there was still opposition to complying with the U.S. Supreme Court's decision to end segregation as ruled in *Brown v. Board of Education of Topeka, Kansas,* 347 U.S. 483 (1954). The president did not attempt to pass any civil rights legislation during his first year in office, and if he had it would have not have been supported by Congress, since it was controlled by southern Democrats. However, in May 1961 Kennedy appointed Thurgood Marshall to the U.S. Court of Appeals for the Second Circuit.

Marshall's appointment was quite contentious:

Six days of hearings were eventually held but over a three month period. The hearings focused on Thurgood's membership with the NAACP, American Civil Liberties Union, and other organizations rather than his qualifications to serve as a judge. Ultimately he was confirmed after a year of extensive hearings on September 11, 1962 by a Senate vote of 56 to 14. Thurgood had been serving as a judge for eleven months but was officially sworn in on October 23, 1961. (Starks and Brooks 2012)

Kennedy made his support for civil rights apparent during his first State of the Union Address on January 30, 1961:

The denial of constitutional rights to some of our fellow Americans on account of race—at the ballot box and elsewhere—disturbs the national conscience, and subjects us to the charge of world opinion that our democracy is not equal to the high promise of our heritage. Morality in private business has not been sufficiently spurred by morality in public business. A host of problems and projects in all 50 States, though not possible to include in this Message, deserves—and will receive—the attention of both the Congress and the Executive Branch. On most of these matters, Messages will be sent to the Congress within the next two weeks. (Kennedy 1960)

The majority of the address focused on the Cold War.

Kennedy was cautious about getting involved in civil rights. Attorney General Robert Kennedy shared the president's cautious stance. The president needed southern backing in order to gain support for both international and domestic issues such as antipoverty legislation. However, the president's stance on civil rights was first tested by the Freedom Riders, who were a group of more than 400 blacks and whites who traveled on buses and trains through the Deep South from May 4, 1961, through November 1961. The first bus left Washington, D.C., with only 13 riders, including student John Lewis who would later become a U.S. congressman from Georgia's 5th District. Although the Supreme Court had ruled in *Morgan v. Virginia* (1946), *Sarah Keys v. Carolina Coach Company* (1955), and *Boynton v. Virginia* (1960) that segregated public buses and interstate commerce were unconstitutional, the ruling was not enforced in most southern states due to Jim Crow laws. Most of the riders were members of the Congress of Racial Equality (CORE), founded in 1942. They tested Jim Crow laws and challenged southern restrictions against segregated travel. In some states, they sat together in segregated restaurants, at lunch counters, and in hotels. Only a few arrests occurred until the Freedom Riders entered Alabama. They ate dinner with Dr. Martin Luther King, Jr. in Georgia, who warned them of pending violence if they continued into Alabama.

Once entering the Deep South starting with Alabama, the Freedom Riders were subjected to violent racial mob attacks supported by police nonaction. Riders were beaten and arrested, and buses were burned. In Birmingham, Alabama, Police Commissioner Eugene "Bull" Connor and Police Sergeant Tom Cook organized violence against the Freedom Riders by aligning with the Ku Klux Klan. As the violence against the riders gained both national and international attention, the violence against them increased. This prompted Robert Kennedy to lead the administration's call for a "cooling off period." The administration was concerned about the coverage on television and in newspapers around the globe. The details of the entire event and the violence were featured on the front pages of leading publications such as *Time, Life,* and *Newsweek*. Kennedy used special assistant John Seigenthaler as an intermediary between the administration and the Freedom Riders, since he was also a white southerner from Tennessee. James Farmer, head of CORE, responded to the attorney general's request by stating, "We have been cooling off for 350 years, and if we cooled off any more, we'd be in a deep freeze" (Dierenfield 2013). Even Seigenthaler was subjected to violence during the

Freedom Rides. While trying to assist riders during a riot in Montgomery, Alabama, on May 20, he was knocked unconscious after telling the assailants that he was a federal authority.

At one point Robert Kennedy urged the riders to "get off the buses and leave the matter to peaceful settlement in the courts" (Bevel 2018, 218). During his run for office, the president had promised that he would not use federal troops in southern racial conflicts as had been done by his predecessor, President Dwight D. Eisenhower, in the integration of high schools in Little Rock, Arkansas. Instead, President Kennedy assigned federal marshals to protect the riders. Robert Kennedy reached a compromise with Mississippi senator James O. Eastland to have the riders jailed for their safety rather than face violence.

Federal Bureau of Investigation (FBI) Director J. Edgar Hoover saw civil rights activists as subversives and communist sympathizers. Although he had information from Gary Thomas Rowe, an FBI operative, about a planned riot against the Freedom Riders in a Birmingham bus terminal on May 14, he would not report it to Attorney General Kennedy. During a riot on May 20 at a Montgomery, Alabama bus station, FBI agents remained in a parked van and took photographs of the incident.

On May 21, 1961, civil rights leaders, including Dr. King, met at Reverend Ralph D. Abernathy's First Baptist Church in Montgomery to discuss the violence, along with 1,500 community members and supported by federal marshals. A violent mob surrounded the church until the National Guard was able to come in the next day to safely escort them out. On May 23, 1961, martial law was declared in the city by Alabama governor John Patterson. Two days later, Robert Kennedy defended the U.S. record on race relations on Voice of America and stated that "there is no reason that in the near or the foreseeable future, a Negro could [not] become President of the United States" (PBS 2018). On May 29, 1961, he sent a formal petition to the Interstate Commerce Commission requesting that it comply with the ruling in *Sarah Keys v. Carolina Coach Company,* 64 MCC 769 (1955), to end public bus segregation. An order was finally issued on September 22 and became effective on November 1, requiring the removal of segregated signs and the end of segregation in waiting rooms, at water fountains, and in restrooms in interstate bus terminals.

On March 6, 1961, President Kennedy issued Executive Order 10925, requiring affirmative action in government contracting. This order was historic in that it was the first time the term "affirmative action" was used in federal legislation, which would have implications for the next four decades in terms of addressing public and private programs to ensure equality for minorities. Part of the order stated:

> The contractor will not discriminate against any employee or applicant for employment because of race, creed, color, or national origin. The contractor will take affirmative action to ensure that applicants are employed, and that employees are treated during employment, without regard to their race, creed, color, or national origin. Such action shall include, but not be limited to, the following: employment, upgrading, demotion or transfer; recruitment or recruitment advertising; layoff or termination; rates of pay or other forms

of compensation; and selection for training, including apprenticeship. The contractor agrees to post in conspicuous places, available to employees and applicants for employment, notices to be provided by the contracting officer setting forth the provisions of this nondiscrimination clause.

The order also established the President's Committee on Equal Employment Opportunity, chaired by the vice president, with the purpose "to scrutinize and study employment practices of the Government of the United States, and to consider and recommend additional affirmative steps which should be taken by executive departments and agencies to realize more fully the national policy of nondiscrimination within the executive branch of the Government" (U.S. Equal Employment Opportunity Commission 2018).

Still, civil rights leaders wanted the president to take a more aggressive stand on ending segregation. In October 1961, King presented Kennedy with the proposal for a proclamation known as the Second Emancipation Proclamation. This new proclamation, to be released on June 6, 1962, in the words of Dr. King, would serve to support the vision of President Abraham Lincoln for a nation that could not exist with segregation. The 64-page document was presented on May 17, 1962, on the eighth anniversary of the Supreme Court's decision in *Brown v. Board of Education of Topeka, Kansas.* The document cited Lincoln's Gettysburg Address, Frederick Douglass's autobiography, President Kennedy's *The Strategy of Peace,* and precedents set by President Harry S. Truman's executive order to desegregate the military and called for the overturning of all laws requiring segregation and discrimination. Kennedy would not issue the proclamation.

James Meredith attended the all-black Jackson State College from 1960 to 1962 and repeatedly applied, unsuccessfully, to the all-white University of Mississippi (nicknamed "Ole Miss") in Oxford, Mississippi. With the assistance of the NAACP, he filed suit against the university in 1961 based on discrimination and claimed that the school violated the Supreme Court's decision in *Brown v. Board of Education of Topeka, Kansas.* The case was appealed to the Supreme Court, which ruled in Meredith's favor in September 1962. The governor of Mississippi, Ross Barnett, refused to abide by the Supreme Court's decision and argued that the federal government had no right to enforce desegregation on a sovereign state. Barnett was a strict segregationist who won the election to become governor based on that issue. On September 13, 1962, he made a statewide speech on television and radio declaring, "I speak to you now in the moment of our greatest crisis since the War Between the States," Barnett declared. "We must either submit to the unlawful dictates of the federal government or stand up like men and tell them, never! I submit to you tonight, no school will be integrated in Mississippi while I am your governor!" (American RadioWorks 2018). He negotiated with the Kennedy administration to block Meredith's admission, not knowing that President Kennedy was taping the secret telephone calls.

On September 27, 1962, Robert Kennedy issued an official statement of the Department of Justice:

It has been clear from the time of the court's decision ordering the University of Mississippi to accept Mr. Meredith that there would be but one resolution to these difficulties. The orders of the federal courts can and will be enforced. It is important to our country, however, that if possible, that this be accomplished without force and without civil disorder.

Every American has the duty to obey the law and the right to expect that the law will be enforced.

It is fundamental in our system that there be respect for the law and compliance with all laws—not just those with which we happen to agree. The course which Governor Barnett is following is, therefore, incompatible with the principles upon which this Union is based.

As the Legislature of the State of Mississippi stated in solemn resolve 129 years ago:

This state owes a duty to the Union above all minor consideration. . . . The doctrine of Nullification is contrary to the letter and spirit of the Constitution, and in direct conflict with the welfare, safety and independence of every State in the Union; and to no one of them would its consequences be more deeply disastrous, more ruinous, than to the State of Mississippi. . . .

This matter will be before the court again tomorrow in New Orleans. At that time, Governor Barnett will have an opportunity to state his case before all the judges of the Court of Appeals for the Fifth Circuit. I hope that this matter will be resolved peacefully and without violence or further action by the federal government.

However, if this is not to be, the federal government will see to it that the orders which are presently outstanding are maintained and enforced, whatever action that ultimately may require. (Sullivan 1965)

Meredith arrived at the campus on Sunday, September 20, escorted by federal officials, including 123 deputy federal marshals, 316 U.S. border guards, and 97 federal prison guards. President Kennedy made a national broadcast addressing the situation while the governor made a state announcement. Mobs descended on the university campus and assaulted the federal marshals with such objects as rocks and bottles, and the marshals responded with tear gas. Two people were killed, including a French journalist, and dozens of others were injured. On another day, 2,000 people, including students, farmers, and other protestors, stormed the campus, forcing the attorney general to now allow Meredith and his federal protectors to enter the campus. President Kennedy deployed 16,000 troops to restore order and to protect Meredith during his entire time at the university. Governor Barnett held several tense telephone calls with Robert Kennedy during the event and finally backed down when he was found guilty of civil contempt by the Fifth Circuit Court of Appeals and faced arrest and fines of $10,000 a day. Meredith graduated from the university on August 18, 1963, with a degree in political science.

On November 20, 1962, President Kennedy issued Executive Order 11063 to prohibit racial discrimination, and thus segregation, in public housing and related facilities because of race, color, creed, or national origin. The order cited the

Housing Act of 1949, signed by President Harry S. Truman as part of his Fair Deal program, and covered any housing owned, sold, leased, or rented where federal funds were provided. The act required the reporting of all programs that fell under the order to the President's Committee on Equal Opportunity in Housing. Specifically, the order barred discrimination based on race, color, religion (creed), sex, or national origin in the following areas:

(a) in the sale, leasing, rental, or other disposition of residential property and related facilities (including land to be developed for residential use), or in the use or occupancy thereof, if such property and related facilities are—

(i) owned or operated by the Federal Government, or

(ii) provided in whole or in part with the aid of loans, advances, grants, or contributions hereafter agreed to be made by the Federal Government, or

(iii) provided in whole or in part by loans hereafter insured, guaranteed, or otherwise secured by the credit of the Federal Government, or

(iv) provided by the development or the redevelopment of real property purchased, leased, or otherwise obtained from a State or local public agency receiving Federal financial assistance for slum clearance or urban renewal with respect to such real property under a loan or grant contract hereafter entered into; and

(b) in the lending practices with respect to residential property and related facilities (including land to be developed for residential use) of lending institutions, insofar as such practices relate to loans hereafter insured or guaranteed by the Federal Government.

Defiance to integration in the South and continued protests by African Americans pushed President Kennedy to address civil rights. Dr. King was arrested in the spring of 1963 while protesting in Birmingham, Alabama. While in jail he wrote "Letter from Birmingham Jail," one of his most prolific writings on racial injustice. James Bevel, another leader in the Southern Christian Leadership Conference, led a march in the streets of the city. Millions around the world watched on television as the demonstrators were attacked by police dogs and battered with high-pressure fire hoses at the command of Birmingham Police Commissioner Eugene "Bull" Connor. President Kennedy reacted by sending in troops.

While these events were occurring at the University of Alabama, on June 12, 1963, civil rights activist Medgar Evers was assassinated by Byron De La Beckwith, a white supremacist and member of the Ku Klux Klan in Jackson, Mississippi. Evers himself had challenged segregation in Mississippi by applying to the law school of the University of Mississippi as part of the NAACP's systematic testing of enforced desegregation in September 1954 but was not accepted. He was an active member of the NAACP, serving as a field representative in Mississippi, and had received many threats against his life. His house was firebombed in May 1963. On June 12 at 12:40 a.m., he was shot in the driveway of his house. He was first taken to a local hospital but initially was not admitted because he was black. Once his family explained who he was, he was admitted but died from his injuries less than an hour later. He thus became the first black person admitted to an all-white hospital in the state of Mississippi. On June 12, President Kennedy sent the following letter to Medgar Evers's wife, Myrlie:

Dear Mrs. Evers,

I extend to you and your children my sincerest condolences on the tragic death of your husband. Although comforting thoughts are difficult at a time like this, surely there can be some solace in the realization of the justice of the cause for which your husband gave his life. Achievement of the goals he did so much to promote will enable his children and the generations to follow to share fully and equally in the benefits and advantages our Nation has to offer.

John F. Kennedy
(Marshall 2018, 193)

Evers was buried on June 19 in Arlington National Cemetery before a crowd of more than 3,000, receiving full military honors. De La Beckwith, who was not convicted by two all-white juries in 1964, was finally convicted of the crime on February 5, 1994. The Evers family and civil rights leaders pressed for the new trial. During his initial trial, De La Beckwith was supported by some of the most prominent white lawyers in the state. Governor Ross Barnett attended his first trial and shook De La Beckwith's hand in full view of the jury. During the 1994 trial, De La Beckwith was given life imprisonment at age 73. He died in 2001. In 1969 Medgar's brother, Charles Evers, became the first African American mayor of Fayette, Mississippi, the first racially mixed southern town since Reconstruction.

In June 1963 the governor of Alabama fought to prevent black students from attending the University of Alabama in Tuscaloosa. The university had denied all applications for black students up to that time. This was especially supported by the state's governor, George Wallace, who stated in his inaugural address in January 1963 after being sworn in, "segregation now, segregation tomorrow, segregation forever." The state would not abide by the Supreme Court's ruling in *Brown v. Board of Education of Topeka, Kansas.* African American applicants Vivian Malone and James Hood applied to the university and were denied but filed suit and were ordered to be admitted by the U.S. District Court for the Northern District of Alabama in June 1963. The students were supported by the NAACP Legal Defense and Educational Fund. President Kennedy had previously sought to have Robert Kennedy attempt to persuade Governor Wallace to comply with the university's desegregation on April 25, 1963, but those talks failed.

During the morning of June 11, Malone and Hood preregistered for courses at the Birmingham courthouse. Later that day they arrived on the campus at Foster Auditorium to enroll as part of a three-car motorcade including federal marshals and U.S. Deputy Attorney General Nicholas Katzenbach. Wallace blocked the door, accompanied by state troopers, and fulfilled his campaign promise to personally block the door if he was ever faced with having to abide by a desegregation order. Katzenbach approached Wallace and demanded that he step aside to allow the black students to be admitted. Wallace replied in a symbolic speech:

The unwelcomed, unwanted, unwarranted and force-induced intrusion upon the campus of the University of Alabama today of the might of the Central Government offers frightful example of the oppression of the rights, privileges and sovereignty of this State by officers of the Federal Government. This intrusion results solely from force, or threat of force, undignified by any reasonable application of the principle of law, reason and justice. It is important that the people of this State and nation understand that this action is in violation of rights reserved to the State by the Constitution of the United States and the Constitution of the State of Alabama. While some few may applaud these acts, millions of Americans will gaze in sorrow upon the situation existing at this great institution of learning. (Ward and Gainty 2012, 367)

President Kennedy issued Presidential Proclamation 3542 ordering Wallace to comply with the federal court's order and step aside and also ordering all those acting with him to cease and desist from obstructing justice. Once notified by Katzenbach that the governor would not comply, the president issued Executive Order 11111 federalizing the Alabama National Guard. Just a few hours after Wallace had blocked the door to Foster Auditorium, National Guard general Henry Graham confronted him and stated, "Sir, it is my sad duty to ask you to step aside under the orders of the President of the United States" (Rice 2017). Wallace made another statement before stepping aside and allowing Malone and Hood to complete their registration at the university. Once they entered the auditorium, Malone and Hood were surprised to be greeted with applause from whites who supported integration. The National Guard remained on the campus, and Executive Order 11111 was used to integrate other all-white schools across the state. In September 1963 President Kennedy issued Executive Order 11118, titled "Providing Assistance for Removal of Unlawful Obstructions of Justice in the State of Alabama," granting the secretary of defense authority to use military force to support integration in Alabama. Malone graduated in 1965 with a bachelor of arts in business management. Hood left the university after two months in 1963 but returned in 1997 to earn a PhD in interdisciplinary studies. Wallace actually planned to give Hood his degree in 1997 but could not attend the ceremony due to poor health.

An interesting note is that while Vivian Malone waited in the dormitory as President Kennedy federalized the Alabama National Guard, she went to the lunchroom to eat. Some white students from the university joined her in support. Governor Wallace later unsuccessfully made four attempts to run for president of the United States. He died in 1998.

President Kennedy took his strongest stance on civil rights by issuing an omnibus bill called the Civil Rights Act of 1963 to Congress on June 19, 1963. A great deal of planning went into developing the bill. In May and June of that year, he held a series of meetings with governors, business executives, union leaders, religious and civil rights leaders, and others to gain both their input and mostly their support. On June 11, he made a nationally televised address outlining the need for the bill, promising to deliver it to Congress by the end of the year. He opened by addressing the need to send the Alabama National Guard to the University of

Alabama to ensure that the two "clearly qualified young Alabama residents who happened to have been born Negro" were admitted. He asked every American to examine their conscience on this and related incidents and to reflect on how the United States was engaged in a worldwide struggle to promote and protect the rights of all who wanted to be free. He then outlined his bill being sent to Congress:

> I am, therefore, asking the Congress to enact legislation giving all Americans the right to be served in facilities which are open to the public—hotels, restaurants, theaters, retail stores, and similar establishments.

> This seems to me to be an elementary right. Its denial is an arbitrary indignity that no American in 1963 should have to endure, but many do.

> I have recently met with scores of business leaders urging them to take voluntary action to end this discrimination and I have been encouraged by their response, and in the last 2 weeks over 75 cities have seen progress made in desegregating these kinds of facilities. But many are unwilling to act alone, and for this reason, nationwide legislation is needed if we are to move this problem from the streets to the courts.

> I am also asking the Congress to authorize the Federal Government to participate more fully in lawsuits designed to end segregation in public education. We have succeeded in persuading many districts to desegregate voluntarily. Dozens have admitted Negroes without violence. Today a Negro is attending a State-supported institution in every one of our 50 States, but the pace is very slow.

> Too many Negro children entering segregated grade schools at the time of the Supreme Court's decision 9 years ago will enter segregated high schools this fall, having suffered a loss which can never be restored. The lack of an adequate education denies the Negro a chance to get a decent job.

> The orderly implementation of the Supreme Court decision, therefore, cannot be left solely to those who may not have the economic resources to carry the legal action or who may be subject to harassment.

> Other features will also be requested, including greater protection for the right to vote. But legislation, I repeat, cannot solve this problem alone. It must be solved in the homes of every American in every community across our country.

> In this respect I want to pay tribute to those citizens North and South who have been working in their communities to make life better for all. They are acting not out of a sense of legal duty but out of a sense of human decency.

> Like our soldiers and sailors in all parts of the world they are meeting freedom's challenge on the firing line, and I salute them for their honor and their courage.

My fellow Americans, this is a problem which faces us all—in every city of the North as well as the South. Today there are Negroes unemployed, two or three times as many compared to whites, inadequate in education, moving into the large cities, unable to find work, young people particularly out of work without hope, denied equal rights, denied the opportunity to eat at a restaurant or lunch counter or go to a movie theater, denied the right to a decent education, denied almost today the right to attend a State university even though qualified. It seems to me that these are matters which concern us all, not merely Presidents or Congressmen or Governors, but every citizen of the United States.

This is one country. It has become one country because all of us and all the people who came here had an equal chance to develop their talents.

We cannot say to 10 percent of the population that you can't have that right; that your children cannot have the chance to develop whatever talents they have; that the only way that they are going to get their rights is to go into the streets and demonstrate. I think we owe them and we owe ourselves a better country than that.

Therefore, I am asking for your help in making it easier for us to move ahead and to provide the kind of equality of treatment which we would want ourselves; to give a chance for every child to be educated to the limit of his talents.

As I have said before, not every child has an equal talent or an equal ability or an equal motivation, but they should have an equal right to develop their talent and their ability and their motivation, to make something of themselves.

We have a right to expect that the Negro community will be responsible, will uphold the law, but they have a right to expect that the law will be fair, that the Constitution will be color blind, as Justice Harlan said at the turn of the century.

This is what we are talking about and this is a matter which concerns this country and what it stands for, and in meeting it I ask the support of all our citizens. (Kennedy, John, 1963)

Kennedy's speech was hailed as historic by civil rights leaders and international partners. Dr. King sent a telegram to the president and called the speech one of the most eloquent and profound in history drawing attention to the moral issue of integration:

I have just listened to your speech to the nation it was one of the most eloquent profound and unequivocal pleas for justice and the freedom of all men ever made by any president you spoke passionately to the moral issues involved in the integration struggle I am sure that your encouraging words will bring a new sense of hope to the millions of disinherited people of our country your message will become a hallmark in annals of American history. (Sandler 2013, 222)

The speech was not received well by southern Democrats, and there was concern from those afraid of black militancy and leaders such as the Nation of Islam's Malcolm X. Senator Richard Russell Jr. from Georgia stated that what the president was proposing would transform the country into a socialist or communist state. Senator Strom Thurmond from South Carolina called on all southern Democrats to block any legislation put forth by Kennedy until he backed down from supporting civil rights. A day after the speech, the House of Representatives voted against a bill to increase funding to the Area Redevelopment Administration due to opposition from southern Democrats.

Still, Kennedy sent the actual bill to Congress on June 19, 1963. While some members of Congress argued for changes, some civil rights leaders stated that it needed to be even more aggressive. Robert Kennedy testified before the Senate Judiciary Committee on July 18, 1963, about the proposed bill and its need. This was part of the president's strategy to get the bill passed before the November 1964 elections so it would not be used as a campaign issue. Robert Kennedy opened by stating the following:

> We are today in the midst of a great debate, whether or not this nation, the champion of freedom throughout the world, can now extend full freedom to twenty million of our own citizens who have yet to achieve it.

> In view of the urgency of the bill before you, I welcome the opportunity to appear before this Committee to state the views of the Administration to answer any questions that may arise.

> It seems to me that no reasonable examination of this or any similar measure can proceed until we have answered one fundamental question: Is it needed or not?

> Clearly, it is needed. No American can condone the injustices under which many American Negroes and other of our fellow citizens are forced to live— injustices that vary in kind and in cause from place to place—injustices which are sometimes so intense that in one of our States, with a non-white population of more than one million, of which 442,000 are of voting age, less than twenty-five thousand of those Negroes are registered to vote.

> Consider also, the innumerable difficulties that face a Negro just traveling from State to State in our country[,] something the rest of us take for granted. If he makes reservations in advance, they may not be honored.

> If he seeks accommodations along the way, he is likely to be rejected time after time, until, just to obtain lodging and food, he must detour widely from his route—and if he does find accommodations available to him, they are likely to be inferior. (Kennedy, Robert, 1963)

To increase attention to the issue and raise international awareness on the condition of blacks in the United States, the March on Washington for Jobs and Freedom took place in Washington, D.C., on August 28, 1963. The event was a call for social, political, and legal equality for African Americans. Approximately 250,000 of all races gathered before the Lincoln Memorial on the anniversary of the Emancipation Proclamation. The event was organized by several civil rights leaders, including A. Philip Randolph; Roy Wilkins of the NAACP; Bayard Rustin, chief aid to Randolph; and Whitney Young of the National Urban League. Other organizers included James Farmer of CORE, John Lewis of the Student Nonviolent Coordinating Committee (SNCC), Walter Reuther of the United Auto Workers, Joachim Prinz of the American Jewish Congress, Eugene Carson Blake of the Commission on Religion and Race of the National Council of Churches, Matthew Ahmann of the National Catholic Conference for Interracial Justice, and Dorothy Height of the National Council of Negro Women. All of the primary leaders of the event gave speeches. However, the most memorable event of the march was the speech delivered by Dr. King titled "I Have a Dream."

The leadership efforts of the Negro American Labor Council led by Randolph, formerly head of the Brotherhood of Sleeping Car Porters, with support from the Southern Christian Leadership Conference, led by Dr. King, as well as other groups including SNCC and the American Federation of Labor made the march possible. Randolph had threatened such a march to President Dwight D. Eisenhower before the passage of the Civil Rights Act of 1957. President Kennedy met with civil rights leaders with two concerns. First, he was concerned that the march would lead to violence. Second, he was concerned that the meeting was ill-timed given the push to get the civil rights bill passed in Congress. The leaders insisted that the march would take place, with King stating "Frankly, I have never engaged in any direct-action movement which did not seem ill-timed" (Schlesinger 2007). The president asked Robert Kennedy to support the march with added security, and the march organizers agreed to end at the Lincoln Memorial rather than the U.S. Capitol so as not to give Congress the impression that it was being attacked. The crowd was supported by 5,000 Washington, D.C., police officers and 6,000 National Guard soldiers. No incidents of violence were reported by the police. In addition to the speakers, performers at the event included Mahalia Jackson, Marian Anderson, Joan Baez, Bob Dylan, and Peter, Paul, and Mary.

After the rally at the Lincoln Memorial, the speakers met with President Kennedy and Vice President Lyndon Johnson at the White House at 5:00 p.m. In attendance were King; Secretary of Labor Willard Wirtz; Mathew Ahmann, executive director of the National Catholic Conference for Interracial Justice; John Lewis, representative for SNCC; Joachim Prinz, president of the American Jewish Congress; Reverend Eugene Carson Blake, president of the National Council of the Churches of Christ in the USA; A. Philip Randolph, president of the Negro American Labor Council; Walter P. Reuther, president of the United Auto Workers; Whitney M. Young Jr., president of the National Urban League; and Floyd McKissick, national chairman of CORE. President Kennedy viewed the event as a success that would increase support for the passage of his civil rights bill. John Lewis commented that "After the March on Washington was over, President Kennedy had invited us back down to the White House. He stood in the door of the Oval Office and he greeted each one of us. He was like a beaming, proud father. He was so pleased. So happy that everything had gone so well" (Matthews 2013).

Not all black leaders supported the event. Militant Nation of Islam leader Malcolm X called the event the "Farce on Washington." He espoused an aggressive approach to civil rights that included no support from whites for blacks to fight for equality in what has become his famous words "by any means necessary." Speaking during a press conference in 1963, he said,

> As long as they thought that Martin Luther King had things under control in Birmingham, Kennedy didn't see fit to send any troops down there. As long as the dogs were biting little black babies and black women and black children, Kennedy never thought of sending any troops into Birmingham. It was only after the Negroes showed that they were fed up and that they were capable of retaliating against the injustices that were being inflicted upon them by the whites that Kennedy called for the troops. (Malcolm X 1964)

In his 1964 book, Malcolm X further elaborated on the March on Washington:

> The marchers had been instructed to bring no signs—signs were provided. They had been told to sing one song: "We Shall Overcome." They had been told how to arrive, when, where to arrive, where to assemble, when to start marching, the route to march. First aid stations were strategically located— even where to faint!

> Yes, I was there. I observed that circus. Who ever heard of angry revolutionists all harmonizing "We Shall Overcome . . . S-u-u-m Day . . ." while tripping and swaying along arm-in-arm with the very people they were supposed to be angrily revolting against? Who ever heard of angry revolutionists swinging their bare feet together with their oppressor in lily-pad park pools, with gospels and guitars and "I Have A Dream" speeches? And the black masses in America were—and still are—having a nightmare. (Malcolm X 1964, 323)

Another event that impacted support for the civil rights bill was the bombing of the 16th Street Baptist Church in Birmingham, Alabama, on September 15, 1963. The church was targeted as a meeting place for civil rights leaders and organizations. Four members of the Ku Klux Klan used dynamite to bomb the church, resulting in the deaths of four young girls: Addie Mae Collins (age 11), Cynthia Wesley (age 14), Carole Robertson (age 14), and Carol Denise McNair (age 11). Over 20 others were injured. As unrest and riots grew in the city, Robert Kennedy sent 25 FBI agents to investigate the bombing. International outrage ensued over the event, particularly because of the deaths of the innocent girls. Even Alabama governor Wallace offered a reward for the perpetrators of the bombing. Wallace also blamed the climate of racism in the state. Dr. King sent Wallace a telegram, stating that "The blood of four little children . . . is on your hands. Your irresponsible and misguided actions have created in Birmingham and Alabama the atmosphere that has induced continued violence and now murder" (Olson 2015). The prosecution of the four Klansman was delayed until 2002. Evidence revealed that the FBI had information on the identities of the bombers as early as 1965, but FBI Director J. Edgar Hoover did not support the Civil Rights Movement.

During the same month as the bombing, northern Democrats added provisions to the civil rights bill, and it passed the House Judiciary subcommittee. These provisions included eliminating segregation in all public facilities and not just schools, giving greater protections to black voters, and authorizing the attorney general to file lawsuits on behalf of those whose rights were violated. Southern Democrats supported the revised bill in the belief that it would be defeated in the full House of Representatives vote. President Kennedy and Robert Kennedy met with a small group of congressional leaders in October 1963 to draft another version of the bill that they felt would gain support, even from conservatives. The bill was referred to the Rules Committee in November 1963, where its chairman, Howard Smith, a southern Democrat from Virginia who strongly supported segregation, made it known that he would do all he could to keep the bill tied up indefinitely.

President Kennedy was assassinated in Dallas, Texas, on November 22, 1963. Vice President Lyndon Johnson became president, and with national sympathy for Kennedy's death, the passage of the Civil Rights Act became a reality on July 2, 1964. Dr. King described Kennedy's death as a loss for the nation and stated that the greatest tribute to the slain president was the implementation of the domestic and foreign policies that he had spearheaded. Not all civil rights leaders made such heartfelt and supportive statements. Malcolm X caused national outrage in stating that the president's assassination was a matter of the "chickens coming home to roost." There was already growing division within the Nation of Islam between its leader Elijah Muhammad and Malcolm X, and the statement about President Kennedy caused Malcolm X's suspension from the Nation of Islam and ultimately his split with the group.

FURTHER READING

American RadioWorks. 2018. The Riot at Ole' Miss, http://americanradioworks.public radio.org/features/mississippi/f1.html.

Barnes, John A. 2007. *John F. Kennedy on Leadership: The Lessons and Legacy of a President.* New York: Amacom, American Management Association.

Brinkley, Alan. 2012. *John F. Kennedy: The American Presidents Series; The 35th President, 1961–1963.* New York: Times Books.

Dalek, Robert. 2013. *An Unfinished Life: John F. Kennedy, 1917–1963.* New York: Little, Brown.

Kennedy, John F. 1960. "Annual Message to the Congress on the State of the Union, January 30, 1961." The American Presidency Project, http://www.presidency.ucsb.edu /ws/index.php?pid=8045.

Kennedy, John F. 1963. "Excerpt from a Report to the American People on Civil Rights, 11 June 1963." John F. Kennedy Presidential Library and Museum, https://www .jfklibrary.org/Asset-Viewer/LH8F_0Mzv0e6Ro1yEm74Ng.aspx.

Kennedy, Robert F. 1963. "Robert F. Kennedy's Testimony on Civil Rights Act of 1963, July 18, 1963." National Archives Catalog, https://catalog.archives.gov/id/193988.

Malcolm X. 1964. *The Autobiography of Malcolm X.* New York: Random House.

Marshall, James P. 2018. *The Mississippi Civil Rights Movement and the Kennedy Administration, 1960–1964.* Baton Rouge: Louisiana State University Press.

Matthews, David. 2013. "Kennedy White House Had Jitters Ahead of 1963 March on Washington." Fox, http://fox13now.com/2013/08/28/kennedy-white-house-had -jitters-ahead-of-1963-march-on-washington/.

Sabato, Larry J. 2013. *The Kennedy Half-Century: The Presidency, Assassination, and Lasting Legacy of John F. Kennedy.* New York: Bloomsbury.

Sandler, Martin W., ed. 2013. *The Letters of John F. Kennedy.* New York: Bloomsbury.

Starks, Glenn L., and Erik Brooks. 2012. *Thurgood Marshall: A Biography.* Santa Barbara, CA: Greenwood.

Sullivan, Donald Francis. 1965. *The Civil Rights Programs of the Kennedy Administration: A Political Analysis.* Norman: University of Oklahoma.

Ward, Walter D., and Denis Gainty. 2012. *Sources of World Societies,* Vol. 2, *Since 1450.* Boston: Bedford/St. Martin's.

Lyndon Baines Johnson

36th President of the United States
Presidential Term: November 22, 1963–January 20, 1969
Political Party: Democratic
Vice President: None (1963–1965), Hubert Humphrey (1965–1969)

Lyndon Baines Johnson (commonly referred to as LBJ) was born on August 27, 1908, near the central Texas community of Johnson City. As vice president, Johnson assumed the presidency after the assassination of John F. Kennedy on November 22, 1963. It was one of the most solemn events in U.S. history, and Johnson was thrust into the highest point of the Civil Rights Movement. President Johnson formulated policies under his Great Society and War on Poverty programs. The first combated poverty and racial injustice, while the second was focused on combating a large percentage of Americans living in poverty. The president continued many domestic programs that Kennedy began under his New Frontier program, to include focusing on civil rights. At the same time that he focused on these domestic policies, Johnson escalated U.S. involvement in the Vietnam War, which was facing growing opposition by American citizens.

Lyndon B. Johnson was the 36th president of the United States. He made legislative history on August 6, 1965, when he signed the Voting Rights Act. The new law was passed to end state and local barriers to African Americans being able to vote as guaranteed under the Fifteenth Amendment. (Library of Congress)

President Kennedy and the vice president had been working to pass a civil rights bill before Kennedy was assassinated, and President Johnson used the national sadness of the assassination to rally support for the passage of the bill. Johnson made an address before a joint session of Congress on November 27, 1963. He opened by stating, "The greatest leader of our time has been struck down by the foulest deed of our time. Today John Fitzgerald Kennedy lives on in the immortal words and works that he left behind. He lives on in the mind and memories of mankind. He lives on in the hearts of his countrymen. No words are sad enough to express our sense of loss. No words are strong enough to express our determination to continue the forward thrust of America that he began" (Johnson 1963).

In the address Johnson asked Congress to support the civil rights bill, a tax bill, and pending education bills. In speaking for support of the civil rights bill, he stated the following (Johnson 1963):

First, no memorial oration or eulogy could more eloquently honor President Kennedy's memory than the earliest possible passage of the civil rights bill for which he fought so long. We have talked long enough in this country about equal rights. We have talked for one hundred years or more. It is time now to write the next chapter, and to write it in the books of law.

I urge you again, as I did in 1957 and again in 1960, to enact a civil rights law so that we can move forward to eliminate from this Nation every trace of discrimination and oppression that is based upon race or color. There could be no greater source of strength to this Nation both at home and abroad.

He ended his speech with the following words:

We meet in grief, but let us also meet in renewed dedication and renewed vigor. Let us meet in action, in tolerance, and in mutual understanding. John Kennedy's death commands what his life conveyed—that America must move forward. The time has come for Americans of all races and creeds and political beliefs to understand and to respect one another. So let us put an end to the teaching and the preaching of hate and evil and violence. Let us turn away from the fanatics of the far left and the far right, from the apostles of bitterness and bigotry, from those defiant of law, and those who pour venom into our Nation's bloodstream.

I profoundly hope that the tragedy and the torment of these terrible days will bind us together in new fellowship, making us one people in our hour of sorrow. So let us here highly resolve that John Fitzgerald Kennedy did not live—or die—in vain. And on this Thanksgiving eve, as we gather together to ask the Lord's blessing, and give Him our thanks, let us unite in those familiar and cherished words:

America, America,
God shed His grace on thee,
And crown thy good
With brotherhood
From sea to shining sea.

The civil rights bill was eventually pushed through the House of Representatives by Johnson, who threatened to use a discharge petition to get it out of the Rules Committee. This would allow the majority of the House to vote on the bill, taking away control of House leaders. The bill had been stuck in the Rules Committee since November 1963, where its chairman, Howard Smith, southern Democrat from Virginia who strongly supported segregation, made it known that he would do all he could to keep the bill tied up indefinitely. After passing the House in February 1964, it was threatened by a filibuster in the Senate. Johnson and Senator Hubert Humphrey from Minnesota (who later became Johnson's vice president) and Senate minority leader Everett Dirksen of Illinois were able to gain the support of enough Republican senators to overcome the filibuster in March 1964, which led to the bill's passage after 75 hours of debate.

Johnson signed the Civil Rights Act of 1964 on July 2, 1964. Among those present at the signing was Dr. King. Others included Attorney General Robert Kennedy, Senator Hubert Humphrey (D-MN), Senator Everett Dirksen (R-IL), A. Philip Randolph, James Forman, Roy Wilkins, Clarence Mitchell, Dorothy Height, and leaders representing congressional, civic, labor, and religious organizations. The president then gave remarks on the law on live television and radio at 6:45 p.m. In part of his address he stated the following:

> That law is the product of months of the most careful debate and discussion. It was proposed more than one year ago by our late and beloved President John F. Kennedy. It received the bipartisan support of more than two-thirds of the Members of both the House and the Senate. An overwhelming majority of Republicans as well as Democrats voted for it.

> We believe that all men are entitled to the blessings of liberty. Yet millions are being deprived of those blessings—not because of their own failures, but because of the color of their skin.

> The reasons are deeply imbedded in history and tradition and the nature of man. We can understand—without rancor or hatred—how this all happened.

> But it cannot continue. Our Constitution, the foundation of our Republic, forbids it. The principles of our freedom forbid it. Morality forbids it. And the law I will sign tonight forbids it.

> It has received the thoughtful support of tens of thousands of civic and religious leaders in all parts of this Nation. And it is supported by the great majority of the American people.

> The purpose of the law is simple.

> It does not restrict the freedom of any American, so long as he respects the rights of others.

> It does not give special treatment to any citizen.

> It does say the only limit to a man's hope for happiness, and for the future of his children, shall be his own ability.

It does say that there are those who are equal before God shall now also be equal in the polling booths, in the classrooms, in the factories, and in hotels, restaurants, movie theaters, and other places that provide service to the public.

I am taking steps to implement the law under my constitutional obligation to take care that the laws are faithfully executed. (Johnson 1964)

The final law was divided into 11 sections called titles. In summary, the law was an act to enforce the constitutional right to vote, confer jurisdiction on the district courts of the United States, provide injunctive relief against discrimination in public accommodations, authorize the attorney general to institute suits to protect constitutional rights in public facilities and public education, extend the Commission on Civil Rights, prevent discrimination in federally assisted programs, establish a Commission on Equal Employment Opportunity and for other purposes.

The act also prohibited voting discrimination within any government agency that received federal funds (see https://www.ourdocuments.gov/doc.php?flash =false&doc=97 for full text of law). Discrimination was prohibited on the basis of race, color, religion, sex, and national origin. "Sex" was not part of the original proposed bill but was later added by Representative Howard W. Smith, a Democrat from Virginia. Smith was chairman of the House Rules Committee and did not support civil rights. Historians agree that he had the prohibition against "sex" added as a means to increase opposition to the law being passed.

One of the first tests of the constitutionality of the Civil Rights Act was the case *Heart of Atlanta Motel, Inc. v. United States,* 379 U.S. 241 (1964). It dealt with a hotel in Atlanta, Georgia, that refused to rent rooms to black patrons. The defendants argued that the Civil Rights Act enforcement under the Commerce Clause exceeded the powers of Congress and that the owner's Fifth Amendment rights were violated in depriving him of property without due process by forcing him to rent to patrons he did not want to rent to. The U.S. Supreme Court ruled that Congress acted within its authority in passing the Civil Rights Act and could regulate interstate commerce. Since the hotel allowed patrons from out of state, it was in violation of the act.

An interesting historical fact about the passage of the Civil Rights Act is that it was also the only occasion that Dr. King and Malcolm X met in person. They met on March 26, 1964, before the Senate debate on the act. The meeting lasted for only about a minute. A month later, Malcolm X gave a speech at Cory Methodist Church in Cleveland, Ohio, urging African Americans to exercise their right to vote. He stated that election time was "When all of the white political crooks will be right back in your and my community with their false promises which they don't intend to keep" (Sargent 1997, 392). However, he urged blacks to take up arms if they did not achieve full equality, given that neither Johnson or Congress had taken substantial action to support African American full equality. Malcolm X specifically called out Johnson by saying the following in what is now known as his "The Ballot or the Bullet" speech:

Lyndon B. Johnson is the head of the Democratic Party. If he's for civil rights, let him go into the Senate next week and declare himself. Let him go in there right now and declare himself. Let him go in there and denounce the Southern branch of his party. Let him go in there right now and take a moral stand—right now, not later. Tell him, don't wait until election time. If he waits too long, brothers and sisters, he will be responsible for letting a condition develop in this country which will create a climate that will bring seeds up out of the ground with vegetation on the end of them looking like something these people never dreamed of. In 1964, it's the ballot or the bullet. (Hammond, Hardwick, and Lubert 2007, 673)

In 1964 Johnson struggled with the idea but eventually decided to nominate Thurgood Marshall to the post of U.S. solicitor general. Johnson's reservations were due to his knowledge of the level of opposition from southern politicians, but he also wanted Marshall to serve as a role model for and of African Americans. The president knew that appointing Marshall would strengthen African American support of the Democratic Party. Marshall's confirmation was rather quick and without a great deal of controversial debate. When President Kennedy had nominated Marshall for the U.S. Court of Appeals for the Second Circuit, the hearings were contentious. On August 11, 1965, Marshall became the 33rd U.S. solicitor general and the first African American to hold the position.

On June 13, 1967, Johnson announced his nomination of Marshall to serve as the first African American on the Supreme Court. During a news conference in the Rose Garden of the White House on June 13, 1967, the president stated that this was "the right thing to do, the right time to do it, the right man and the right place" (Williams and Cohen 2007). Critics of Marshall's appointment, led by West Virginia senator Robert Byrd and South Carolina senator Strom Thurmond, searched for information that would derail his confirmation hearing. J. Edgar Hoover did an extensive background check of Marshall to see if any negative information could be found and used against him. Despite the attempts to block Thurgood's appointment, he was confirmed by the Senate on August 30, 1967, after a vote of 69 to 11. Two days later, Associate Justice Hugo Black swore in the 59-year-old Marshall during a private ceremony.

Another legislative milestone in 1964 was an amendment to the U.S. Constitution. On January 23, 1964, the Twenty-Fourth Amendment to the Constitution was ratified by states, prohibiting the assessment of poll taxes as a condition for voting in federal elections. The amendment was actually sent to the states for ratification on August 27, 1962. Efforts to end the poll tax had been in action since Reconstruction. President Franklin D. Roosevelt unsuccessfully fought to end it, and southern senators blocked it for years with filibusters. Southern Democrats were needed for other legislations over the decades in which the proposed amendment languished in Congress. President Kennedy was able to push support to get the amendment through Congress before it was sent to the states. When ratified, only Virginia, Alabama, Texas, Arkansas, and Mississippi still had poll taxes. In 1966, the Supreme Court ruled that the amendment covered all elections at every level of government, not just federal elections, as in the case of *Harper v. Virginia*

Board of Elections, 383 U.S. 663 (1966). The court held that state poll taxes violated the Fourteenth Amendment's Equal Protection Clause.

In early 1964, three civil rights workers and members of the Congress of Racial Equality (CORE) traveled to Mississippi to organize efforts to combat segregation. Michael "Mickey" Schwerner and Andrew Goodman were both white New Yorkers, and James Chaney was a local African American member of CORE. They disappeared on June 21, 1964, and their abandoned station wagon was found burned on June 23. This led to national attention and resulted in Attorney General Robert Kennedy pushing the Federal Bureau of Investigation (FBI) to send hundreds of agents and troops to the area to assist with search efforts. Hoover opened a new bureau office there in July 1964. One of the perpetrators of the murder, Delmar Dennis, was paid $30,000 in exchange for immunity and his information on the murders. The FBI found the bodies of the slain CORE members on August 4, 1964. They had been shot and buried beneath a damn in Philadelphia, Mississippi. Still, no arrests were made or indictments pursued by state or local officials.

On December 4, 19 men were indicted by the Department of Justice for violating the civil rights of Schwerner, Goodman, and Chaney. It took three years for the case to come to trial, and the Supreme Court defended the federal indictments before the case was heard in Jackson, Mississippi, before U.S. district judge William Cox. He was a strong supporter of segregation, and it took federal pressure for him to try the case fairly. An all-white jury found seven of the men guilty on October 27, 1967, and Judge Cox sentenced them to only a range of three to seven years in prison. His explanation for the light sentences was that "They killed one n---r, one Jew, and a white man. I gave them what I thought they deserved" (Windell 2015, 122). On June 21, 2005, the 41st anniversary of the murders, Edgar Ray Killen was found guilty on three counts of manslaughter in the case and sentenced to 60 years in prison. He was then 80 years old. This entire case gave further support to passage of the Civil Rights Act in 1964.

In November 1964, Johnson ran for reelection against Republican senator Barry Goldwater of Arizona. Johnson won by a landslide, garnering 61.1 percent of the popular vote (leading to 486 electoral votes compared to 52 for Goldwater). This was the greatest win for a presidential candidate since James Monroe's reelection in 1820. Johnson carried 44 of the 50 states. The District of Columbia voted for the president for the first time, and Johnson carried the district. He received 94 percent of the black vote, and the election marked the beginning of African Americans predominantly recognizing themselves as Democrats. The national sympathy from the assassination of President Kennedy, the passage of the Civil Rights Act, and Johnson's support of civil rights gained overwhelming African American support. Humphrey ran as Johnson's running mate and became vice president.

On February 21, 1965, Malcolm X was assassinated by members of the Nation of Islam while giving a speech at Manhattan's Audubon Ballroom in New York. The autopsy revealed that he had been shot 21 times in various parts of his body. He was 39 years old. Given the comments that he had made about Kennedy's death as well as his stance on the federal government ignoring black rights and his earlier radical views of civil rights, it was not surprising that President Johnson did not make a statement.

President Kennedy first referenced the term "affirmative action" to remedy past discrimination against African Americans when he issued Executive Order 10925 on March 6, 1961. Johnson is credited with defining what affirmative action means in a commencement address to the graduating class of Howard University on June 4, 1965:

> That beginning is freedom; and the barriers to that freedom are tumbling down. Freedom is the right to share, share fully and equally, in American society—to vote, to hold a job, to enter a public place, to go to school. It is the right to be treated in every part of our national life as a person equal in dignity and promise to all others.

> But freedom is not enough. You do not wipe away the scars of centuries by saying: Now you are free to go where you want, and do as you desire, and choose the leaders you please.

> You do not take a person who, for years, has been hobbled by chains and liberate him, bring him up to the starting line of a race and then say, "you are free to compete with all the others," and still justly believe that you have been completely fair.

> Thus it is not enough just to open the gates of opportunity. All our citizens must have the ability to walk through those gates.

> This is the next and the more profound stage of the battle for civil rights. We seek not just freedom but opportunity. We seek not just legal equity but human ability, not just equality as a right and a theory but equality as a fact and equality as a result.

> For the task is to give 20 million Negroes the same chance as every other American to learn and grow, to work and share in society, to develop their abilities—physical, mental and spiritual, and to pursue their individual happiness.

> To this end equal opportunity is essential, but not enough, not enough. Men and women of all races are born with the same range of abilities. But ability is not just the product of birth. Ability is stretched or stunted by the family that you live with, and the neighborhood you live in—by the school you go to and the poverty or the richness of your surroundings. It is the product of a hundred unseen forces playing upon the little infant, the child, and finally the man. (Johnson 1965a)

Johnson made legislative history again on August 6, 1965, when he signed the Voting Rights Act. The new law was passed to end state and local barriers to African Americans being able to vote, as guaranteed under the Fifteenth Amendment. The law banned the use of literacy tests as a requirement for voting, authorized the U.S. attorney general to investigate the use of poll taxes, and allowed federal oversight of voter registration in any area where less than 50 percent of the non-white population had not registered to vote.

The passage of the Voting Rights Act was spurred by a civil rights march in Alabama to protest blacks' disenfranchisement from voting. Dr. King and the Southern Christian Leadership Conference (SCLC) decided to focus on Selma, Alabama, in 1965 to increase black voter registration, given that only 2 percent of the city's eligible black voters had actually been allowed to vote. The Student Non-violent Coordinating Committee (SNCC) had been leading a black voter registration drive in Selma since 1961. King had won the Nobel Peace Prize in 1964, and this would add attention to the efforts. SNCC and the SCLC were also joined by the Dallas County Voters League and other local activists. However, on February 18, 1965, white segregationists attacked peaceful demonstrators in Marion, Alabama, leading to an Alabama state trooper shooting one of the black demonstrators, Jimmie Lee Jackson, a 26-year-old deacon and Vietnam War veteran who was trying to protect his mother from state troopers beating demonstrators.

This led Dr. King and the SCLC, along with John Lewis and SNCC, to plan a protest march from Selma to the state capital of Montgomery, some 54 miles away. On Sunday, March 7, 1965, 600 people left Selma to begin the march. King was in Atlanta, Georgia, on this day, which would become known as Bloody Sunday. Once the marchers reached Edmund Pettus Bridge over the Alabama River, they were beaten with whips and nightsticks by Alabama state troopers and assaulted with tear gas. Many were injured, and over 50 people were hospitalized. The brutal scene was broadcast on national television and ultimately around the world, causing international outrage. Alabama Governor George Wallace and Police Commissioner Eugene "Bull" Connor were partly blamed for the event, given that they both were steadfast in their opposition to segregation and abiding by the Civil Rights Act. John Lewis commented, "I don't see how President Johnson can send troops to Vietnam—I don't see how he can send troops to the Congo—I don't see how he can send troops to Africa and can't send troops to Selma" (Carson 2005, 18).

The broadcasting of Bloody Sunday on national television only increased support for the march. On March 9, King led more than 2,000 marchers across Edmund Pettus Bridge. When their path was blocked, he turned the crowd around for fear of being attacked by state troopers again. Although some criticized King's decision to turn around, this garnered support from Johnson, who admired his restraint. The president made a public statement that "Americans everywhere join in deploring the brutality with which a number of Negro citizens of Alabama were treated when they sought to dramatize their deep and sincere interest in attaining the precious right to vote" (Johnson 1965b). That night, white segregationists attacked and killed Reverend James Reeb, a young white Unitarian minister who had come to join the march from Massachusetts. Reverends Clark Olsen and Orloff Miller were also beaten but survived. President Johnson called Reeb's widow with his condolences and met with Governor Wallace to demand protection for the marchers and local voting rights for African Americans.

This led to even greater national support. Johnson addressed a joint session of Congress on March 15 to support the Selma protestors and to call for a new voting rights bill to be passed by Congress. This speech was historic in that Johnson identified with the marchers to the point of using the phrase "we shall overcome." In his speech, he stated the following:

> There is no Negro problem. There is no Southern problem. There is no Northern problem. There is only an American problem. And we are met here tonight as Americans—not as Democrats or Republicans—we are met here as Americans to solve that problem.

> This was the first nation in the history of the world to be founded with a purpose. The great phrases of that purpose still sound in every American heart, North and South: "All men are created equal"—"government by consent of the governed"—"give me liberty or give me death." Well, those are not just clever words, or those are not just empty theories. In their name Americans have fought and died for two centuries, and tonight around the world they stand there as guardians of our liberty, risking their lives.

> Those words are a promise to every citizen that he shall share in the dignity of man. This dignity cannot be found in a man's possessions; it cannot be found in his power, or in his position. It really rests on his right to be treated as a man equal in opportunity to all others. It says that he shall share in freedom, he shall choose his leaders, educate his children, and provide for his family according to his ability and his merits as a human being. (Johnson 1965c)

The next day, the Selma demonstrators submitted a detailed plan of the march to federal judge Frank M. Johnson Jr. and obtained approval for the march. This overturned an earlier restraining order issued against the march by Judge Johnson. On March 21, 2,000 marchers left Selma to march to Montgomery. They were protected by U.S. Army troops and members of the Alabama National Guard, which had been federalized by President Johnson. Among the marchers were such celebrities as Harry Belafonte and Lena Horne. They reached Montgomery on March 25, where they were met by nearly 50,000 supporters of all races. Among the crowd were Assistant Attorneys General John Doar and Ramsey Clark and former assistant attorney general Burke Marshall. King spoke to the gathering, along with other notable speakers such as 1950 Nobel Peace Prize winner Ralph Bunche (he was the first African American to win the prize, for his efforts in mediation of an Arab-Israeli truce in Palestine in the 1940s). After the march to Montgomery, white Michigan housewife Viola Liuzzo was shot and killed by four members of the Ku Klux Klan for her participation in the march. Three of the perpetrators were eventually prosecuted by Doar for violating Liuzzo's civil rights.

When Johnson signed the Voting Rights Act of 1965, among those present were King, Reverend Ralph D. Abernathy Sr., Senator Robert Kennedy, and a host of politicians and other civil rights leaders. Johnson expanded legislation by issuing Executive Order 11246 on September 24, 1965, which enforced affirmative action for the first time. The order prohibited employment discrimination based on race, color, religion, and national origin by any federal department or agency and any organization receiving federal contracts and subcontracts. The Civil Service Commission was charged with implementing policy and oversight to ensure equal employment in federal positions. The secretary of labor was charged with oversight of fair employment by government contractors and subcontractors. The President's Committee on Equal Employment Opportunity had been created by President Kennedy under Executive Order 10925 on March 6, 1961. With the passage of the Civil Rights Act of 1964, the committee's functions were divided between the Equal Employment Opportunity Commission and the Office of Federal Contract Compliance (which in 1975 was renamed the Office of Federal Contract Compliance Programs). These new offices were part of enforcing Executive Order 11246.

Racial unrest continued in the country, and not just in the South. On August 11, 1965, a young African American motorist, Marquette Frye, and his stepbrother, Ronald, were pulled over while driving their mother's car and arrested by a white California highway patrolman, Lee W. Minikus, under suspicion of drunk driving. Two white policemen got into a scuffle with the Fryes. As a watching crowd grew in number, tensions also grew between police officers and the crowd, as the local residents believed that this was yet another incident of racially motivated police abuse. The mother of the two young men even got into a fight with police when she arrived on the scene. The incident escalated as more police arrived, and the crowd grew larger and more vocally and physically aggressive, as did the police.

This eventually sparked a riot in the Watts neighborhood, a poor neighborhood in South Central Los Angeles. Over the course of six days of riots that spanned over 50 square miles, cars were burned, stores were looted, buildings were burned, whites were beaten, and police and firefighters were fired upon by snipers. The riots only intensified when Police Commissioner William Parker first refused local leaders' requests to deploy more local black police officers to ease tensions and then later made the statement that the rioters were "monkeys in a zoo" and implied that Muslims were infiltrating the city and agitating the situation. Eventually, 14,000 California National Guard troops and a curfew spanning over 45 miles were put in place.

When the riots finally ended on August 17, 4,000 people had been arrested, more than 1,000 were injured, 34 had been killed, and the property damage exceeded $45 million. California governor Pat Brown's investigation found that the riot resulted from the residents of the Watts community being fed up with high unemployment, substandard housing, and inadequate schools. Still, state and city leaders did nothing to improve the conditions of the community.

The riot in Watts was just one of several that took place in urban cities in the 1960s. Three days of riots in Rochester, New York, began with the arrest of a 19-year-old black man on July 24, 1964. Order was finally restored when 450 state troopers and 1,500 National Guardsmen were deployed to occupy the city. Almost 900 arrests were made, 350 people were injured, 4 were killed, over 200 stores were looted, and property damage was over $1 million. The impetus for the riot was the social and economic depression of blacks in the area, including poor housing and high unemployment.

On July 16, 1964, a 15-year-old black student, James Powell, was fatally shot by an off-duty white policeman, Thomas Gilligan, in Yorkville, New York. Although two days of peaceful protests ensued, violence broke out when protestors then surrounded the police precinct calling for Gilligan's arrest. They were met by police officers swinging clubs. This led to six nights of riots in Harlem and Bedford-Stuyvesant in Brooklyn. Stores were looted, and rioters pelted police officers with bottles and bricks. In the end, one person was killed, several hundred were injured, and hundreds were arrested. During the summer of 1964, riots also broke out in Dixmoor, Illinois, near Chicago from August 15 through August 17, and in Philadelphia, Pennsylvania, from August 28 to August 30. In 1967, 159 race riots occurred in cities throughout the United States including Newark and Plainfield, New Jersey, as well as Milwaukee, Detroit, Atlanta, Boston, Cincinnati, Tampa, and Buffalo. What most of the riots had in common were tensions between blacks and the local police, with blacks suffering from such issues as poverty, poor housing, and unemployment.

One impetus for the riots in the 1960s was blacks migrating to urban cities and whites and businesses moving to the suburbs, leaving the inner cities in greater poverty. While most riots occurred in 1964 and especially in 1967, there were also race riots in 1961 and 1965. Perhaps the worst occurred on the night of April 4, 1968, after Dr. King was assassinated, leading to violent riots in over 100 cities. According to Postrel (2004), "Consider the wave of race riots that swept the nation's cities. From 1964 to 1971, there were more than 750 riots, killing 228 people and injuring 12,741 others. After more than 15,000 separate incidents of arson, many black urban neighborhoods were in ruins."

In 1964, Johnson feared that the riots would jeopardize his chances for election. He made a statement to an aide that "One of my political analysts tells me that every time one occurs, it costs me 90,000 votes" (Flamm 2005, 37). He also feared backlash from whites. He and Dr. King had several discussions on needed actions after the Watts Riot in 1965. King told the president that people were in poverty and despair and that the incident could be the impetus for a full-scale race war. Johnson remarked on all his accomplishments made with the Civil Rights Act and Voting Rights Act: "I've spent the biggest part of my life the last four years on civil rights bills, but it doesn't, all of it comes to naught if you have a situation like war in the world or a situation in Los Angeles" (Zelizer 2015).

While the riots were occurring during Johnson's administration, another historical event was the appointment of the first African American to a U.S. cabinet-level position. In 1966 Johnson appointed Robert Clifton Weaver as head of the new Department of Housing and Urban Development. Previously, President Kennedy had appointed Weaver to head the Housing and Home Finance Agency. Weaver served under Johnson until 1968.

Johnson took action to quell the riots in 1967. On July 23 he ordered 4,700 federal troops to Detroit. Between July 23 and July 30, more than 40 people were killed and 2,000 injured. Johnson outlined his decision to send troops per the executive order during televised remarks to the nation on July 24, 1967:

> Pillage, looting, murder, and arson have nothing to do with civil rights. They are criminal conduct. The Federal Government in the circumstances here presented had no alternative but to respond, since it was called upon by the Governor of the State and since it was presented with proof of his inability to restore order in Michigan.

We will not tolerate lawlessness. We will not endure violence. It matters not by whom it is done or under what slogan or banner. It will not be tolerated. This Nation will do whatever it is necessary to do to suppress and to punish those who engage in it.

I know that, with few exceptions, the people of Detroit, and the people of Newark, and the people of Harlem, and of all of our American cities, however troubled they may be, deplore and condemn these criminal acts. I know that the vast majority of Negroes and Whites are shocked and outraged by them.

So tonight, your President calls upon all of our people, in all of our cities, to join in a determined program to maintain law and order—to condemn and to combat lawlessness in all of its forms—and firmly to show by word and by deed that riots, looting, and public disorder will just not be tolerated.

In particular, I call upon the people of the ravaged areas to return to their homes, to leave the streets, and to permit the authorities to restore quiet and order without further loss of life or property damage. Once this is done, attention can immediately be turned to the great and urgent problems of repairing the damage that has been done.

I appeal to every American in this grave hour to respond to this plea. (Johnson 1967)

After the riots during the summer of 1967, Johnson issued Executive Order 11365 on July 29, 1967, establishing the Kerner Commission to investigate the riots over the 1960s. The 11-member commission was headed by Governor Otto Kerner Jr. of Illinois and included Democratic and Republican members, Roy Wilkins from the NAACP, Atlanta police chief Herbert Turner Jenkins, and I. W. Abel, president of the U.S. Steelworkers of America. The commission issued its final report on February 29, 1968, titled *Report of the National Advisory Commission on Civil Disorders* (also called the Kerner Report). The report outlined how state and federal policies had failed to address housing, social services, and education equality. It also criticized the media: "The press has too long basked in a white world looking out of it, if at all, with white men's eyes and white perspective." White racism was blamed for the riots, and the commission warned that "Our nation is moving toward two societies, one black, one white—separate and unequal."

Johnson rejected the commission's recommendations that included the creation of 2 million new jobs over the next three years, federally subsidized job training programs, implementation of housing policies, and racial integration in communities across the nation. Still, he knew the issue would not get better. For example, on August 18, 1967, he told former Central Intelligence Agency Director John McCone that these "groups they got really absolutely nothing to live for. Forty percent of them are unemployed. These youngsters, they live with rats and they've got no place to sleep. . . . [B]roken homes and illegitimate families and all the narcotics are circulating around them. . . . And we've isolated them, and they're all in one area, when they move in why we move out" (Zelizer 2015).

Efforts to pass a fair housing law had languished in Congress since 1966. The NAACP, the American GI Forum, and the National Committee against Discrimination in Housing were among the groups that lobbied the president and Congress for the bill's passage. Democratic senator Edward Kennedy (brother of John F. and Robert Kennedy) from Massachusetts and Senator Edward Brooke of Massachusetts, the first African American U.S. senator since Reconstruction, were the primary advocates of the bill. It eventually passed the Senate in early April 1968, after Senate Republican leader Everett Dirksen defeated a filibuster. It was expected to face strong opposition in the more conservative House due to growing lack of support because of the urban riots and the Black Power movement.

On April 4, 1968, the same day the Senate voted on the fair housing bill, Dr. Martin Luther King, Jr. was assassinated in Memphis, Tennessee, while visiting the city to support striking sanitation workers. At a little after 6:00 p.m. as he was standing on a balcony of the Lorraine Motel, he was shot in the neck by a sniper. He was rushed to the hospital but was pronounced dead an hour later. He was only 39 years old. The impact of his death was felt around the world. Johnson addressed the nation on King's assassination on April 4, offering condolences and praying for peace and understanding throughout the country. The president spoke of the need to join and work together to achieve equality. On April 5 he issued Proclamation 3839, "Death of Martin Luther King, Jr.":

To the People of the United States:

The heart of America grieves today. A leader of his people—a teacher of all people—has fallen.

Martin Luther King, Jr., has been struck down by the violence against which he preached and worked.

Yet the cause for which he struggled has not fallen. The voice that called for justice and brotherhood has been stilled—but the quest for freedom to which he gave eloquent expression, continues.

Men of all races, all religions, all regions must join together in this hour to deny violence its victory—and to fulfill the vision of brotherhood that gave purpose to Martin Luther King's life and works.

Now, Therefore, I, Lyndon B. Johnson, President of the United States, do call upon all Americans to observe Sunday next, the seventh day of April, as a day of national mourning throughout the United States. In our churches, in our homes, and in our private hearts, let us resolve before God to stand against divisiveness in our country and all its consequences.

I direct that until interment the flag of the United States shall be flown at half-staff on all buildings, grounds and naval vessels of the Federal Government in the District of Columbia and throughout the United States and its Territories and possessions.

I also direct that the flag shall be flown at half-staff for the same length of time at all United States embassies, legations, consular offices, and other facilities abroad, including all military facilities and naval vessels and stations.

In Witness Whereof, I have hereunto set my hand this fifth day of April, in the year of our Lord nineteen hundred and sixty-eight and of the Independence of the United States of America the one hundred and ninety-second.

LYNDON B. JOHNSON

Johnson declared April 7, 1968, a national day of mourning. While there was international mourning, riots, burning, and looting broke out in over 100 cities across the United States. The King assassination riots, also called the Holy Week Uprising, was the greatest show of social unrest in the United States since the American Civil War. In Washington, D.C., crowds of up to 20,000 overwhelmed the 3,100 local police, 13,600 federal troops, and 1,700 National Guardsmen. Over 1,000 buildings were burned. Some parts of the city were so badly destroyed that communities didn't recover under the early 1990s. In Chicago, 10,500 police, 6,700 state National Guardsmen, and 5,000 U.S. Army soldiers were needed to deal with the riots. By April 7, 500 were injured, 11 were killed, and over 2,000 had been arrested. Property damage exceeded $10 million. In Baltimore, 500 Maryland police and thousands of National Guardsmen were called in, and over 4,000 arrests were made. Across the country, property damage amounted to an estimated $65 million (which is almost $400 million in current dollars), and 39 people were killed, over 20,000 were injured, and an estimated 21,000 were arrested.

Dr. King's funeral was held at the Ebenezer Baptist Church in Atlanta, Georgia, on April 9. Over 100,000 people attended the funeral and procession to Morehouse College (King's alma mater), although the church could only seat 750.

King had lobbied for the passage of a fair housing law and marched in Chicago along with making speeches for its passage. Johnson wanted the bill passed as a testimony to King and before his funeral in Atlanta. The House of Representatives had a limited debate on the bill and passed it on April 10. On April 11, 1968, Johnson signed the Civil Rights Act of 1968, also known as the Fair Housing Act. It guaranteed equal housing opportunities regardless of race, color, religion, national origin, disability, family status, or sex and made it illegal to use force, threat, injury, intimidation, or interference in violating the act. Equal housing opportunities pertained to the sale, rental, lease, advertising, and financing of housing.

On Sunday, March 31, 1968, Johnson made the surprise announcement "I shall not seek, and I will not accept, the nomination of my party for another term as your President." This announcement came at the end of a televised speech he gave on the state of U.S. forces in Vietnam. Some attribute his decision partly due to declining support for the U.S. involvement in the war. He also stated, "With American sons in the field far away, with the American future under challenge right here at home, with our hopes and the world's hopes for peace in the balance every day, I do not believe that I should devote an hour or a day of my time to any personal partisan causes or to any duties other than the awesome duties of this office, the Presidency of your country" (Wicker 1968).

Another devastating event occurred on June 5, 1968, when Robert F. Kennedy was assassinated while campaigning as the Democratic candidate for the presidency at the Ambassador Hotel in Los Angeles, California. He was shot by 22-year-old Sirhan Sirhan, a Palestinian. Sirhan reported that he was upset at Kennedy's support of Israel, and the day of the shooting was the first anniversary of the start of the Six-Day War between Israel and its surrounding Arab countries. On June 6, 1968, Johnson addressed the nation and issued Proclamation 3853, "Death of Robert F. Kennedy," after describing the events as a time of tragedy and loss:

To the People of the United States:

A noble and compassionate leader, a good and faithful servant of the people, in the full vigor of his promise, lies dead from an assassin's bullet.

The tragedy and the senseless violence of Robert F. Kennedy's death casts a deep shadow of grief across America and across the world.

This is a moment for all Americans to join hands and walk together through this dark night of common anguish into a new dawn of healing unity.

Now, Therefore, I, Lyndon B. Johnson, President of the United States, do call upon all Americans to observe Sunday next, the ninth day of June, as a day of national mourning in his memory throughout the United States. In our churches, in our homes, and in our hearts let us resolve before God and before each other that the purpose of progress and justice for which Robert F. Kennedy lived shall endure.

I direct that until interment the flag of the United States shall be flown at half-staff on all buildings, grounds and naval vessels of the Federal Government in the District of Columbia and throughout the United States and its Territories and possessions.

I also direct that the flag shall be flown at half-staff for the same length of time at all United States embassies, legations, consular offices, and other facilities abroad, including all military facilities and naval vessels and stations.

In Witness Whereof, I have hereunto set my hand this sixth day of June, in the year of our Lord nineteen hundred and sixty-eight and of the Independence of the United States of America the one hundred and ninety-second.

LYNDON B. JOHNSON

The White House
June 6, 1968

Johnson was instrumental in passing laws that changed the history of civil rights. However, he was known for using racist terms. For example, he often used the term "n----r" when referring to blacks. In his appointment of Thurgood Marshall to the Supreme Court, Johnson was reported as stating "Son, when I appoint a n----r to the court, I want everyone to know he's a n----r." When once asked if he consulted his wife on policy, he replied, "I have a n----r maid, and I talk things over with her too." In response to King denouncing the U.S. policy in Vietnam, Johnson fumed, "What is that goddamn n----r preacher trying to do to me?" Johnson was born and raised in Texas. While his use of racist terms cannot be excused, it does reflect his southern background of the times.

FURTHER READING

Califano, Joseph A., Jr. 1991. *The Triumph & Tragedy of Lyndon Johnson: The White House Years.* New York: Touchstone.

Carson, Clayborne. 2005. "1965: A Decisive Turning Point in the Long Struggle for Voting Rights." *The Crisis* 112, no. 4 (July–August): 16–20.

Dallek, Robert. 1998. *Flawed Giant: Lyndon Johnson and His Times, 1961–1973.* New York: Oxford University Press.

Goodwin, Doris Kearns. 1991. *Lyndon Johnson and the American Dream.* New York: Open Road Integrated Media.

Hammond, Scott J., Kevin R. Hardwick, and Howard L. Lubert, eds. 2007. *Classics of American Political and Constitutional Thought,* Vol. 2, *Reconstruction to the Present.* Indianapolis: Hackett Publishing.

Johnson, Lyndon B. 1963. "Address before a Joint Session of the Congress, November 27." The American Presidency Project, http://www.presidency.ucsb.edu/ws/?pid =25988.

Johnson, Lyndon B. 1964. "Radio and Television Remarks upon Signing the Civil Rights Bill, July 2, 1964." The American Presidency Project, http://www.presidency .ucsb.edu/ws/?pid=26361.

Johnson, Lyndon B. 1965a. "Commencement Address at Howard University: 'To Fulfill These Rights,' June 4, 1965." The American Presidency Project, http://www .presidency.ucsb.edu/ws/?pid=27021.

Johnson, Lyndon B. 1965b. "Special Message to the Congress: The American Promise, March 15, 1965." The American Presidency Project, http://www.presidency.ucsb .edu/ws/?pid=26805.

Johnson, Lyndon B. 1965c. "Statement by the President on the Situation in Selma, Alabama, March 9, 1965." The American Presidency Project, http://www.presi dency.ucsb.edu/ws/?pid=26802.

Johnson, Lyndon B. 1967. "Remarks to the Nation after Authorizing the Use of Federal Troops in Detroit, July 24, 1967." The American Presidency Project, http://www .presidency.ucsb.edu/ws/?pid=28364.

Peters, Charles. 2010. *Lyndon B. Johnson: The American Presidents Series; The 36th President, 1963–1969.* New York: Times Books.

Postrel, Virginia. 2004. "The Consequences of the 1960's Race Riots Come into View." *New York Times,* December 30, 2004, https://www.nytimes.com/2004/12/30 /business/the-consequences-of-the-1960s-race-riots-come-into-view.html.

Watson, W. Marvin, and Sherwin Markman. 2004. *Chief of Staff: Lyndon Johnson and His Presidency.* New York: St. Martin's.

Wicker, Tom. 1968. "Johnson Says He Won't Run." *New York Times,* April 1.

Windell, James O. 2015. *Looking Back in Crime: What Happened on This Date in Criminal Justice History?* Boca Raton, FL: CRC Press.

Zelizer, Julian. 2015. "A 1965 Failure That Still Haunts America." CNN, January 19, https://www.cnn.com/2015/01/19/opinion/zelizer-lbj-watts-riots/index.html.

Post–Civil Rights Era

Although the Civil Rights Movement officially ended in 1968 with passage of major laws guaranteeing equal rights for blacks, it did not mark the end of African Americans' fight for equality. Over the next few decades, African Americans sought to reverse the vestiges of hundreds of years of discrimination and racial oppression in politics, housing, education, and social justice. A key battleground for equality was in the area of education. Affirmative action programs were seen as a way to support African Americans attending colleges and universities of their choice but also with financial support from federal and state funding. It was not long before this became the new background of resistance.

A second issue that impacted African Americans was attacks on social programs by both Republican and Democratic presidents. Although these attacks were not based on race, they disparately impacted African Americans, who had greater percentages in poverty. Presidents sought to reduce federal spending on welfare, housing assistance, and even education. At the same time, states were given more authority to run their own affairs while federal financial support to the states increased.

The relationship between the African American community and presidents during this era was dynamic. This was predominantly because there were really no organized African American organizations as there were in the 1950s and 1960s such as the Southern Christian Leadership Conference. This was coupled with what some described as the declining significance of race but a greater concern for policies that didn't address income inequality. In the African American community, educational and professional opportunities led to a growing middle class. These families and individuals moved to the suburbs and sometimes exclusive housing communities, just as whites did. This left blacks in poverty separated in urban cities and poor rural areas. Without a common organization focused on civil rights and with equality concerns that were no longer in parallel, sects of the African American community were unable to have the same leverage or even concerns over common issues to forge a united agenda in which to influence presidential action on behalf of the African American community.

Richard Milhous Nixon

37th President of the United States
Presidential Term: January 20, 1969–August 4, 1974
Political Party: Republican
Vice President: Spiro Agnew (1969–1973), Gerald Ford (1973–1974)

Richard Milhous Nixon was born on January 9, 1913, in Yorba Linda, California. He had previously served as vice president to Dwight D. Eisenhower, a member of the U.S. House of Representatives, and a U.S. senator. Nixon assumed office of the presidency when opposition to the Vietnam War was at its height, the nation was still mourning the assassinations of Dr. Martin Luther King, Jr. and Robert F. Kennedy, and urban cities were trying to rebuild from the most recent race riots of

Richard M. Nixon was the 37th president of the United States. During his run for president, Nixon was accused of pandering to the racism of white southerners as part of his "Southern strategy." Although he never used overtly racist statements, Nixon did campaign based on a platform of states' rights and "law and order." (Library of Congress)

1967 and 1968. With all his successes as president, he is the only U.S. president to resign from office, a result of the Watergate scandal. During the election of 1968, 85 percent of nonwhites voted for Hubert Humphrey, who had been vice president under President Lyndon B. Johnson. Nixon won by receiving 47 percent of the white vote. It was a three-candidate race, as former governor George C. Wallace also ran for the presidency. Wallace is best known for his staunch support of segregation while serving as governor of Alabama.

President Nixon's domestic programs were based on his adoption of New Federalism, in which greater powers would go back to the states versus being held and exercised by the federal government. This included allowing states and localities to have more control in dealing with such issues as desegregation. During his run for office, he was accused of pandering to the racism of white southerners as part of his Southern Strategy. Although Nixon was not using racist statements, he did campaign based on a platform of states' rights and "law and order." He also pledged to southern politicians that he would make conservative appointments to the U.S. Supreme Court. This was seen as a means of converting southern white Democrats to Republicans and especially tapping into southern whites who were dissatisfied with more liberal democratic policies. However, Nixon supported many policies for African Americans that would later upset those still supporting segregationist stances.

Nixon appointed Robert J. Brown as a special assistant to the president. Brown, an African American, had campaigned on behalf of Nixon and advised him on education and economic opportunities for African Americans. Brown noted to the president in 1969 that black colleges were only receiving 3 percent of the annual allocation of $4 billion to higher education. Brown arranged a meeting between Nixon and a dozen presidents of historically black colleges and universities (HBCUs). As a result, Nixon pledged an additional $100 million in redirected federal funding to HBCUs and an additional $30 million in the following years. Federal funding to HBCUs increased from $108 million in 1969 to $400 million by 1973.

Nixon made several appointments to the Supreme Court that would alter its more liberal stance on civil rights issues since the early 1950s. Under Chief Justice Earl Warren, the Supreme Court had ruled in favor of desegregation in *Brown v. Board of Education of Topeka, Kansas,* 347 U.S. 483 (1954). The addition of Thurgood Marshall as associate justice in 1967 by President Lyndon B. Johnson further increased Supreme Court support of plaintiffs with valid discrimination cases. However, Warren announced his intentions to retire in 1968. Johnson nominated sitting associate justice Abe Fortas to serve as chief justice, but the nomination was blocked by a Senate filibuster. Nixon was able to then nominate Warren E. Burger, whom the Senate confirmed on June 9, 1969. Burger was nominated due to his strict constructionist view of the U.S. Constitution. Fortas resigned from the Supreme Court in 1969, allowing Nixon to successfully nominate Harry Blackmun in 1970, who was confirmed on May 12, 1970. The two prior nominations that Nixon made before Blackmun were not confirmed due to their histories of ruling for segregation in prior cases in lower courts. Associate Justice Blackmun would go on to be a very liberal judge, voting in favor of such issues as a woman's right to abortion. In 1971, both Justice Hugo Black and Justice John M. Harlan retired from the Supreme Court due to poor health. Nixon made two nominations that were eventually confirmed. The first nominee, Lewis F. Powell Jr., was easily confirmed by the Senate. The second nominee, William H. Rehnquist, was contentious and was not supported by some Democrats, the NAACP, and labor unions. However, both Powell and Rehnquist were sworn in on January 7, 1972. Both went on to be conservative judges on the court.

On August 8, 1969, Nixon signed Executive Order 11478 that forbade discrimination in the competitive service of the federal government workforce. Discrimination was prohibited based on race, color, religion, sex, national origin, handicap, and age, and all departments and agencies were required to take affirmative action steps to promote employment opportunities. The Equal Employment Opportunity

Commission (EEOC) was directed to "issue such rules, regulations, orders, and instructions and request such information from the affected departments and agencies as it deems necessary and appropriate to carry out this Order" (United States Department of Labor 2018a). The order was amended on April 23, 1971, with Executive Order 11590 to apply to the recently organized U.S. Postal Service and the Postal Rate Commission.

However, Nixon was aggressive when it came to school desegregation. In 1968 before he took office, 68 percent of black children in the South were attending all-black schools. States were in defiance of the Supreme Court's decision in *Brown v. Board of Education of Topeka* and also *Brown II* in which the Supreme Court ordered states to implement desegregation with deliberate speed. The Department of Health and Human Services was originally called the Department of Health, Education, and Welfare (HEW). The original HEW's functions included executing educational policies before the Department of Education became an actual federal department in 1979. One of HEW's functions was thus implementing the desegregation of schools. In the 1960s HEW was hampered by resistance from southern states, where most segregated schools were located. At one point, HEW was forced to focus on both northern and southern schools so its funding from Congress would not be threatened.

The Civil Rights Division of the Department of Justice and the NAACP Legal Defense Fund began lawsuits to challenge school districts. The Supreme Court heard cases that forced a more aggressive stance on school desegregation. In *Green v. County School Board of New Kent County,* 391 U.S. 430 (1968), the court ruled that schools must formulate plans and steps to ensure a desegregated school system and not rely on a plan based on freedom of choice. In *Alexander v. Holmes County Board of Education,* 396 U.S. 19 (1969), the Supreme Court ordered the immediate desegregation of public schools in the South. This last ruling was in contradiction to a decision by Nixon and HEW secretary Robert Finch in July 1969 that allowed granted delays to five southern districts to delay their desegregation plans or face loss of funding. Finch had stated, "A policy requiring all school districts, regardless of the difficulties they face, to complete desegregation by the same terminal date is too rigid to be either workable or equitable" (Bond 1979). Nixon was now forced to support the Supreme Court's decision.

On February 16, 1970, Nixon established the Cabinet Committee of Education as an informal cabinet-level working group to examine how the federal government could assist school districts in immediately desegregating schools. The committee was chaired by Vice President Spiro Agnew and included Secretary of Labor George P. Shultz as vice chairman; Attorney General John Mitchell; Postmaster General Winton M. Blount; Robert H. Finch, secretary of health, education, and welfare; Donald Rumsfeld, director of the Office of Economic Opportunity; and presidential counselors Daniel P. Moynihan and Bryce Harlow. A staff, headed first by Robert C. Mardian and then by Edmond L. Morgan, carried out the day-to-day activities of the committee. The committee developed methods to peacefully desegregate southern schools through several advisory panels staffed by a cross section of southern leaders, including leaders both opposed to and in support of desegregation.

On March 24, 1970, Nixon made a statement about desegregation of elementary and secondary schools and outlined his specific objectives:

—To reaffirm my personal belief that the 1954 decision of the Supreme Court in *Brown v. Board of Education* was right in both constitutional and human terms.

—To assess our progress in the 16 years since Brown and to point the way to continuing progress.

—To clarify the present state of the law, as developed by the courts and the Congress, and the administration policies guided by it.

—To discuss some of the difficulties encountered by courts and communities as desegregation has accelerated in recent years, and to suggest approaches that can mitigate such problems as we complete the process of compliance with *Brown*.

—To place the question of school desegregation in its larger context, as part of America's historic commitment to the achievement of a free and open society. (Gannon 2010)

Nixon also passed the Emergency School Aid Act to help school districts deal with the costs of desegregation. He gave a special message to Congress proposing the act on May 21, 1970:

Successfully desegregating the nation's schools requires more than the enforcement of laws. It also requires an investment of money.

In my statement on school desegregation on March 24, I said that I would recommend expenditure of an additional $1.5 billion—$500 million in fiscal 1971, and $1 billion in fiscal 1972—to assist local school authorities in meeting four special categories of need:

—The special needs of desegregating (or recently desegregated) districts for additional facilities, personnel and training required to get the new, unitary system successfully started.

—The special needs of racially impacted schools where de facto segregation persists—and where immediate infusions of money can make a real difference in terms of educational effectiveness.

—The special needs of those districts that have the furthest to go to catch up educationally with the rest of the nation.

—The financing of innovative techniques for providing educationally sound interracial experiences for children in racially isolated schools.

To achieve these purposes, I now propose the Emergency School Aid Act of 1970.

Under the terms of this Act, the four categories of need I outlined would be met through three categories of aid:

(I) Aid to districts now eliminating de jure segregation either pursuant to direct Federal court orders or in accordance with plans approved by the Secretary of Health, Education and Welfare, for special needs incident to compliance.

(II) Aid to districts that wish to undertake voluntary efforts to eliminate, reduce or prevent de facto racial isolation, with such aid specifically targeted for those purposes.

(III) Aid to districts in which de facto racial separation persists, for the purpose of helping establish special interracial or inter-cultural educational programs or, where such programs are impracticable, programs designed to overcome the educational disadvantages that stem from racial isolation. (Nixon 1970a)

As stated earlier, when Nixon took office, 68 percent of black children in the South were attending all-black schools. By the end of 1970 that rate had fallen to 18.5 percent and then to 8 percent by 1974. Over 1,000 small school districts were persuaded by HEW to desegregate, while others demanded administrative hearings on their funding being threatened. By 1970, seven states continued to have separate schools for whites and blacks: Alabama, Arkansas, Georgia, Louisiana, Mississippi, North Carolina, and South Carolina. The NAACP sued HEW in 1970 for continuing to give funds to schools that the organization felt were in violation of Title VI of the Civil Rights Act of 1964. HEW acknowledged that Louisiana, Mississippi, Oklahoma, North Carolina, Florida, Arkansas, Pennsylvania, Georgia, Maryland, and Virginia were still operating segregated schools, but the states were given 120 days to desegregate them in early 1970. Some states that refused to desegregate ignored demands by HEW to integrate but were still receiving funding. The case was heard in the U.S. Court of Appeals for the District of Columbia on several dates from 1972 through 1983. In 1972 and 1973, Judge John H. Pratt ruled in favor of the plaintiffs.

Nixon supported peaceful solutions to racial problems and remained open with meeting with committees and organizations supporting that aim. On June 24, 1970, he met with the Mississippi State Advisory Committee on Civil Rights at the White House and two months later with Louisiana's state advisory committee in New Orleans. He met with many other state advisory committees and continued to seek funding from Congress for minority schools.

On March 5, 1969, Nixon issued Executive Order 11458, establishing the Office of Minority Business Enterprise (OMBE) (renamed the Minority Business Development Agency in 1979 and transferred to the Department of Commerce). The purpose of the office was to increase business opportunities for minority companies, and the executive order established the Advisory Council for Minority Business Enterprise to support this. Nixon made a statement about a national program for minority business enterprise on March 5, 1969:

I have often made the point that to foster the economic status and the pride of members of our minority groups we must seek to involve them more fully in our private enterprise system. African Americans, Mexican-Americans,

Puerto Ricans, Indians, and others must increasingly be encouraged to enter the field of business, both in the areas where they now live and in the larger commercial community—and not only as workers, but also as managers and owners. (Nixon 1969a)

The scope of the OMBE was expanded when Nixon issued Executive Order 11625 on October 13, 1971, to supersede Executive Order 11458. Executive Order 11625 gave the secretary of commerce the power "(a) to implement Federal policy in support of the minority business enterprise program; (b) provide additional technical and management assistance to disadvantaged businesses; (c) to assist in demonstration projects; and (d) to coordinate the participation of all Federal departments and agencies in an increased minority enterprise effort" (National Archives 2018).

As the number of African Americans increased in Congress they felt a need to establish a group, as they each felt somewhat isolated because there were at first so few. In the late 1960s, Representative Charles Diggs (D-MI) created the Democracy Select Committee. Due to court-ordered redistricting to serve black communities around the country, the number of African American congressional representatives increased to 13 by 1971. Thus, they established the Congressional Black Caucus (CBC) on June 18, 1971, with Diggs as its first chairman. The following are the founding members of the CBC:

Shirley A. Chisholm (D-NY)

William L. Clay Sr. (D-MO)

George W. Collins (D-IL)

John Conyers Jr. (D-MI)

Ronald V. Dellums (D-CA)

Charles C. Diggs Jr. (D-MI)

Walter E. Fauntroy (D-DC)

Augustus F. Hawkins (D-CA)

Ralph H. Metcalfe (D-IL)

Parren J. Mitchell (D-MD)

Robert N. C. Nix Sr. (D-PA)

Charles B. Rangel (D-NY)

Louis Stokes (D-OH)

Nixon refused to meet with the CBC in 1970, so it boycotted his January 1971 State of the Union Address. The president finally met with the CBC on March 25, 1971, and the CBC outlined 61 recommendations to support improved education, housing, and civil rights and expanded involvement for African Americans in government ("CBC Letter to Nixon" 1971). The president responded to their recommendations in a 115-page report, but the CBC felt that he did not issue any policies supporting their requests. Part of Nixon's letter to Diggs in response to recommendations of the CBC, dated May 19, 1971, stated:

The Administration has examined these recommendations in depth over the past seven weeks. A fresh assessment of all the alternatives in each area characterized this review process, both at the operating department level and then at the White House. Present policies served as a starting point, but we went beyond these in attempting to draw our conclusions on the merits in each case. We found that your broad goals are largely the same as those of the Administration, and we used this review as an occasion for measuring actual results against these goals and for considering appropriate changes where results seemed inadequate.

This review, culminating in the preparation of detailed responses to each of your proposals, was conducted under the overall supervision of the Domestic Council and the Office of Management and Budget. At the same time, George Shultz, Director of OMB, prepared at my request a summary report on this Administration's major programs and activities in the field of civil rights and related social and economic programs. Having reviewed and concurred in this report and the sixty responses, I am pleased to transmit them to you and your colleagues herewith. (Nixon 1971a)

On June 3, 1971, Diggs presented the CBC's "A Report to the Nation," formally outlining its disappointment with the president's response. The CBC continued to work on its recommendations with other members of Congress.

President Lyndon B. Johnson signed the Voting Rights Act in 1965. Its first amendment was signed by Nixon in 1970. The amendment focused on Section 5 of the act, which was only temporary when the original act was passed for a term of five years. The amendment required jurisdictions with a history of voter discrimination to obtain approval from the Department of Justice before being able to implement changes to voting laws. This would allow the department to determine if these changes harmed minority voters. The 1970 amendment extended this requirement for another five years, until 1975.

One important note about the Voting Rights Act of 1970 is that it also attempted to lower the voting age from 21 to 18 for all elections at every level of government. Senator Ted Kennedy proposed this change to the act, and it was included in the law signed by Nixon. Nixon did comment that "Despite my misgivings about the constitutionality of this one provision, I have signed the bill. I have directed the attorney general to cooperate fully in expediting a swift court test of the constitutionality of the 18-year-old provision" (Nixon 1970b). This was challenged in court. In the case *Oregon v. Mitchell,* 400 U.S. 112 (1970), the Supreme Court ruled that Congress could only lower the voting age to 18 for federal elections. The Supreme Court's decision led Congress to amend the Constitution. The proposal for the Twenty-Sixth Amendment was issued in Congress on March 23, 1971. It was driven by 18-year-olds fighting in Vietnam who were unable to vote. The amendment was ratified quickly and became part of the Constitution on July 1, 1971.

In 1971, the issue of school desegregation continued but this time with an emphasis on busing. Busing was a means to transport black children from their communities with poor schools to other communities with better schools that were located in white communities. A decade after the ruling in *Brown,* the Charlotte-Mecklenburg, North Carolina, school system still had approximately 14,000 black students attending schools that were at least 99 percent black. On April 20, 1971, the Supreme Court ruled in the case *Swann v. Charlotte-Mecklenburg Board of Education,* 402 U.S. 1 (1971) that busing was an acceptable means to achieve desegregation. The court held that busing addressed racial imbalances in schools and gave all children an equal opportunity for a quality education. Additionally, it was permissible to use mathematical ratios or quotas in school enrollments to ensure a proper mix of students by race. The plaintiffs in the case were represented by the NAACP Legal Defense Fund. Both white and black opponents called this "forced busing," as black students were forced to endure long commutes to and from schools. Still, Charlotte, North Carolina, was seen as a model for other cities and was called the "city that made desegregation work." The use of busing continued across the United States until the 1990s. The issue of busing didn't end with the court's decision in this one case but was an issue during the 1972 presidential election. Nixon used opposition to forced busing as one of his popular points. Some localities were forced by the courts to desegregate using busing, such as in Denver, Colorado, in 1973 and Boston, Massachusetts, in 1974.

In a news conference on April 29, 1971, Nixon was asked his position on busing to overcome racial segregation and the Supreme Court's decision. He responded,

> This problem involves some very technical legal distinctions. I will not go into them in detail.
>
> I will, however, say this: I expressed views with regard to my opposition to busing for the purpose of achieving racial balance and in support of the neighborhood school in my statement of March of last year. I stated those views at that time with the preface that this was an area that the Supreme Court had not yet spoken on and that it was my responsibility, therefore, to speak on it and to give guidance to our executive agencies.
>
> Now that the Supreme Court has spoken on that issue, whatever I have said that is inconsistent with the Supreme Court's decision is now moot and irrelevant, because everybody in this country, including the President of the United States, is under the law; or, putting it another way, nobody, including the President of the United States, is above the law as it is finally determined by the Supreme Court of the United States.
>
> Now, what is the law in this instance? The law is that where we have segregation in schools as a result of governmental action—in other words, de jure—that then busing can be used under certain circumstances to deal with that problem. And so we will comply with that situation, and we will work with the Southern school districts, not in a spirit of coercion, but one of cooperation as we have during the past year in which so much progress has been made in getting rid of that kind of a system that we have had previously.
>
> Second, however, the Court explicitly by dictums did not deal with the problem of de facto segregation as it exists in the North and perhaps as it may eventually

exist in the South. That matter the Court still has not decided on explicitly. It will probably have that opportunity, because I noted a California case a couple of days ago from San Francisco which said that busing would be required to deal with segregation which was a result, not of what a governmental body did, but as a result of housing patterns coming from individual decisions.

Now, until the Court does move in that field, I still will hold to my original positions of March: That I do not believe that busing to achieve racial balance is in the interests of better education. Where it is de jure, we comply with the Court; where it is de facto, until the Court speaks, that still remains my view. (Nixon 1971b)

President Johnson issued Executive Order 11246 on September 24, 1965, that forbade discrimination in federal government hiring and also by contractors doing business with the government. The following was a specific requirement for contractors to practice affirmative action:

The contractor will not discriminate against any employee or applicant for employment because of race, creed, color, or national origin. The contractor will take affirmative action to ensure that applicants are employed, and that employees are treated during employment, without regard to their race, creed, color, or national origin. Such action shall include, but not be limited to the following: employment, upgrading, demotion, or transfer; recruitment or recruitment advertising; layoff or termination; rates of pay or other forms of compensation; and selection for training, including apprenticeship. The contractor agrees to post in conspicuous places, available to employees and applicants for employment, notices to be provided by the contracting officer setting forth the provisions of this nondiscrimination clause. (United States Department of Labor 2018b)

The Department of Labor found that government construction contractors in Philadelphia, Pennsylvania, were violating the order by not hiring minority workers. Specifically, blacks comprised 1 percent or less of workers in the fields of ironworkers, steam fitters, sheet metal workers, electricians, elevator construction workers, and plumbers and pipe fitters. In 1967 the department implemented the Philadelphia Plan, requiring the contractors to meet the goals of affirmative action. However, the original plan was found to be illegal in 1968 by the comptroller general of the United States because it set hiring quotas revised by the Nixon administration in September 1969. The Department of Labor announced in February 1970 that the plan would be extended to other cities if they did not devise their own methods to end job discrimination in the construction industry. The Contractors Association of Eastern Pennsylvania challenged the plan in 1971, arguing that it was beyond the authority of the president per the Constitution and was in violation of the Civil Rights Act of 1964 and the National Labor Relations Act. The U.S. Court of Appeals for the Third Circuit ruled in favor of the federal government in *Contractors Association of Eastern Pennsylvania v. Secretary of Labor,* 442 F. 2d 159 (3rd Cir. 1971), and the Supreme Court refused to hear the case. The Philadelphia Plan initially included government contracts in excess of $500,000 in the construction trade and later expanded to include contracts of $50,000 or more in all areas of industry.

Nixon made a statement about congressional action on the Philadelphia Plan on December 23, 1969, in support of Congress's vote to an amendment that in effect would have rejected the plan:

I am deeply gratified that the Congress has acted responsibly to allow continuation of the Philadelphia Plan and our program of positive steps to assure equal job opportunity. The Members of the Congress who contributed to this wise action have my thanks and congratulations.

There is no civil right more central to the American system than the right of equal opportunity. Every American should have equal opportunity for new jobs created by the taxes paid by all Americans. I have worked for implementation of this principle since 1953 when President Eisenhower appointed me Chairman of the President's Committee on Government Contracts. This administration is determined to see that this right—so long denied or given lip service—becomes national policy.

The Philadelphia Plan has been opening new jobs for minority workers in the construction industry, an industry with a severe labor shortage in skilled crafts. With this action by the Congress, this program of economic opportunity can go forward as planned. (Nixon 1969b)

Nixon made a proclamation on September 30, 1972, that publicly outlined how he embraced the nation's diversity and to show that his administration was "ethnically aware." With Proclamation 4160, he established National Heritage Day on October 1, 1972. His proclamation stated the following:

The special quality of the United States is the interaction of many peoples from many lands, each asserting the freedom to be different, each respecting and honoring his own ethnic heritage, while contributing to a nation in which all are Americans together.

The shining guarantee of our national future is precisely the repeated rebirth, the reinvigoration, the gift of renewal, implicit in this constant meeting of the world's peoples here in our own land.

The unusual virtue of the United States is that all men and women are accepted for what they are, with friendship and respect founded upon knowledge and understanding of all races, creeds, and national origins.

The "melting pot" is one of unity, but never of uniformity.

The national pride of the United States is, in this sense, pride of our people in the heritage we draw from all nations.

In order that we may pause for a moment to express our appreciation of America's heritage, the Congress, by House Joint Resolution 1304, has requested the President to issue a proclamation designating Sunday, October 1, 1972, as National Heritage Day.

Now, Therefore, I, Richard M. Nixon, President of the United States of America, do hereby proclaim Sunday, October 1, 1972, as National Heritage Day. I call upon all Americans to reflect upon the composite vitality, enthusiasm and tenacity of the many separate peoples who have built our beloved country, and to celebrate, with appropriate ceremonies, the fact that our one nation is many nations, and our many nations are one nation, dedicated to freedom, under God.

In Witness Whereof, I have hereunto set my hand this thirtieth day of September, in the year of our Lord nineteen hundred seventy-two, and of the Independence of the United States of America the one hundred ninety-seventh. (Nixon 1972a)

Still, Nixon was unable to win the black vote. After the election of Lyndon B. Johnson, African Americans were predominantly Democrat. In the election of 1972, Nixon only received 13 percent of the nonwhite vote. At the same time, African Americans began gaining prominence in politics. For example, Shirley Chisholm became the first African American to campaign for a presidential nomination in 1972. She ran for the Democratic presidential nomination although unsuccessfully. In 1968 Chisholm became the first black woman elected to Congress and served the 12th Congressional District of New York for seven terms, from 1969 until 1983. Barbara Jordon of Houston, Texas, and Andrew Young of Atlanta, Georgia, became the first black congressional members elected from southern states since 1898. In 1973, Maynard H. Jackson Jr. was elected the first black mayor of Atlanta and Coleman Young the first black mayor of Detroit.

In 1972 Congress passed and Nixon signed the Equal Employment Opportunity Act, giving greater enforcement power to the EEOC. He made a statement on March 25, 1972, outlining some expansions made to federal powers:

The most significant aspect of this legislation is a new authority consistently advocated by this Administration since 1969—a provision arming the Equal Employment Opportunity Commission with power to bring lawsuits in the Federal district courts to enforce the rights guaranteed by title VII of the Civil Rights Act of 1964. . . .

Additionally, the legislation extends the protections of title VII to millions of American citizens previously excluded from its coverage. The experiences of both the Justice Department and the EEOC under title VII have demonstrated that considerable discrimination problems have existed in State and local governments, with small employers, and in some educational institutions. Individuals employed in these areas have not heretofore been protected by title VII. This bill corrects that defect. . . .

Also created by this legislation is the Equal Employment Opportunity Coordinating Council, a new interagency group which will coordinate, monitor, and report on the Government's enforcement drive against all remaining job discrimination. (Nixon 1972b)

The following are specific amendments made per the 1972 act:

1. EEOC has litigation authority. If the agency cannot secure an acceptable conciliation agreement, it has the option of suing nongovernment respondents—employers, unions, and employment agencies.

2. Educational institutions are subject to Title VII. Congress found that discrimination against minorities and women in the field of education was just as pervasive as discrimination in any other area of employment.

3. State and local governments are no longer exempt from Title VII. Removal of this exemption results in 10 million more employees being immediately added to Title VII's coverage.

4. The Federal Government is subject to Title VII. Federal executive agencies and defined units of the other branches must make all personnel actions free from discrimination based on race, color, sex, religion or national origin.

5. The number of employers covered by Title VII is increased by reducing the number of employees (from 25 to 15) needed for an employer to be covered by the Act.

6. Charging parties have a longer period of time to file their charges, 180 or 300 days rather than 90 or 210 days.

   Additionally, charging parties now have 90 days rather than 30 days to file a lawsuit after EEOC has informed them that it is no longer working on their charge. This extension of time affords charging parties a better chance to find a lawyer if they wish to pursue their charges in court.

The issue of busing became violent as a series of protests and riots broke out in Boston, Massachusetts, from 1974 through 1976. The Massachusetts legislature passed the Racial Imbalance Act in 1965 that mandated the desegregation of public schools. This caused whites to leave the urban areas for the suburbs and was supported by a court ruling by the U.S. District Court for the District of Massachusetts. The NAACP successfully filed a class-action lawsuit against the Boston School Committee in 1972 in the case *Morgan v. Hennigan,* 379 F. Supp. 410 (1974), alleging violation of the Thirteenth and Fourteenth Amendments as well as the 1964 Civil Rights Act because segregated schools were still being maintained. In the final ruling in the case on June 21, 1974, U.S. district judge Arthur Garrity Jr. ordered black students to be bused to predominantly white schools and, in turn, white students to be bused to predominantly black schools.

Over 4,000 white demonstrators protested the court's decision at the Boston Common on September 9, 1974. Senator Edward Kennedy tried to address the crowd and was booed and pelted with eggs. The protestors also expressed outrage with Senator Edward Brooke and Judge Garrity. Protests continued as forced busing began on September 12, 1974. Many parents kept their children home, and the National Guard was mobilized in October to enforce the desegregation orders.

Boston School Committee chairwoman Louise Day Hicks then formed Restore Our Alienated Rights (ROAR) in 1974. ROAR used sit-ins, public prayers, and marches to oppose school desegregation. Violence erupted with injuries, and some people were killed. A black student was attacked by a white student using an American flag. A white teenager was stabbed by a black student on a different occasion at a different school. When black students arrived at predominantly white schools, some were greeted with jeers, and rocks were thrown at them. Black and white students engaged in a huge brawl outside Hyde Park High School on February 11, 1975. The NAACP organized marches in Boston on May 17, 1975, in favor of busing and to bring attention to whites opposing desegregation. The unrest in Boston continued for a decade until the busing program was transferred to the Boston School Committee in 1988. The busing program was not replaced until 2013.

Boston was not the only place in the country to face violence due to busing. On March 2, 1970, up to 200 white men attacked buses bringing black students to a predominantly white school in Lamar, South Carolina. While police used tear gas to disperse the mob and get the children inside the school, the mob overturned two empty buses. On August 30, 1971, six members of the Ku Klux Klan bombed 10 buses that were to be used to integrate schools in Pontiac, Michigan, as part of a court-ordered busing plan.

The Supreme Court heard a case on busing in Detroit in 1974. In *Milliken v. Bradley,* the NAACP filed suit against the State of Michigan. William Milliken, the governor of Michigan, was named as a defendant in this lawsuit. African Americans were kept out of many white neighborhoods, and this resulted in the majority of inner-city Detroit schools becoming predominantly black, while white students attended schools in the suburbs and counties. The lower courts ruled in favor of desegregation, even if it meant integration between districts. The Supreme Court ruled in favor of the defendants and against forced integration in districts. It held that there was "no showing of significant violation by the 53 outlying school districts and no evidence of any interdistrict violation or effect" (Cornell Law School 2018), and the lower court's ruling was not permissible or justified by the Supreme Court's ruling in *Brown v. Board of Education of Topeka, Kansas.* The Supreme Court also emphasized the importance of local control over how schools were operated. In his dissent, Justice Thurgood Marshall stated, "School district lines, however innocently drawn, will surely be perceived as fences to separate the races when, under a Detroit-only decree, white parents withdraw their children from the Detroit city schools and move to the suburbs in order to continue them in all-white schools."

Nixon was consumed by the Watergate investigation for much of 1974. On August 9, 1974, he became the only president to resign from office. Because there were still efforts in place to convict Nixon, his former vice president, Gerald Ford, granted him a full pardon on September 8, 1974, once Ford was president.

Like President Lyndon B. Johnson, President Nixon often used racist terms to refer to blacks. For example in 1969 while discussing policies with his national security adviser, Henry Kissinger, Nixon told him to leave African policy to Secretary of State William Rogers: "Henry, let's leave the n----rs to Bill and we'll take care of the rest of the world" (Waters 2009, ix). Richard M. Nixon passed away on April 22, 1994, in New York City.

FURTHER READING

Aitken, Jonathan. 1993. *Nixon: A Life.* Washington, DC: Regnery History.

Black, Conrad. 2007. *Richard M. Nixon: A Life in Full.* New York: PublicAffairs.

Bond, Julian. 1979. "Just Schools: A Special Report Commemorating the 25th Anniversary of the Brown Decision." *Southern Exposure* 7, no. 2 (Summer).

Drew, Elizabeth. 2007. *Richard M. Nixon: The American Presidents Series; The 37th President, 1969–1974.* New York: Times Books.

Farrell, John A. 2017. *Richard Nixon: The Life.* New York: Doubleday.

Gannon, Frank. 2010. "3.24.70." Richard Nixon Foundation, Library and Museum, https://www.nixonfoundation.org/2010/03/3-24-70/.

Nixon, Richard M. 1969. "Statement about Congressional Action on the Philadelphia Plan, December 23, 1969." The American Presidency Project, http://www.presidency.ucsb.edu/ws/?pid=2382.

Nixon, Richard M. 1970a. "Special Message to the Congress Proposing the Emergency School Aid Act of 1970, May 21, 1970." The American Presidency Project, http://www.presidency.ucsb.edu/ws/?pid=2509.

Nixon, Richard M. 1970b. "Statement on Signing the Voting Rights Act Amendments of 1970, June 22, 1970." The American Presidency Project, http://www.presidency.ucsb.edu/ws/index.php?pid=2553.

Nixon, Richard M. 1971. "The President's News Conference, April 29, 1971." The American Presidency Project, http://www.presidency.ucsb.edu/ws/index.php?pid=2993.

Nixon, Richard M. 1972. "Statement about Signing the Equal Employment Opportunity Act of 1972, March 25, 1972." The American Presidency Project, http://www.presidency.ucsb.edu/ws/?pid=3358.

Nixon, Richard. 2012. *RN: The Memoirs of Richard Nixon.* New York: Simon and Schuster.

Thomas, Evan. 2015. *Being Nixon: A Man Divided.* New York: Random House.

Waters, Robert Anthony, Jr. 2009. *Historical Dictionary of United States–Africa Relations.* Lanham, MD: Scarecrow.

Gerald Rudolph Ford Jr. (born Leslie Lynch King Jr.)

38th President of the United States
Presidential Term: August 4, 1974–January 20, 1977
Political Party: Republican
Vice President: None (August–December 1974),
Nelson Rockefeller (1974–1977)

Gerald Rudolph Ford Jr. was born in Omaha, Nebraska, on July 14, 1913, as Leslie Lynch King Jr. but changed his name as a result of his mother's divorce and remarriage to Gerald Rudolph Ford in 1917. Ford was never legally adopted by his stepfather but legally changed his name in 1935.

Ford is the only president not to be elected to the positions of president and vice president. He became vice president under Richard Nixon on October 12, 1973, after Vice President Spiro T. Agnew resigned as part of a plea bargain for charges of conspiracy, tax evasion, and bribery. Ford became president after the resignation of Nixon while under investigation in the Watergate scandal.

President Ford's pardon of Nixon did not garner support from black leaders. It was seen as another example of political corruption and as evidence of an American justice system that had one standard for whites and another standard for blacks. Ford's selection of Nelson Rockefeller as vice president was supported by African American groups and leaders due to Rockefeller's outspoken support of civil rights. Rockefeller's father and grandfather had both supported African Americans and civil rights. His grandfather, John D. Rockefeller, founded Standard Oil and financially supported the historically black Spelman College and Morehouse College. Nelson Rockefeller funded the rebuilding of bombed churches in the South, and he was an active supporter of the efforts of Dr. Martin Luther King, Jr. and the Southern Christian Leadership Conference even while serving as governor of New York. Ford selected Rockefeller over then U.S. ambassador Donald Rumsfeld (who would later become secretary of defense under George W. Bush) and George H. W. Bush (who would later become 41st president of the United States).

While serving in the House of Representatives, Congressman Ford supported the Civil Rights Act of 1964 and the Voting Rights Act of 1965. He also supported desegregation on legal and moral grounds. However, as president of the United States, he was not supportive of busing to combat school segregation. The issue of busing continued into the administration of President Ford, who believed that the use of busing was a local issue rather than mandated by the federal government. He made his position on the issue clear on August 21, 1974, when he stated, "In general, I am opposed to the forced busing of school children because it does not lead to better education and it infringes upon traditional freedoms in America" (Ford 1974a). When violence broke out in Boston, Massachusetts, after a federal judge ruled in favor of busing, Ford refused to send in U.S. marshals to help restore order. Instead, on October 9, 1974 he stated,

> I deplore the violence that I have read about and seen on television. I think that's most unfortunate. The court decision in that case, in my judgment, was not the best solution to quality education in Boston. I have consistently opposed forced busing to achieve racial balance as a solution to quality education. And therefore I respectfully disagree with the Judge's order. I hope and trust that it's not necessary to call in Federal officials or Federal law enforcement agencies. The marshals, if my information is accurate, are under the jurisdiction of the court, not directly under my jurisdiction. As far as I know, no specific request has come to me for any Federal involvement and therefore I'm not in a position to act under those circumstances. (Ripley 1974)

On the same day, Ford met with the Congressional Black Caucus (CBC). At this time members of the CBC were members of the Democratic Party. There was a bit of tension before the meeting, as only one member of the CBC, Representative Andrew Young of Georgia, had voted to confirm Ford as vice president under Nixon. This was a warm meeting, as Nixon had refused to meet with the group when it was first founded. Ford actually invited the members of the caucus to the meeting. The CBC left the president with recommendations on policies supporting African Americans, and Ford assured them that he would consider them and that the Oval Office would always be open to their concerns and advice. Ford also made a promise to the CBC to appoint more blacks to key White House positions.

On January 23, 1975, Ford made remarks before the members of the National Newspaper Publishers Association, a trade association for hundreds of African American–owned community newspapers around the country. He outlined policies that his administration was putting forward to support African Americans, including an extension of the Voting Rights Act of 1965 and economic policies to tackle the recession. He outlined his policies by first stating that "Blacks in our society have too often been mentally segregated by some thinkers and planners who acted as if blacks did not have the same expectations and problems as other Americans. I promised at the very beginning of my Administration to be President of all the people, and I am keeping that pledge" (Ford 1975c).

On March 7, 1975, Ford appointed the first African American to serve as U.S. secretary of transportation. William Thaddeus "Bill" Coleman served in that position through Ford's tenure as president. He was the second African American to hold a presidential cabinet post, after Robert C. Weaver served as secretary of housing and urban development under President Lyndon B. Johnson.

Ford spoke at the annual convention of the NAACP on July 1, 1975. In his speech, he outlined his administration's support of civil rights and domestic policies that would support African Americans. The nation was facing a recession, and inflation and reduced federal spending were seen as having a particularly negative impact on African Americans. Ford outlined how "A policy of fiscal restraint does not mean that this Nation will turn its back on major problems of employment, housing, transportation, health care, and education. In fact, my budget for the fiscal year of 1976, which starts today—it increases the total of these human resources programs by more than $17 billion over fiscal year 1975." He also stated,

In fiscal year 1975 that ended at midnight last night, minority enterprise programs of the Small Business Administration [SBA] alone created or saved 63,000 jobs. Twenty-five percent of all SBA loans and 16 percent of the total dollars went to minority business. To make certain that job opportunities in the Federal Government are open to all Americans, each department and each agency will vigorously enforce the equal opportunity employment laws. To make sure, to make certain job opportunities are open in the private sector, I have emphasized to Lowell Perry, the new Chairman of the Equal Employment Opportunity Commission, this Administration's commitment to the elimination of all vestiges of job discrimination because of race, religion, or sex.

He closed his remarks with the statement "The entire Nation is at last waking up to the contribution and potential of black people. And along with Roy Wilkins, I believe that if America's blacks are permitted to do for themselves, according to their own likes, they will do like nobody ever dreamed" (Ford 1975b).

In 1975, Ford not only supported the extension of the temporary provisions of the Voting Rights Act of 1975 but also asked for its expansion. In a letter to the

Senate minority leader on July 23, 1975, Ford asked for support of the expansions already approved by the House of Representatives:

> The House of Representatives, in H.R. 6219, has broadened this important law in this way: (1) The House bill would extend the temporary provisions of the Act for ten years, instead of five; and (2) the House bill would extend the temporary provisions of the Act so as to include discrimination against language minorities, thereby extending application of the Act from the present seven States to eight additional States, in whole or in part. In light of the House extension of the Voting Rights Act for ten years and to eight more States, I believe this is the appropriate time and opportunity to extend the Voting Rights Act nationwide. (Ford 1975a)

The final amendment expanded the Voting Rights Act and made permanent the temporary provision of the law forbidding literacy tests. The amendment extended other temporary provisions such as the Department of Justice's oversight of states with a history of voting discrimination that changed voting laws from five to seven years. It also expanded the law to all states by requiring protections for those whose first language was not English and where they represented more than 5 percent of the population. This required voting information to be provided in other than English for Hispanics, Asian Americans, native Alaskans, and Native Americans.

Black History Month was celebrated nationally for the first time in February 1976. Prior to this month-long celebration, African American scholar Dr. Carter G. Woodson began Negro History Week in 1926. On February 2, 1976, Ford issued a statement celebrating the month during the celebration of the U.S. bicentennial:

> In the Bicentennial year of our Independence, we can review with admiration the impressive contributions of black Americans to our national life and culture.

> One hundred years ago, to help highlight these achievements, Dr. Carter G. Woodson founded the Association for the Study of Afro-American Life and History. We are grateful to him today for his initiative, and we are richer for the work of his organization.

> Freedom and the recognition of individual rights are what our Revolution was all about. They were ideals that inspired our fight for Independence: ideals that we have been striving to live up to ever since. Yet it took many years before ideals became a reality for black citizens.

> The last quarter-century has finally witnessed significant strides in the full integration of black people into every area of national life. In celebrating Black History Month, we can take satisfaction from this recent progress in the realization of the ideals envisioned by our Founding Fathers. But, even more than this, we can seize the opportunity to honor the too-often neglected accomplishments of black Americans in every area of endeavor throughout our history.

> I urge my fellow citizens to join me in tribute to Black History Month and the message of courage and perseverance it brings to all of us. (Ford 1976a)

As President Ford's term in office continued, he faced opposition from black leaders due to issues such as unemployment, the recession, and federal programs that they felt were not supporting the needs of African Americans. During a press conference on April 10, 1976, Ford was asked how he would attract the black vote during his upcoming presidential election campaign. A reporter specifically stated, "Mr. Ford, several members of the Congressional Black Caucus and other black political leaders have said that they will not endorse a Presidential candidate right now because they are not addressing themselves to the specific needs of black Americans, i.e., unemployment, welfare, and things like that. What will you do to get the black American vote, and just how important is that vote to you?" President Ford responded:

I want the votes, to the maximum degree possible, of all elements of our society. I don't believe that one should make a specific appeal to any segment of our society for a vote on the basis of what I promise. It is my aim and objective—it has been, it is, and it will be—to have a program that meets the needs of all segments of our society.

I recognize that there are certain interests that one group or another may have. In the case of blacks, the minority economic assistance program. We have done well in that. We have done very well in trying to provide summer youth employment. I recommended the maximum possible under the law, and that has a particular impact on minority youth because they have the highest rate of unemployment.

So, what we try to do is to recognize a problem that affects all of our citizens. If it affects one group more than another, and we get an answer, it, in my opinion, is the right approach. But to offer as a specific program to a particular group in order to get their votes, I don't think that is the way a candidate for the Presidency should operate. I don't intend to do so. (Ford 1976b)

On June 24, 1976, Ford asked Congress to support limited court-ordered desegregation plans with his School Desegregation Standards and Assistance Act of 1976, which would also establish a National Community and Education Committee. As part of this message, he stated:

While I personally believe that every community should effectively desegregate on a voluntary basis, I recognize that some court action is inevitable.

In those cases where Federal court actions are initiated, however, I believe that busing as a remedy ought to be the last resort, and that it ought to be limited in scope to correcting the effect of previous Constitutional violations.

The goal of the judicial remedy in a school desegregation case ought to be to put the school system, and its students, where they would have been if the acts which violate the Constitution had never occurred.

The goal should be to eliminate "root and branch" the Constitutional violations and all of their present effects. This is the Constitutional test which the Supreme Court has mandated—nothing more, nothing less.

Therefore, my bill would establish for Federal courts specific guidelines concerning the use of busing in school desegregation cases. It would require the court to determine the extent to which acts of unlawful discrimination by governmental officials have caused a greater degree of racial concentration in a school or school system than would have existed in the absence of such acts. It would further require the court to limit the relief to that necessary to correct the racial imbalance actually caused by those unlawful acts. This would prohibit a court from ordering busing throughout an entire school system simply for the purpose of achieving racial balance.

In addition, my bill recognizes that the busing remedy is transitional by its very nature and that when a community makes good faith efforts to comply, busing ought to be limited in duration. Therefore, the bill provides that three years after the busing remedy has been imposed a court shall be required to determine whether to continue the remedy. Should the court determine that a continuation is necessary, it could do so only for an additional two years. Thereafter, the court could continue busing only in the most extraordinary circumstances, where there has been a failure or delay of other remedial efforts or where the residual effects of unlawful discrimination are unusually severe. (Ford 1976d)

Roy Wilkins of the NAACP called the president's proposal a "craven, cowardly, despicable retreat and recapitulation to lawlessness, ignorance and the forces of race" (Simmons 1984, 30). Congress took no action on Ford's proposal.

As the presidential election of 1976 neared, Ford and members of his administration campaigned around the county. This included his secretary of agriculture, Earl Butz. However, Butz was already criticized for his racist views. In 1974, he used a mock Italian accent to criticize Pope Paul VI's opposition to the use of artificial birth control to solve world food problems. Ford admonished Butz for his statement. Then in August 1976 while traveling from the Republican National Convention, Butz referred to blacks as "coloreds" and outlined how "coloreds" don't vote Republican because of the following: "I'll tell you what the coloreds want. It's three things: first, a tight pussy; second, loose shoes; and third, a warm place to shit" (Carroll 2000, 203). Butz received extreme criticism from the media, Republican leaders, and citizens. Under pressure from the White House, he apologized and resigned. On October 4, 1976, Ford made remarks upon accepting the resignation of Butz and stated, "Yet Earl Butz is also wise enough and courageous enough to recognize that no single individual, no matter how distinguished his past public service, should cast a shadow over the integrity and good will of the American Government by his comments. For that reason, I have accepted the resignation of this decent and good man" (Ford 1976c).

In December 1976, Ford created the National Advisory Committee on Black Higher Education and Black Colleges and Universities (HBCUs). Its first meeting did not occur until September 1977 because its formation was not published in the Federal Register until June 1977 for public comment, as required for new federal policies. The committee's purpose was to develop recommendations for increased support to HBCUs and black college-age students.

Ford was able to win the Republican National Convention nomination to run for president against Ronald Reagan, who would later become the 40th president of the United States. However, Ford lost the general election to Georgia governor James "Jimmy" Carter. In that election, 85 percent of blacks voted for Carter. Ford later commented that despite his positive record on civil rights, he knew that as a Republican he would be unable to sway blacks to abandon the Democratic Party.

Ford did not cease his support for civil rights once he left office. In 1999, affirmative action was a heated political and legal topic. The University of Michigan was under fire for its use of affirmative action in admissions. Ford wrote an op-ed in the *New York Times* strongly supporting this practice:

> At its core, affirmative action should try to offset past injustices by fashioning a campus population more truly reflective of modern America and our hopes for the future. Unfortunately, a pair of lawsuits brought against my alma mater pose a threat to such diversity. Not content to oppose formal quotas, plaintiffs suing the University of Michigan would prohibit that and other universities from even considering race as one of many factors weighed by admission counselors.
>
> So drastic a ban would scuttle Michigan's current system, one that takes into account nearly a dozen elements—race, economic standing, geographic origin, athletic and artistic achievement among them—to create the finest educational environment for all students.
>
> This eminently reasonable approach, as thoughtful as it is fair, has produced a student body with a significant minority component whose record of academic success is outstanding. (Ford 1999)

Gerald Ford passed away on December 26, 2006, in California.

FURTHER READING

Brinkley, Douglas. 2007. *Gerald R. Ford: The American Presidents Series; The 38th President, 1974–1977.* New York: Times Books.

Cannon, James. 2013. *Gerald R. Ford: An Honorable Life.* Ann Arbor: University of Michigan Press.

Carroll, Peter N. 2000. *It Seemed Like Nothing Happened: America in the 1970s.* New Brunswick, NJ: Rutgers University Press.

DeFrank, Thomas M., and Gerald Ford. 2007. *Write It When I'm Gone: Remarkable Off-the-Record Conversations with Gerald Ford.* New York: Penguin Group.

Ford, Gerald R. 1974. "Statement by the President." The White House, https://www.fordlibrarymuseum.gov/library/document/0248/whpr19740821-008.pdf.

Ford, Gerald R. 1975a. "Letter to the Senate Minority Leader Urging Extension of the Voting Rights Act of 1965, July 23, 1975." The American Presidency Project, http://www.presidency.ucsb.edu/ws/index.php?pid=5097.

Ford, Gerald R. 1975b. "Remarks at the Annual Convention of the National Association for the Advancement of Colored People, July 1, 1975." The American Presidency Project, http://www.presidency.ucsb.edu/ws/index.php?pid=5037.

Ford, Gerald R. 1975c. "Remarks to Members of the National Newspaper Publishers Association, January 23, 1975." The American Presidency Project, http://www .presidency.ucsb.edu/ws/index.php?pid=5105.

Ford, Gerald R. 1976a. "Message on the Observance of Black History Month, February 1976, February 10, 1976." The American Presidency Project, http://www.presi dency.ucsb.edu/ws/?pid=6288.

Ford, Gerald R. 1976b. "The President's News Conference, April 10, 1976." The American Presidency Project, http://www.presidency.ucsb.edu/ws/index.php?pid=5828.

Ford, Gerald R. 1976c. "Remarks upon Accepting the Resignation of Earl L. Butz as Secretary of Agriculture, October 4, 1976." The American Presidency Project, http:// www.presidency.ucsb.edu/ws/index.php?pid=6408.

Ford, Gerald R. 1976d. "Special Message to the Congress Transmitting Proposed School Busing Legislation, June 24, 1976." The American Presidency Project, http:// www.presidency.ucsb.edu/ws/index.php?pid=6150.

Ford, Gerald R. 1999. "Inclusive America, under Attack." *New York Times,* August 8, https://www.nytimes.com/1999/08/08/opinion/inclusive-america-under-attack .html.

Mieczkowski, Yanek. 2005. *Gerald Ford and the Challenges of the 1970s.* Lexington: University Press of Kentucky.

Simmons, Althea T. L. 1984. "The Civil Rights Act of 1964 Revisited." *The Crisis* no. 91, 9 (November): 28–34.

James Earl "Jimmy" Carter Jr.

39th President of the United States
Presidential Term: January 20, 1977–January 20, 1981
Political Party: Democratic
Vice President: Walter Mondale

James Earl Carter Jr. (nicknamed Jimmy) was born on October 1, 1924, in Plains, Georgia. He served as the governor of Georgia from 1971 to 1975, and his early political career included a hard stance against racial segregation and discrimination. His victory over Gerald Ford in the 1976 presidential election was due in part to his receiving 90 percent of the black vote. This demonstrates how in only a few decades African Americans were solidly Democrat, to the point of overwhelmingly support for a southern Democrat. Carter was a longtime advocate of desegregation and civil rights, which reflected the changing views of some southern Democrats. When Carter was sworn in as governor of Georgia, he pledged to forever end segregation in the state. He also appointed African Americans to prominent positions in state government. As governor, Carter declared January 15, 1973, Martin Luther King, Jr. Day in Georgia and even hung King's portrait in the state capitol. He did so against the advice of both his political opponents and his closest advisers. He defeated former Alabama governor George C. Wallace for the Democratic nomination for president with the support of such black leaders as Barbara Jordan, congresswoman from Texas, and Andrew Young, congressman from Georgia. Carter also won the election in part because he was seen as an outsider and not a tainted member of the Washington establishment, which was popular to voters after the resignation of President Richard Nixon and his pardon by

President Gerald Ford. Carter promised to bring honesty and morality back to the federal government.

One of the most surprising personal actions President Carter took when he arrived in Washington, D.C., was to send his daughter Amy not only to a public school but to the historic African American Thaddeus Stevens School. Amy went on to attend the District of Columbia Public Schools. This was a rare decision by any president before or after Carter; even most congressional representatives sent their children to private schools.

Carter made several notable federal appointments of African Americans. Patricia Robert Harris was appointed secretary of the Department of Housing and Urban Development, becoming the first ever African American female presidential cabinet member. Drew S. Days III was appointed as the first African American division head in the

In 1976, Jimmy Carter of Georgia was elected president of the United States. President Carter appointed more African Americans, Latinos, and women to federal judiciary positions than all previous presidents before him combined. (Library of Congress)

Department of Justice, serving as assistant attorney general for civil rights. Other appointments were Wade H. McCree as solicitor general, John B. Slaughter as director of the National Science Foundation, Eleanor Holmes Norton as chair of the Equal Employment Opportunity Commission (EEOC), Franklin Delano Raines as assistant director of the White House Domestic Policy Staff, and Marry Berry as assistant secretary for education in the Department of Health, Education, and Welfare (as the Department of Education had yet to be established). Clifford Leopold Alexander Jr. was appointed the first African American secretary of the U.S. Army on February 14, 1977. He served in the position until January 20, 1981. One of President Carter's most notable appointments was Andrew Young as U.S. ambassador to the United Nations (UN) in 1977. Young was the first African American to hold this position and was sworn in on January 30, 1977, by U.S. Supreme Court Justice Thurgood Marshall. However, Young held a secret meeting with the UN representative for the Palestine Liberation Organization (PLO) in 1979 over his concerns about a pending report on the creation of a Palestinian state. The UN had promised Israel that no meetings would be held with the PLO due to diplomatic tensions. Young resigned, and Carter replaced him with another African American, Donald Franchot McHenry. Carter also appointed more African Americans, Latinos, and women to federal judiciary positions than all previous presidents before him combined.

Two other notable advancements for African Americans took place during Carter's tenure in office: the promotion of Frank Emanuel Peterson Jr. on February 23, 1979, to become the first African American general in the U.S. Marine Corps, and Hazel Winifred Johnson-Brown, to become the first African American female general in the U.S. Army, also in 1979. She was also the first African American chief of the U.S. Army Nurse Corps.

Carter pledged his support for preserving civil rights legislation such as the Civil Rights Act of 1964 and the Voting Rights Act of 1965. In February 1977 he stated, "There will never be any attempt while I am President to weaken the great civil rights acts that have passed in years gone by" (Califano 1981, 243). To that end, on July 20, 1977, he issued a memorandum for the heads of executive departments and agencies on the enforcement of Title VI of the Civil Rights Act:

Title VI of the Civil Rights Act of 1964 writes into law a concept which is basic to our country—that the government of all the people should not support programs which discriminate on the grounds of race, color, or national origin. There are no exceptions to this rule; no matter how important a program, no matter how urgent the goals, they do not excuse violating any of our laws—including the laws against discrimination.

This Administration will enforce Title VI. This means, first, that each of you must exert firm leadership to ensure that your department or agency enforces this law.

Second, there must be central guidance and oversight of Title VI enforcement. Executive Order 11764 places with the Attorney General the responsibility for coordinating Title VI enforcement and for approving rules, regulations and orders which departments or agencies issue under Title VI. I want the Attorney General to work closely with each of you to help you make sure that your department or agency is doing an effective job, and I have asked him to give this matter a high priority. The Department of Justice will shortly be contacting each department and agency to determine what action has been taken to comply with the Attorney General's Title VI regulations. You should insist that your staff cooperate fully with the Department of Justice staff as they carry out this task and their other responsibilities under the Executive Order.

Finally, as you know, Title VI was intended to provide an administrative mechanism for insuring equal treatment in Federal programs. Consequently, administrative proceedings leading to fund terminations are the preferred method of enforcing Title VI, and this sanction must be utilized in appropriate cases. There may be some instances, however, where litigation is in order. You must make sure such cases are referred to the Department of Justice. The effective use of the sanctions provided by Title VI is an essential element of this Administration's effort to guarantee that Federal funds do not flow to discriminatory programs.

Carter achieved a foreign policy victory in March 1977 that was supported by the Congressional Black Caucus (CBC). The United Nations had instituted sanctions against the white majority–governed country of Rhodesia (now modern-day Zimbabwe and Zambia) in 1966. The Rhodesian government remained under control by white supremacists even though Rhodesia declared independence from Great Britain in 1965. Due to the Byrd Amendment that was passed in 1971, the United States had been importing chrome from the country. Carter was able to convince Congress to repeal the amendment and support enforcement of the embargo.

Due to school integration, many elementary and high schools labeling themselves "Christian academies" were opened in southern states. Some were really all-white schools using religion as an excuse for their existence. In 1978, the Internal Revenue Service (IRS) announced that it would close such schools by taking away their tax-exempt status if they were actually found to be segregated schools. The Supreme Court had already ruled in the case *Runyon v. McCrary*, 427 U.S. 160 (1976) against private schools discriminating on the basis of race. In 1978, Prince Edward Academy in Virginia lost its tax-exempt status when it was found to be refusing black students. Opposition to the IRS was fierce, and in 1979 Congress placed an appropriation limit on the Department of Treasury so that the IRS could not implement its policy against private religious schools. Ronald Reagan ended the guideline when he became president. The initial move by the IRS is credited with starting the Religious Right Movement in the United States and specifically its involvement in politics.

Carter expressed his support of historically black colleges and universities (HBCUs) during remarks at a meeting of the United Negro College Fund on November 11, 1977:

> One of the obvious purposes is to give a superb education to those students in our Nation who could not otherwise afford it. Another one is to preserve the uniqueness of a curriculum and a student body commitment that mirror quite often the yearnings and the frustrations and the desires and the hopes and the dreams and aspirations of families of those students who, because of racial prejudice and discrimination, did not have a chance for a good education or to broaden their hearts and their minds. And in many ways these modern-day students of minority groups represent not only themselves but they represent their families and their other ancestors who have been so severely deprived. (Carter 1977)

Carter was an advocate of Affirmative Action. When asked during an interview on April 5, 1978, if he felt it was a form of reverse discrimination he said,

> Most Americans, particularly myself as a southerner, can still see the very difficult circumstances under which minority families live on the average—there are obvious exceptions both ways—because of past legal discrimination, plus the illegal discrimination that still exists in some areas. That's why, under civil service reform, under equal employment opportunity program reform, we're trying to root out those last vestiges of discrimination in government and set a pattern for the private sector. (Carter 1978)

The president's views were in line with that of the Supreme Court at the time. On October 12, 1977, the court heard the case *Regents of the University of California v. Bakke,* 438 U.S. 265 (1978), in which a white plaintiff argued that he was not admitted while the university system admitted less qualified black applicants. The state set aside admission slots for blacks as part of its affirmative action program. The Supreme Court ruled on June 28, 1978, that racial quotas were not allowed but that race could be used as one of several factors in admission policies. The amicus brief (supported by those with special interest in the case) filed by the U.S. solicitor general on behalf of the Carter administration on October 3, 1977, outlined support for affirmative action to remedy past discrimination as well as opposition to strict set-asides.

Another important Supreme Court ruling that took place during Carter's administration was its ruling in the case *United Steelworkers of America, AFL-CIO v. Weber,* 444 U.S. 888 (1979). The court ruled that employers could favor women and minorities in their hiring practices as part of their affirmative action plans to correct past discrimination. Further, this was not a violation of the Civil Rights Act of 1964; however, these programs must be temporary and must not violate the rights of white employees. In this case, the training program under question was open to all races, although the plaintiff's complaint was based on his company offering training to blacks and whites on a one-to-one basis.

The relationship between Carter and the Congressional Black Caucus somewhat soured when the president initially did not support the Humphrey and Hawkins full-employment bill, an amendment to the Employment Act of 1946 signed by President Harry S. Truman. The proposed law initially set a goal of 3 percent unemployment within four years of its passage. However, Carter was leery of the cost of implementation and the ability to achieve such a lofty goal. The proposed bill was watered down by the time Carter signed it on October 27, 1978, and was criticized for being a symbolic versus material law to combat unemployment. The aggressive goals originally proposed were not part of the final law, as "full unemployment" was not clearly defined, and guaranteed job provisions that allowed someone to sue if not given a job were removed.

Although Carter was clearly in favor of desegregation, particularly in schools, he did not favor the use of busing. During an interview with reporters on September 23, 1980, he outlined his views:

> I'm against busing, and Jim Corman is against busing, and others are, too. I have never known a massive busing system that was mandated in this country to work with effectiveness. Both the minority parents and students and those in the majority races in a particular community soon find out that the mandatory massive busing programs just do not work.

> What is necessary under the American law and the Constitution is that if the school boards and the parents and the teachers cannot come up with a way to treat the minority students fairly and equitably and give them equal quality of education, then the courts move in as a last resort and mandate that students be bused to one another's schools. That's a last resort that ought to be

avoided. And in my judgment, the best thing that parents and teachers and others can do to avoid the injection of the Federal courts into the situation is to guarantee equality of opportunity in the school systems as they exist.

But I'm against massive busing, do not think it works, and have to acknowledge the fact that as President I'm sworn to uphold the law once it's implemented by the courts. That summarizes it. And my hope is that in Los Angeles and other places this massive busing can be avoided. (Carter 1980b)

On August 8, 1980, Carter issued Executive Order 12232 that supported increased federal funding to HBCUs. This support from the federal government began under President Richard Nixon. Carter's order also led to the establishment of the White House Initiative on HBCUs within the Department of Education. Carter's order outlined the following:

By the authority vested in me as President by the Constitution of the United States of America, and in order to overcome the effects of discriminatory treatment and to strengthen and expand the capacity of historically Black colleges and universities to provide quality education, it is hereby ordered as follows:

1-101. The Secretary of Education shall implement a Federal initiative designed to achieve a significant increase in the participation by historically Black colleges and universities in Federally sponsored programs. This initiative shall seek to identify, reduce, and eliminate barriers which may have unfairly resulted in reduced participation in, and reduced benefits from, Federally sponsored programs.

1-102. The Secretary of Education shall, in consultation with the Director of the Office of Management and Budget and the heads of the other Executive agencies, establish annual goals for each agency. The purpose of these goals shall be to increase the ability of historically Black colleges and universities to participate in Federally sponsored programs.

1-103. Executive agencies shall review their programs to determine the extent to which historically Black colleges and universities are unfairly precluded from participation in Federally sponsored programs.

1-104. Executive agencies shall identify the statutory authorities under which they can provide relief from specific inequities and disadvantages identified and documented in the agency programs.

1-105. Each Executive agency shall review its current programs and practices and initiate new efforts to increase the participation of historically Black colleges and universities in the programs of the agency. Particular attention should be given to identifying and eliminating unintended regulatory barriers. Procedural barriers, including those which result in such colleges and universities not receiving notice of the availability of Federally sponsored programs, should also be eliminated.

1-106. The head of each Executive agency shall designate an immediate subordinate who will be responsible for implementing the agency responsibilities set forth in this Order. In each Executive agency there shall be an agency liaison to the Secretary of Education for implementing this Order.

1-107. (a) The Secretary of Education shall ensure that an immediate subordinate is responsible for implementing the provisions of this Order.

(b) The Secretary shall ensure that each President of a historically Black college or university is given the opportunity to comment on the implementation of the initiative established by this Order.

1-108. The Secretary of Education shall submit an annual report to the President. The report shall include the levels of participation by historically Black colleges and universities in the programs of each Executive agency. The report will also include any appropriate recommendations for improving the Federal response directed by this Order.

Carter strongly supported policies to ensure equal rights in housing. He held a reception for the CBC at the White House on September 25, 1980, and outlined two priorities that were being considered in Congress:

One is to implement a bill that was passed in 1968 to guarantee Americans equality in seeking adequate housing. We must have enforcement powers for the Fair Housing Act. This is the most significant civil rights legislation of the last 10 years, and I ask you to help us all get it passed through the United States Senate before this Congress adjourns for the year. It's crucial. We must have it.

And the other request I have to you is to remember that although we've made great strides forward in making available to Americans 8 1/2 million more new jobs, 1.3 million of those jobs being for black people, we still have an extremely high unemployment rate among young minority citizens of this country. We must provide additional help for them, because as the economic recovery takes place, many people can go back to the jobs they had, but too many young black Americans have never had a job to which they can return. And a $2 billion program on our youth bill now before the Senate must pass. That's the other item on the agenda that I want to discuss with you, and I ask you to join with me as a full partner in getting this legislation passed. (Carter 1980a)

June is now recognized as African-American Music Appreciation Month. This tradition was started by Carter, who decreed on June 7, 1979, that June would be recognized as Black Music Month. In his remarks commemorating the recognition and honoring the Black Music Association, Carter stated:

It's important, in my opinion, for our own Nation and the rest of the world to know the importance that the President of the United States and his family and friends attach to black music, because in many ways, the feelings of our own black citizens throughout the history of our country has been accurately expressed in the music. And it presents a kind of history of our Nation when you go back and see the evolution of black music. It's meant a lot to me as a young boy and a young man and adult in Georgia. . . .

And I've learned one thing about black music, and that is that people who talk before the performance are not appreciated nearly so much as the performance itself. So, I'm ready now to join the audience, but to express on behalf of the 220 million people in our country my thanks to superb black musicians throughout the history of our country and my congratulations to the Black Music Association for spending your first birthday party here at the White House with us. (Carter 1979)

On October 12, 1977, Carter signed the Community Reinvestment Act. The law was passed to combat discriminatory credit practices by banks and thrift institutions against those living and having businesses in low-income neighborhoods. The president attempted to persuade Congress to make amendments to the Fair Housing Act in 1980. It passed the House of Representatives but not the Senate. On December 31, 1980, Carter issued Executive Order 12259, "Leadership and Coordination of Fair Housing in Federal Programs." The order strengthened the Fair Housing Act originally passed as part of the Civil Rights Act of 1968 by stipulating the following:

- reemphasizes HUD's authority and responsibility to administer the Fair Housing Act;
- stipulates the leadership and coordination role of HUD and the responsibilities of all other agencies with respect to the preparation and implementation of regulations and procedures which will further fair housing;
- requires all agencies to use informal and formal means to remedy violations of regulations or procedures adopted pursuant to the order;
- sets a timetable for implementation of these requirements by all Federal agencies;
- directs HUD to submit an annual report to the President noting the progress made by the Federal Government in furthering fair housing objectives. (Carter 1981)

As outlined in his remarks to the CBC, Carter also tried to obtain Congress's approval of a $2 billion youth bill to tackle the high unemployment rate of African American youths. This also failed in Congress in 1980. During his term in office Carter had a relatively poor relationship with Congress, even though both chambers were controlled by Democrats. He was quick to criticize Congress in public, increasing tensions. Because of his inability to get passage on some bills supporting African Americans, Carter faced criticism from the CBC. The CBC felt that he spent more time on issues such as the Strategic Arms Limitation Talks (SALT) Treaty, the Panama Canal Treaty, and energy than advancing civil rights.

On September 24, 1965, President Lyndon B. Johnson had issued Executive Order 11246 that divided the responsibilities of preventing discrimination in federal contracts and hiring from the single President's Committee on Equal Employment

Opportunity that had been created by President Kennedy under Executive Order 10925 on March 6, 1961. Under Johnson's executive order, the EEOC and the Office of Federal Contract Compliance (which in 1975 was renamed the Office of Federal Contract Compliance Programs) were created. On October 5, 1978, Carter issued Executive Order 12086 to transfer under the Department of Labor functions across the government related to affirmative action and contract compliance as well as equal employment opportunity all under the Department of Labor. This created the Office of Federal Contract Compliance Programs all under the Department of Labor.

Civil rights leader A. Philip Randolph died on May 16, 1979. He founded and led the Brotherhood of Sleeping Car Porters in 1925; led the March on Washington for Jobs and Freedom on August 28, 1963; and was instrumental in President Franklin D. Roosevelt issuing Executive Order 8802 in 1941 to ban discrimination in defense industries. On May 17, 1979, President Carter issued an official statement on the death of the civil rights leader:

> It can be said of few individuals in our time that they helped transform the face of the American Nation. A. Philip Randolph was one of those giants. His leadership in the trade union and civil rights movements has left an indelible mark on almost every area of our national life. A. Philip Randolph helped sweep away longstanding barriers of discrimination and segregation in industry and labor unions, in our schools and armed services, in politics and government.

> For each new generation of civil rights leaders, he was an inspiration and an example. His dignity and integrity, his eloquence, his devotion to nonviolence, and his unshakable commitment to justice all helped shape the ideals and spirit of the civil rights movement.

> His voice and inspiration will long be missed, but America will always be a more just, more humane, and more decent nation because A. Philip Randolph lived among us.

Carter also spoke at the memorial for Randolph held at the Metropolitan African Methodist Episcopal Church in Washington, D.C., on June 3, 1979. On October 10, 1980, Carter announced the establishment of two African American sites in recognition of the contributions of blacks. In remarks made by the president on October 10, 1980, he outlined two bills:

> First, I will sign a bill that designates and establishes the Martin Luther King, Junior, National Historic Site and Preservation District in Atlanta to preserve the area where Dr. Martin Luther King, Jr., lived and worked and worshiped and where he's buried, as a living memorial to the civil rights movement which he came to symbolize.

> The second bill establishes a Boston African American National Historical Site, including the African-American Meeting House, which was the center of the 19th century free African American community on Beacon Hill. That bill also provides for the establishment of a national center for the study of

Afro-American history and culture with headquarters in Wilberforce, Ohio. (Carter 1980c)

In 1980, President Carter lost his bid for reelection due in part to the Iranian Hostage Crisis and surging unemployment as the economy worsened. He still received 86 percent of the nonwhite vote. Carter remained active in politics after leaving office. He has been a tireless worker for Habitat for Humanity, building homes for needy families. He has also become a noted author by writing over 30 books, many of them best sellers. In perhaps his most notable achievement, Carter was awarded the Nobel Peace Prize in 2002 "for his decades of untiring effort to find peaceful solutions to international conflicts, to advance democracy and human rights, and to promote economic and social development" ("The Nobel Prize for 2002" 2002).

FURTHER READING

Califano, Joseph A., Jr. 1981. *Governing America: An Insider's Report from the White House and the Cabinet.* New York: Simon and Schuster.

Carter, Jimmy. 1977. "United Negro College Fund Remarks at a Meeting With Officials of the Fund, November 11, 1977." The American Presidency Project, http://www.presidency.ucsb.edu/ws/index.php?pid=6917.

Carter, Jimmy. 1978. "Interview with the President: Remarks in an Interview Lot 'Black Perspective on the News,' April 5, 1978." The American Presidency Project, http://www.presidency.ucsb.edu/ws/index.php?pid=30620.

Carter, Jimmy. 1979. "Black Music Association Remarks at a White House Dinner Honoring the Association, June 7, 1979." The American Presidency Project, http://www.presidency.ucsb.edu/ws/?pid=32450.

Carter, Jimmy. 1980a. "Congressional Black Caucus Remarks at a White House Reception for Members of the Caucus, September 25, 1980." The American Presidency Project, http://www.presidency.ucsb.edu/ws/?pid=45142.

Carter, Jimmy. 1980b. "Los Angeles, California: Remarks in an Interview with Reporters from Newscenter 4, KNBC-TV, September 23, 1980." The American Presidency Project, http://www.presidency.ucsb.edu/ws/index.php?pid=45118.

Carter, Jimmy. 1980c. "Martin Luther King, Junior, and Boston African American National Historic Sites Remarks on Signing H.R. 7218 and H.R. 7434 into Law, October 10, 1980." The American Presidency Project, http://www.presidency.ucsb.edu/ws/index.php?pid=45253.

Eizenstat, Stuart E. 2018. *President Carter: The White House Years.* New York: St. Martin's.

Hargrove, Erwin C. 1988. *Jimmy Carter as President: Leadership and the Politics of the Public Good.* Baton Rouge: Louisiana State University Press.

Morris, Kenneth E. 1996. *Jimmy Carter: American Moralist.* Athens: University of Georgia Press.

"The Nobel Peace Prize for 2002." 2002. Nobel Prize, https://www.nobelprize.org/nobel_prizes/peace/laureates/2002/.

Padgett, Dorothy. 2016. *Jimmy Carter: Elected President with Pocket Change and Peanuts.* Macon, GA: Mercer University Press.

Selizer, Julian E. 2010. *Jimmy Carter: The American Presidents Series; The 39th President, 1977–1981.* New York: Times Books.

Ronald Wilson Reagan

40th President of the United States
Presidential Term: January 20, 1981–January 20, 1989
Political Party: Republican
Vice President: George H. W. Bush

Ronald Reagan was the 40th president of the United States. Reagan won the election in a landslide victory. President Reagan was criticized for his administration's stances on African Americans, women, and Hispanics. (U.S. Department of Defense)

Ronald Wilson Reagan was born on February 6, 1911, in Tampico, Illinois, and grew up in Dixon, Illinois. He began his campaign for the 1980 presidential election in Neshoba County, Mississippi. This is the same city where civil rights activists James Chaney, Andrew Goodman, and Michael Schwerner were murdered on June 21, 1964. Before an all-white crowd at the county's state fair on August 3, 1980, Reagan declared his support for states' rights and curbing federal powers: "I still believe the answer to any problem lies with the people. I believe in states' rights and I believe in people doing as much as they can for themselves at the community level and at the private level. I believe we have distorted the balance of our government today by giving powers that were never intended to be given in the Constitution to that federal establishment" (Hayward 2001, 696).

Reagan's views on civil rights were well known, as he opposed the Civil Rights Act of 1964, the Voting Rights Act of 1965, and the Fair Housing Act of 1968.

Incumbent president Jimmy Carter commented on Reagan's speech while visiting Ebenezer Baptist Church in Atlanta, Georgia, where Dr. Martin Luther King, Jr. was the former preacher. On September 16, 1980, Carter stated:

> You've seen in this campaign the stirrings of hate and the rebirth of code words like "States rights" in a speech in Mississippi, in a campaign reference to the Ku Klux Klan, relating to the South. That is a message that creates a cloud on the political horizon. Hatred has no place in this country. Racism has no place in this country. Daddy King says in his book, "Nothing that a

man does makes him lower than when he allows himself to hate anyone. Hatred is not needed," he says, "to stamp out evil. Despite what some people have been taught, people can accomplish all things God wills in this world. Hate cannot." (Carter 1980)

Still, Carter would go on to lose the election to Reagan. Carter's receipt of 88 percent of the black vote was not enough to overcome Reagan's national appeal with white voters, to include Reagan winning southern states that had voted for Carter in the 1976 presidential election. Reagan's win in the South was attributed to his adoption of the Southern Strategy that had been used by President Richard Nixon, based on words and rhetoric that would attract the votes of southern whites. Reagan also ran on the campaign slogan "Make American Great Again," referring to the need to improve the economy and reduce inflation. This slogan would be recycled and used by Republican Party candidate Donald Trump in 2016. The slogan also became a tool when Trump's marketing machine put it on red baseball caps and sold them to the public.

Once in office, President Reagan appointed one African American cabinet member, Samuel R. Pierce Jr., as secretary of housing and urban development. Pierce gained the nickname "Silent Sam" by civil rights leaders due to his silence on issues important to African Americans. The cabinet did not include any women. Reagan only appointed one African American, Lawrence W. Pierce, to the 83 federal appeals court positions he filled while in office and only one African American, Clarence Thomas (who was later nominated to the U.S. Supreme Court by President George H. W. Bush in 1991), in the 32 appointments he made to federal courts of appeal.

Reagan appointed conservatives to top posts in his administration. For example, he appointed Clarence M. Pendleton to chair the U.S. Civil Rights Commission. Although an African American, Pendleton characterized affirmative action as "immoral," was against busing to combat segregation, and did not support racial quotas or set-asides. He also did not support equal pay for men and women and described comparable pay for women as "the looniest idea since Looney Tunes came on the screen" (Associated Press 1984).

Maxine Waters, congresswoman from California, espoused the views of other black leaders in describing the few blacks whom Reagan did appoint as "Uncle Toms" and "Aunt Tomasinas." The appointees were not well known in the African American community, had no record of supporting black causes, and were not good at selling the intended policies of the Reagan administration to the black community. Reagan made three Supreme Court appointments that created an even more conservative court, causing concern for black leaders: William Rehnquist's promotion to chief justice of the Supreme Court in 1986, Sandra Day O'Conner (the first woman to serve on the Supreme Court) in 1981, and Antonin Scalia in 1986.

A troubling figure in Reagan's administration was Henry LeRoy "Lee" Atwater. He served as one of the president's aides and managed Reagan's reelection campaign in 1984 (and also managed George H. W. Bush's campaign in the presidential election of 1988) before becoming chairman of the Republican National Committee. Atwater gave an interview in 1981 to a political science professor at

Case Western Reserve University in which he stated the following in explaining the Southern Strategy to appeal to white voters:

> You start out in 1954 by saying, "N----r, n----r, n----r." By 1968 you can't say "n----r"—that hurts you. Backfires. So you say stuff like forced busing, states' rights and all that stuff. You're getting so abstract now [that] you're talking about cutting taxes, and all these things you're talking about are totally economic things and a byproduct of them is [that] blacks get hurt worse than whites. And subconsciously maybe that is part of it. I'm not saying that. But I'm saying that if it is getting that abstract, and that coded, that we are doing away with the racial problem one way or the other. You follow me—because obviously sitting around saying, "We want to cut this," is much more abstract than even the busing thing, and a hell of a lot more abstract than "n----r, n----r." (Singer 1997, 13–14)

Reagan attempted to gain support of the NAACP by addressing its 72nd Annual Convention in Denver, Colorado, on June 29, 1981. In his address, he outlined areas of his intended policies that were consistent with the desires of African Americans. For example, the following is an excerpt from his speech:

> Our dialog must also include discussions on how we can best protect the rights and privileges of all our citizens. My Administration will root out any case of government discrimination against minorities and uphold and enforce the laws that protect them. I emphasize that we will not retreat on the nation's commitment to equal treatment of all citizens. Now, that, in my view, is the primary responsibility of national government. The Attorney General is now carefully studying the decennial redistricting plans being submitted under the current Voting Rights Act. As soon as we have all the information there will be a decision regarding extension of the Act.

> Until a decision is announced, you should know this: I regard voting as the most sacred right of free men and women. We have not sacrificed and fought and toiled to protect that right so that now we can sit back and permit a barrier to come between a secret ballot and any citizen who makes a choice to cast it. Nothing, nothing will change that as long as I am in a position to uphold the Constitution of the United States.

> In the months ahead, our dialog also will include tough and realistic questions about the role of the federal government in the black community. I'm not satisfied with its results, and I don't think you are either. And the failures of the past have been particularly hard on the minority poor, because their hopes have failed as surely as the federal programs that built those hopes. But I must not be the only one who has questions about government policies. (Reagan 1981c)

Reagan issued Executive Order 12320 on September 15, 1981, to support historically black colleges and universities. This was an executive action began by President Richard Nixon and then continued by President Jimmy Carter. The first two sections of Executive Order 12320 outlined the stance of the Reagan administration on this issue:

Section 1. The Secretary of Education shall supervise annually the development of a Federal program designed to achieve a significant increase in the participation by historically Black colleges and universities in Federally sponsored programs. This program shall seek to identify, reduce, and eliminate barriers which may have unfairly resulted in reduced participation in, and reduced benefits from, Federally sponsored programs. This program will also seek to involve private sector institutions in strengthening historically Black colleges.

Sec. 2. Annually, each Executive Department and those Executive agencies Designated by the Secretary of Education shall establish annual plans to increase the ability of historically Black colleges and universities to participate in Federally sponsored programs. These plans shall consist of measurable objectives of proposed agency actions to fulfill this Order and shall be submitted at such time and in such form as the Secretary of Education shall designate. In consultation with participating Executive agencies, the Secretary of Education shall undertake a review of these plans and develop an integrated Annual Federal Plan for Assistance to Historically Black Colleges for consideration by the President and the Cabinet Council on Human Resources (composed of the Vice President, the Secretaries of Health and Human Services, Agriculture, Labor, Housing and Urban Development, and Education, the Attorney General, the Counsellor to the President, and the White House Chief of Staff).

One of the first political and legal issues that Reagan tackled when he took office was affirmative action. He saw associated policies and programs as supporting "reverse discrimination" against whites. During a news conference on January 29, 1981, he stated, "I think there are some things . . . that may even be distorted in the practice, such as some affirmative action programs becoming quota systems. And I'm old enough to remember when quotas existed in the United States for the purpose of discrimination, and I don't want to see that happen again" (Reagan 1981a).

When Reagan took office, the Supreme Court had recently ruled in *United Steelworkers of America v. Weber,* 443 U.S. 193 (1979), that affirmative action programs with preferences to women and minorities were constitutional as long as they were needed to reverse past discrimination, were temporary in nature, were flexible toward nonminorities, and did not bar the hiring of nonminorities. Yet, critics argued, the court's decision supported reverse discrimination. The Reagan administration agreed and saw affirmative action programs as setting racial quotas and cut funding to the Equal Employment Opportunity Commission (EEOC) and the Civil Rights Division of the Department of Justice. This resulted in the EEOC filing 60 percent fewer cases by 1984. The Supreme Court then ruled in *Fullilove v. Klutznick,* 448 U.S. 448 (1980), that Congress could use spending to combat past discrimination and that 10 percent of federal funds for local public works programs could be set aside for minority-owned companies. This supported the use of quotas.

In 1982 Reagan and his attorney general, William French Smith, wanted to ease state restrictions in the renewal of the Voting Rights Act of 1965. Reagan had previously stated in 1980 that the act was humiliating to southern states and should be applied to all 50 states. Part of this desired plan was to pass a 10-year extension that would require plaintiffs to prove that any discrimination they faced was intentional and also have the law apply to all states and not just southern states, which were the target of the original act given their history of racial discrimination in voting.

A grassroots movement and legislative campaign forced Reagan to agree to a 25-year extension of the act and include stronger provisions. Section 2 of the act that prohibits discrimination against minorities whether intentional or not was made permanent. The president's advisers informed him that he was losing support from both minorities and moderate whites because of a perception that he was prejudiced against blacks. The president then invited black leaders to the signing ceremony of the amendment on June 30, 1982, in an attempt to gain their support. Still, NAACP president Benjamin Hooks and Operation Push president Jesse Jackson Sr. were among the civil rights leaders who commented on the president's reluctance and delay in signing the amendment extension. Besides Hooks and Jackson, other notable blacks at the signing included Joseph Lowery, head of the Southern Christian Leadership Conference; Urban League president John Edward Jacob; and Coretta Scott King, widow of Dr. Martin Luther King, Jr. Dr. King was present when President Lyndon B. Johnson signed the original Voting Rights Act on August 6, 1965.

On October 14, 1982, Reagan declared a War on Drugs in an announcement of federal initiatives against drug trafficking and organized crime. Declaring the drug trade a threat to national security, the Reagan administration established tougher sentencing for even minor infractions, which also led to the seizure of cash and property of those convicted. The perception of this policy on drugs depicted blacks as the primary culprits of both drug use and distribution, particularly given the increased use of crack in the inner cities; the rhetoric on the topic, however, ignored the rampant use of cocaine by whites. Blacks were targeted for arrests and given harsher prison sentences due to the establishment of mandatory minimum sentences. The number of blacks, particularly black males, dramatically increased in prisons. According to data from the Sentencing Project (2016), "The state and federal prison population grew from 218,466 in 1974 to 1,508,636 in 2014, which is a nearly 600 percent increase. For comparison, the overall United States population has increased just 51 percent since 1974" (Carroll 2016).

Critics contended that federal funding was going to countries known to be leading producers of cocaine that was then trafficked into the United States. First Lady Nancy Reagan started the "Just Say No" program that promoted an antidrug message to children. This was indicative of the efforts by the Reagan administration to focus on drug users rather than drug producers and distributors. This supply-side focus on drug crimes was seen as ineffective in achieving results.

As the media increased its coverage of celebrities dying from drug overdoses, such as black University of Maryland basketball star Len Bias, and as politicians used communication strategies to increase fear in parents, Congress passed the

Anti-Drug Abuse Act in 1986. The act authorized billions of dollars in spending, set the first ever mandatory minimum sentencing for possession of cocaine, and established minimum standards for crack cocaine offenses. For example, this zero-tolerance policy resulted in a minimum sentence of five years for possession of 5 grams of crack cocaine or 500 grams of cocaine. The disparate impact on African Americans was devastating. According to the American Civil Liberties Union (ACLU), "In 1986, before the enactment of federal mandatory minimum sentencing for crack cocaine offenses, the average federal drug sentence for African Americans was 11% higher than for whites. Four years later, the average federal drug sentence for African Americans was 49% higher" (Vagins and McCurdy 2006).

The Reagan administration, and particularly Drug Enforcement Agency official Robert Putnam, assisted in pushing stories about "crack babies" and "crack whores" and the resulting crimes of drug use. However, rather than reducing drug crime, the rates of drug-related crimes continued to increase. As a result, Congress passed the Omnibus Anti-Drug Abuse Act of 1988 to target crack cocaine abuse. Among other stipulations, the act established a 5-year mandatory minimum sentence and a 20-year maximum sentence for possession of five grams or more of crack cocaine.

The issue of tax-exempt status for religious universities accused of discrimination began under President Jimmy Carter and continued during the Reagan administration. The Reagan administration tried to intervene on behalf of religious schools before pending cases reached the Supreme Court. This issue was part of the 1980 presidential election when, as part of its platform, the Republican Party announced that it would "halt the unconstitutional regulatory vendetta launched by Mr. Carter's IRS [Internal Revenue Service] Commissioner against independent schools" (Weber, Hiers, and Flesken 2016, 125). This was an appeal to conservative republicans and Christian far-right religious leaders, such as Bob Jones and Jerry Falwell, who were active in the election and helped Republican candidates to win the Senate in 1980. These religious leaders banded to form the Moral Majority.

On January 8, 1982, the U.S. Treasury Department announced that in acting "without further guidance from Congress, the Internal Revenue Service will no longer revoke or deny tax-exempt status for religious, charitable, educational, or scientific organizations on the grounds that they don't conform with fundamental public policies" (Devins 1983, 153). A motion was filed the same day for the Supreme Court to vacate decisions on Bob Jones University and Goldsboro Christian Schools. Both had policies and practices deemed racially discriminatory toward blacks in admissions and were both threatened by the IRS to have their tax-exempt statuses revoked. The Reagan administration restored tax-exempt status to both schools.

Reagan and the Department of Justice were barraged by criticism from civil rights groups, Democratic leaders, some Republicans, members of the Justice Department, and the media. The president attempted to quell critical outrage by asking Congress to pass legislation prohibiting racially discriminatory organizations from tax-exempt status. His administration's leadership claimed that the president did not support racial discrimination but had concerns over administrative agencies that exercised powers that were only delegated to Congress in the U.S.

Constitution. Congress refused to take up any new legislation because it felt that the matter was sufficiently settled by laws already in place that barred such discrimination. However, the Reagan administration and some members of Congress still argued that the IRS had no power granted by Congress to revoke tax-exempt status. The Supreme Court received petitions from many groups to hear the case, including the NAACP and the ACLU.

On October 12, 1982, the Supreme Court heard arguments in the case *Bob Jones University v. United States,* 461 U.S. 574 (1983). This was actually two cases being heard together. The first issue was whether Bob Jones University, a private religious university in Greenville, South Carolina, could retain its tax-exempt status from the IRS while forbidding interracial dating and marriage. Students involved in such relationships were not allowed to attend the university. University officials argued that this was against the school's interpretation of the Bible and that the IRS had no right to revoke its tax-exempt status because of the school's stance. The second issue was the Goldsboro Christian Schools' racially discriminatory practice of admitting white applicants only, resulting in being denied tax-exempt status and being required to pay federal social security and unemployment taxes. The Supreme Court ruled in favor of the IRS's rejection of tax-exempt status to both schools. The court held that the schools both engaged in discriminatory practices and violated national public policy. However, the court outlined that its ruling was specific to schools and not to purely religions organizations such as churches. Bob Jones University lost its tax-exempt status, as the ban on interracial relationships was not lifted until 2000 following a media uproar after an announcement about a pending visit by President George W. Bush.

In 1983, Reagan faced criticism as his administration abandoned the review of cases with civil rights violations. Mary Frances Berry was appointed to the U.S. Commission on Civil Rights by President Carter. Reagan removed her and two others in 1983 for criticizing the administration's stances on blacks, women, and Hispanics. Berry wrote a scathing report on the commission:

> The commission has for the most part abandoned its responsibility to monitor the activities of the civil rights enforcement agencies of the Federal government. Not one report or statement about any Federal body has been issued since the takeover. Indeed, the commission has become so much a public relations operation for the Administration that its members have been referred to in the media as Administration spokespersons. (Booker 2017)

The three remaining commission members were all Republican. President Reagan was criticized for his actions by both Democratic and Republican members of Congress and the NAACP. Since the members were serving in an independent agency, some questioned if the president had the authority to remove members without Senate approval. Berry sued Reagan in federal court and was able to retain her seat. Reagan's appointees Commissioners Linda Chavez and Clarence Pendleton Jr. were openly critical of civil rights, affirmative action, and black leaders. Although an African American, Pendleton made such statements as "Civil rights won't make you educated. They won't make you rich. And they won't make you socially acceptable" (Williams 1988).

Others in the Reagan administration were also in strong opposition to affirmative action. Reagan appointed Edwin Meese as attorney general of the United States in 1985. Meese had served as chief of staff when Reagan was governor of California and as a counselor to the president during his first term in office. Meese was a conservative and staunchly opposed affirmative action. On September 17, 1985, he made the statement that "the idea you can use discrimination in the form of racially preferential quotas, goals, and set-asides to remedy the lingering social effects of past discrimination makes no sense in principle; in practice, it is nothing short of a legal, moral, and constitutional tragedy" (Booker 2017).

On November 2, 1983, Reagan signed legislation establishing Dr. Martin Luther King, Jr. Day as a federal holiday. This was not without political controversy. The president did not support the proposed law, citing cost concerns in establishing it as a holiday. However, Congress had passed the legislation with a majority vote of 338 to 90 in the House of Representatives and 78 to 22 in the Senate. If Reagan had not signed it, the law would have been passed with a congressional override of a presidential veto. The holiday was first observed in the United States on January 20, 1986.

Reagan won reelection in 1984 against Democratic contender Walter Mondale, who had served as vice president under Jimmy Carter. It was a landslide victory for Reagan, as he won 49 of the 50 states and a record 525 of the 538 electoral votes. It was a historic election in that Mondale's vice presidential running mate was a woman, Geraldine Ferraro, the first woman to appear on a major presidential party ticket. Although Reagan won the election by gaining 59 percent of the overall vote, 91 percent of blacks voted for Mondale.

In 1988, Congress passed the Civil Rights Restoration Act of 1987 after overriding a veto by Reagan. The act, also called the Grove City Act, required all recipients of federal funds to comply with civil rights laws in all areas and not just in the program for which they received federal funding. Thus, the 1987 act amended Title IX of the Education Amendments of 1972, the 1973 Rehabilitation Act, Title VI of the Civil Rights Act of 1964, and the Age Discrimination in Employment Act by extending the law to civil rights compliance in all areas.

Reagan vetoed the act because he felt that it applied unjustifiable enforcement on the states, private businesses, and churches. It was the first veto of a civil rights act since President Andrew Johnson vetoed the Civil Rights Act of 1866. The president vetoed the act even though it passed with widespread bipartisan support, passing in the Senate with a vote of 75 to 14 and in the House with a vote of 315 to 28. The passage of the Civil Rights Restoration Act thus overturned a 1984 ruling by the Supreme Court in the case *Grove City College v. Bell,* 465 U.S. 555 (1984). Grove City College was a private school that only received federal grants for some student scholarships, and the Supreme Court agreed with its argument that only its financial aid department was subject to compliance with the nondiscrimination requirements of Title IX of the Education Amendments of 1972.

Reagan was also criticized for this stance on South Africa and its apartheid policy that sanctioned racial segregation and discrimination. Since 1972 Congress had been attempting to pass a law imposing sanctions, including U.S. investments and trade, on South Africa to force it to end its policy. The Comprehensive

Anti-Apartheid Act was sponsored in 1972 by Senator William Victor Roth Jr., a Republican from Delaware, and initiated by Congressman Ronald V. Dellums, a Democrat from California. The passage of the act was halted by a Republican filibuster in 1985. Reagan did not support the act, as he viewed it as an infringement on his authority to lead in foreign policy. He also said that sanctions would hurt the black population of South Africa, who made up the working class. In a speech given on July 22, 1986, Reagan stated, "The primary victims of an economic boycott of South Africa would be the very people we seek to help. Most of the workers who would lose jobs because of sanctions would be black workers. We do not believe the way to help the people of South Africa is to cripple the economy upon which they and their families depend for survival" (Reagan 1986c).

Yet, it was not forgotten that Reagan had previously outlined support for South Africa. In an interview in 1981, he stated that "a country that has stood by us in every war we've ever fought, a country that, strategically, is essential to the free world in its production of minerals" (Myre 2013). Reagan also espoused a "constructive engagement" strategy with South Africa, designed by his assistant secretary of state for African affairs, Chester Crocker. As South Africa was anticommunist and supported the United States during the Cold War, the Reagan administration sought to increase relations with the South African government. Reagan also criticized Nelson Mandela, the renowned revolutionary and leader who fought apartheid in South Africa, and his African National Congress as using terrorist tactics as well as having goals of creating a communist state. In July 1986 both Republicans and Democrats opposed Reagan, who asked South Africa's president P. W. Botha to establish a timetable for when apartheid would be eliminated and all political prisoners released. Reagan also stated that Mandela should be freed from prison but outlined that sanctions were a "historic act of folly for the United States and the West—out of anguish and frustration and anger—to write off South Africa. . . . As one African leader remarked recently, southern Africa is like zebra. If the white parts are injured, the black parts die too" (Boyd 1986).

The president issued his own set of sanctions that Democrats particularly criticized as being "watered down." The act was reintroduced in 1986 and passed after bipartisan compromise. Reagan vetoed the bill on September 26, 1986, and called it economic warfare. As part of his opposition he stated,

> Let us not forget our purpose. It is not to damage or destroy any economy, but to help the black majority of South Africa and southern Africa enjoy a greater share of the material blessings and bounties their labor has helped to produce—as they secure as well their legitimate political rights. That is why sweeping punitive sanctions are the wrong course to follow, and increased American and Western investment—by firms that are breaking down apartheid by providing equal opportunity for the victims of official discrimination—is the right course to pursue. Our goal is a democratic system in which the rights of majorities, minorities, and individuals are protected by a bill of rights and firm constitutional guarantees. (Reagan 1986a)

The president was criticized not only domestically but also internationally. Antiapartheid South African leader Desmond Tutu said that Reagan would be judged harshly by history. Congress overrode Reagan's veto on September 29, 1986. U.S. sanctions weren't lifted until the South African government passed legislation to end apartheid in 1993.

Mandela was released on February 11, 1990, after serving 27 years in prison because of his antiapartheid efforts. He became president of South Africa in 1994 and served until 1999.

On February 15, 1986, Reagan outlined his administration's focus on welfare reform during a radio address. Although more whites than blacks were on welfare, this was an area that caused a racial divide because of the stereotype of black women being "welfare queens" defrauding the government. Reagan actually began this public controversy over "welfare queens" when he was at a campaign rally in 1976 when he stated, "She used 80 names, 30 addresses, 15 telephone numbers to collect food stamps, Social Security, veterans' benefits for four nonexistent deceased veteran husbands, as well as welfare. Her tax-free cash income alone has been running $150,000 a year" (Black and Sprague 2016). His statement was based on the actual case of Linda Taylor, a Chicago woman accused of welfare fraud in the 1970s. In his 1986 address, Reagan declared the welfare system broken; he argued that the funding given to recipients perpetuated poverty and did not solve the problem of funding to single mothers:

> Perhaps the most insidious effect of welfare is its usurpation of the role of provider. In States where payments are highest, for instance, public assistance for a single mother can amount to much more than the usable income of a minimum wage job. In other words, it can pay for her to quit work. Many families are eligible for substantially higher benefits when the father is not present. What must it do to a man to know that his own children will be better off if he is never legally recognized as their father? Under existing welfare rules, a teenage girl who becomes pregnant can make herself eligible for welfare benefits that will set her up in an apartment of her own, provide medical care, and feed and clothe her. She only has to fulfill one condition— not marry or identify the father. (Reagan 1986b)

The Reagan administration began cutting federal funding to social programs when the president took office in 1981. The number of people receiving food stamps, Medicaid, Aid to Families with Dependent Children, and cash benefits was drastically reduced in 1981 and 1982. The public service employment program was eliminated. Critics contended that the funding cuts to these programs was used to increase military spending and to fund tax cuts to the wealthy and that the results drastically increased the working poor. Reagan's welfare reform policies and his economic programs based on trickle-down economics, or Reaganomics, were seen as negative programs that impacted minorities and the poor. The administration supported tax cuts and government incentives to wealthy individuals and large corporations, believing that they in turn would increase hiring and wages for their workers. In theory, the benefits to the wealthy would trickle down to the middle class and poor.

In 1988 Reagan signed the Fair Housing Amendments Act of 1988, which expanded federal coverage combating housing discrimination prohibited in the original Fair Housing Act of 1968. In his remarks upon signing the act on September 13, 1988, Reagan recognized support for Dr. Martin Luther King, Jr.'s dream in signing "the most important civil rights legislation in 20 years" and also outlined changes based on the amendment to the original law:

> The bill I sign today has a number of significant features. First, the law extends protection to families with children and persons with handicaps and continues to recognize and protect the special needs of the elderly. Second, for the first time, aggrieved parties may avail themselves of an administrative enforcement procedure. Moreover, the administrative law judge may assess penalties against those who discriminate. The penalties are a $10,000 fine for the first violation, $25,000 for the second, and $50,000 for the third. Third, for the first time, in cases initiated by the Department of Justice, the Department may obtain monetary relief for victims and civil penalties of $50,000 for a first violation and $100,000 for subsequent violations. Fourth, the constitutional rights of all parties are protected. Both defendant and plaintiff have the option of a jury trial, or they can agree to the faster, simpler administrative procedure. (Reagan 1988)

Reagan continues to be criticized for his lack of action to address the HIV/AIDS crisis that began in 1981, the very year he took office. He failed to recognize the issue until 1985, when actor Rock Hudson announced that he had the disease and the president was directly asked about the issue by reporters. His response indicated that if he had school-age children, he would not support sending them to school with a child having the disease:

> I can well understand the plight of the parents and how they feel about it. I also have compassion, as I think we all do, for the child that has this and doesn't know and can't have it explained to him why somehow he is now an outcast and can no longer associate with his playmates and schoolmates. On the other hand, I can understand the problem with the parents. It is true that some medical sources had said that this cannot be communicated in any way other than the ones we already know and which would not involve a child being in the school. And yet medicine has not come forth unequivocally and said, This we know for a fact, that it is safe. And until they do, I think we just have to do the best we can with this problem. I can understand both sides of it. (Reagan 1985)

Nancy Reagan was also criticized for not speaking out about the issue or taking steps to sway her husband to take action; meanwhile, she aggressively campaigned against drugs in her "Just Say No" program. President Reagan's communications director, Pat Buchanan, declared that AIDS was "nature's revenge on gay men" (Axelrod-Sokolov 2011). This was in line with similar statements from members of the Christian Right. Reagan did not address the issue in speeches until 1987, although Surgeon General C. Everett Koop went against administration wishes and issued policies and communications that strongly supported education, research, the distribution of condoms and a rejection of mandatory AIDS testing. Reagan's support of research eventually led to increased federal funding for research in

1988. By then thousands had died from the disease in the United States alone, and especially impacted was the African American community.

Reagan was troubled that some considered him a racist or at least unsympathetic to the needs of African Americans. During an interview in 1989, the last year of his presidency, he stated that "One of the great things that I have suffered is this feeling that somehow I'm on the other side" of the Civil Rights Movement (Beckman 2014, 155). Ronald Reagan passed away on June 5, 2004, in California.

FURTHER READING

Associated Press. 1984. "Concept of Pay Based on Worth Is the 'Looniest,' Rights Chief Says." *New York Times,* November 17, http://www.nytimes.com/1984/11/17/us /concept-of-pay-based-on-worth-is-the-looniest-rights-chief-says.html.

Beckman, James A., ed. 2014. *Controversies in Affirmative Action: Historical Dimensions.* Santa Barbara, CA: Praeger.

Black, Rachel, and Aleta Sprague. 2016. "The Rise and Reign of the Welfare Queen." *New America,* September 22, https://www.newamerica.org/weekly/edition-135 /rise-and-reign-welfare-queen/.

Booker, Christopher B. 2017. *The Black Presidential Nightmare: African-Americans and Presidents, 1789–2016.* Bloomington, IN: Xlibris.

Boyd, Gerald M. 1986. "President Opposes Additional Steps on South Africa." *New York Times,* July 23, 1986, https://www.nytimes.com/1986/07/23/world/president -opposes-additional-steps-on-south-africa.html.

Brands, H. W. 2015. *Reagan: The Life.* New York: First Anchor Books.

Carroll, Lauren. 2016. "How the War on Drugs Affected Incarceration Rates." Politifact, July 10, http://www.politifact.com/truth-o-meter/statements/2016/jul/10/cory-booker /how-war-drugs-affected-incarceration-rates/.

Carter, Jimmy. 1980. "Atlanta, Georgia Remarks at a Meeting with Southern Black Leaders, September 16, 1980." The American Presidency Project, http://www .presidency.ucsb.edu/ws/index.php?pid=45059.

Devins, Neal. 1983. "Tax Exemptions for Racially Discriminatory Private Schools: A Legislative Proposal." Faculty Publications, College of William and Mary, http: //www.academia.edu/28479250/Tax_Exemptions_for_Racially_Discriminatory _Private_Schools_A_Legislative_Proposal.

Edwards, Lee. 2005. *The Essential Ronald Reagan: A Profile in Courage, Justice, and Wisdom.* Lanham, MD: Rowman and Littlefield.

Hayward, Steven F. 2001. *The Age of Reagan: The Fall of the Old Liberal Order: 1964–1980.* New York: Crown Publishing Group.

Johns, Andrew L. 2015. *A Companion to Ronald Reagan.* Malden, MA: Wiley.

Myre, Greg. 2013. "Now Praised by Presidents, Mandela Wasn't Always Admired In The U.S." National Public Radio, https://www.npr.org/sections/parallels/2013/12/09/249 708436/now-praised-by-presidents-mandela-wasnt-always-admired-in-the-u-s.

Reagan, Ronald. 1981a. "The President's News Conference, January 29, 1981." The American Presidency Project, http://www.presidency.ucsb.edu/ws/?pid=44101.

Reagan, Ronald. 1981b. "Remarks in Denver, Colorado, at the Annual Convention of the National Association for the Advancement of Colored People, June 29, 1981." The American Presidency Project, http://www.presidency.ucsb.edu/ws/index.php?pid =44016&st=NAACP&st1=Denver.

Reagan, Ronald. 1985. "The President's News Conference, September 17, 1985." The American Presidency Project, http://www.presidency.ucsb.edu/ws/?pid=39125.

Reagan, Ronald. 1986a. "Message to the House of Representatives Returning without Approval a Bill Concerning Apartheid in South Africa, September 26, 1986." The American Presidency Project, http://www.presidency.ucsb.edu/ws/?pid=36504.

Reagan, Ronald. 1986b. "Radio Address to the Nation on Welfare Reform, February 15, 1986." The American Presidency Project, http://www.presidency.ucsb.edu/ws/?pid=36875.

Reagan, Ronald. 1986c. "Remarks to Members of the World Affairs Council and the Foreign Policy Association, July 22, 1986." The American Presidency Project, http://www.presidency.ucsb.edu/ws/?pid=37643.

Reagan, Ronald. 1988. "Remarks on Signing the Fair Housing Amendments Act of 1988, September 13, 1988." The American Presidency Project, http://www.presidency.ucsb.edu/ws/?pid=36361.

Reagan, Ronald. 1990. *An American Life: Ronald Reagan.* New York: Simon and Schuster.

Reagan, Ronald. 2003. *Reagan: A Life In Letters.* New York: Free Press.

Singer, Alan J. 1997. *Social Studies for Secondary Schools: Teaching to Learn, Learning to Teach, Third Edition.* New York: Routledge.

Vagins, Deborah J., and Jesselyn McCurdy. 2006. "Cracks in the System: Twenty Years of the Unjust Federal Crack Cocaine Law." American Civil Liberties Union, https://www.aclu.org/files/assets/cracksinsystem_20061025.pdf.

Weisberg, Jacob. 2016. *Ronald Reagan: The American Presidents Series; The 40th President, 1981–1989.* New York: Times Books.

Williams, Juan. 1988. "The Harsh Message for Blacks from Clarence Pendleton." *Washington Post,* June 12, https://www.washingtonpost.com/archive/opinions/1988/06/12/the-harsh-message-for-blacks-from-clarence-pendleton/7ecb1fa6-6089-4914-aa8e-241f32c37d1f/?utm_term=.74b62fe3d115.

George Herbert Walker Bush

41st President of the United States
Presidential Term: January 20, 1989–January 20, 1993
Political Party: Republican
Vice President: Dan Quayle

George Herbert Walker Bush was born on June 12, 1924, in Milton, Massachusetts. His son George W. Bush later became the 43rd president of the United States, and his son Jeb Bush served as governor of Florida from 1999 through 2007. Jeb unsuccessfully ran for the Republican nomination for president in the 2016 election, when he and other contenders lost the nomination to Donald Trump.

President George H. W. Bush won the presidential election in 1988 based on the popularity of Ronald Reagan, for whom Bush had served as vice president. Bush defeated Michael Dukakis by obtaining 53 percent of the overall vote. However, 89 percent of black voters supported Dukakis. When in office, President Bush continued the programs established by the Reagan administration, and like Reagan, Bush opposed affirmative action programs. Bush was criticized by Reverend Jesse Jackson for the vice president's campaign position on affirmative action as a quota system. In 1988 Jackson stated, "It's a sad day when an American president consciously promotes racial fear and division in our country as his main means of governing and of being reelected" (Booker 2017).

Before becoming president, Bush was asked by such leaders as Benjamin L. Hooks of the NAACP and Joseph Lowery of the Southern Christian Leadership Conference to change policies under Reagan that had been damaging to African Americans. While campaigning, however, Bush seized on the actions of Willie Horton as a case about being soft on crime. Horton was a black man and a prisoner in Massachusetts during the time Dukakis served as governor of the state. As part of a furlough program, Horton was released on a weekend pass in June 1986, although he was in prison for robbery and murder charges. Horton fled to Florida and eventually went to Maryland in April 1987, where he assaulted and raped a woman twice after beating her fiancé with a gun, stabbing him, and tying him to a pole in the basement of the couple's home. Horton then robbed the house and stole the fiancé's car and was eventually captured in Maryland. He was sentenced to more than two consecutive life terms. Bush was criticized for using the Horton case as a means to attract white voters, as Horton's two victims were white. While Bush's message was intended to address a tough stance on crime and an end to the "revolving door" of the prison system caused by liberals such as Dukakis, it was criticized as a call to white voters to be wary of black criminals, given commercials featuring the wild-eyed face of Horton. Notably, the first to criticize the weekend pass program was Al Gore in his Democratic debates with Dukakis for the party's nomination to run for president. However, Lee Atwater, Bush's political strategist, convinced Bush to seize the opportunity to use the Horton case.

Once in office, President Bush was praised for his appointment in August 1989 of Colin Powell as the first African American chairman of the Joint Chiefs of Staff. Powell achieved the rank of a Four-Star general in the U.S. Army in April of that year and had served as national security adviser under President Reagan. As chairman of the Joint Chiefs of Staff, Powell held the most powerful position an African American had ever held in the executive department. At the time, he was also the youngest in history to be appointed to the position. Powell went on to develop the Powell Doctrine, hailed as a premiere military strategy for using maximum force to combat an enemy while minimizing casualties. He became a national figure during Operations DESERT SHIELD and DESERT STORM.

President Bush also appointed Louis Wade Sullivan as secretary of the U.S. Department of Health and Human Services, Constance Ernestine Berry Newman as head of the Office of Personnel Management, and Fred McClure as head of congressional liaison. Other notable posts held by African Americans under Bush were Gwendolyn S. King as commissioner of the Social Security Administration (she was formally the White House director of intergovernmental affairs) and Edward J. Perkins as the U.S. ambassador to South Africa and later director general of the Foreign Service (he was the U.S. ambassador to Liberia under Reagan).

President Bush aggressively continued the War on Drugs that began under the Reagan administration. During an address to the nation on September 5, 1989, Bush outlined his National Drug Control Strategy. He held up a bag of crack cocaine during the televised speech, noting that it had been seized in a park across the street from the White House by undercover agents. It was later revealed that a drug seller was lured to the park so that the president could make the statement of the drugs being seized in the park. In part of his address he outlined the following:

Let me address four of the major elements of our strategy. First, we are determined to enforce the law, to make our streets and neighborhoods safe. So, to start, I'm proposing that we more than double Federal assistance to State and local law enforcement. Americans have a right to safety in and around their homes. And we won't have safe neighborhoods unless we're tough on drug criminals—much tougher than we are now. Sometimes that means tougher penalties, but more often it just means punishment that is swift and certain. We've all heard stories about drug dealers who are caught and arrested again and again but never punished. Well, here the rules have changed: If you sell drugs, you will be caught. And when you're caught, you will be prosecuted. And once you're convicted, you will do time. Caught—prosecuted—punished.

I'm also proposing that we enlarge our criminal justice system across the board—at the local, State, and Federal levels alike. We need more prisons, more jails, more courts, more prosecutors. So, tonight I'm requesting—all together—an almost $1.5 billion increase in drug-related Federal spending on law enforcement. (Bush 1989)

The impact of Bush's strategy was criticized for having an adverse impact on African Americans. Describing the drug crisis as "the greatest domestic threat facing our nation today," Bush approved the use of surplus military-grade equipment to be used by local and state police departments around the country under the 1208 Program (later changed to the 1033 Program) as well as over $1 billion in spending for new prisons. Police raids led to the seizure of property, the use of such tactics as wiretaps and mail searches to catch offenders, and increased incarcerations for even minor offenses. At the same time, some police departments were cited for using excessive force, seizing property with a lack of evidence of wrongdoing, and keeping cash and property for personal use. The incarceration rates escalated from a few hundred thousand in the early 1980s to over 1 million by the early 2000s, particularly for young African American males.

In 1990, Bush vetoed an amendment to the Civil Rights Act. He would not support expanded protections that he described as legally destructive quotas. The primary goal of the amendment was to allow punitive and compensatory damages to women and minorities for intentional and unintentional discrimination by employers. This in turn, according to critics including Bush, would cause companies to use quotas in hiring to ensure a representation of female and minority employees. In a message to the Senate on returning the bill on October 22, Bush outlined his specific concerns. Among them, he stated the need for Congress to act on the alternative bill he sent it for approval on October 20, 1990. He also outlined the following:

Despite the use of the term "civil rights" in the title of S. 2104, the bill actually employs a maze of highly legalistic language to introduce the destructive force of quotas into our Nation's employment system. Primarily through provisions governing cases in which employment practices are alleged to have unintentionally caused the disproportionate exclusion of members of certain groups, S. 2104 creates powerful incentives for employers to adopt hiring and promotion quotas. These incentives are created by the bill's new and very technical rules of litigation, which will make it difficult for employers to defend legitimate employment practices. In many cases, a defense against unfounded allegations will be impossible. Among other problems, the plaintiff often need not even show that any of the employer's practices caused a significant statistical disparity. In other cases, the employer's defense is confined to an unduly narrow definition of "business necessity" that is significantly more restrictive than that established by the Supreme Court in Griggs and in two decades of subsequent decisions. Thus, unable to defend legitimate practices in court, employers will be driven to adopt quotas in order to avoid liability. (Bush 1990)

Bush was only the third president in history to veto an amendment to the Civil Rights Act. The other two were Reagan and Andrew Jackson. In the case of Bush, Congress did not override his veto. Bush directed his staff to work with Congress to amend the bill, and it was reintroduced in 1991. He eventually signed the Civil Rights Act of 1991 on November 21, 1991. The act still made it easier for employees to sue employers for discrimination and, among its provisions, allowed plaintiffs to request a jury trial and to sue for both compensatory and punitive damages up to $300,000. The 1991 law was much narrower than the 1990 bill, was specific to hiring discrimination, and was not seen as a law that would result in hiring quotas. The amendments proposed in 1990 and 1991 both resulted from a number of U.S. Supreme Court rulings, including *Ward's Cove Packing Company, Inc. v. Atonio,* 490 U.S. 642 (1989), and *Patterson v. McLean Credit Union,* 491 U.S. 164 (1989). The rulings in these cases led Congress to pass the 1991 act to allow plaintiffs to sue for even unintentional discrimination, force businesses to prove that they were not disparately impacting minorities in employment, and allow plaintiffs to receive damages, as the Supreme Court had ruled against these remedies in the afore cited cases.

In 1991, Bush's nomination of Clarence Thomas to replace Thurgood Marshall on the Supreme Court led to national controversy. First, Thomas was a conservative and openly criticized affirmative action. His nomination was not supported by the Congressional Black Caucus, some democratic congressional representatives, and black leaders. He was criticized for his conservative views and the failure of the Equal Employment Opportunity Commission to tackle racial discrimination cases when he led the agency. The most detrimental thing facing his Senate confirmation was allegations by Anita Hill of past sexual harassment. During open testimony before the Senate Judiciary Committee, chaired by Democrat Joe Biden (who later became vice president under President Barack Obama), Hill detailed Thomas's use of sexually explicit language and requests for sexual acts while she served as his assistant when Thomas worked at the Department of Education and the Equal Employment Opportunity Commission. Hill was discredited during the hearings, and a political compromise between Republicans and Biden to get Thomas confirmed was revealed. Other witnesses who supported Hill's claims were not allowed to testify. Hill passed a polygraph test verifying that she was telling the truth. Thomas, however, was not asked to take a polygraph test. Later evidence revealed that there were other women who claimed to have been sexually harassed by Thomas. Thomas called Hill's testimony part of a "high-tech lynching" geared to stop his confirmation because he was black. He was eventually confirmed on October 15, 1991, and Hill's testimony led to new laws and policies dealing with sexual harassment as well as continued national debate on the issue.

The issue of the treatment of blacks by police officers became the focus of national debate while President Bush was in office due to the beating of motorist Rodney King by police officers in Los Angeles, California, on March 3, 1991. King was sighted speeding on the freeway at approximately 12:30 a.m. and then pursued by police officers. He attempted to outrun police, as he was intoxicated and on parole. After being pursued by police in patrol cars and a helicopter, he was eventually forced to stop. King and two others in his car were ordered to the ground. While the incident was being videotaped by a local bystander, George Holliday, from a nearby balcony, King was tasered by police twice then repeatedly and brutally beaten with batons as well as kicked by a group of police officers. Over a dozen other police officers stood by and watched as four officers continued to beat King while he was lying on the ground. The brutality of the incident led to the video as well as photos of King's battered face, broken bones, and bruises airing repeatedly on news outlets around the world. Police officers Stacey Koon, Laurence Powell, Theodore Briseno, and Timothy Wind were charged with using a deadly weapon and excessive force on March 14, 1991. The initial judge was removed after telling prosecutors "You can trust me," and the case led to an acquittal of 3 of the officers by a jury on April 29, 1992. The trial was moved from Los Angeles to the predominantly white suburb of Simi Valley to ensure a fair trial. The jury consisted of 10 white members, 1 Hispanic, and 1 Asian.

The verdict in the trial led to rioting in Los Angeles that lasted for six days by enraged residents who felt that the verdict was based on race and was yet another example of the mistreatment of blacks by the justice system. Order was restored after the deployment of local police, federal agents, and members of the U.S. Army, the U.S. Marine Corps, and the National Guard. The riots resulted in 53 deaths, over 2,000 injuries, more than 9,000 arrests, and nearly $1 billion in property damage. King made a television appearance on May 1, 1992, in which he spoke the now famous words "I just want to say—you know—can we all just get along? Can we, can we get along?" (Bates 2012).

President Bush stated before reporters during a meeting with Attorney General Dick Thornburgh that he was sickened by the scenes of the event: "Those terrible scenes stir us all to demand an end to gratuitous violence and brutality. Law enforcement officials cannot place themselves above the law that they are sworn to defend. It was sickening to see the beating that was rendered and there's no way, no way in my view, to explain that away. It was outrageous" (Bush 1991). Thornburgh announced on March 15, 1991, that the Justice Department would review every police brutality complaint the federal government had received over the past six years. The president later met with congressional leaders and members of the cabinet to discuss problems in urban communities around the country.

Bush made an address to the nation on May 1, 1992, as the riots took place. After speaking of efforts to work with state and local officials to restore order, he stated,

Now let's talk about the beating of Rodney King, because beyond the urgent need to restore order is the second issue, the question of justice: Whether Rodney King's Federal civil rights were violated. What you saw and what I saw on the TV video was revolting. I felt anger. I felt pain. I thought: How can I explain this to my grandchildren?

Civil rights leaders and just plain citizens fearful of and sometimes victimized by police brutality were deeply hurt. And I know good and decent policemen who were equally appalled.

I spoke this morning to many leaders of the civil rights community. And they saw the video, as we all did. For 14 months they waited patiently, hopefully. They waited for the system to work. And when the verdict came in, they felt betrayed. Viewed from outside the trial, it was hard to understand how the verdict could possibly square with the video. Those civil rights leaders with whom I met were stunned. And so was I, and so was Barbara, and so were my kids. (Bush 1992)

Two of the four police officers in the King case, Koon and Powell, were finally convicted on federal charges by the U.S. Department of Justice in 1993, while two were acquitted. King eventually sued the city and was awarded $3.8 million in a civil trial. Rodney King died by drowning in 2012. Los Angeles Police Department chief Darryl Gates, who was viewed as symbolizing racial intolerance in the department, resigned. He was replaced by Willie Williams, an African American, who implemented changes to the department recommended by an independent investigatory commission.

On June 22, 1992, Bush signed a supplemental appropriation law that provided funding to Los Angeles to recover from the Rodney King riots, funding to Chicago to recover from flooding, and funding for other cities with urgent needs. The appropriation provided $300 million for Federal Emergency Management Agency disaster assistance, $500 million for summer youth jobs programs, and $143.8 million for Small Business Administration disaster loans.

One notable point is that Bush published an autobiography titled *Looking Forward* in 1987. Proceeds from the book's sale were donated to the United Negro College Fund as well as medical research on leukemia. He died at the age of 94 on November 30, 2018.

FURTHER READING

Booker, Christopher B. 2017. *The Black Presidential Nightmare: African-Americans and Presidents, 1789–2016.* Bloomington, IN: Xlibris.

Bush, George H. W. 1989. "Address to the Nation on the National Drug Control Strategy, September 5, 1989." The American Presidency Project, http://www.presidency.ucsb.edu/ws/?pid=17472.

Bush, George H. W. 1990. "Message to the Senate Returning without Approval the Civil Rights Act of 1990, October 22, 1990." The American Presidency Project, http://www.presidency.ucsb.edu/ws/index.php?pid=18948.

Bush, George H. W. 1991. "Remarks on Police Brutality and an Exchange with Reporters, March 21, 1991." The American Presidency Project, http://www.presidency .ucsb.edu/ws/index.php?pid=19410&st=police&st1=.

Bush, George H. W. 1992. "Address to the Nation on the Civil Disturbances in Los Angeles, California, May 1, 1992." The American Presidency Project, http://www.pres idency.ucsb.edu/ws/?pid=20910.

Bush, George H. W. 2009. *Speaking of Freedom: The Collected Speeches.* New York: Scribner.

Bush, George H. W. 2013. *All the Best, George Bush: My Life in Letters and Other Writings.* New York: Scribner.

Elston, Heidi M. D. 2009. *George H. W. Bush: 41st President of the United States.* Edina, MN: ABDO Publishing.

Naftali, Timothy. 2007. *George H. W. Bush: The American Presidents Series; The 41st President, 1989–1993.* New York: Times Books.

William Jefferson Clinton
(born William Jefferson Blythe III)

42nd President of the United States
Presidential Term: January 20, 1993–January 20, 2001
Political Party: Democratic
Vice President: Albert "Al" Gore

William Jefferson Clinton was born on August 19, 1946, as William Jefferson Blythe III. His father died in a car accident three months before his son's birth. Clinton's mother married a car dealer named Roger Clinton Sr., thus leading to Clinton's last name change. Clinton, more commonly called "Bill" Clinton, solidly won the presidential election of 1992 against incumbent George H. W. Bush. Clinton won 370 electoral votes, compared to Bush's 168 and 0 for independent candidate Ross Perot. Clinton also won 83 percent of the African American vote. While Clinton's campaign was plagued by assertions of extramarital affairs, Bush ultimately lost in part due to the lagging economy.

During the campaign, Clinton took an action that led to the permanent political term "Sister Souljah moment." Speaking before Jesse Jackson's Rainbow Coalition in June 1992, Clinton denounced the rap lyrics of Sister Souljah and the organization itself for giving her a forum by allowing her to speak at the event. Clinton was referencing her former comments in a *Washington Post* interview that included such statements as "If black people kill black people every day, why not have a week and kill white people?" in reference to the riots in Los Angeles after the acquittal of police officers charged with beating Rodney King. Clinton compared her hate speech to that of Klansman David Duke: "If you took the words 'white' and 'black,' and you reversed them, you might think David Duke was giving that speech" (Chang 2005, 395).

While Clinton's statement in front of an African American audience shocked some, it was done to intentionally portray his bravery to address the issue. This event led to Clinton's rise in the polls, particularly against Democrats who were competing for the party's nomination to run for president. Ever since the event, a "Sister Souljah Moment" has referred to candidates taking a bold stance on a controversial topic.

Clinton's popularity among African Americans earned him the informal title the "first black president." This reference was for his attraction to blacks based on his southern background, his appeal to black voters on such programs as the *Arsenio Hall Show,* and his ability to appeal to poor blacks and give them a sense of hopefulness. Clinton also supported black voters, and blacks could relate to how Republicans and conservatives waged personal attacks against Clinton.

Once in office, President Clinton accomplished one of the most diverse presidential appointments in history. His

William "Bill" Jefferson Clinton was the 42nd president of the United States. After the election, Pulitzer Prize–winning novelist Toni Morrison wrote an article about him in the *New Yorker,* designating Clinton as "the first black president." (Library of Congress)

cabinet appointments alone totaled nine African Americans over the course of his two terms in office. These included Rob Brown as secretary of commerce, Mike Espy as secretary of agriculture, Hazel O'Leary as secretary of energy, Alexis Herman as secretary of labor, Rod Slater as secretary of transportation, Jesse Brown and later Togo West as secretary of veterans affairs, Franklin Raines as director of the Office of Management and Budget, and Eric Holder as deputy attorney general. According to the White House,

> Over the past eight years, he has appointed seven African American Cabinet Secretaries, and women make up 44 percent of Clinton Administration appointees, including the first woman to serve as Secretary of State, Madeline Albright, and the first to serve as Attorney General, Janet Reno. The President also appointed the first Asian American to serve in a Cabinet, Commerce Secretary Norman Mineta. The President has appointed more African Americans to federal judgeships than were appointed during the last sixteen years combined and 14 percent of all Clinton Administration appointees are African American, twice as many as in any previous Administration. President Clinton appointed three times as many female judges as the

two previous administrations and the most Hispanic judicial nominees of any President. Record numbers of people with disabilities are also serving in the White House and throughout the Clinton Administration. (The Clinton Presidency: Building One America 2018)

With the goal of creating an administration that looked like America, Clinton's appointments are also summarized in the archives of the Clinton White House:

The President appointed the most diverse Cabinet and Administration in history. The Clinton Cabinet includes three African Americans: Rodney Slater, Secretary of the Department of Transportation; Togo West, Jr., Secretary of Veterans Affairs and Alexis Herman, Secretary of Labor. Additionally, African Americans serve in the Administration as Surgeon General, Deputy Attorney General for the Department of Justice, Director of the National Park Service, Deputy Secretary of Commerce, Department of Education General Counsel and as the Department of Education's Chief of Staff. Thirteen percent of Clinton Administration appointees are African American, which is twice as many African Americans as any previous administration. White House appointees include: Bob Nash, Assistant to the President and Director of Presidential Personnel; Thurgood Marshall, Jr., Assistant to the President and Director of Cabinet Affairs; Minyon Moore, Assistant to the President and Director of Political Affairs; Cheryl Mills, Deputy Assistant to the President and Deputy Counsel and Ben Johnson, Deputy Assistant to the President and Deputy Director of Public Liaison; Alphonso (Al) Maldon, Deputy Assistant to the President for Legislative Affairs; and Tracey Thornton, Deputy Assistant to the President for Legislative Affairs. (White House 1999)

President Clinton was concerned about political conflict with conservative lawmakers when making two nominations. This resulted in his withdrawal of the nominations of two prominent African Americans from political appointment posts. The first was Lani Guinier as head of the Department of Justice's Civil Rights Division. Guinier remained a law professor at Harvard University and the first woman of color to receive tenure at Harvard's Law School. After her nomination, her writings were criticized for being antidemocratic, such as her support of racial quotas and all-black voting districts. Critics dubbed her the "quota queen." Clinton explained his withdrawal of her nomination in remarks given on June 3, 1993:

At the time of the nomination I had not read her writings. In retrospect, I wish I had. Today, as a matter of fairness to her, I read some of them again in good detail. They clearly lend themselves to interpretations that do not represent the views that I expressed on civil rights during my campaign and views that I hold very dearly, even though there is much in them with which I agree. I have to tell you that had I read them before I nominated her, I would not have done so.

Now, I want to make it clear that that is not to say that I agree with all the attacks on her. She has been subject to a vicious series of willful distortions on many issues, including the quota issue. And that has made this decision all the more difficult. (Clinton 1993)

The second was Jocelyn Elders, who served as the first African American surgeon general until she was fired in 1994 for making controversial remarks on encouraging masturbation education. She also supported legalizing drugs and handing out condoms in school and criticized the Catholic Church for opposing abortions. On December 9, 1994, Clinton remarked, "Dr. Elders's public statements reflecting differences with administration policy and my own convictions have made it necessary for her to tender her resignation" (Clinton 1994b). After Elders's stint as surgeon general, she returned to the University of Arkansas Medical School as a professor of pediatrics.

During his first year in office, President Clinton signed the Violent Crime Control and Law Enforcement Act. The legislation allowed the funding of $30 billion for prisons, new police officers, and increases in punitive actions for offenses. While the bill included spending more than $6 billion on crime prevention measures, it also included over $9 billion to fund new prisons. One of its more controversial requirements mandated life sentences for repeat offenders, commonly known as the "three strikes" policy. The act also expanded the death penalty to cover 60 new offenses including terrorist homicides, murder of a federal law enforcement officer, large-scale drug trafficking, drive-by shootings resulting in death, and carjackings resulting in death. On September 13, 1994, Clinton made remarks on the signing of the law. In two excerpts from his speech he stated:

> Gangs and drugs have taken over our streets and undermined our schools. Every day we read about somebody else who has literally gotten away with murder. But the American people haven't forgotten the difference between right and wrong. The system has. The American people haven't stopped wanting to raise their children in lives of safety and dignity, but they've got a lot of obstacles in their way. . . .

> When this bill is law, "three strikes and you're out" will be the law of the land; the penalty for killing a law enforcement officer will be death; we will have a significant—we will have the means by which we can say punishment will be more certain. We will cut the Federal work force over a period of years by 270,000 positions to its lowest level in 30 years and take all that money to pay for this crime bill. The savings will be used to put 100,000 police officers on the street, a 20 percent increase. It will be used to build prisons to keep 100,000 violent criminals off the street. It will be used to give our young people something to say yes to, places where they can go after school where they are safe, where they can do constructive things that will help them to build their lives, where teachers replace gang leaders as role models. All of these things should be done and will be done. (Clinton 1994a)

The law was seen as producing a disparaging impact on African Americans, particularly black male youths who were more prone to being stopped by police. In some ways, critics outlined how the law seemed to target crime in urban areas. First

Lady Hillary Clinton was equally criticized for using the term "super-predator" to describe youths who had no empathy for their actions, a reference that many contended referred to black youths. The law was also criticized for not focusing enough on rehabilitation and eliminating such programs as Pell Grants for higher education for prison inmates. It also funded new prisons by prodding states to force offenders to serve 85 percent of their sentence in prison rather than being allowed early parole. The end result was an increase in millions of people placed in prison. Supporters of the act outlined the need to tackle the increase in crime at the time. These supporters included several black mayors of urban cities and a group of black pastors who lobbied the Congressional Black Caucus to support the bill. In a statement issued on August 16, 1994, they outlined the following:

> The White House today released the following statement by African-American religious leaders supporting the crime bill.
>
> "In the words of an African proverb 'It takes an entire village to raise a child.' We believe there is no more important responsibility of society than to raise its children to become upstanding adults. Parents and families must shoulder the burden of this duty, but all of society—including government—must pitch in. That is why we support the President's crime bill.
>
> While we do not agree with every provision in the crime bill, we do believe and emphatically support the bill's goal to save our communities, and most importantly, our children.
>
> We believe and support the $8 billion in the bill to fund prevention programs such as grants for recreation, employment, anti-gang and comprehensive programs to steer our young people away from crime.
>
> We believe in drug treatment to help get federal and state inmates out of the cycle of dependency.
>
> We believe in programs to fight violence against women.
>
> We believe in banning assault weapons, and preventing these deadly devices from falling into the hands of criminals and drug dealers.
>
> We believe in putting 100,000 well-trained police officers on the streets of our most violence-plagued communities and urban areas.
>
> We believe that 9-year-olds like James Darby of New Orleans, who was killed by a stray bullet only days after writing a plea to President Clinton to stop the violence, must have the opportunity to live and learn and grow in safe, decent communities.
>
> For all these reasons, we support the crime bill and we urge others to join us in this crusade." (The Clinton White House 1994)

Note that later both Bill and Hillary Clinton expressed regrets at many facets of the law, including the negative impact it had on African Americans.

The Clinton administration took actions to address hate crimes based on race, sexuality, and other factors as early as 1994. According to White House archives,

> The Clinton-Gore Administration has fought hate crimes and racial profiling by fighting for the Hate Crimes Sentencing Enhancement Act, which increased penalties for hate crimes as part of the 1994 Crime Bill. As a result of Presidential leadership, the number of law enforcement agencies across the country reporting hate crimes to the Justice Department has risen from 2,771 in 1991 to 12,122 in 1999—giving authorities a more accurate picture of the problem. President Clinton is also working to end racial profiling, by directing Cabinet agencies to collect data on the race, ethnicity, and gender of individuals subject to certain stops by federal law enforcement to help determine where and when racial profiling occurs. (The Clinton White House 2018)

The attack on affirmative action that had begun under President Reagan continued while President Clinton was in office. This was particularly the case when Republicans gained a majority in Congress after the 1994 midterm elections. Rather than supporting the total discontinuation of these programs, Clinton outlined the need to evaluate the use of affirmative action and made changes where needed. In a speech given at the White House on July 9, 1995, he stated the following:

> The job of ending discrimination in this country is not over. That should not be surprising. We had slavery for centuries before the passage of the 13th, 14th and 15th Amendments. We waited another hundred years for the civil rights legislation. Women have had the vote less than a hundred years. We have always had difficulty with these things, as most societies do. But we are making more progress than many people. Based on the evidence, the job is not done. So here is what I think we should do. We should reaffirm the principle of affirmative action and fix the practices. We should have a simple slogan: Mend it, but don't end it. (Clinton 1995)

Clinton's remarks were in response to the U.S. Supreme Court's ruling in *Adarand Constructors, Inc. v. Pena,* 515 U.S. 200 (1995), that called for strict scrutiny in determining if race should or should not be a factor in federal, state, or local affirmative action programs. This case involved the Department of Transportation giving additional compensation to a company that used minority subcontractors such as African Americans, Hispanic Americans, Native Americans, or Asian Pacific Americans. Adarand was not awarded the contract even though it was the lowest bidder because it did not use minority contractors. The Supreme Court ruled against the Department of Transportation.

Under the leadership of Harvard law professor Christopher Edley, a report titled *Review of Federal Affirmative Action Programs: Report to the President* was issued. It is commonly known as the Clinton Report on Affirmative Action. Due to opposition from conservatives and concerns over political fallout, Clinton did not act on any of the report's recommendations.

Clinton attempted to improve economically depressed areas by issuing Executive Order 13005 on May 21, 1996. The order mandated policies to ensure that federal agencies were given incentives to companies in these areas in federal procurements. As stated in the order,

> In order to promote economy and efficiency in Federal procurement, it is necessary to secure broad-based competition for Federal contracts. This broad competition is best achieved where there is an expansive pool of potential contractors capable of producing quality goods and services at competitive prices. A great and largely untapped opportunity for expanding the pool of such contractors can be found in this Nation's economically distressed communities. (Clinton 1996)

On August 22, 1996, Clinton signed the Personal Responsibility and Work Opportunity Act. The bill was designed to address the growing number of people receiving assistance from Aid to Families with Dependent Children. This increase partly stemmed from the recessions that persisted under President George H. W. Bush before Clinton took office. Options that were debated before the law passed included strategies to push those on welfare to work and denying benefits to single mothers under the age of 21. As outlined by the U.S. Department of Health and Human Services (1996), "The law contains strong work requirements, a performance bonus to reward states for moving welfare recipients into jobs, state maintenance of effort requirements, comprehensive child support enforcement, and supports for families moving from welfare to work—including increased funding for child care and guaranteed medical coverage."

However, some saw these options as an attack on the poor and minorities. For example, noted political activist Barbara Ehrenreich stated that these proposed policies were "an implicit attack on the dignity and personhood of every woman, black or white, poor or posh" (Health and Human Services 1996, 193). Others criticized the proposals as continuing the stereotypes espoused by President Ronald Reagan of "welfare queens." Clinton finally signed the act but with trepidation, calling it a "decent welfare bill wrapped in a sack of shit" given that it was part of his campaign promise to deal with welfare reform. He had vetoed previous bills, and the new measures were pushed by conservative legislators such as Newt Gingrich.

President Clinton easily won his bid for reelection in 1996 against Republican challenger Bob Dole. Clinton received 49.2 percent of the popular vote, compared to 40.7 percent for Dole and 8.4 percent for Ross Perot. Clinton garnered 84 percent of votes from African Americans.

On April 3, 1996, Ronald "Ron" Brown was killed in a plane crash along with 34 others in Croatia. Brown was President Clinton's secretary of commerce and the first African American to hold that position. In Brown's eulogy, Clinton stated,

> Ron Brown—a trailblazer, a builder, a patriot. A husband, a father, a wonderful friend, and a great American. Let us remember these things about Ron. Let us always have our joy in the morning. Let us be determined to carry on his legacy. Let us always be vigilant, as he was, in fighting against any shred of racism and prejudice. Let us always be vigilant, as he was, in remembering that we cannot lift ourselves up by tearing other people down,

that we have to go forward together. Let us always remember, as he did, that Alexis de Tocqueville was right when he said so many years ago, America is great because America is good. He knew we had to keep working and striving to be better. In his last sermon from the pulpit, Martin Luther King asked God to grant us all a chance to be participants in the newness and magnificent development of America. That is the cause for which Ron Brown gave his life, and the cause for which he gave up his life. (The Clinton White House 1996)

On June 14, 1997, Clinton announced the establishment of the "One America in the 21st Century: The President's Initiative on Race" during his speech to the graduating class of the University of California–San Diego. The intent of the initiative was to have a panel that would spearhead a discussion on race relations and best practices to make improvements in this area. During his speech, Clinton outlined its intent by stating,

I want this panel to help educate Americans about the facts surrounding issues of race, to promote a dialog in every community of the land to confront and work through these issues, to recruit and encourage leadership at all levels to help breach racial divides, and to find, develop, and recommend how to implement concrete solutions to our problems, solutions that will involve all of us in Government, business, communities, and as individual citizens.

I will make periodic reports to the American people about our findings and what actions we all have to take to move America forward. This board will seek out and listen to Americans from all races and all walks of life. They are performing a great citizen service, but in the cause of building one America, all citizens must serve. As I said at the Presidents' Summit on Service in Philadelphia, in our new era such acts of service are basic acts of citizenship. Government must play its role, but much of the work must be done by the American people as citizen service. The very effort will strengthen us and bring us closer together. In short, I want America to capture the feel and the spirit that you have given to all of us today. (Clinton 1997)

To support this initiative Clinton signed Executive Order 13050, President's Advisory Board on Race, on June 13, 1997. Per the order, the advisory board was empowered to advise the president on matters of race and racial reconciliation, including the following four ways the president could:

(1) Promote a constructive national dialogue to confront and work through challenging issues that surround race;

(2) Increase the Nation's understanding of our recent history of race relations and the course our Nation is charting on issues of race relations and racial diversity;

(3) Bridge racial divides by encouraging leaders in communities throughout the Nation to develop and implement innovative approaches to calming racial tensions;

(4) Identify, develop, and implement solutions to problems in areas in which race has a substantial impact, such as education, economic opportunity, housing, health care, and the administration of justice.

Members of the advisory board included John Hope Franklin, noted historian and author of *Up From Slavery;* Linda Chavez-Thompson, a former executive vice president of the American Federation of Labor and Congress of Industrial Organizations; Susan D. Johnson Cook, noted pastor, author, and activist; and former New Jersey governor Thomas Kean. President Clinton officially received the report, titled *One America in the 21st Century: Forging a New Future,* from the advisory council on September 19, 1998. In a ceremony held before an audience including civil rights veterans Rosa Parks and Representative John Lewis, Clinton stated, "It comes from, yes, opportunity; it comes from, yes, learning; it comes from, yes, the absence of discrimination. But it also has to come from the presence of reconciliation, from a turning away from the madness that life only matters if there is someone we can demean, destroy or put down" (Clinton 1998). While the report outlined such actions as funding for schools in minority communities, getting youth leaders engaged to build racial bridges, and creating a permanent Presidential Council on Race, it was criticized for not including more bold recommendations. The report did lead to greater dialogue in the media and in academic discussions, but the entire initiative was hurt by criticisms from conservatives and overshadowed by the administration's focus on a scandal involving President Clinton's affair with Monica Lewinsky.

Clinton faced possible impeachment in 1998 as a result of a revealed affair he had with then 22-year-old Lewinsky, a White House intern. He first flatly denied any relationship with Lewinsky by stating "I did not have sexual relations with that woman, Miss Lewinsky," during a January 1998 press conference. He later recanted his denial and admitted to wrongdoing as evidence surfaced. On the charges of perjury, the president was convicted by the U.S. House of Representatives. However, he was not convicted by the U.S. Senate. The scandal did not negatively impact support of the president by African Americans. Representative Maxine Waters explained how this was due in part to how President Clinton treated blacks: "The black community knows the difference between individuals who patronize them and are forced to get to know black leaders and those who genuinely look you in the eye, know you and call you by your name. His eyes are not glazed over when he looks at blacks" (Connolly and Pierre 1998). Clinton continued to have overwhelming support from black voters, the Congressional Black Caucus, and black leaders.

As a result of political attempts to impeach Clinton, the discussion around his role as the nation's first black president gained popularity. Some viewed attacks against Clinton's actions as hypocritical. For example, in October 1998, noted novelist Toni Morrison wrote an article in the *New Yorker* titled "Clinton as the First Black President" in which she stated the following:

African-American men seemed to understand it right away. Years ago, in the middle of the Whitewater investigation, one heard the first murmurs: white skin notwithstanding, this is our first black President. Blacker than any actual black person who could ever be elected in our children's lifetime. After all, Clinton displays almost every trope of blackness: single-parent household, born poor, working-class, saxophone-playing, McDonald's-and-junk-food-loving boy from Arkansas. And when virtually all the African-American Clinton appointees began, one by one, to disappear, when the President's body, his privacy, his unpoliced sexuality became the focus of the persecution, when he was metaphorically seized and body-searched, who could gainsay these black men who knew whereof they spoke? The message was clear: "No matter how smart you are, how hard you work, how much coin you earn for us, we will put you in your place or put you out of the place you have somehow, albeit with our permission, achieved. You will be fired from your job, sent away in disgrace, and—who knows?—maybe sentenced and jailed to boot. In short, unless you do as we say (i.e., assimilate at once), your expletives belong to us." (Morrison 1998)

On June 9, 1998, Clinton signed the Transportation Equity Act for the 21st Century into law. Its primary provisions were to authorize federal surface transportation programs for highways, highway safety, and transit for the six-year period 1998–2003. Within the law was a provision to support the Disadvantage Business Enterprise program by guaranteeing that "not less than 10 percent of the amounts made available for any program under titles I, III, and V of this Act shall be expended with small business concerns owned and controlled by socially and economically disadvantaged individuals" (U.S. Department of Transportation 2018). Socially and economically disadvantaged individuals included women and minorities.

In 1999, Clinton recognized and attempted to combat racial profiling used by law enforcement across the country. His actions were in part a reaction to the murder of Amadou Diallo, a 23-year-old immigrant from Guinea who was shot almost 20 times by four police officers in New York after they mistook him for a rape suspect. The officers, who actually fired 41 shots in total, were acquitted of criminal charges, but the family successfully sued the city in a civil case. The event led to protests and a national debate on racial profiling as well as greater scrutiny of the practice by law enforcement agencies across the country. In a statement given as part of his opening remarks at a roundtable discussion on increasing trust between communities and law enforcement officers on June 9, 1999, he stated the following:

We also must stop the morally indefensible, deeply corrosive practice of racial profiling. Last year I met with a group of black journalists, and I asked how many of them had been stopped by the police, in their minds for no reason other than the color of their skin, and every single journalist in the room raised his hand—every one.

People of color have the same reaction wherever you go. Members of Congress can tell this story. Students, professors, even off-duty police officers, can tell this story. No person of color is immune from such humiliating experiences. A racial profiling is, in fact, the opposite of good police work,

> where actions are based on hard facts, not stereotypes. It is wrong; it is destructive; and it must stop.
>
> As a necessary step to combat it, we, too, need hard facts. Today, I am directing my Cabinet agencies to begin gathering detailed information on their law enforcement activities. The Justice Department will then analyze this data to assess whether and where law enforcement engage in racial profiling and what concrete steps we need to take at the national level to eliminate it anywhere it exists. We are committed to doing this, and we hope that all of you will support us in this endeavor. (Clinton 1999)

The president's remarks were part of the Strengthening Police-Community Relationship conference held in Washington, D.C., during June 9–10, 1999, also attended by Attorney General Janet Reno, civil rights leaders, and government and police leaders from around the country. The president ordered law enforcement agencies across the country to compile data on profiling. This greatly increased data collection nationwide and even led to the Department of Justice taking action against the New Jersey and New York attorneys general to find police guilty of the practice.

Clinton expanded the categories of prohibited discrimination in federal employment by forbidding the use of genetic information. This benefited all races and particularly African Americans, who have a history of genetic health issues such as diabetes. Executive Order 13145 was issued on February 8, 2000, and on that day President Clinton remarked on the act:

> The fear of misuse of private genetic information is already very widespread in our nation. Americans are genuinely worried that their genetic information will not be kept secret, that this information will be used against them. As a result, they're often reluctant to take advantage of new breakthroughs in genetic testing—making a point I think we cannot make too often—if we do not protect the right to privacy, we may actually impede the reach of these breakthroughs in the lives of ordinary people, which would be a profound tragedy.
>
> A Pennsylvania study, for example, showed that nearly a third of women at high risk for inherited forms of breast cancer refused to be tested to determine whether they carry either of the two known breast cancer genes because they feared discrimination based on the results.
>
> That is simply wrong. We must not allow advances in genetics to become the basis of discrimination against any individual or any group. We must never allow these discoveries to change the basic belief upon which our government, our society, and our system of ethics is founded—that all of us are created equal, entitled to equal treatment under the law. (Clinton 2000)

Clinton was credited with supporting policies that improved the economic well-being of blacks. As Kurtzleben pointed out, "The Clinton years were also known for a booming economy. During that time, the median household income in African American households grew by 25 percent, twice as fast as it did for all households nationwide. In addition, African American unemployment plummeted from 14.1 percent to 8.2 percent (of course, the unemployment rate also fell for other groups). And the administration touted its record of boosting loans to minorities" (2016). The president's support of increased enforcement of the Community Reinvestment Act is credited with increasing minority and low-income ownership. The act required banks to lend to people living in low-income neighborhoods and allowed Fannie Mae and Freddie Mac to subsidize mortgages to low-income borrowers. A list of professed benefits to African Americans by President Clinton can be found at "Working on Behalf of African Americans" (Clinton White House 1999).

FURTHER READING

Carter, Daryl A. 2016. *Brother Bill: President Clinton and the Politics of Race and Class.* Fayetteville: University of Arkansas Press.

Chang, Jeff. 2005. *Can't Stop Won't Stop: A History of the Hip-Hop Generation.* New York: St. Martin's.

Clinton, William J. 1993. "Remarks on the Withdrawal of the Nomination of Lani Guinier to Be an Assistant Attorney General and an Exchange with Reporters, June 3, 1993." The American Presidency Project, http://www.presidency.ucsb.edu/ws/index.php?pid=46657.

Clinton, William J. 1994a. "Remarks on Signing the Violent Crime Control and Law Enforcement Act of 1994, September 13, 1994." The American Presidency Project, http://www.presidency.ucsb.edu/ws/?pid=49072.

Clinton, William J. 1994b. "Statement on the Resignation of Joycelyn Elders as Surgeon General, December 9, 1994." The American Presidency Project, http://www.presidency.ucsb.edu/ws/index.php?pid=49574.

Clinton, William J. 1995. "Remarks on Affirmative Action at the National Archives and Records Administration, July 19, 1995." The American Presidency Project, http://www.presidency.ucsb.edu/ws/index.php?pid=51631.

Clinton, William J. 1996. "Executive Order 13005—Empowerment Contracting, May 21, 1996." The American Presidency Project, http://www.presidency.ucsb.edu/ws/?pid=52845.

Clinton, William J. 1997. "Commencement Address at the University of California San Diego in La Jolla, California, June 14, 1997." The American Presidency Project, http://www.presidency.ucsb.edu/ws/?pid=54268.

Clinton, William J. 1998. "Remarks on Receiving the Report of the President's Advisory Board on Race, September 18, 1998." The American Presidency Project, http://www.presidency.ucsb.edu/ws/index.php?pid=54937.

Clinton, William J. 1999. "Opening Remarks at a Roundtable Discussion on Increasing Trust between Communities and Law Enforcement Officers, June 9, 1999." The American Presidency Project, http://www.presidency.ucsb.edu/ws/index.php?pid=57700.

Clinton, William J. 2000. "Remarks on Signing an Executive Order To Prohibit Discrimination in Federal Employment Based on Genetic Information, February 8, 2000." The American Presidency Project, http://www.presidency.ucsb.edu/ws/index.php?pid=58108.

Clinton, Bill. 2004. *My Life.* New York: Knopf.

Connolly, Ceci, and Robert Pierre. 1998. "African American Voters Standing by Clinton." *Washington Post,* September 17, 1998, https://www.washingtonpost.com/wp-srv/politics/special/clinton/stories/blacks091798.htm.

Ehrenreich, Barbara. 1995. *The Snarling Citizen: Essays.* New York: Farrar, Straus and
    Giroux.
Hamilton, Nigel. 2007. *Bill Clinton: Mastering the Presidency.* New York: PublicAffairs.
Kurtzleben, Danielle. 2016. "Understanding The Clintons' Popularity with Black Voters."
    National Public Radio, March 1, https://www.npr.org/2016/03/01/468185698/under
    standing-the-clintons-popularity-with-black-voters.
Maraniss, David. 1995. *First In His Class: A Biography of Bill Clinton.* New York: Simon
    and Schuster.
Morrison, Toni. 1998. "Clinton as the First Black President." *New Yorker,* October 1998,
    http://ontology.buffalo.edu/smith/clinton/morrison.html.
Tomasky, Michael. 2017. *Bill Clinton: The American Presidents Series; The 42nd Presi-
    dent, 1993–2001.* New York: Times Books.
U.S. Department of Health and Human Services. 1996. "The Personal Responsibility and
    Work Opportunity Reconciliation Act of 1996." Office of the Assistant Secretary
    for Planning and Evaluation, https://aspe.hhs.gov/report/personal-responsibility
    -and-work-opportunity-reconciliation-act-1996.
Wickham, DeWayne. 2002. *Bill Clinton and Black America.* New York: Ballantine Books.

George Walker Bush

43rd President of the United States
Presidential Term: January 20, 2001–January 20, 2009
Political Party: Republican
Vice President: Richard "Dick" Cheney

George Walker Bush was born on July 6, 1946, in New Haven, Connecticut. He is
the son of 41st president of the United States George Herbert Walker Bush and
Barbara Bush. George W. Bush was elected president of the United States in 2000
by defeating Al Gore in one of the slimmest margins in American presidential
election history. This made Bush and his father the only son and father to become
president of the United States since John Adams and John Quincy Adams. In fact,
Bush lost the popular vote but won the Electoral College. In doing so, he became
the first president to be elected after having lost the popular vote since Benjamin
Harrison in 1888. In 2016, Donald J. Trump would become the third president
elected without winning the popular vote. Before becoming president of the United
States, Bush served as a business entrepreneur and the governor of Texas from
1995 until 2000.

Bush was a legacy at Yale University, as both his father and grandfather were
alumni of the institution. Bush received a bachelor's degree in history from Yale
University in 1968 and then joined the Texas National Guard but had unremark-
able service in the military and received an honorable discharge to begin graduate
school. Bush received a master's degree in business administration from Harvard
University in 1975. He then began working for a family friend's oil company. In
1977 he married Laura Welch, who was a teacher and librarian. In 1994 Bush
challenged incumbent Ann Richards for governor of Texas. Bush defeated Richards by a margin of 53 percent to 46 percent. He became the first governor of
Texas to win consecutive four-year terms. As governor, Bush appropriated more
money to elementary and secondary schools but tied this increase in funding

teacher salary increases to student performances on standardized achievement examines.

Bush announced his run for president of the United States in June 1999 and ran as a compassionate conservative. The term "compassionate conservative" entails a political philosophy that stresses using traditionally conservative techniques and concepts in order to help the general welfare of society. This term has been credited to historian and politician Doug Weed, who used it in the title of a speech in 1979. In Bush's view, the term "compassionate conservative" is a combination of traditional Republican economic policies and concern for the underprivileged. Although President Bush called himself as a compassionate conservative, prisoner executions increased under his administration, as did the number of crimes to which juveniles could be tried and sentenced as adults. In Bush's tenure as governor of Texas, 152 prisoners were executed, more than any previous governor in modern history. In only one case did Bush intervene and commute the death sentence of a prisoner. He received international attention for swift sentencing, the use of the death penalty, and the high number of executions in Texas. This issue was brought up during Bush's presidential campaign.

The murder of James Byrd brought Bush to the center of the race and hate crime debates in America during the 1990s. In 1998 in Jasper, Texas, Byrd was walking home from his parents' house during the early morning hours. He accepted a ride from three white men, who beat him, chained him to the back of a truck, and dragged him to death. His head and right arm were severed from his body. Byrd's headless torso was dumped on the side of the road, with his clothes scattered nearby. In 2001, the Texas Senate passed a hate crimes bill. Texas Democrats had been attempting to strengthen the state's hate crime law but were blocked in 1999. A similar bill passed, but Governor Bush refused to sign bill into law. Byrd's daughter even lobbied the governor to sign the bill in memory of her father. Bush would not budge, stating that crime is a crime no matter who commits it. He refused to sign the bill under pressure from religious and social conservatives because it included language providing protection for gays and lesbians. All three of Byrd's killers were convicted of capital murder. One of Byrd's killers was executed by the State of Texas on September 2011, marking the very first time in Texas history that a white person received a death sentence for killing a black person.

In 2000 while running for president, Bush spoke at the annual convention of the National Association for the Advancement of Colored People (NAACP) in Baltimore, Maryland. Traditionally a hostile crowd toward Republican Party candidates, Bush had the most to gain from a positive appearance in front of this group. The Republican Party had a fractured history with the civil rights organization. President Ronald Reagan refused to go and declined invitations from the organization. Bush's father, Vice President George H. W. Bush, received audible boos from the NAACP crowd when he addressed the group in 1983. Vice President Bush returned to the NAACP convention in 1988 and was received better than during his previous visit. In his address, he implicitly criticized his own administration's sensitivity on racial issues in 1996. Former Senate majority leader Bob Dole, a Republican Party presidential nominee, drew criticism for withdrawing from a scheduled appearance at the NAACP's annual convention. Dole said that he cancelled because he was afraid that the group's leadership was trying to "set me up" for a hostile reception. Dole also added that he preferred to speak to audiences he "could relate to" ("Bush Reaches Out to Minority Voters" 2006).

On the campaign trail and at the NAACP's convention, Bush defined himself as "a different kind of Republican." He indicated that he had tried to bring a more inclusive image to the Republican Party. Bush conceded that there was a gulf between the Republican Party and the African American community. Bush said, "I recognize the history of the Republican Party and the NAACP had not been one of regular partnership. . . . While some in our party have avoided the NAACP, and while some in the NAACP have avoided my party, I am proud to be here." During his remarks, candidate Bush promised "strong civil rights enforcement as a cornerstone of his administration" and acknowledged that "discrimination is still a reality even when it takes different forms." Bush also stressed his theme of expanding upward economic mobility. He did not reveal any new policy initiatives in his remarks at the conference but promised to make a strong commitment to civil rights if he won the presidency. He declared, "Strong civil rights enforcement will be a cornerstone of my administration. And I will confront another form of bias: the soft bigotry of lowered expectations" ("Bush Reaches Out to Minority Voters" 2006). There were protesters who spoke out against Bush and the State of Texas's hasty use of the death penalty. As Bush was being introduced, protesters held up signs saying "Abolish the racist death penalty." Other protesters chanted "Remember Gary Graham!"—referring to the controversial case of an African American man who was convicted of murder and executed in Texas earlier in 2000. The protesters were escorted out by security.

In 2006, President Bush returned to address the NAACP convention. It was the first time he spoke to the group as the president of the United States. Bush reiterated many of the same themes from his previous 2000 address to the organization. He talked about the gulf between the Republican Party and the African American community. Bush asserted, "I consider it a tragedy that the party of Abraham Lincoln let go of its historic ties with the African-American community." Emphasizing his point, he also stated, "For too long my party wrote off the African-American vote, and many African-Americans wrote off the Republican Party" (Stolberg 2006). Bush called for the U.S. Senate to renew the 1965 Voting Rights Act. After this call for action, the room erupted into applause. However, when Bush began to address education policies, housing policies, and employment policies, the crowd grew silent.

Bush was booed when he raised the topic of charter schools. Similar to when he gave the speech to the organization in 2000, he was interrupted by a heckler who shouted about the president's policies in the Middle East. Bush did not respond to these interruptions, overlooked the outburst, and plowed ahead, addressing the audience.

As the general election campaign advanced toward election day, the gap in the polls between Bush and Gore narrowed to the closest in any election in the previous 40 years. On election day, the electoral vote of Florida became the center of the country's attention. Florida's 25 electoral votes hung in the balance in a race that was too close to call. Gore called Bush on the night of the election to concede, then retracted his concession after learning how close the Florida vote count was. Bush led Gore by fewer than 1,000 popular votes after a mandatory statewide machine recount. The Florida Supreme Court got involved to sort out this wrangled election.

The Gore campaign asked for manual recounts in four counties that are known to traditionally lean toward the Democratic Party. In response, the Bush campaign filed suit in federal court to stop the voting recounts. For five weeks, the election remained unresolved as Florida state courts and federal courts heard numerous legal challenges by both the Bush and Gore campaigns. The Florida Supreme Court decided in a decision of 4 to 3 to cease the statewide manual recount of the approximately 45,000 ballots that voting machines recorded as an undetermined presidential vote (*New York Times* 2000). The deadline for certifying the state electors was December 18, 1999. The Bush campaign filed an appeal with the U.S. Supreme Court and asked that any recount be delayed until the case could be heard in front of the court. The court agreed with the Bush campaign, and a stay was issued on December 9, 1999. The court stated that an adequate and fair recount could not be conducted in time to certify the election. Essentially, this decision awarded the electoral votes of Florida and the presidency. In the end, Bush had 271 electoral votes to Gore's 266. Gore finally conceded the race on December 13, 2000, via a nationally televised event.

On January 29, 2001, Bush created the Office of Faith-Based and Community Initiatives with an executive order. The faith-based initiative was established with the premise that people could be better served by nonprofits and local groups than the federal government.

There were a number of critics of this initiative because it appropriated federal money to faith-based charities, which some believed violated the U.S. Constitution and separation of church and state. Thousands of faith-based and community organizations received federal grants because of Bush's faith-based initiative. Bush used these initiatives to make grand overtures to the African American community, unlike past presidents. He centered his message to the African American community on a faith-based approach and partnering with the community. The most important issues in the African American community were social, economic, and educational policies. Bush looked to partner with local organizations active in housing, job creation, drug rehabilitation, and other fields. He also met with African American clergy and others involved in these programs and hoped to push for legislation to provide federal support for their efforts.

In some ways, Bush exceeded the expectations of the African American community in diversifying his presidential cabinet. He appointed women and people of color. As president, Bush named five women, four African Americans, three Latinos, and two Asian Americans. He also appointed African Americans to more high-profile positions than any other previous president of the United States. African Americans in his first administrative cabinet included Secretary of State Colin L. Powell and Education Secretary Roderick R. Paige, both of whom left after the first term of President Bush. During Bush's second term, Al Jackson and Condoleezza Rice joined the cabinet.

Bush twice named African Americans as secretary of state. In January 2001, Colin L. Powell became the first African American to serve as secretary of state and served in this position for one term before resigning.

After Powell's resignation, Condoleezza "Condi" Rice was named secretary of state. She became the first African American woman to hold this position. She was also the first African American woman to serve as the U.S. national security adviser and the second woman to hold this post. Prior to joining the Bush administration, she had been a political science professor and provost at Stanford University. She served during the George H. W. Bush administration as a special assistant and director of Soviet and East European affairs with the National Security Council. As secretary of state in the George W. Bush administration, she devoted her agency to "transformational diplomacy." The State Department's mission under her watch was to build and sustain democratic states around the world and particularly in the Middle East. Rice supported the invasion of Iraq in 2003 after the United States made the case to the United Nations that Iraq had weapons of mass destruction.

Roderick "Rod" Paige served as secretary of education in the Bush administration from 2001 until 2005. Prior to that, Paige helped create the "No Child Left Behind" law. This law was based in part on his work as superintendent of the Houston Independent School District. Paige seemed to have widespread support when he was appointed to the post and advocated for more partnerships between states and districts to implement "No Child Left Behind" legislation. By 2003, every state had approved an accountability plan. The goal of these plans was to ensure that every student was learning and meeting goals. Paige focused on curtailing fraud and waste within the Department of Education. He pushed for streamlining operations and promoting excellence in the Department of Education. As a result of this work, the department received its second clean financial audit in a row in fiscal year 2003. This accomplishment was only the third clean audit in the history of the Department of Education. As a result, the department received the highest praise from the U.S. Office of Management and Budget.

In February 2001, Bush wanted to spur long-term economic growth and proposed tax cuts as a way to create jobs and stimulate the economy, calling for a $1.6 trillion reduction in taxes. The proposal doubled the child tax credit, incentivized more retirement savings, and phased out federal estate taxes. All income brackets received a tax cut, including new rebates for taxes paid in 2001. This bill was lauded by the Republicans, while Democrats believed that it amounted to tax breaks for the wealthiest Americans. Senate Democrats forced a compromise that reduced the final tax cut to $1.35 trillion, with an expiration date in 2011. Even with Democrats forcing a compromise, the tax cuts were a major victory for Bush. He was able to pass another modest tax cut in 2006 that reduced federal revenue by an estimated $4 trillion over a period of 10 years, worsening wealth inequality in the United States. These tax cuts also significantly increased the federal deficit.

Bush signed the "No Child Left Behind Act" into law on January 8, 2002. The program's reliance on testing was controversial. Critics charged that implementing this policy was too costly and that it usurped local power, local authority, and local autonomy, which formed the bedrock of the U.S. education system. By the time Bush left office, fourth-grade reading and math scores and eighth-grade math scores had reached their highest levels in history. Both parents and teachers complained about "teaching to the test," and administrators struggled to meet requirements. In 2015, Congress replaced "No Child Left Behind" with a new education bill.

In 2004, Bush named Alphonso Jackson as secretary of housing and urban development. Jackson joined the Bush administration in June 2001 as the Department of Housing and Urban Development's (HUD) deputy secretary and chief operating officer. As deputy secretary, he managed the day-to-day operations of the $32 billion agency and instilled a new commitment to ethics and accountability within HUD's programs and among its workforce and grant partners. Prior to working in the Bush administration, Jackson was president and CEO of the Housing Authority of the City of Dallas, Texas; the director of Public Safety for the City of St. Louis, Missouri; and a special assistant to the chancellor at the University of Missouri. After his stint in the Bush administration, Jackson returned to private-sector employment.

In 2005, Hurricane Katrina hit the Gulf Coast of the United States. The storm was classified as a Category 3 when it hit landfall, meaning that winds were between 100 and 140 miles per hour and stretched some 400 miles across. The states of Louisiana, Alabama, and Mississippi bore the brunt of the storm. Hurricane Katrina caused the displacement of hundreds of thousands of people from their homes, more than $100 billion in damages, and the loss of 2,000 people. The city of New Orleans became the focal point during this hurricane and its aftermath.

New Orleans was at high risk because the city is below sea level. Over the years, the Army Corp of Engineers had constructed a system of levees and seawalls to prevent the city from flooding, but levee breaches led to massive flooding. Nearly 80 percent of the city of New Orleans was under some quantity of water. Many people charged that the federal government was slow to meet the needs of the people affected by the storm. Bush later said he thought that New Orleans had dodged a bullet. The Bush administration failed to realize the gravity of the storm and its aftermath.

Bush spoke to the nation at historic Jackson Square in New Orleans. He stated that "four years after the frightening experience of September the 11th, Americans have every right to expect a more effective response in a time of emergency. When the federal government fails to meet such an obligation, I, as President, am responsible for the problem, and for the solution." Bush directed a comprehensive review of the federal government's response to Hurricane Katrina. He believed that a comprehensive review would better prepare the country for any future disasters. In a Pew Research poll, 66 percent of blacks said that the federal government's response in the wake of Katrina would have been faster if most of the victims were white. Only 16 percent of whites polled agreed with the response that it would have been handled in a timelier manner.

In September 2005 during a telethon benefit for victims of Hurricane Katrina, Mike Myers and Kanye West stood in front of a teleprompter and encouraged viewers to donate to the Red Cross. In his impromptu speech, West stated that

I hate the way they portray us in the media. If you see a black family, it says, "They're looting." You see a white family, it says, "They're looking for food." And you know that it's been five days because most of the people are black. And even for me to complain about it, I would be a hypocrite because I've tried to turn away from the TV because it's too hard to watch. I've even been shopping before, even giving a donation. So now I'm calling my business manager right now to see what's, what is the biggest amount I can give, and, and just to imagine if I was down there, and those are my people down there. So anybody out there that wants to do anything that we can help with the set-up, the way America is set up to help the, the poor, the black people, the less well-off, as slow as possible. I mean, this Red Cross is doing everything they can. We already realize a lot of people that could help are at war right now, fighting another way and they've given them permission to go down and shoot us. (Harris-Perry 2011, 10)

West concluded his impromptu speech with "George Bush doesn't care about black people!" The camera had not cut away in time, and millions of Americans heard his words. West's statement became the title of a song by the hip-hop group K-OTIX. The group used the music from Kanye West's hit song "Gold Digger" to create "George Bush Don't Like Black People." This implied that President Bush was a deliberate racist. Bush would later call West's words the worst moment of his presidency. Responding to West's comments, Bush stated, "I resent it, it's not true, and it's one of the most disgusting moments of my presidency" (Thomas 2015).

When asked about his views on affirmative action during presidential debates, Bush switched the topic and said that he "did not like quotas." In 2003 he sided with three white students who filed a discrimination suit at the University of Michigan. The U.S. Supreme Court heard a case that considered reversing a decision that upheld the use of affirmative action at universities as a means to obtaining diversity. Bush caved to conservative Republicans who believe that race should never be a factor in admissions and ordered a friend of the court to brief the Supreme Court case. Alberto Gonzales, who was the White House counsel, and Colin Powell, the secretary of state, favored using affirmative action as a policy to diversify the undergraduate student body. The Supreme Court struck down the admissions policy at the University of Michigan in 2003. In a turn, however, the Supreme Court, by a slim vote of five to four vote, upheld the affirmative action program at the Michigan Law School. During the presidential debate against John Kerry in Tempe, Arizona, in 2004, Bush clarified and summed up his views on affirmative action:

- He supported "affirmative access" to open the opportunities by using programs such as the Texas 10 percent plan. Under the Texas 10 percent plan, students who graduate in the top 10 percent of their class were automatically admitted to any state college or university.

- He advocated needs-based contracting and segmenting federal government contracts into smaller sizes to encourage entrepreneurship with minorities and people of color.

- He opposed quotas and racial preferences.

President Bush nominated several unwavering conservatives to U.S. courts of appeal, including two politically conservative African Americans: Janice Rogers Brown, who had been confirmed to the D.C. Circuit, and Jerome A. Holmes, who became the first African American judge to serve on the Tenth Circuit Court of Appeals when he was nominated and confirmed in 2006.

Bush nominated Brown for the U.S. Court of Appeals for the District of Columbia circuit, but her nomination stalled when Democrats took issue with her past opinions on abortion, affirmative action, and speeches denouncing government regulations. Ultimately, she was confirmed in 2005. As a justice of the California Supreme Court, Brown wrote the majority decision upholding the legality of Proposition 209. Most of Bush's appointments to the U.S. Commission on Civil Rights and the Office for Civil Rights at the U.S. Department of Education were staunch conservatives who were opposed to affirmative action. During Bush's administration, the Office for Civil Rights at the Department of Education pressured colleges and universities to abandon programs that were specifically designed to increase the number of minority students at colleges and universities.

Under the Bush administration, median incomes dropped for both African Americans and whites. In 2004 the median black income was $35,158, or 3 percent lower than the median income in 2000 ("Demographic Trends and Economic Well-Being" 2016). For whites, the median income dropped 1.2 percent. When Bush took office in 2001, the African American unemployment rate was 8.2 percent. During his first term in office the unemployment rate for African Americans fluctuated between 8.2 percent and 10.7 percent. The highest unemployment rate for African Americans was 11.3 percent in 2002. During his second term, the unemployment rate lowered for African Americans in 2005, 2006, and 2007. In these years, the numbers dipped below 10 percent. However, in 2008 the unemployment rate for African Americans was 12.1 percent.

In 2007, the economy in the United States began to decline. In an attempt to prop up the economy, the Federal Reserve lowered the interest rate. Financial firms skidded, and financial markets teetered toward failure. In February 2008, the Bush administration responded to the economic slowdown with a $168 billion stimulus package. In October 2008, consumer spending fell to historic low levels because hundreds of thousands of people lost their jobs. The national housing market went into a tailspin. The housing market crash was based on banks bundling mortgages and charging high interests to people who wanted to buy homes. Many of these individuals were African American or from poor economic backgrounds. Federal loan agencies lowered standards for mortgages due to pressure from Congress to increase home ownership among the poorer sectors of society. When lower-income borrowers began defaulting on their loans, the housing bubble burst and sent shockwaves through the country; the number of repossessed houses doubled over a one-year period. President Bush and Republicans who backed limited government went against their principles and intervened in this financial crisis. Bush signed the Emergency Economic Stabilization Act, which established the Troubled Assets Relief Program (TARP). TARP authorized $700 billion of expenditures to stabilize banks, restart credit markets, and support the U.S. auto industry. The act also provided assistance to help people avoid foreclosure on their homes.

Bush made two trips to Africa while he was in office. President Bill Clinton traveled to the slave ports at Gorée Island during an African tour in 1998 and 2004, and President Barack Obama would make two trips to Africa, in 2009 and 2013. In 2003 Bush visited five nations over a five-day period in an attempt to build relations with several nations. He traveled to Senegal, South Africa, Botswana, Uganda, and Nigeria. In 2008 on his second trip to the continent, he traveled to Benin, Tanzania, Rwanda, Ghana, and Liberia. There were very tight security measures taken for both trips, which led to security clashes between these African governments and the U.S. Secret Service. Measures were taken to manage the cultural clashes between security forces. Some believed that his first trip to Africa was an attempt to placate African American voters ahead of his reelection bid. Bush was accompanied by Condoleezza Rice and Colin Powell when he visited the slave ports on Gorée Island. The slave ports off of the coast of Senegal were the last site where millions of Africans were captured into slavery and shipped to the Americas. Bush visited slave quarters on Gorée Island off the coast of Senegal and followed the steps that were taken by countless terrified Africans who were chained and herded down the narrow passage toward the "Door of No Return," or the last point on the continent of Africa before the six-month torturous passage to America.

Bush gave an address at the site of the slave castles to about 300 people. During this speech in the blistering sun, the president called "slavery one of the greatest crimes in history" and said that "Christian men and women became blind to the clearest commands of their faith and added hypocrisy to injustice. . . . A republic founded on equality for all became a prison for millions" (Henry 2007). Bush confessed to the original sin of slavery in the United States and promised to make amends by directing funds to the development of Africa and addressing the AIDS epidemic through an African AIDS initiative. Also during this speech, he openly discussed U.S. participation in the transatlantic slave trade and the horrid conditions of the Middle Passage:

> Mr. President and Madam first lady, distinguished guests, and residents of Goree Island, citizens of Senegal, I'm honored to begin my visit to Africa in your beautiful country. For hundreds of years on this island, peoples of different continents met in fear and cruelty. Today, we gather in respect and friendship, mindful of past wrongs and dedicated to the advance of human liberty.

> At this place, liberty and life were stolen and sold. Human beings were delivered and sorted and weighed and branded with the marks of commercial enterprises and loaded as cargo on a voyage without return. One of the largest migrations of history was also one of the greatest crimes of history. Below the decks, the middle passage was a hot, narrow, sunless nightmare; weeks and months of confinement and abuse and confusion on a strange and lonely sea.

> Some refused to eat, preferring death to any future their captors might prefer for them. Some who were sick were thrown over the side. Some rose up in violent rebellion, delivering the closest thing to justice on a slave ship. Many

acts of defiance and bravery are recorded. Countless others we will never know. (Whitehouse.gov, Bush 2003)

Bush then moved to discussing the conditions and brutal treatment of the enslaved Africans once they landed in America. He discussed the freedoms that were ripped away from these individuals as they were kidnapped from Africa:

> Those who lived to see land again were displayed, examined and sold at auctions across nations in the Western Hemisphere. They entered society indifferent to their anguish and made prosperous by their unpaid labor. There was a time in my country's history where one in every seven human beings was the property of another. In law, they were regarded only as articles of commerce, having no right to travel or to marry or to own possessions. Because families were often separated, many were denied even the comfort of suffering together. (Marable and Agard-Jones 2018, 313)

President Bush took aim and admonished fellow Christians for the hypocrisy used to justify enslaving Africans in America and the contradictions of the founding principles of America and its practices. He wrapped Christianity in the country's founding but also pointed to the hardness of the hearts and consciences of slave owners and a dullness of sympathy to humanity:

> For 250 years the captives endured an assault on their culture and their dignity. The spirit of Africans in America did not break. Yet the spirit of their captors was corrupted. Small men took on the powers and airs of tyrants and masters. Years of unpunished brutality and bullying and rape produced a dullness and hardness of conscience. Christian men and women became blind to the clearest commands of their faith and added hypocrisy to injustice. A republic founded on equality for all became a prison for millions.

> And yet in the words of the African proverb, no fist is big enough to hide the sky. All of the generations oppressed under the laws of man could not crush the hope of freedom and defeat the purposes of God. In America, enslaved Africans learned the story of the exodus from Egypt and set their own hearts on a promised land of freedom. Enslaved Africans discovered a suffering savior and found he was more like themselves than their masters.

> Enslaved Africans heard the ringing promises of the Declaration of Independence and asked the self-evident question, "Then why not me?" In the era of America's founding, a man named Olaudah Equiano was taken in bondage to the New World. He witnessed all of slavery's cruelties, the ruthless and the petty. He also saw beyond the slave-holding piety of a time to a higher standard of humanity.

> "God tells us," wrote Equiano, "that the oppressor and the oppressed are both in his hands. And if these are not the poor, the broken-hearted, the blind, the captive, the bruised which our Savior speaks of, who are they?" Down through the years, African-Americans have upheld the ideals of America by exposing laws and habits contradicting those ideals. The rights

of African-Americans were not the gift of those in authority. Those rights were granted by the author of life and regained by the persistence and courage of African-Americans themselves. (CNN/World, Bush 2003)

Bush took the opportunity in the speech to discuss African American heroes who rose to prominence despite the legacy of slavery in America. He discussed the many ways in which these individuals faced the struggle for equality and fought against injustice and also discussed whites who abhorred the institution of slavery in America:

> Among those Americans was Phillis Wheatley, who was dragged from her home here in West Africa in 1761 at the age of 7. In my country she became a poet and the first noted black author in our nation's history. Phillis Wheatley said, "In every human breast God has implanted a principle which we call love of freedom. It is impatient of oppression and pants for deliverance." That deliverance was demanded by escaped slaves named Frederick Douglass and Sojourner Truth, educators named Booker T. Washington and W. E. B. Du Bois and ministers of the Gospel named Leon Sullivan and Martin Luther King, Jr. At every turn, the struggle for equality was resisted by many of the powerful. And some have said we should not judge their failures by the standards of a later time, yet in every time there were men and women who clearly saw this sin and called it by name. We can fairly judge the past by the standards of President John Adams, who called slavery "an evil of colossal magnitude." We can discern eternal standards in the deeds of William Wilberforce and John Quincy Adams and Harriet Beecher Stowe and Abraham Lincoln.

> These men and women, black and white, burned with a zeal for freedom and they left behind a different and better nation. Their moral vision caused Americans to examine our hearts, to correct our Constitution and to teach our children the dignity and equality of every person of every race. By a plan known only to Providence, the stolen sons and daughters of Africa helped to awaken the conscience of America. The very people traded into slavery helped to set America free. (CNN/World, Bush 2003)

Bush acknowledged that slavery did not end when it was outlawed in the United States. He reminded all that freedom cannot be held by one race or one nation and is the possession of all humankind. He admitted that slavery was still affecting the American experience today as the country still strives toward liberty and peace:

> My nation's journey toward justice has not been easy and it is not over. The racial bigotry fed by slavery did not end with slavery or with segregation, and many of the issues that still trouble America have roots in the bitter experience of other times. But however long the journey, our destination is set: liberty and justice for all.

> In the struggle of the centuries, America learned that freedom is not the possession of one race. We know with equal certainty that freedom is not the possession of one nation. This belief in the natural rights of man, this

conviction that justice should reach wherever the sun passes, leads America into the world.

With the power and resources given to us, the United States seeks to bring peace where there is conflict, hope where there's suffering, and liberty where there's tyranny. And these commitments bring me and other distinguished leaders of my government across the Atlantic to Africa. African peoples are now writing your own story of liberty. Africans have overcome the arrogance of colonial powers, overcome the cruelty of apartheid, and made it clear that dictatorship is not the future of any nation on this continent. (CNN/World, Bush 2003)

Bush acknowledged that Africa has its own heroes and leadership and that America has been arrogant and paternalistic in dealing with African countries. He promised that America and the nations of Africa would form trade partnerships and bring about prosperity. He pledged to stand with the nations of Africa to pursue political and economic freedom and to fight against the spread of AIDS:

In the process, Africa has produced heroes of liberation, leaders like Mandela, Senghor, Nkrumah, Kenyatta, Selassie and Sadat. And many visionary African leaders, such as my friend, have grasped the power of economic and political freedom to lift whole nations and put forth bold plans for Africa's development. Because Africans and Americans share a belief in the values of liberty and dignity, we must share in the labor of advancing those values. In a time of growing commerce across the globe, we will ensure that the nations of Africa are full partners in the trade and prosperity of the world.

Against the waste and violence of civil war, we will stand together for peace. Against the merciless terrorists who threaten every nation, we will wage an unrelenting campaign of justice. Confronted with desperate hunger, we will answer with human compassion and the tools of human technology. In the face of spreading disease, we will join with you in turning the tides against AIDS in Africa. We know that these challenges can be overcome because history moves in the direction of justice. The evils of slavery were accepted and unchanged for centuries, yet eventually the human heart would not abide them. (CNN/World, Bush 2003)

Bush concluded his speech by using the imagery of Dr. Martin Luther King, Jr. and Nelson Mandela to call on people to let their conscience guide them and voice injustice anywhere they see it:

There is a voice of conscience and hope in every man and woman that will not be silenced, what Martin Luther King called a certain kind of fire that no water could put out. That flame could not be extinguished at the Birmingham (Alabama) jail. It could not be stamped out at Robben Island (South Africa) prison. It was seen in the darkness here at Goree Island, where no chain could bind the soul. This untamed fire of justice continues to burn in the affairs of man, and it lights the way before us. (CNN/World, Bush 2003)

After he left office, Bush again gave poignant comments about the historical significance of slavery in America at the opening of the National Museum of African American History and Culture in Washington, D.C., in 2016. He reminded the country that John Adams voiced his opposition to slavery and that the museum was a testament to telling the entire history of America's story. Bush also acknowledged the African American heroes who faced America's cruelty with courageous acts and their faith:

> This museum is an important addition to our country for many reasons. Here are three. First, it shows our commitment to truth. A great nation does not hide its history. It faces its flaws and corrects them. This museum tells the truth that a country founded on the promise of liberty held millions in chains. That the price of our union was America's original sin. From the beginning, some spoke to truth. John Adams, who called slavery an "evil of colossal magnitude." Their voices were not heeded, and often not heard. But they were always known to a power greater than any on earth, one who loves his children and meant them to be free.
>
> Second, this museum shows America's capacity to change. For centuries, slavery and segregation seemed permanent. Permanent parts of our national life, but not to Nat Turner or Frederick Douglass; Harriet Tubman; Rosa Parks; or Martin Luther King, Jr. All answered cruelty with courage and hope. Our country is better and more vibrant because of their contributions and the contributions of millions of African Americans. No telling of American history is neither complete nor accurate without acknowledging them. And finally, the museum showcases the talent of some of our finest Americans. The galleries celebrate not only African American equality, but African American greatness. (Yahr 2016)

Bush concluded this speech by saying the new museum is home to all Americans and by staying true to the founding principles of the country and acknowledging our total history, the country will be empowered.

President Bush also celebrated the significance of the museum and its purpose. He believed the country would be stronger with a comprehensive telling of the country's history: "The lesson in this museum is that all Americans share a past and a future by staying true to our principles, righting injustice, and encouraging the empowerment of all. We will be an even greater nation for generations to come. I congratulate all those who played a role in creating this wonderful museum" (CNN/World, Bush 2003).

After the attacks of September 11, 2001, there were repeated complaints that the government singled out people with Islamic, Arabic, or Middle Eastern ties for increased scrutiny at the country's borders. There were also complaints of greater law enforcement surveillance and longer detention for immigration violations. Under the Bush administration, Middle Eastern men drew greater attention at airports. In 2003, the Bush administration ordered a broad ban on racial and ethnic profiling at all 70 federal law enforcement agencies. Critics believed the policy asserted that profiling could still be permissible when government mandated. The Justice Department issued guidelines that impacted some 120,000 U.S. law enforcement officers at the Federal Bureau of Investigation; the Drug Enforcement Agency; the Homeland Security Department; the Bureau of Alcohol, Tobacco, Firearms and Explosives; the Coast Guard; and other agencies.

In 2006, President Bush reauthorized the legislation that extended the Voting Rights Act for 25 years. The Voting Rights Act of 1965 opened polls to millions of African Americans by outlawing racist voting practices in the South. Bush signed the bill with lots of fanfare at the White House. He stated, "Congress has reaffirmed its belief that all men are created equal." The event was attended by Congress, civil rights leaders, and family members of civil rights leaders. It was one of a series of high-profile ceremonies that the president held to sign popular bills into law. Civil rights leaders attending the event included Reverend Al Sharpton and Reverend Jesse Jackson as well as the friends and relatives of Reverend Dr. Martin Luther King, Jr. and Rosa Parks; Dorothy Height, chairwoman of the National Council of Negro Women; and Marc Morial, the National Urban League head. The NAACP also sent an envoy that included its president Bruce Gordon, Chairman Julian Bond, and former head Benjamin Hooks. The bill passed the Senate by a vote of 98 to 0 and the House of Representatives by a vote of 390 to 33 (Tate 2014). The overwhelming majorities belied the difficulties getting to that point. Some southern lawmakers rebelled against renewing a law that requires their states to continue to use preclearance. In preclearance, states that have shown racist practices in voting must obtain Justice Department approval before changing any voting rules. These states contended that they were being punished for racist practices that had been eliminated. The states whose voting procedures still are overseen by the federal government are Alabama, Alaska, Arizona, Georgia, Louisiana, Mississippi, South Carolina, Texas, and Virginia.

FURTHER READING

Bush, George W. 2010. *Decision Points.* New York: Crown Publishers.

"Bush Reaches Out to Minority Voters." 2006. ABC News Archives, https://abcnews .go.com/US/story?id=96571&page=1.

Corn, David. 2004. *The Lies of George W. Bush.* New York: Three Rivers.

"Demographic Trends and Economic Well-Being." 2016. Pew Research Center, June 27, http://www.pewsocialtrends.org/2016/06/27/1-demographic-trends-and-economic -well-being/.

Ferguson, Michaele L., and Lori Jo Marso. 2007. *W Stands for Women: How the George W. Bush Presidency Shaped a Politics of Gender.* Durham, NC: Duke University Press.

Henry, Charles P. 2007. *Long Overdue: The Racial Politics of Racial Reparations.* New York: New York University Press.

Mann, James. 2015. *George W. Bush: The American Presidents Series; The 43rd President, 2001–2009.* New York: Times Books.

Peleg, Ilan. 2009. *The Legacy of George W. Bush's Foreign Policy: Moving beyond Neo-conservatism.* New York: Routledge.

Smith Edward, Jean. 2016. *Bush.* New York: Simon and Schuster.
Stolberg, Sheryl Gay. 2006. "In Speech to N.A.A.C.P., Bush Offers Reconciliation." *New York Times,* July 21.
Tate, Katherine. 2014. *Concordance: Black Lawmaking in the U.S. Congress from Carter to Obama.* Ann Arbor: University of Michigan Press.

Barack Hussein Obama II

44th President of the United States
Presidential Term: January 20, 2009–January 20, 2017
Political Party: Democratic
Vice President: Joseph R. Biden Jr.

Although Toni Morrison referred to Bill Clinton as the first black president of the United States, the first African American president of the United States was elected in 2008 with the election of Barack Obama. He was 45 years old when he was elected and a graduate of Harvard University Law School and Columbia University. Obama was the first African American president of the *Harvard Law Review.* He entered politics in Illinois, where he practiced civil rights law and taught at the University of Chicago Law School. Obama's first venture into politics came when he took his seat in the Illinois state assembly in 1997, serving from 1997 until 2005. In 2005, he was elected as a U.S. senator representing the state of Illinois.

Barack Hussein Obama II was born on August 4, 1961, in Honolulu, Hawaii, to a white woman from Kansas and a black man from Kenya. His parents met while they were students at the University of Hawaii. Obama wrote two best-selling books, *Dreams from My Father,* published in 1996 and reprinted in 2004, and *The Audacity of Hope,* published in 2006.

On January 20, 2009, Barack Obama was sworn in as the first African American president of the United States. President Obama helped improve the lives of African Americans through legislation such as the JOBS Act, the Affordable Care Act, and the My Brother's Keeper Alliance. He also became the first president to address the African Union. (U.S. Senate)

The United States first took notice of the charismatic Obama when he gave a keynote address at the 2004 Democratic National Convention. After this electrifying speech, combined with his victory in the U.S. senatorial race in 2004, he quickly gained popularity in the polls. A source of great speculation was whether or not he would run for president. And if he did run, could an African American man win? Initially, Obama denied that he would run for president. Celebrities called for him to throw his name in the ring for the presidency. On January 16, 2007, Obama released a video with the announcement that he was forming a committee to explore his viability as a candidate for president. On February 10, 2007, he formally announced his candidacy. Illinois state senator Barack Obama stood before a crowd of about 15,000 people in Springfield, Illinois, to announce his run for president of the United States. He stated, "I know I haven't spent a lot of time learning the ways of Washington. But I've been there long enough to know that the ways of Washington must change" (Dupuis and Boeckelman 2008).

The 2007 Democratic Party presidential nomination contest included several formidable candidates including Senator Hillary Rodham Clinton from New York, Senator John Edwards from North Carolina, Senator Joe Biden of Delaware, Representative Dennis Kucinich of Ohio, Bill Richardson of New Mexico, and Iowa Governor Tom Vilsack. Obama was the only African American serving in the U.S. Senate at the time he announced his run. Edwards and Clinton emerged as Obama's biggest rivals for the Democratic nomination. Clinton was the overwhelming favorite to win the nomination. Until 2006, most assumed that Edwards would be the biggest challenger to her candidacy.

Obama announced his run for the presidency at the Old State Capitol building in Springfield, Illinois, where President Abraham Lincoln gave his "House Divided" speech in 1858. During Obama's announcement he invoked the spirit of Lincoln, saying "And that is why, in the shadow of the Old State Capitol, where Lincoln once called on a divided house to stand together, where common hopes and common dreams still live, I stand before you today to announce my candidacy for president of the United States of America" (Berry and Gottheimer 2010). He heralded the decency of the citizens in the United States and expressed a desire to restore hope in the country. He specifically stated, "It was here, in Springfield, where North, South, East and West come together that I was reminded of the essential decency of the American people where I came to believe that through this decency, we can build a more hopeful America." Obama was interrupted several times with chants of "Obama! Obama! Obama!"

One of Obama's presidential opponents would become his vice presidential running mate. In 2007 Biden, senator from Delaware, launched his second bid for the presidency. On the day he officially filed his paperwork with the Federal Election Commission to start his campaign, he made some comments about Obama that some interpreted as being disparaging and others thought were borderline racist. In an interview with in the *New York Observer* Biden stated, "I mean you got the first mainstream African American who is articulate, bright, clean, and a nice-looking guy" (Nagourney 2007). He noted that Obama's life narrative was "storybook."

Biden's description drew scrutiny from his critics. A contrite Biden stated that his comments were taken out of context and apologized, saying "I deeply regret any offense my remark in the *New York Observer* might have caused anyone. That was not my intent, and I expressed that to Senator Obama." Biden noted he was using an expression his mother used in describing someone who was a good example, "clean as a whistle, sharp as a tack." Obama was not offended by Biden's comment. When Biden called to apologize, Obama told him it was unnecessary and that there were more important matters to worry about such as the Iraq War, health care, and energy. Obama stated, "I have no problem with Joe Biden." Later, Obama reiterated that he was not offended by Biden's comments. Obama also stated, "I didn't take Senator Biden's comments personally, but obviously they were historically inaccurate. African American presidential candidates like Jesse Jackson, Shirley Chisholm, Carol Moseley Braun and Al Sharpton gave a voice to many important issues through their campaigns, and no one would call them inarticulate" (Gregory 2007).

Obama faced the decision as to who he wanted as his running mate. After an initial list of about 20 people, two people rose to the top. A large contingent of people wanted Obama to choose Clinton as his vice president. Instead, he narrowed it down to Biden and Indiana senator Evan Bayh. Obama was looking for a partner and someone he could connect with for many years to come. Biden's enthusiasm and personality are the characteristics that nudged him forward to receive the vice presidential nod.

Obama downplayed being African American on the campaign trail, and while reluctant to get Secret Service protection, he acknowledged there had been death threats directed at him because he was an African American. In analyzing how his race would impact his campaign to become president, he stated, "You know, I don't spend a lot of time thinking about it or considering the details of this, but just to broaden the issue, are there people who would be troubled with an African-American president? Yes." He also said, "Are there folks who might not vote for me because I'm African-American? No doubt." Obama also continued and said if he did not become president it would not be because of his race. He stated, "It's going to be because I didn't project a vision of leadership that gave people confidence. It's going to be because of something I didn't do as opposed to because I'm African-American." When Obama was campaigning, he addressed his views on affirmative action. He believed that African Americans from high-income families should not receive any advantages. He used his daughters as examples when they apply for college and noted that his daughters are advantaged individuals and admission officers should treat them as such. He went on to say, "I think that we should take into account white kids who have been disadvantaged and who have been brought up in poverty and shown themselves to have what it takes to succeed." Obama, to not appear as slighting African American students and families, said, "There are a lot of African-American kids who are still struggling." Obama then added, "If we have done what needs to be done to ensure that kids who are qualified to go to college can afford it, that affirmative action becomes a diminishing tool for us to achieve racial equality in this society" (Wilson 2016, 66).

A video of Reverend Dr. Jeremiah Wright's controversial sermon surfaced and increased attention and scrutiny, and Obama addressed the issue of race and Wright's comments. Wright was Obama's pastor at Trinity Church of Christ in Chicago. In Wright's sermon, he describes a Marine Corps veteran who denounced the United States as being racist and described the attacks of September 11 as chickens coming home to roost because of the country's foreign policy. Critics attacked Wright as unpatriotic and un-American and tied Obama to Wright's rhetoric. In response to the negative media he had received and his association with Wright in an attempt to remain the front-runner in the Democratic Party nomination for president, Obama gave a speech on race at the National Conventional Center in Philadelphia, Pennsylvania, on March 18, 2008. The speech, titled, "A More Perfect Union," addressed inequality in the United States. Obama presented examples from his own life to show the complexity of the racial experience in America. He also covered "white privilege" and "black anger" during portions of the speech. In this critical speech, he offered healing and hope for America's future but also insisted that racism is still prevalent in society. In explaining black anger, Obama insisted "The anger is real; it is powerful; and to simply wish it away, to condemn it without understanding its roots, only serves to widen the chasm of misunderstanding that exists between the races" (Obama, *A More Perfect Union* 2008). Obama continued to show the complexity of race in America. He attempted to contrast the maternal and paternal sides of his family. He discussed being raised by his white grandmother and grandfather in Hawaii. He also discussed his white mother from Kansas and his black father from Kenya.

Obama continued to discuss his wife Michelle's blended heritage also. In discussing her heritage he stated, "I am married to a black American who carries within her the blood of slaves and slave owners, an inheritance we pass on to our two precious daughters." In addressing the contradictions both his grandmother and Wright presented in his narrative, Obama stated that he could not disown either of them. Noting Wright's status in his life, he said that he could not disown Wright, who officiated his wedding and baptized his children. Obama said, "I can no more disown him than I can my white grandmother." He further elaborated on the complexity of race in America and his grandmother: "She was a woman who loves me as much as she loves anything in this world, but a woman who once confessed her fear of black men who passed by her on the street, and who on more than one occasion has uttered racial or ethnic stereotypes that made me cringe" (Obama 2008).

Obama called for an end to the racial stalemate that the country had been stuck in for years. Some of his aides advised him to not give this unvarnished speech on race. They believed that a speech about racial issues in America of any kind would alienate white voters and bring his race center stage to his presidential campaign. The speech did not upend his campaign and appeared to endear him to whites while shoring up more support in the African American community.

Obama was not the first billion-dollar president but came very close to achieving the title in 2008. Over two years, he raised $750 million. These financial figures surpassed those of all of his opponents in the race for the White House. Obama's prowess was so impressive that he declined to participate in the public financing system for elections. After the Democratic National Convention, Obama had amassed about $200 million more than Republican Party nominee and Arizona senator John McCain. In an attempt to keep up with Obama fundraising, McCain received a large infusion of money from the Republican

National Committee. McCain raised $238 million from donors and also accepted $84 million in federal grant money for participating in the public financing system (Bradley 2008). Obama chose to spend his campaign dollars on television advertisements and spent $100 million more than McCain (Bradley 2008). The Obama campaign paid $5 million for a 30-minute network infomercial that aired on several broadcast networks and cable stations (Carter 2008).

The 2012 presidential race broke all previous fundraising totals for any presidential contest and became the most expensive in history. Obama raised $1.123 billion, while his opponent, Mitt Romney, raised $1.019 billion. As in his previous presidential race, Obama used a combination of small donors and a strong grassroots ground game to raise money. He also used large donations but relied on more small donors. Romney and the Republican Party relied on large donations. In the final weeks, Romney's committee outspent Obama's committee (Vogel, Levinthal, and Parti 2012).

Obama received overwhelming support from the African American community in both of his campaigns for president. He became a symbol of pride and hope for many African Americans. In May 2009 two African American boys, one eight years old and another five years old, visited the Oval Office with their father for a family photograph with President Obama. One of the boys asked the president, "I want to know if your hair is like mine." President Obama lowered his head so the young man could feel the texture of his hair. A White House photographer captured the moment. Later at a fundraiser, Michelle Obama stated that all pictures are changed out periodically in the White House except the one of the young boy touching President Obama's hair. It is a reminder that change is possible. She affirmed, "I want you to think of that little black boy in the Oval Office of the White House touching the head of the first black president" (Cockburn 2016). African Americans embraced the Obama presidency, which became an iconic symbol to the African American community and a marketing bonanza for some black entrepreneurs. Obama's image was plastered on items from T-shirts to car tags. The image of Obama became as iconic as the pictures of Reverend Dr. Martin Luther King, Jr. No other groups were more loyal to Obama in voting and support than the African American community.

While African Americans were psychologically uplifted with Obama's presidential win and years in the White House, African Americans overall appeared to fare worse in unemployment than in previous years. The wealth and income gap increased between blacks and whites. Black unemployment also increased under Obama's terms in office. According to the Bureau of Labor Statistics, the African American unemployment rate was 12.7 percent when Obama took office in January 2008. The lowest rate of African American unemployment during the Obama administration was 9.5 percent in June 2015, compared with 7.7 percent during the George W. Bush administration in August 2007. The highest number under Bush was 12.1 percent in December 2008, and under Obama it was 16.8 percent in March 2011 (Bureau of Labor Statistics 2018). This was the highest since the Ronald Reagan administration.

In November 2008, Obama won the Iowa Caucus. This winning finish in the caucus was due in part to record participation in the caucus by young Iowans.

John Edwards finished second, while Hillary Clinton finished third. This victory was crucial in Obama's presidential campaign. The Iowa win showed doubters of all races that he was a viable presidential candidate. Many potential voters reasoned that if Obama could win in an overwhelmingly white-populated state such as Iowa, it was possible he could win the presidency. In February 2008, veteran civil rights leader Congressman John Lewis, who had endorsed Clinton's run for the Democratic nomination, switched his support to Obama because his district strongly supported Obama. At the time of his endorsement of Clinton, Lewis stated, "She is the best-prepared to lead this country at a time when we are in desperate need of strong leadership." Lewis had been a longtime friend and supporter of President Bill Clinton and proclaimed he had a deep abiding love for both Bill and Hillary but felt compelled to switch his support to reflect the will of the people in his district. Lewis proclaimed, "I think the candidacy of Senator Obama represents the beginning of a new movement in American political history that began in the hearts and minds of the people of this nation. And I want to be on the side of the people, on the side of the spirit of history" (Zeneley 2008). Lewis's announcement came days before the Democratic primaries in the states of Texas and Ohio. Hillary Clinton was hoping to break Obama's winning streak of 11 straight wins in the primary races.

As Obama secured the Democratic nomination, debates were set with Republican Party presidential nominee John McCain. A series of debates was scheduled by the Commission on Presidential Debates, a bipartisan group, and three debates were scheduled for the presidential nominees at the University of Mississippi in Oxford; Belmont University in Nashville, Tennessee; and Hofstra University in Long Island, New York. At a McCain rally in Minnesota during a question-and-answer session, an elderly white lady expressed her fear that Obama was an Arab and a Muslim. McCain quickly corrected her: "No ma'am, Obama is a decent family man and citizen that I just happen to have disagreements with on fundamental issues" (Douglas and Talev 2008).

Misinformation was spread about Obama to fan the flames of fear that he was a Muslim, a terrorist, or a socialist. This misinformation campaign smacked of a racist attempt to play up the tragedy of 9/11 and the ethnicity and religious affiliation of those who carried out the attack, conflate these issues, and transfer them onto Obama. Handbills and pamphlets filled with misinformation were disseminated to white neighborhoods erroneously portraying Obama as an Arab, a Muslim, and a terrorist. The term "Birtherism" grew out of these controversies. Birtherism is the falsehood that Obama was not born in the United States, which would make him ineligible to serve as president. Reality show star Donald Trump was one of the main champions of this falsehood and pushed the idea so convincingly that some believed him and began to question whether Obama was actually born in Hawaii. Trump challenged Obama to show his birth certificate and even offered money to any individual who would find Obama's "real birth certificate." In an attempt to cut down this controversy laced with racism, the hospital where Obama was born released his birth certificate, but this still did not quell the controversy. Trump continued to whip those who believed this lie into a frenzy about the possibility of having an illegitimate president. Letter-writing campaigns were also initiated, and anti-Obama letters filled with misinformation were mailed out in a concerted effort to destroy his presidential campaign and reputation.

On November 4, 2008, Obama won the presidential election with more than 69 million votes, defeating McCain to become the 44th president of the United States. Obama was 47 years old; he received 365 Electoral College votes and accumulated almost 53 percent of the popular vote. He was the first sitting U.S. senator to win the presidency since John F. Kennedy in 1960. Obama was able to win traditional strongholds such as Virginia and Indiana and battleground states such as Florida and Ohio that had been held by the Republican Party in the previous elections.

After Obama's victory, a huge rally was held in Grant Park in Chicago. His presidential victory came 140 years after the conclusion of the American Civil War and state-sanctioned slavery. Obama appeared with his wife, Michelle, and daughters, Malia and Sasha, to an enormous crowd. In his victory speech, President Obama opened by affirming the power of America's democracy and acknowledging the history-making moment. He opened with "If there is anyone out there who still doubts that America is a place where all things are possible, who still wonders if the dream of our founders is alive in our time, who still questions the power of our democracy, tonight is your answer." Obama then thanked his supporters, acknowledged their diversity and unity, and said, "It's the answer spoken by young and old, rich and poor, Democrat and Republican, black, white, Hispanic, Asian, Native American, gay, straight, disabled and not disabled. Americans who sent a message to the world that we have never been just a collection of individuals or a collection of red states and blue states. We are and always will be, the United States of America" (Obama Speech, "This Is Your Victory," 2008). He wanted the crowd gathered at Grant Park to share and revel in his victorious moment with him and his family:

> This is our chance to answer that call. This is our moment. This is our time, to put our people back to work and open doors of opportunity for our kids; to restore prosperity and promote the cause of peace; to reclaim the American dream and reaffirm that fundamental truth, that, out of many, we are one; that while we breathe, we hope. And where we are met with cynicism and doubts and those who tell us that we can't, we will respond with that timeless creed that sums up the spirit of a people: Yes, we can! (Obama Speech, "This Is Your Victory," 2008)

On January 20, 2009, at noon on the west front of the U.S. Capitol and before a crowd of more than 1 million onlookers, Obama was sworn in as president of the United States. The inaugural theme was "A New Birth of Freedom." This phrase was taken from and paid homage to Abraham Lincoln's Gettysburg Address and honored the 200th anniversary of his birthday. Obama was sworn in under the tightest security ever for a president. He was shielded by a heavily armed Cadillac limousine with bullet-resistant glass, fighter planes, and Secret Service SWAT teams with automatic weapons. Snipers were also positioned on rooftops and balconies along Pennsylvania Avenue, with at least 58 law enforcement and other agencies working on the president's security detail. All individuals attending the actual swearing-in ceremony were screened with walk-through or handheld metal detectors.

Obama's inaugural address aimed to encourage a sense of hope in the nation and reassure citizens that America was not in decline and had the fortitude to rise to meet the challenges that faced the nation:

> These are the indicators of crisis, subject to data and statistics. Less measurable, but no less profound, is a sapping of confidence across our land; a nagging fear that America's decline is inevitable, that the next generation must lower its sights. Today I say to you that the challenges we face are real, they are serious and they are many. They will not be met easily or in a short span of time. But know this America: They will be met. On this day, we gather because we have chosen hope over fear, unity of purpose over conflict and discord. On this day, we come to proclaim an end to the petty grievances and false promises, the recriminations and worn-out dogmas that for far too long have strangled our politics. (Obama, Inaugural Address, 2009)

With this address, Obama also hoped to calm the fear about economic instability in the country and restore the nation's confidence in the economy. The American people were skittish, as the economy had been locked into a downward spiral. Obama stated,

> For everywhere we look, there is work to be done. The state of our economy calls for action: bold and swift. And we will act not only to create new jobs but to lay a new foundation for growth. We will build the roads and bridges, the electric grids and digital lines that feed our commerce and bind us together. We will restore science to its rightful place and wield technology's wonders to raise health care's quality and lower its costs. We will harness the sun and the winds and the soil to fuel our cars and run our factories. And we will transform our schools and colleges and universities to meet the demands of a new age. All this we can do. All this we will do. (Obama, Inaugural Address, 2009)

Obama also addressed the nation's security and how the nation would thwart threats and seek corporation and understanding with other nations. He also sent a stern warning to the nation's enemies that America's resolve would not be broken:

> They understood that our power alone cannot protect us, nor does it entitle us to do as we please. Instead, they knew that our power grows through its prudent use. Our security emanates from the justness of our cause; the force of our example; the tempering qualities of humility and restraint. We are the keepers of this legacy; guided by these principles once more, we can meet those new threats that demand even greater effort, even greater cooperation and understanding between nations. We'll begin to responsibly leave Iraq to its people and forge a hard-earned peace in Afghanistan. With old friends and former foes, we'll work tirelessly to lessen the nuclear threat and roll back the specter of a warming planet. We will not apologize for our way of

life nor will we waver in its defense. And for those who seek to advance their aims by inducing terror and slaughtering innocents, we say to you now that our spirit is stronger and cannot be broken. You cannot outlast us, and we will defeat you. (Obama, Inaugural Address, 2009)

A few days after the inauguration and as the governing phase of Obama's presidency began, Republicans in Congress plotted ways to win and recapture political power and limit Obama's legislative agenda. Eric Cantor, the Republican minority whip from Virginia, and U.S. Senate minority leader Mitch McConnell from Kentucky were two of the key architects of this resistance strategy. Cantor got the House Republicans to stand against Obama's economic stimulus plan. In an interview, McConnell told reporters, "The single most important thing we want to achieve is for President Obama to be a one-term president" (Capehart 2012). The Republicans believed that their party could return to the seat of power by resisting President Obama and limiting him as a one-term president. Vice President Biden stated that several Republican congressman made their obstructionist views plain when they stated, "For the next two years, we can't let you succeed in anything. That's our ticket to coming back" (Sargent 2012).

President Obama continued the banking bailout, begun under President George W. Bush, as a means to curb the financial crisis that began in 2007. Obama's administration enacted an $800 billion stimulus program under the American Recovery and Reinvestment Act of 2009, and over the next two years, jobs began to increase. In 2010, the Patient Protection and Affordable Care Act (ACA) was passed. This law assisted 23 million people with health insurance through state health care exchanges and an extension of Medicaid. Some states opted out of the Medicaid expansion option. One of the features of this law was that it aimed to help the poor, those who were sick, and those who had difficulty finding insurance coverage. Under the law, insurance companies could no longer deny coverage to people with preexisting conditions or drop individuals when they are sick. Another feature aimed to help people who were too poor to afford health care insurance and who make too much money to qualify for Medicaid. An expansion of Medicaid and the Children's Health Insurance Program helped these individuals. Before the new law was put into place, there was an issue with lifetime and annual dollar limits that did not cover expensive treatments. This law also eliminated lifetime limits. The only reason that subscribers could be dropped on the new ACA-protected health plans was through fraud.

The ACA was dubbed "Obamacare," a term coined by conservative Republicans as derogatory slang for a law they vehemently opposed. It was also a way of tainting Obama's attempt to reform America's health care system. At first Obama resisted having his name associated with the law, but then he embraced it. Obama stated, "You want to call it Obamacare, that's okay, because I do care" (Delreal 2014). The White House capitalized on Obama's embracing of the term and created a Twitter hashtag. Obamacare cut the number of blacks uninsured by a third.

Critics and opponents challenged part of the ACA, with portions of the law challenged all the way to the U.S. Supreme Court. The court's decision allowed the federal government to continue providing subsidies to Americans who purchase health care through exchanges regardless of whether they are state or federally operated. Sonia Sotomayor, whom President Obama nominated to the Supreme Court, is credited as a key force in the ruling, having presented cautionary arguments against the potential dismantling of the law.

Obama appointed African Americans, Latinos, and women to his cabinet. Many thought he would appoint a large number of African Americans, and some African American congressmen were disappointed that he did not. Charles Rangel, congressman from New York, was one of the most vocal critics of the lack of diversity within the Obama cabinet: "Obama's lack of diversity is embarrassing as hell" (Killough 2013). Obama did appoint Eric Holder, attorney general from 2009 to 2015, and Loretta Lynch, attorney general from 2015 to 2017; Susan Rice, ambassador to the United Nations and special adviser; Ron Kirk, U.S. trade representative; Jeh Johnson, secretary of homeland security; Anthony Foxx, secretary of transportation; and John King Jr., secretary of education. Van Jones was set to become the nation's first green jobs czar, but his appointment was nixed because of disparaging comments he made toward the Republican Party regarding 9/11. Jones's comments fit the erroneously constructed narrative that Obama and those associated with him were radical leftists and socialists. On August 2009, President Obama nominated Sonia Sotomayor to the Supreme Court. The U.S. Senate confirmed her by a margin of 68 to 31, and she became the Supreme Court's first Latino justice.

In July 2009, Harvard University professor Dr. Henry Louis Gates Jr. was arrested at his Cambridge, Massachusetts, home by local police. After coming home from a trip to China, Gates found his front door jammed. He and his driver pushed their way into the house. One of Gates's neighbors thought he was robbing the house and called the police.

Gates was in the house when the police arrived. The police officer asked him to step outside for questioning, but Gates refused. He then showed the officer his driver's license and Harvard University faculty identification card. The driver's license showed Gates's address, which confirmed that the house was his residence. According to police, Gates became angry and belligerent and followed the police outside. He was then arrested for disorderly conduct, but the charge was later dropped. During a press conference on health care reform, Obama was asked about Gates's arrest. The president weighed in on the situation and stated that the police officer acted "stupidly." Obama said that he understood Gates's frustration and if he were to attempt to "jigger into" his old house in Chicago, he anticipated that the police would be called on him as well. Obama continued:

> Now, I don't know, not having been there and not seeing all the facts, what role race played. But I think it's fair to say, number one, any of us would be pretty angry; number two, that the Cambridge police acted stupidly in arresting somebody when there was already proof that they were in their own home. (Goodnough 2009)

Obama reminded the country of its long history of racial profiling and the role that race has played in American policing. He stated, "What I think we know, separate and apart from this incident, is that there's a long history in this country of African Americans and Latinos being stopped by law enforcement disproportionately. That's just a fact." He continued: "And yet the fact of the matter is, is that, you know, this still haunts us. And even when there are honest misunderstandings, the fact that blacks and Hispanics are picked up more frequently, and often time for no cause, casts suspicion, even when there is good cause" (Khan and McPhee 2009).

As a legislator in Illinois, Obama had pushed for the passage of legislation to address racial profiling. He also reminded the country that progress had been made on the racial front and his being elected president of the United States was a testament to that fact. His critics issued torrid responses to his comments. Obama backed off, hoping not to racialize this situation even though he rarely spoke about race issues.

During a 2009 speech to a joint session of Congress, Congressman Joe Wilson, a Republican from South Carolina, shouted "You lie!" after President Obama stated that the proposed health care legislation and plan would not cover undocumented immigrants in the address. After Wilson's disrespectful outburst, Obama calmly stopped and looked at him and replied "That's not true," then continued with his address. People inside the chamber and those watching on television were shocked at this outburst. While this act received much media attention, several other disrespectful acts took place during the State of the Union Address. Congressman Louie Gohmert from Texas wore a sign around his neck that said "What bill?" During the address when President Obama requested that Republicans share their health reform ideas with him, a small group of them raised a stack of papers above their heads. Republican Arizona senator John McCain, Obama's opponent in the 2008 presidential election, called these actions "totally disrespectful." Republican senator Lindsey Graham expressed disappointment in the actions of his Republican colleagues: "Our nation's president deserves to be treated with respect. It was an inappropriate remark, and I am glad an apology has been made" (CNN Politics 2009).

In response to Wilson's outburst, former president Jimmy Carter stated that it "was based on racism. . . . [T]here is an inherent feeling among many in this country that an African American should not be president" (Meikle 2009). Minority whip Democratic congressman James Clyburn from South Carolina expressed his hope that Wilson would publicly apologize to President Obama on the same floor where the insolent infraction occurred (Rowland 2009). After the speech, Wilson issued a statement apologizing for his outburst:

> This evening, I let my emotions get the best of me when listening to the president's remarks regarding the coverage of illegal immigrants in the health care bill. While I disagree with the president's statement, my comments were inappropriate and regrettable. I extend sincere apologies to the president for this lack of civility. (Bresnahan and Gerstein 2009)

The U.S. House of Representatives formally reprimanded Wilson. In a vote of 240 to 179, the House of Representatives passed a resolution of disapproval, which was a mild rebuke for his discourteous actions during the speech at the joint session of Congress. Following the incident, Wilson's campaign donations increased.

President Obama accepted Wilson's apology and expressed his understanding that people make mistakes.

In 2009 in one of his first international trips as president, Obama visited Africa. He traveled to Ghana and Egypt. In his speech, he discussed the relationship between the United States and Africa and the partnerships needed to ensure transformational change across the continent:

> I've come here to Ghana for a simple reason: The 21st century will be shaped by what happens not just in Rome or Moscow or Washington, but by what happens in Accra, as well. This is the simple truth of a time when the boundaries between people are overwhelmed by our connections. Your prosperity can expand America's prosperity. Your health and security can contribute to the world's health and security. And the strength of your democracy can help advance human rights for people everywhere. So, I do not see the countries and peoples of Africa as a world apart. I see Africa as a fundamental part of our interconnected world as partners with America on behalf of the future we want for all of our children. That partnership must be grounded in mutual responsibility and mutual respect. (Obama, A New Moment of Promise Speech, 2009)

In 2013 Obama returned to Africa and visited Senegal, South Africa, and Tanzania. During this trip he met with a wide array of leaders from government, business, and civil society to discuss strategic partnerships on bilateral and global issues. Just as he did in his first trip to Africa, Obama stressed the importance that the United States places on the deep and growing relationships with countries in Africa. In doing so, he expressed his desire to expand economic growth, investment, and trade and reinforce democratic institutions by investing in the next generation of African leaders.

In 2012, Obama was reelected to a second presidential term, defeating the Republican Party nominee Mitt Romney. Obama received about 51 percent of the vote, while Romney received 47 percent. Other minor political party candidates made up the remaining voting percentage. This was the first time a Democratic president won the Electoral College and over 51 percent of the popular vote in two elections. Among white male voters Obama lost by a large margin, but he performed strongly among African Americans. Obama also performed well with women of all races, winning this demographic by double digits. He also won the majority of the Latino vote.

In July 2013, President Obama again waded into the issue of race when George Zimmerman was acquitted of killing Trayvon Martin, an African American teenager. Obama did not hesitate in discussing this African American teenager's killing. The president talked about the problematic issues facing black men in this country. He also explained why the Zimmerman verdict hit close to home for him and other African Americans:

> You know, when Trayvon Martin was first shot I said that this could have been my son. Another way of saying that is Trayvon Martin could have been me 35 years ago. And when you think about why, in the African American

community at least, there's a lot of pain around what happened here, I think it's important to recognize that the African American community is looking at this issue through a set of experiences and a history that doesn't go away. (Washington Post Staff 2013)

Obama may have felt more freedom to speak on racial issues and other controversial matters because he was serving in his second term and did not have the pressure of being reelected to office. In 2014, a group of young African American activists met privately with Obama in the White House. These young activists did not believe that Obama understood their pain, and they wanted him to speak more about race issues. They believed that if Obama spoke out more on these issues, he could create and secure his presidential legacy. On February 18, 2014, the president invited civil rights activists and leaders to the White House to discuss a range of civil rights issues including criminal justice reform. The event was billed as an intergenerational meeting with young and old civil rights leaders. Aislinn Pulley, a cofounder of Black Lives Matter Chicago, chose not to attend the meeting, believing that it was just a photo opportunity for President Obama. She said, "The struggle is not a soundbite." In 2016 at a rally in London, England, Obama met a group of young people. One young person suggested that the president had not done enough to address racial profiling at airports in the United States. Obama then turned his attention to the Black Lives Matter movement. He praised the movement as "really effective in bringing attention to problems" (Shear and Stack 2016). However, he believed that young activists should be more willing to work with political leaders to craft solutions instead of criticizing from outside the political process. He specifically stated:

Once you've highlighted an issue and brought it to people's attention and shined a spotlight, and elected officials or people who are in a position to start bringing about change are ready to sit down with you, then you can't just keep on yelling at them. And you can't refuse to meet because that might compromise the purity of your position. . . . The value of social movements and activism is to get you at the table, get you in the room, and then to start trying to figure out how is this problem going to be solved. (Shear and Stack 2016)

Several civil rights leaders and other leaders in the African American community believed that the president had not done enough. Obama pushed back on his critics and touted his administration's support for sentencing guidelines that were more fair-minded to African Americans. The administration had reached out to young black men with the "My Brother's Keeper" initiative and created a task force to address tensions between African Americans and the police and other law enforcement units.

Tavis Smiley and Cornell West, two well-respected African American intellectuals, were critical of Obama's presidency. Smiley, an author and media personality, had a national following from his syndicated shows on Black Entertainment Television and the Public Broadcasting System. He had been a commentator on the *Tom Joyner Morning* syndicated radio show but left the show after being critical of Obama and receiving condemnation from radio listeners. Obama had been on Smiley's PBS show several times prior to becoming president of the United States. After Obama made public comments about the killing of Trayvon Martin, Smiley referred to Obama's comments as "weak as presweetened Kool-Aid." In 2014, Smiley defended his criticisms of Obama. He believed that he was being respectful and speaking truth to power. Smiley stated:

> As Cornell West and I said many years ago; I respect the president, I will protect the president against white supremacist attacks or anything else he's unfairly targeted for. So you're respecting, you're protecting, but you're correcting when he's wrong. Not because he's Barack Obama, but because he's the president. (Williams 2014)

Cornell West, an author, scholar, professor, public intellectual, and professor at Princeton University and Harvard University, had initially supported Obama and spoke on his behalf at campaign rallies in 2008. West became critical after Obama won the Nobel Peace Prize in 2009. In 2011 West directed harsh comments toward Obama, calling him a "black mascot" for the Wall Street oligarchy, a "black Muppet" for corporate plutocrats, and a "Rockefeller Republican in black face." West also called Obama counterfeit and someone who posed as a progressive. He defined Obama's presidency as a "drone presidency" because of the continued use of drones to drop bombs in Afghanistan and a "Wall Street presidency" because of corporate bank bailouts. Smiley and West started a tour in which they hoped to highlight poverty in America through a radio show and on Smiley's PBS television show. The tour took place prior to the 2012 presidential race, and they hoped it would showcase poverty, as many of the presidential candidates had failed to adequately address the issue. West and Smiley authored a book, *The Rich and the Rest of Us,* that chronicled their poverty tour and did not cease their criticism of Obama.

Minister Louis Farrakhan, the leader of the Nation of Islam, was also a critic of President Obama. Farrakhan lambasted the president over the bombing and killing of Muammar Gaddafi, the prime minister of Libya. Gaddafi led Libya for 40 years. His leadership was bolstered by the country's oil wealth and autocratic leadership. Gaddafi was thought to be a sponsor of terrorism and to have had a hand in the bombing of Pan Am Flight 103 in 1988 that killed 189 Americans. In 2011, Libyans rose up against his dictatorship and overthrew him. After many years of economic sanctions, Libya and Gaddafi began to make overtures to Western nations in an attempt to rebuild relationships with them. Gaddafi also relinquished the country's nuclear weapons, renounced his support for terrorist groups, and gave up his pursuit of nuclear weapons. He began to move toward a domestic policy that featured privatization and international investments. Sanctions were gradually lifted, but when the revolt occurred in 2011, Western nations backed the rebel forces. After the uprising, Gaddafi was caught and killed.

Obama addressed the situation in Libya in the White House Rose Garden after a video was shown of Gaddafi's bloody corpse. President Obama said, "One of the world's longest-serving dictators is no more." He also stated, "The Libyans had won their revolution and "the dark shadow of tyranny has been lifted." President

Obama, when later asked what his biggest mistake was, replied, "Probably failing to plan for the day after what I think was the right thing to do in intervening in Libya" (Tierney 2016).

Farrakhan had harsh criticism for President Obama and his foreign policy advisers: "You have made your president an assassin. The only value that he has now is that he was responsible for the death of Osama bin Laden. He was captured without a weapon. He should have been brought to America, put on trial for the American people to see this man" (Haggerty 2011). Farrakhan's heated rhetoric and criticism may have been based on his friendship and business relationship with Gaddafi. *The Chicago Tribune* reported that Farrakhan had received a $3 million loan from Gaddafi to build the Mosque Maryam, the Nation of Islam's international headquarters in Chicago. Farrakhan went on to describe Obama's advisers as "wicked demons" and said the United States and its allies are "in for a shock" if they believe that new governments in Libya, Egypt, and other Arab countries will automatically be pro-America. Farrakhan noted, "We voted for our brother Barack, a beautiful human being with a sweet heart. . . . But he has turned into someone else. Now he's an assassin" (Haggerty 2011).

Farrakhan continued to denounce the U.S. government and President Obama. He stated: "America puts her trust in her weapons of war. She threatens the nations of the earth and has my brother calling for the assassination of Brother Muammar Gaddafi. What has he done? I can defend that man. You don't know that man." Farrakhan believed that Obama's advisers gave him wrong intelligence regarding Libya. Farrakhan used the comparison between U.S. intervention in Libya and the wars in Iraq and Afghanistan as an example of past deceptive American foreign policy.

Farrakhan said, "You talk about a man killing his own people. When you lie to the American people saying that Saddam Hussein had weapons of mass destruction. When you lie and then take innocent young men who come to serve their country, and send them to die in Iraq, in Afghanistan, over lies, that's a murderer in the White House" (Huffington Post 2017). After Gaddafi was killed, Libya plunged into chaos, with militias taking over and rival governments claiming power. Obama has said the worst mistake of his presidency was to underestimate the tribal differences and lack of planning for the aftermath of a post-Gadaffi Libya.

In July 2015, Obama became the first U.S. president to address the African Union. The African Union is an intergovernmental organization formed to promote unity and solidarity in all 55 countries of Africa. The African Union was established in 2001 in Ethiopia and replaced the Organization of African Unity, which operated from 1963 to 2002. Obama's appearance before the African Union was part of a five-day two-nation tour of East Africa. His keynote address was at the African Union headquarters in Mandela Hall in Addis Ababa, Ethiopia. During his address, Obama criticized some African leaders and their quest to hold on to power even after their presidential terms ended. His address was interrupted several times with thunderous applause. Obama stated, "Africa's democratic progress is also at risk when leaders refuse to step aside when their terms end. Now, let me honest with you, I don't understand this" (VOA 2015). Obama also addressed corruption and the mistreatment of women in African countries. This echoed sentiments of the speech he had given earlier in the week in Nairobi,

Kenya. Obama's visit to Africa was different than his first visit in 2009. Many nations in Africa have built relationships with China. Chinese investments have helped to eliminate some of the stereotypes of an Africa overrun by poverty and war. China has invested in many African nations, which has made them less inclined to take policy direction from the United States and other Western powers. Obama addressed ending the culture of corruption in some countries in Africa that prevented these countries from reaching their full economic potential.

In March 7, 2015, Obama went to Selma, Alabama, to commemorate the 50th anniversary of the Selma-to-Montgomery march and the passage of the Voting Rights Act of 1965. More than 100,000 people showed up to participate in the festivities. President Obama and former presidents George W. Bush and Bill Clinton were present to remember the tragic events known as Bloody Sunday on the Edmund Pettus Bridge.

Back in 1965 during the apex of the modern Civil Rights Movement, activists organized a march from Selma to Montgomery, the state capital. The marchers wanted to bring attention to African Americans being denied the right to vote and participate in the electoral process. On March 7, some 600 people assembled at a downtown church, prayed, and began to walk slowly and solemnly through the streets of Selma. When they approached the Edmund Pettus Bridge, the marchers were met by Alabama state troopers swinging nightsticks, clubs, and whips to break up a civil rights voting march. Five months after this incident, President Lyndon B. Johnson signed the Voting Rights Act of 1965 into law. The act protected African Americans' right to vote that had been granted in 1870 by the Fifteenth Amendment but had not been followed in some states.

Obama opened his speech, reminding the audience of Reverend Dr. Martin Luther King, Jr. and Addie Mae Collins, Cynthia Wesley, Carole Robertson, and Denise McNair, the four girls who died in the 16th Street Baptist Church bombing in 1963. Obama exclaimed that the civil rights battles of the past were clashes in determining the true meaning of America and its ideals. He then acknowledged that the civil rights leaders and foot soldiers of the era endeavored to create a more inclusive and just society. He noted that the events that transpired on the bridge could be analyzed not in isolation but instead as part of a long history of the struggle for freedom:

> In one afternoon fifty years ago, so much of our turbulent history, the stain of slavery and anguish of civil war; the yoke of segregation and tyranny of Jim Crow; the death of four little girls in Birmingham, and the dream of a Baptist preacher met on this bridge. It was not a clash of armies, but a clash of wills; a contest to determine the meaning of America. And because of men and women like John Lewis, Joseph Lowery, Hosea Williams, Amelia Boynton, Diane Nash, Ralph Abernathy, C. T. Vivian, Andrew Young, Fred Shuttlesworth, Dr. King, and so many more, the idea of a just America, a fair America, an inclusive America, a generous America that idea ultimately triumphed. As is true across the landscape of American history, we cannot examine this moment in isolation. The march on Selma was part of a broader campaign that spanned generations; the leaders that day part of a long line

of heroes. They saw that idea made real in Selma, Alabama. They saw it made real in America. (Obama Remarks, 50th Anniversary of Selma to Montgomery 2015)

Obama acknowledged that the events that took place on the Edmund Pettus Bridge and the subsequent march from Selma to Montgomery impacted the African American community. He understood that the moment was a shining one in paving the way to opening doors for other minority communities. He understood that the events on the Edmund Pettus Bridge were key to him becoming the first African American president of the United States:

> Because of campaigns like this, a Voting Rights Act was passed. Political, economic, and social barriers came down, and the change these men and women wrought is visible here today in the presence of African-Americans who run boardrooms, who sit on the bench, who serve in elected office from small towns to big cities; from the Congressional Black Caucus to the Oval Office.

> Because of what they did, the doors of opportunity swung open not just for African-Americans, but for every American. Women marched through those doors. Latinos marched through those doors. Asian Americans, gay Americans, and Americans with disabilities came through those doors. Their endeavors gave the entire South the chance to rise again, not by reasserting the past, but by transcending the past. (Obama Remarks, 50th Anniversary of Selma to Montgomery 2015)

Obama used the historical events and the anniversary of the Voting Rights Act of 1965 to connect the era to contemporary issues and injustices facing America. He urged people to use their imaginations to search for solutions, because change depends on individuals exacting change. Reminiscent of his speech at the Democratic National Convention in 2004, Obama called on Americans to look past race and recognize that change is needed:

> This is work for all Americans, and not just some. Not just whites. Not just blacks. If we want to honor the courage of those who marched that day, then all of us are called to possess their moral imagination. All of us will need to feel, as they did, the fierce urgency of now. All of us need to recognize, as they did, that change depends on our actions, our attitudes, the things we teach our children. And if we make such effort, no matter how hard it may seem, laws can be passed, and consciences can be stirred, and consensus can be built. (Obama Remarks, 50th Anniversary of Selma to Montgomery 2015)

Obama then noted what could be accomplished if people stuck together. He believed that trust between police and the African American community could improve if just policies are created. He addressed the injustice prevalent in the American criminal justice system, in particular overcrowded prisons and unfair sentencing. He suggested the system needed to be fixed because it is a main contributor to breaking up families and poverty:

With such effort, we can make sure our criminal justice system serves all and not just some. Together, we can raise the level of mutual trust that policing is built on the idea that police officers are members of the communities they risk their lives to protect, and citizens in Ferguson and New York and Cleveland just want the same thing young people here marched for—the protection of the law. Together, we can address unfair sentencing, and overcrowded prisons, and the stunted circumstances that rob too many boys of the chance to become men, and rob the nation of too many men who could be good dads, and workers, and neighbors. With effort, we can roll back poverty and the roadblocks to opportunity. Americans don't accept a free ride for anyone, nor do we believe in equality of outcomes. But we do expect equal opportunity, and if we really mean it, if we're willing to sacrifice for it, then we can make sure every child gets an education suitable to this new century, one that expands imaginations and lifts their sights and gives them skills. We can make sure every person willing to work has the dignity of a job, and a fair wage, and a real voice, and sturdier rungs on that ladder into the middle class. (Obama Remarks, 50th Anniversary of Selma to Montgomery 2015)

Obama noted the efforts to roll back voting statutes such as the federal government monitoring elections and the creation of voting districts that either weaken or strengthen a political party's hold. He affirmed that voting is the bedrock of a functioning democracy and again acknowledged that the events and the efforts were the product of sacrifice of those willing to put their lives on the line for the right to vote:

And with effort, we can protect the foundation stone of our democracy for which so many marched across this bridge and that is the right to vote. Right now, in 2015, fifty years after Selma, there are laws across this country designed to make it harder for people to vote. As we speak, more of such laws are being proposed. Meanwhile, the Voting Rights Act, the culmination of so much blood and sweat and tears, the product of so much sacrifice in the face of wanton violence, stands weakened, its future subject to partisan rancor. (Obama Remarks, 50th Anniversary of Selma to Montgomery 2015)

Three months after this speech, Obama would face another tragic racial event with the mass killing of African Americans in a Charleston, South Carolina, church.

On June 17, 2015, Dylann Roof, a white man, gunned down nine African American churchgoers while they prayed and held Bible study at Emanuel African Methodist Episcopal Church in downtown Charleston. Reverend Clementa Pinckney, a South Carolina state legislator who was also the pastor of the church, was one of those killed in this shooting. The gunman was later found in North Carolina and extradited to South Carolina. The shooter was charged with several crimes including a hate crime. This church had historic roots in slave resistance, and this may have been the reason it was targeted. In 1833, the historic church was investigated for its involvement in a planned slave revolt in Charleston. Denmark Vesey, one of the church's founders, was hanged for organizing a slave uprising.

In the 2015 shooting, Roof confessed to police and admitted that the act of violence was influenced by the race of the congregants. He had also been photographed with symbols of white supremacy on his clothing, and his car had a Confederate States of America license plate on it. The shooter's roommates stated that Roof was "into segregation" and "wanted to start a race war" (Mosendz 2015). As he shot the victims in the church, Roof reportedly yelled, "You rape our women, and you're taking over our country" (Mosendz 2015). President Obama spoke to the nation about these tragic events. In his remarks he said, "Michelle and I know several members of Emanuel AME Church. We knew their pastor, Reverend Clementa Pinckney, who, along with eight others, gathered in prayer and fellowship and was murdered last night" (Time Staff 2015). Obama continued: "And to say our thoughts and prayers are with them and their families, and their community doesn't say enough to convey the heartache and the sadness and the anger that we feel" (Time Staff 2015). Obama eulogized Reverend Pinckney and utilized tradition well observed in the African American church; he delivered Pinckney's eulogy by concluding with the hymn "Amazing Grace."

By the conclusion of President Obama's second term in office in 2016, a CNN and Opinion Research Corporations poll found that the majority of Americans believe that race relations between blacks and whites had worsened under Obama. Overall, 54 percent of people polled said that relations between blacks and whites have gotten worse since Obama became president. These numbers include 57 percent of whites and 40 percent of African Americans.

In 2018, a photograph surfaced of Obama and Farrakhan that was taken in 2005 at a Congressional Black Caucus event. Askia Muhammad, the photographer who captured the photo, gave up the photograph and was sworn to secrecy. The photograph was kept secret because the photographer believed it would have turned people against Obama and dashed the chances of the presidential hopeful.

Barack Obama's election in 2008 as the first African American president of the United States was misjudged as the beginning of a "postracial America." Some believe it was penitence for America's original sin of slavery and the scar of segregation. In 2014, President Obama told a group of young black activists that change was "hard and incremental" (Shear and Stack 2016). He ended his presidency with some of the highest approval ratings for a president. Many in the nation underestimated the significance of race on his presidency.

FURTHER READING

Dupuis, Martin, and Keith Boeckelman. 2008. *Barack Obama, the New Face of American Politics.* Westport, CT: Greenwood.

Dyson, Michael Eric. 2016. *The Black Presidency: Barack Obama and the Politics of Race in America.* New York: Houghton Mifflin Harcourt.

Ifill, Gwen. 2009. *Break Through: Politics and Race in the Age of Obama.* New York: Anchor Books.

Obama, Barack. 2004. *Dreams from My Father: A Story of Race and Inheritance.* New York: Three Rivers.

Obama, Barack. 2006. *The Audacity of Hope: Thoughts on Reclaiming the American Dream.* New York: Crown/Three Rivers.

Remnick, David. 2010. *The Bridge: The Life and Rise of Barack Obama.* New York: Knopf.

Donald John Trump

45th President of the United States
Presidential Term: Began January 20, 2017
Political Party: Republican
Vice President: Michael Richard Pence

Donald John Trump was born on June 14, 1946, in Queens, New York. His family owned a real estate company, which he inherited from his father. His father began working in the business when he was 15 and continued it later when he married his wife, an immigrant from Scotland, who first worked as a maid when she came to the United States.

The election of Donald Trump to the presidency has been characterized as one of the most stunning presidential victories in history. He defeated Democrat Hillary Clinton, former senator and secretary of state, despite having no experience in politics and without the support of the Republican establishment. Trump was able to win the election by galvanizing citizens with promises to reform the government, shake up the political establishment, tackle illegal immigration, and reduce taxes. He was seen as the anti-establishment candidate who ran on the slogan "Make America Great Again," a phrase borrowed from former president Ronald Reagan. Trump gained 12 percent of the African American vote, which was at least a percentage point higher than previous white presidential candidates over the last three decades.

During the campaign, many had concerns that Trump was attracting racist followers due to his stance on immigration: he wanted to deport illegal immigrants and build a wall on the U.S.-Mexican border. During some of his rallies, black and white attendees engaged in verbal and even physical confrontations. Trump was criticized for not making comments to quell these confrontations. He was accused at times of instigating violence by mocking protestors and counter-activists from the podium and screaming things such as "Get them out!" Trump was also criticized for some of his comments. In August 2016 while campaigning in the majority white Dimondale, Michigan, he commented on why African Americans should vote for him saying, "Look at how much

Donald J. Trump became the 45th president of the United States in 2017. During his presidency, Trump has been accused of being sympathetic with far-right and racist organizations. (The White House)

African American communities are suffering from Democratic control. . . . To those I say the following: What do you have to lose by trying something new like Trump? What do you have to lose? You live in poverty, your schools are no good, you have no jobs, 58 percent of your youth is unemployed—what the hell do you have to lose?" (Brazile 2016).

Before becoming president, Trump had already been criticized by blacks and others for promulgating the falsehood that Barack Obama was not born in the United States and therefore was never truly eligible to run for president. This "Birther Movement" and Trump's allegations continued even after he became president, although proof of President Obama's birth in Hawaii was substantiated. Some saw Trump's stance as racist and targeted at Obama only because he was the first African American president.

Once Trump was in office, African American satisfaction with him quickly plummeted. The president appointed only one African American cabinet member, Dr. Benjamin Solomon Carson Sr., who had little or no experience in working with urban development, as secretary of housing and urban development. During Trump's first year in office 91 percent of his judicial appointments were white, and 81 percent were male. The last president before him to appoint a group who lacked racial and gender diversity was President George H. W. Bush. The only African American appointed to a White House post was Omarose Onee Manigault-Newman, to the post of director of communications for the Office of Public Liaison. However, she resigned on December 23, 2017, with details from the White House confirming that she was actually forcibly removed from her post. On June 29, 2017, Trump nominated African American Jerome Adams to the post of surgeon general of the United States. He was confirmed by the Senate on August 3, 2017. Adams named his top two priorities as tackling the national opioid epidemic and untreated mental illness.

Trump nominated Jefferson B. Sessions III as U.S. attorney general in November 2016. Sessions had been nominated for a federal judge position in the U.S. District Court for the Southern District of Alabama by President Ronald Reagan in 1986 but was not confirmed over charges of his negative views on minorities, led by Senators Joe Biden and Ted Kennedy. This was only the second time in 50 years that such an appointment was blocked by the U.S. Senate.

During the confirmation hearings, a former civil rights attorney testified that Sessions viewed such groups as the National Association for the Advancement of Colored People (NAACP), the National Council of Churches, and the American Civil Liberties Union as un-American and inspired by communism. The attorney also alleged that Sessions considered a white civil rights attorney who had supported a civil rights plaintiff's case in Alabama a disgrace to his race. There were allegations that Sessions had used the word "n----r" to describe a local black government official in Alabama and called a black lawyer "boy" and warned him to be careful what he said to white people. Sessions was also accused of admiring the Ku Klux Klan until he heard that its members smoked marijuana and of indicting activists who were helping elderly African Americans in Alabama vote in the 1980s. During the 1986 hearing, Coretta Scott King was so concerned about his nomination that she wrote a letter to the Senate confirmation committee, stating in part that

"Mr. Sessions has used the awesome powers of his office in a shabby attempt to intimidate and frighten elderly black voters. For this reprehensible conduct, he should not be rewarded with a federal judgeship." Democrats were outraged when Senator Elizabeth Warren from Massachusetts was silenced by Republicans when she tried to read the letter during the 2016–2017 confirmation hearings.

Since 1986, Sessions had been a chief federal prosecutor in Alabama and asserted his support of civil rights groups, including the NAACP. He was elected to the U.S. Senate four times. During that time, he was adamant in not supporting illegal immigration. He changed his responses to questions during this confirmation hearing for U.S. attorney general, particularly on questions regarding allegations of his racist comments and behavior in the past. He was confirmed on February 8, 2017, with a vote of 52 to 47 in the Senate and was sworn in on February 9, 2017, even though 1,100 law school professors from 170 law schools in 48 states around the country sent letters to Congress urging the Senate to reject the appointment. Sessions was fired by Trump on November 7, 2018, after the two disagreed for a year, mostly due to the Department of Justice's investigation of the president's collusion with Russia during his campaign.

Trump's first two years in office were politically tumultuous, given a continuous change in White House staff, his use of tweeting to announce policies, his willingness to wage personal attacks on political figures and private citizens, and his alliance with individuals who were known to have very right-wing views on such issues as equality. He appointed Stephen K. Bannon as White House strategist, a selection hailed by white supremacist individuals and groups. Bannon is a former film producer and also a cofounder of Breitbart News, a news website that was established as "the platform for the alt-right" in 2016. Its content is described as racist, xenophobic, and misogynistic. The website has also supported the views of white supremacist individuals, neo-Nazis, and other organizations. Bannon departed the White House on August 28, 2017. Accounts of whether he was fired or voluntarily resigned conflict, but it was widely believed that he was fired for ill-advising the president on how to handle comments after violence erupted at an alt-right rally in Charlottesville, Virginia, on August 11–12, 2017. During the rally, white supremacists converged on the city in protest of city plans to remove the statue of Robert E. Lee from Emancipation Park. The event led to riots, the death of an attendee when a Nazi sympathizer drove into a crowd or pedestrians, and other cases of racial violence and property damage. When asked for comments on the violence, Trump responded, "You had a group on one side that was bad and you had a group on the other side that was also very violent, there's blame on both sides" (Scott 2018). His failure to denounce white nationalist activities was criticized as supporting hate groups. The United Nations (UN) Committee on the Elimination of Racial Discrimination issued a report expressing concern at the "failure at the highest political level of the United States of America to unequivocally reject and condemn the racist violent events and demonstrations" on August 18, 2017 (Goodenough 2017). The UN committee urged U.S. leaders to "identify and take concrete measures to address the root causes of the proliferation of such racist manifestations, and thoroughly investigate the phenomenon of racial discrimination targeting in particular against people of African descent, ethnic or ethno-religious minorities, and migrants."

Trump's comments and the event itself led to the removal of Confederate stat-utes in cities across the United States. While the president tried to deflect criticism with later statements, he continued to be condemned due to conflicting remarks on the topic. On August 22, 2017, he commented on the removal of Confederate statues: "Does anybody want George Washington's statue [taken down]? No. Is that sad, is that sad? To Lincoln to Teddy Roosevelt. I see they want to take Teddy Roosevelt's down too. They're trying to figure out why, they don't know. They're trying to take away our culture; they're trying to take away our history. And our weak leaders, they do it overnight" (Krieg 2017).

The backlash against the president's comments was immediate from political and social respondents. Former presidents George H. W. Bush and George W. Bush commented that

> America must always reject racial bigotry, anti-Semitism, and hatred in all forms. As we pray for Charlottesville, we are reminded of the fundamental truths recorded by that city's most prominent citizen in the Declaration of Independence: we are all created equal and endowed by our Creator with unalienable rights. We know these truths to be everlasting because we have seen the decency and greatness of our country. (Estepa 2017)

Speaker of the House Paul Ryan stated, "We must be clear. White supremacy is repulsive. This bigotry is counter to all this country stands for. There can be no moral ambiguity" (Siegel 2017).

It can be inferred that Trump doesn't know a lot about African American culture, social norms, perceptions, or history. This lack of knowledge did cause some contention given some of the comments he made, seemingly without malice. For example, in February 2017 he was speaking to some African American supporters at breakfast commemorating the start of African American History month. In referring to one of the most well-known Americans in history, he stated that "Frederick Douglass is an example of somebody who's done an amazing job and is being recognized more and more, I notice." Sean Spicer, then White House press secretary, sought to later clarify the president's comments by stating, "I think he wants to highlight the contributions that he has made, and I think through a lot of the actions and statements that he's going to make, I think the contributions of Frederick Douglass will become more and more" (Merica 2017).

On February 28, 2017, Trump issued a Presidential Executive Order on the White House Initiative to Promote Excellence and Innovation at Historically Black Colleges and Universities (HBCUs). The order charged each agency sup-porting HBCUs with preparing an annual plan "describing its efforts to strengthen the capacity of HBCUs to participate in applicable Federal programs and initia-tives." It also established within the Department of Education the president's Board of Advisors from the public and private sectors to consult on issues related to HBCUs, specifically

(i) improving the identity, visibility, distinctive capabilities, and overall com-petitiveness of HBCUs;

(ii) engaging the philanthropic, business, government, military, homeland-security, and education communities in a national dialogue regarding new HBCU programs and initiatives;

(iii) improving the ability of HBCUs to remain fiscally secure institutions that can assist the Nation in achieving its educational goals and in advancing the interests of all Americans;

(iv) elevating the public awareness of, and fostering appreciation of, HBCUs; and

(v) encouraging public-private investments in HBCUs. (Trump 2017)

On February 27, 2017, Trump met with the presidents of historically black colleges in the White House, but this did not do much to repair his relationship with the African American community or with the HBCU leaders with whom he met when he entered the White House. Since meeting with the group, Trump reduced funding for grant and work-study programs upon which many HBCU students rely. He also refused to attend events organized by traditional civil rights groups such as the NAACP and the National Urban League. Trump questioned whether HBCUs could legally receive aid from the federal government. Apparently, he thought that HBCUs were not open to non-black students and thus were discriminatory. White and nonblack students of color have attended and been faculty members at HBCUs since their inception. U.S. Department of Education secretary Betsy DeVos seemed just as uninformed about HBCUs as Trump. DeVos described historically black colleges as "real pioneers when it comes to school choice" even though they were created because mainstream universities and colleges denied admission to black people (Douglas-Gabriel and Jan 2017).

Trump began another controversy when he made statements about National Football League (NFL) players kneeling during the national anthem. This was an action credited to Colin Kaepernick, the former San Francisco 49ers quarterback, that grew in practice across the league during the 2017 and 2018 football seasons. Participating players reported that they engaged in this practice as a silent protest of the mistreatment of African Americans in the criminal justice system, because of government policies, and in light of continued racism in the country. Trump added to the already controversial issue by making public statements via Twitter that the players should be fired and tweeting comments such as "The NFL has decided that it will not force players to stand for the playing of our National Anthem. Total disrespect for our great country!" and on October 28, 2017, "At least 24 players kneeling this weekend at NFL stadiums that are now having a very hard time filling up. The American public is fed up with the disrespect the NFL is paying to our Country, our Flag and our National Anthem. Weak and out of control!" His comments were hailed by some but criticized by others, who viewed them as divisive, particularly given the concerns on other issues such as the president's remarks after the racial violence in Charlottesville. In protest in September 2017, players, owners, and coaches from most NFL teams either did not come onto the field during the playing of the national anthem or remained in their locker rooms. The controversy continued during much of the season, with divisive debates held in social and political realms. On September 23, 2017, at a campaign-style rally in Alabama, Trump made incendiary remarks about protesting NFL players: "Wouldn't you love to see one of these NFL owners, when somebody disrespects our flag, to say, 'Get that son of a b---h off the field right now. He is fired. He's fired!' And that owner, they don't know it [but] they'll be the most popular person in this country." The crowd erupted into applause and chants of "USA! USA! USA!"

Trump continued: "Total disrespect of our heritage, a total disrespect of everything that we stand for. Everything that we stand for. You know what's hurting the game more than that? When people like yourselves turn on television and you see those people taking the knee when they are playing our great national anthem" (Cillizza 2017).

In May 2018, the NFL passed a rule requiring its players to observe the national anthem or remain in the locker room. Fines would be issued against teams whose players did not observe the national anthem. Trump continued the controversy on June 4, 2018, when he disinvited the Philadelphia Eagles from attending the White House to recognize their recent Super Bowl LII victory. However, many noted that a large number of players were not planning to attend the White House event.

Many African American leaders, celebrities, and even citizens refused to meet with the president. Those who did often faced strong criticism. Comedian and television host Steve Harvey met with Trump in New York City on January 13, 2017. Speaking of the criticisms he received afterward, Harvey stated, "I didn't see that coming. Jesus. It was so vicious that it really threw me. . . . I was being called names that I've never been called: Uncle Tom. A coon. A sellout" (Workneh 2017). He said that his wife had warned him not to meet with the president, and he wished he had taken her advice.

In September 2017 after the Golden State Warriors won the National Basketball Association (NBA) Championship, some players, including Steph Curry, refused the invite. Trump responded in anger with a tweet on September 23, 2017: "Going to the White House is considered a great honor for a championship team. Stephen Curry is hesitating, therefore invitation is withdrawn!" In 2017 some players from the New England Patriots would not meet with the president during a meeting to celebrate their Super Bowl victory, and some players from the Philadelphia Eagles also refused to do so after their Super Bowl win in 2018. In a press conference during the NBA Finals in 2018, LeBron James stated that no matter which team won the NBA Championship, neither team would go the White House.

The Mississippi Civil Rights Museum was officially dedicated on December 9, 2017. The museum was constructed to honor African Americans and others who fought for equality during the Civil Rights Movement from the 1940s through the 1960s. Mississippi's Republican governor Phil Bryant invited Trump to the dedication ceremony, which immediately led many civil rights leaders, politicians, and other attendees to declare that they would not attend the dedication if the president did. Among some of the more vocal individuals who threatened to boycott the event were U.S. representative John R. Lewis, who was a leader in the Civil Rights Movement; U.S. representative Bennie Thompson; and Jackson, Mississippi, mayor Chokwe Antar Lumumba. In a joint statement Lewis and Thompson said, "President Trump's attendance and his hurtful policies are an insult to the people portrayed in this civil rights museum." Lumumba stated, "The martyrs of Mississippi who have died for our civil rights, for our progress, will not allow me to stand with Donald Trump" (Brown and Wootson 2017).

Trump flew to Mississippi on December 9 but did not attend the dedication ceremony. Instead, he was given a private tour and gave a speech before a small invitation-only audience that included Myrlie Evers-Williams, the wife of civil rights activist Medgar Evers who was murdered in Jackson, Mississippi, in 1963. During this private event, protests were held outside the museum directed at the president's attendance. In his speech Trump stated, "Today we pay solemn tribute to our heroes of the past and dedicate ourselves to building a future of freedom, equality, justice, peace" (Brown and Wootson 2017).

Some of the other controversial issues that Trump faced arose from meetings that were deemed private or secure yet resulted in the leaking of his comments to the public. One of the most controversial was during a meeting in January 2018 in which the president allegedly stated, "Why do we want all these people from 's--thole countries' coming here?" in reference to immigrants from Haiti and countries in Africa and South America. Trump indicated that the United States should seek more immigrants from places such as Norway. There were denials and confirmations of the statement from those in attendance, which included Democratic and Republican members of Congress. The allegations caused international outrage; the president stated that his remarks were harsh but that the alleged words were not used.

During his January 31, 2018, State of the Union Address, President Trump touted, "African American unemployment stands at the lowest rate ever recorded. And Hispanic American unemployment has also reached the lowest levels in history" (Trump 2018a). Data support that his assertion was correct. However, many analysts pointed to the fact that Trump was unable to take sole credit for this achievement, since the unemployment rate for minorities started dropping in 2010 under the policies of President Barack Obama. Still, it has not been uncommon for presidents to tout achievements that didn't solely begin under their administrations.

Trump's comments on African American unemployment led to a social media assault with rapper and businessman Jay-Z. While speaking on a television show on January 27, Jay-Z said, referring to increased pay from jobs for African Americans, "It's not about money at the end of the day. Money doesn't equate to happiness. It doesn't. That's missing the whole point. You treat people like human beings. That's the main point. It goes back to the whole thing—'treat me really bad and pay me well.' It's not going to lead to happiness, it's going to lead to, again, the same thing. Everyone's going to be sick." Trump responded in a tweet on January 20, 2018: "Somebody please inform Jay-Z that because of my policies, Black Unemployment has just been reported to be at the Lowest Rate Ever Recorded!" (Jacobson 2018).

Some of the controversies that Trump has encountered have been attributed to his bad choice of words. For example, during a rally in June 2016 he attempted to show his support for African Americans by pointing to a male in the audience and stating, "Oh, look at my African American over here. Look at him. Are you the greatest?" (Diamond 2016).

On January 31, 2018, Trump made an official proclamation recognizing February 2018 as National African American History Month, as most of his presidential predecessors did, since the month was officially recognized as Black History Month by President Gerald R. Ford in 1976. Speaking on the achievements and contributions of African Americans, Trump said,

> This February, we celebrate National African American History Month to honor the significant contributions African Americans have made to our great Nation—contributions that stand as a testament to their resolve, resilience, and courage. Over the course of our Nation's history, African Americans have endured egregious discrimination and bigotry. They have, nevertheless, always been determined to contribute their earnest efforts to America's greatness.
>
> This annual observance is an opportunity to remember the challenges of our past, but also to honor countless African-American heroes who inspire us to shape our country's future. This year's theme, "African Americans in Times of War," calls our attention to the heroic contributions of African Americans during our Nation's military conflicts, from the Revolutionary War to present-day operations. (Trump 2018b)

On February 13, 2018, President Trump and First Lady Melania Trump hosted a reception at the White House honoring Black History Month. Ben Carson, secretary of housing and urban development, and Surgeon General Jerome Adams both attended, the only two African Americans in the president's top administration. During the event Trump stated, "Our thoughts turn to the heroes of the civil rights movement whose courage and sacrifices have really totally inspired us all. From the pews to the picket lines, African American civil rights champions have brought out the best in us" (Diamond 2018).

On January 8, 2018, Trump signed the Martin Luther King, Jr. National Historical Park Act of 2017, designating Dr. King's birthplace, the church where he was baptized, and his burial place as a national historical park and extending the boundaries of the park to include the Prince Hall Masonic Temple. Part of the location was a historic site, but the legislative act upgraded its designation. The temple served as home to the Southern Christian Leadership Conference, which King co-founded. Alveda King, the niece of Dr. King, was present for the signing ceremony. The original bill was sponsored by Representative John Lewis.

On the same day, the president signed the African American Civil Rights Network Act of 2017. The legislation called for the

> Department of the Interior to establish within the National Park Service (NPS) a U.S. Civil Rights Network that encompasses: (1) all NPS units and programs that relate to the African American civil rights movement from 1939 through 1968; (2) with the property owner's consent, other federal, state, local, and privately owned properties that relate or have a verifiable connection to such movement and that are included in, or eligible for, the National Register of Historic Places; and (3) other governmental and nongovernmental facilities and programs of an educational, research, or interpretive

nature that are directly related to such movement. In carrying out the network, Interior must: (1) review civil rights movement studies and reports, such as the Civil Rights Framework Study; (2) produce and disseminate educational materials relating to such movement; (3) provide technical assistance; and (4) adopt an official, uniform symbol or device for the Network and issue regulations for the symbol's use. ("H.R.1927" 2018)

The president also signed the 400 Years of African American History Commission Act to commemorate the arrival of Africans in the English colonies at Port Comfort, Virginia, in 1619. Per the legislation, the commission is charged with four responsibilities:

1. plan programs to acknowledge the impact that slavery and laws that enforced racial discrimination had on the United States;

2. encourage civic, patriotic, historical, educational, artistic, religious, and economic organizations to organize and participate in anniversary activities;

3. assist states, localities, and nonprofit organizations to further the commemoration; and

4. coordinate for the public scholarly research on the arrival of Africans in the United States and their contributions to this country. ("H.R.1242" 2018)

In May 2018, rapper Kanye West was criticized for making disparaging comments about former president Barack Obama, confessing his "love" for Trump, and more so for professing that blacks voluntarily submitted to slavery over the course of 400 years. On April 25, 2018, West tweeted, "You don't have to agree with trump but the mob can't make me not love him. We are both dragon energy. He is my brother. I love everyone. I don't agree with everything anyone does. That's what makes us individuals. And we have the right to independent thought." West received international condemnation for his statements, particularly on slavery, including criticisms from black leaders and celebrities. Trump thanked West for his support and credited him with increasing African American support for the president's policies. On May 4, 2018, Trump tweeted, "I doubled my African-American poll numbers. We went from 11 to 22 in one week" (Kruzel 2018). Critics contended that Trump's statements were false, as the poll surveyed only black males, but admittedly the poll showed overall support of Trump by all African Americans polled and an increase in support even though a very small sample size was used (less than 200).

This is not the first time Trump was recognized by rappers. During the 1980s through the 2000s, he was often referenced in rap and R&B songs as the epitome of success and wealth. For example, Prince wrote a song for the group Time in 1990 titled "Donald Trump (Black Version)," with the lead singer Morris Day touting a black version of Trump who could fulfill a woman's every dream. Mac Miller released a rap song titled "Donald Trump" in 2011. Trump himself issued a statement: "A lot of people are calling me about the Mac Miller rap song. Now, it's named 'Donald Trump.' Maybe you should pay me a lot of money, but it just did over 20 million people, tuning into Mac Miller. So in one way, I'm proud of him. I haven't actually seen the language. . . . Probably, it's not the cleanest language you've ever heard. . . . But the 'Donald Trump' song just hit over 20 million, that's not so bad. I'm very proud of him." Later he unsuccessfully demanded royalties for the song.

In May 2018, Trump's stance on racism was again questioned due to an incident that began with comedienne and actress Roseanne Barr. On May 29, 2018, Barr tweeted that Valerie Jarrett, a black woman and former senior adviser to President Obama, looked like an ape. Her specific comments were "Muslim brotherhood & planet of the apes had a baby=vj." Her hit show, *Roseanne,* which had received high ratings after returning to the air after 20 years, was cancelled by ABC network executives within hours of her tweet. Trump became part of the controversy, as he did not condemn the comments but instead rather criticized the ways in which ABC executives never called him in regard to negative comments made on the network toward him. On May 30, 2018, he tweeted, "Bob Iger of ABC called Valerie Jarrett to let her know that 'ABC does not tolerate comments like those' made by Roseanne Barr. Gee, he never called President Donald J. Trump to apologize for the HORRIBLE statements made about me on ABC. Maybe I just didn't get the call?"

FURTHER READING

Black, Conrad. 2018. *Donald J. Trump: A President Like No Other.* Washington, DC: Regnery.

Brazile, Donna. 2016. "Trump's Pitch to Blacks Is Deluded." *USA Today,* August 24, 2016, https://www.usatoday.com/story/opinion/2016/08/24/trump-black-voters-democrats-donna-brazile/89221932/.

Brown, DeNeen L., and Cleve R. Wootson Jr. 2017. "Trump Ignores Backlash, Visits Mississippi Civil Rights Museum and Praises Civil Rights Leaders." *Washington Post,* December 9, https://www.washingtonpost.com/news/post-politics/wp/2017/12/09/amid-backlash-trump-set-to-attend-private-gathering-as-civil-rights-museum-opens-in-mississippi/?utm_term=.53401f13f402.

Diamond, Jeremy. 2016. "Trump on Black Supporter: 'Look at My African-American over Here.'" CNN, https://www.cnn.com/2016/06/03/politics/donald-trump-african-american/index.html.

Diamond, Jeremy. 2018. "White House Hosts Black History Month Event." CNN, February 13, https://www.cnn.com/2018/02/13/politics/donald-trump-black-history-month/index.html.

Estepa, Jessica. 2017. "George H. W. Bush, George W. Bush: We Must Reject 'Hatred in All Forms.'" *USA Today,* August 16, https://www.usatoday.com/story/news/politics/onpolitics/2017/08/16/george-h-w-bush-george-w-bush-we-must-reject-hatred-all-forms/572468001/.

Goodenough, Patrick. 2017. "UN Experts 'Disturbed' by U.S. 'Failure' to Reject and Condemn Racist Demonstrations." CNSNews.com, August 24, 2017, https://www.cnsnews.com/news/article/patrick-goodenough/un-experts-disturbed-us-failure-reject-and-condemn-racist.

"H.R.1242—400 Years of African-American History Commission Act." 2018. United States Congress, https://www.congress.gov/bill/115th-congress/house-bill/1242.

"H.R.1927—African American Civil Rights Network Act of 2017." 2018. United States Congress, https://www.congress.gov/bill/115th-congress/house-bill/1927.

Jacobson, Louis. 2018. "Donald Trump Is Partly Correct in Response to Jay-Z about Black Unemployment." PolitiFact, January 30, http://www.politifact.com/truth-o-meter /statements/2018/jan/30/donald-trump/donald-trump-partly-correct-rejoinder -jay-z/.

Kessler, Ronald. 2018. *The Trump White House: Changing the Rules of the Game.* New York: Crown Forum.

Kranish, Michael, and Marc Fisher. 2017. *Trump Revealed: The Definitive Biography of the 45th President.* New York: Scribner.

Krieg, Gregory. 2017. "Rally Trump vs. Teleprompter Trump." CNN, August 23, https:// www.cnn.com/2017/08/23/politics/comparing-donald-trump-speeches-afghani stan-phoenix/index.html.

Kruzel, John. 2018. "Donald Trump's Misleading Claim That Kanye West's Praise Doubled His African-American Support." PolitiFact, May 7, http://www.politifact .com/truth-o-meter/statements/2018/may/07/donald-trump/donald-trumps-mis leading-claim-kanye-wests-praise-/.

Merica, Dan. 2017. "Trump: Frederick Douglass 'Is Being Recognized More and More.'" CNN, February 2, https://www.cnn.com/2017/02/02/politics/donald-trump -frederick-douglass/index.html.

Siegel, Josh. 2017. "Paul Ryan: 'We Must Be Clear. White Supremacy Is Repulsive.'" *Washington Examiner,* August 15, 2017, https://www.washingtonexaminer.com /paul-ryan-we-must-be-clear-white-supremacy-is-repulsive.

Trump, Donald, and Tony Schwartz. 2009. *Trump: The Art of the Deal.* New York: Ballantine Books.

Trump, Donald J. 2017. "Presidential Executive Order on the White House Initiative to Promote Excellence and Innovation at Historically Black Colleges and Universities." The White House, https://www.whitehouse.gov/presidential-actions/presi dential-executive-order-white-house-initiative-promote-excellence-innovation -historically-black-colleges-universities/.

Trump, Donald J. 2018a. "President Donald J. Trump Proclaims February 2018 as National African American History Month." The White House, https://www.whitehouse .gov/presidential-actions/president-donald-j-trump-proclaims-february-2018 -national-african-american-history-month/.

Trump, Donald J. 2018b. "President Donald J. Trump's State of the Union Address." The White House, https://www.whitehouse.gov/briefings-statements/president-donald -j-trumps-state-union-address//.

Workneh, Lilly. 2017. "Steve Harvey: My Wife Told Me To Skip Meeting With Trump, I Should've Listened." Huffington Post, September 5, https://www.huffingtonpost .com/entry/steve-harvey-my-wife-told-me-to-skip-meeting-with-trump-i -shouldve-listened_us_59aee344e4b0354e440d0925.

Bibliography

ABC News Archives. (2006). Bush Reaches Out to Minority Voters, https://abcnews.go.com/US/story?id=96571&page=1, January 7, 2006. Accessed June 26, 2018.

ABC News Archives. (2006). Bush to Speak at NAACP Convention, https://abcnews.go.com/Politics/story?id=123423&page=1, July 9, 2006. Accessed June 26, 2018.

Adams, John. (1819). "From John Adams to Robert J. Evans, 8 June 1819." *Founders Online,* National Archives, last modified June 13, 2018, http://founders.archives.gov/documents/Adams/99-02-02-7148

Adams, John. (1851). *The Works of John Adams, Second President of the United States,* Volume 3. Boston, MA: Bolles and Houghton Publishing.

Adams, John. (1881). "From John Adams letter to John Yates." In Hastings, Hugh J., *Ancient American Politics.* New York, NY: Harper & Brothers.

Alton Evening Telegraph. (1891). *Alton Evening Telegraph* from Alton, Illinois, January 23, 1891. Retrieved from https://www.newspapers.com/newspage/16345463/

American RadioWorks. (1951). Korean War Courts Martial: Interview with Thurgood Marshall. Retrieved from http://americanradioworks.publicradio.org/features/marshall/korea.html

American RadioWorks. (2018). The Riot at Ole' Miss. Retrieved from http://americanradioworks.publicradio.org/features/mississippi/f1.html

Ashworth, John. (1995). *Slavery, Capitalism, and Politics in the Antebellum Republic: Commerce and Compromise, 1820–1850,* Volume 1. Cambridge, MA: Cambridge University Press.

Associated Press. (1984). Concept of Pay Based on Worth Is the "Looniest," Rights Chief Says. *The New York Times,* November 17. Retrieved from http://www.nytimes.com/1984/11/17/us/concept-of-pay-based-on-worth-is-the-looniest-rights-chief-says.html

Axelrod-Sokolov, Mark. (2011). Reagan: The Dark Side of the Script. HuffPost. https://www.huffingtonpost.com/mark-axelrod/reagan-the-dark-side-of-t_b_820742.html

Ball, Howard. (1996). *Hugo L. Black: Cold Steel Warrior.* New York: Oxford University Press.

Banneker, Benjamin. (1791). To Thomas Jefferson from Benjamin Banneker, 19
    August 1791. *Founders Online,* National Archives, last modified June 13,
    2018,   http://founders.archives.gov/documents/Jefferson/01-22-02-0049.
    [Original source: *The Papers of Thomas Jefferson,* vol. 22, *6 August 1791–
    31 December 1791,* ed. Charles T. Cullen. Princeton: Princeton University
    Press, 1986, pp. 49–54.]

Baptist, Edward. (2014). *The Half Has Never Been Told: Slavery and the Making
    of American Capitalism.* New York, NY: Basic Books.

Bates, Karen Grigsby. 2012. Rodney King Comes To Grips With "The Riot Within."
    NPR, April 23, https://www.npr.org/2012/04/23/150985823/rodney-king
    -comes-to-grips-with-the-riot-within

Blanchet, Benjamin. (2017). Pride and Shame: Millard Fillmore's Controversial
    Legacy at UB, The Spectrum, May 8, 2017. Accessed May 30, 2018, http://
    www.ubspectrum.com/article/2017/05/millard-fillmore-controversial
    -legacy-at-ub

Bean, Jonathan (ed.). (2009). *Race and Liberty in America: The Essential Reader.*
    Louisville: The University Press of Kentucky.

Beckman, James A. (ed.). (2014). *Controversies in Affirmative Action: Historical
    Dimensions.* Santa Barbara, CA: Praeger.

Bennett, Lerone. (2007). *Forced into Glory: Abraham Lincoln's White Dream.*
    Chicago, IL: Johnson Publishing Company.

Berry, Mary Frances and Josh Gottheimer. 2010. *Power in Words: The Stories
    behind Barack Obama's Speeches, from the State to the White House.* Bos-
    ton, MA: Beacon Press.

Bevel, Helen L. 2018. *The Nonviolent Right to Vote Movement Almanac: From
    Tragedy to Triump, From Violence to Nonviolence.* Chicago, IL: The Peace
    Fellowship.

Bishop, Joseph Bucklin. (1920). *Theodore Roosevelt and His Time: Shown in His
    Own Letters.* New York, NY: Charles Scribner's Sons.

Black, Rachel and Aleta Sprague. (2016). The Rise and Reign of the Welfare
    Queen. *New America,* September 22, 2016. Retrieved from https://www
    .newamerica.org/weekly/edition-135/rise-and-reign-welfare-queen/

Bloom, Jack M. (1987). *Class, Race, and the Civil Rights Movement.* Blooming-
    ton, IN: Indiana University Press.

Bond, Julian. (1979). Just Schools: A Special Report Commemorating the 25th
    Anniversary of the Brown Decision. *Southern Exposure,* 7, 2, Summer.
    Institute for Southern Studies.

Booker, Christopher B. (2000). *"I Will Wear No Chain": A Social History of Afri-
    can American Males.* Westport, CT: Praeger.

Booker, Christopher B. (2017). *The Black Presidential Nightmare: African-
    Americans and Presidents, 1789–2016.* Bloomington, IN: Xlibris.

Borstelmann, Thomas. (2001). *The Cold War and the Color Line: American Race
    Relations in the Global Arena.* Cambridge, MA: Harvard University Press.

Bowers, William T., William M. Hammond, and George K. MacGarrigle. (1996).
    Black Soldier, White Army: The 24th Infantry Regiment in Korea. Wash-
    ington, D.C.: Center of Military History.

Boyd, Gerald M. (1986). President Opposes Additional Steps on South Africa. *The New York Times,* July 23, 1986. Retrieved from https://www.nytimes.com/1986/07/23/world/president-opposes-additional-steps-on-south-africa.html

Bradley, Tahman. (2008). Final Fundraising Figure: Obama's $750M. *ABC News,* December 5, 2008, https://abcnews.go.com/Politics/Vote2008/story?id=6397572&page=1

Brazile, Donna. (2016). Trump's pitch to blacks is deluded. *USA Today,* August 24, 2016. Retrieved from https://www.usatoday.com/story/opinion/2016/08/24/trump-black-voters-democrats-donna-brazile/89221932/

Bresnahan, John and Josh Gerstein. (2009). Tensions Remain after Wilson Apology. *Politico,* September, 10, 2009, https://www.politico.com/story/2009/09/tensions-remain-after-wilson-apology-026985

Brown, DeNeen L. and Cleve R. Wootson Jr. (2017). Trump ignores backlash, visits Mississippi Civil Rights Museum and praises civil rights leaders. *The Washington Post,* December 9, 2017. Retrieved from https://www.washingtonpost.com/news/post-politics/wp/2017/12/09/amid-backlash-trump-set-to-attend-private-gathering-as-civil-rights-museum-opens-in-mississippi/?utm_term=.53401f13f402

Brown, Deneen. (2017). Hunting Down Runaway Slaves: The Cruel Ads of Andrew Jackson and the Master Class. *The Washington Post,* May 1, 2017, https://www.washingtonpost.com/news/retropolis/wp/2017/04/11/hunting-down-runaway-slaves-the-cruel-ads-of-andrew-jackson-and-the-master-class/?noredirect=on&utm_term=.307593ea47f2

Bureau of Labor Statistics. (2018). Unemployment Rate—Black or African American Series Id: LNS14000006, Data extracted on August 25, 2018, https://data.bls.gov/timeseries/LNS14000006

Bush, George H. W. (1989). Address to the Nation on the National Drug Control Strategy, September 5, 1989. *The American Presidency Project.* Retrieved from http://www.presidency.ucsb.edu/ws/?pid=17472

Bush, George H. W. (1990). Message to the Senate Returning without Approval the Civil Rights Act of 1990, October 22, 1990. *The American Presidency Project.* Retrieved from http://www.presidency.ucsb.edu/ws/index.php?pid=18948

Bush, George H. W. (1991). Remarks on Police Brutality and an Exchange with Reporters, March 21, 1991. *The American Presidency Project.* Retrieved from http://www.presidency.ucsb.edu/ws/index.php?pid=19410&st=police&st1=

Bush, George H. W. (1992). Address to the Nation on the Civil Disturbances in Los Angeles, California, May 1, 1992. *The American Presidency Project.* Retrieved from http://www.presidency.ucsb.edu/ws/?pid=20910

Bush, George H. W. (2003). Remarks by the President on Goree Island Senegal, Whitehouse.govBush, 2003, https://georgewbush-whitehouse.archives.gov/news/releases/2003/07/20030708-1.html

Califano, Joseph A., Jr. (1981). *Governing America: An Insider's Report from the White House and the Cabinet.* New York, NY: Simon and Schuster.

Capehart, Johnathan. (2012). Republicans Had It in for Obama before Day 1. *Washington Post,* August 10, 2012, https://www.washingtonpost.com/blogs/post-partisan/post/republicans-had-it-in-for-obama-before-day-1/2012/08/10/0c96c7c8-e31f-11e1-ae7f-d2a13e249eb2_blog.html?noredirect=on&utm_term=.63d8cb411114

Carroll, Lauren. (2016). How the war on drugs affected incarceration rates. *Politifact,* July 10. Retrieved from http://www.politifact.com/truth-o-meter/statements/2016/jul/10/cory-booker/how-war-drugs-affected-incarceration-rates/

Carroll, Peter N. (2000). *It Seemed Like Nothing Happened: America in the 1970s.* New Brunswick, NJ: Rutgers University Press.

Carson, Clayborne (ed.). (2000). *The Papers of Martin Luther King, Jr., Volume IV: Symbol of the Movement, January 1957–December 1958.* Berkeley: University of California Press.

Carson, Clayborne. (2005). 1965: A Decisive Turning Point in the Long Struggle for Voting Rights. *The Crisis,* 112, 4, July/August, pp. 16–20.

Carter, Bill. (2008). Infomercial for Obama Is Big Success in Ratings. *New York Times,* October 30, 2008, https://www.nytimes.com/2008/10/31/us/politics/31rate.html

Carter, Jimmy. (1977). United Negro College Fund Remarks at a Meeting with Officials of the Fund, November 11, 1977. *The American Presidency Project.* Retrieved from http://www.presidency.ucsb.edu/ws/index.php?pid=6917

Carter, Jimmy. (1978). Interview with the President Remarks in an Interview Lot "Black Perspective on the News," April 5, 1978. *The American Presidency Project.* Retrieved from http://www.presidency.ucsb.edu/ws/index.php?pid=30620

Carter, Jimmy. (1979). Black Music Association Remarks at a White House Dinner Honoring the Association, June 7, 1979. *The American Presidency Project.* Retrieved from http://www.presidency.ucsb.edu/ws/?pid=32450

Carter, Jimmy. (1980a). Los Angeles, California Remarks in an Interview with Reporters from Newscenter 4, KNBC-TV, September 23, 1980. *The American Presidency Project.* Retrieved from http://www.presidency.ucsb.edu/ws/index.php?pid=45118

Carter, Jimmy. (1980b). Congressional Black Caucus Remarks at a White House Reception for Members of the Caucus, September 25, 1980. *The American Presidency Project.* Retrieved from http://www.presidency.ucsb.edu/ws/?pid=45142

Carter, Jimmy. (1980c). Martin Luther King, Junior, and Boston African American National Historic Sites Remarks on Signing H.R. 7218 and H.R. 7434 Into Law, October 10, 1980. *The American Presidency Project.* Retrieved from http://www.presidency.ucsb.edu/ws/index.php?pid=45253

Carter, Jimmy. (1980d). Atlanta, Georgia Remarks at a Meeting with Southern Black Leaders, September 16, 1980. *The American Presidency Project.* Retrieved from http://www.presidency.ucsb.edu/ws/index.php?pid=45059

Carter, Jimmy. (1981). Leadership and Coordination of Fair Housing in Federal Programs Statement on Executive Order 12259. *The American Presidency Project.* Retrieved from http://www.presidency.ucsb.edu/ws/?pid=44463

Chang, Jeff. (2005). *Can't Stop Won't Stop: A History of the Hip-Hop Generation.* New York, NY: St. Martin's Press.

Cheathem, Mark, R. (2014). Hannah, Andrew Jackson's Slave. *Humanities,* 35: 2 (March/April), https://www.neh.gov/humanities/2014/marchapril/feature /hannah-andrew-jacksons-slave

Cheney, Albert Loren. (1919). *Personal Memoirs of the Home Life of the Late Theodore Roosevelt as Soldier, Governor, Vice President, and President, in Relation to Oyster Bay.* Washington, D.C.: The Cheney Publishing Company.

Chernow, Ron. (2010). *Washington: A Life.* New York, NY: Penguin Group.

Cillizza, Chris. (2017). The dark racial sentiment in Trump's NBA and NFL criticism. *CNN Politics.* Retrieved from https://www.cnn.com/2017/09/23 /politics/donald-trump-nfl-nba/index.html

Cleveland, Grover. (1885). Inaugural Address, March 4, 1885. *The American Presidency Project.* Retrieved from http://www.presidency.ucsb.edu/ws/index .php?pid=25824

Cleveland, Grover. (1893). Inaugural Address, March 4, 1893. *The American Presidency Project.* Retrieved from http://www.presidency.ucsb.edu/ws/index .php?pid=25826

Cleveland, Grover. (1903). Responsibilities of the Races. *The Florida Magazine,* Vol. 5, No. 1, January 1903, Jacksonville, Virginia.

Clinton, William J. (1993). Remarks on the Withdrawal of the Nomination of Lani Guinier to Be an Assistant Attorney General and an Exchange with Reporters, June 3, 1993. *The American Presidency Project.* Retrieved from http://www.presidency.ucsb.edu/ws/index.php?pid=46657

Clinton, William J. (1994a). Statement on the Resignation of Joycelyn Elders as Surgeon General, December 9, 1994. *The American Presidency Project.* Retrieved from http://www.presidency.ucsb.edu/ws/index.php?pid=49574

Clinton, William J. (1994b). Remarks on Signing the Violent Crime Control and Law Enforcement Act of 1994, September 13, 1994. *The American Presidency Project.* Retrieved from http://www.presidency.ucsb.edu/ws/?pid =49072

Clinton, William J. (1995). Remarks on Affirmative Action at the National Archives and Records Administration, July 19, 1995. *The American Presidency Project.* Retrieved from http://www.presidency.ucsb.edu/ws/index .php?pid=51631

Clinton, William J. (1996). Executive Order 13005—Empowerment Contracting, May 21, 1996. *The American Presidency Project.* Retrieved from http:// www.presidency.ucsb.edu/ws/?pid=52845

Clinton, William J. (1997). Commencement Address at the University of California San Diego in La Jolla, California, June 14, 1997. *The American Presidency Project.* Retrieved from http://www.presidency.ucsb.edu/ws/?pid =54268

Clinton, William J. (1998). Remarks on Receiving the Report of the President's Advisory Board on Race, September 18, 1998. *The American Presidency Project.* Retrieved from http://www.presidency.ucsb.edu/ws/index.php?pid =54937

Clinton, William J. (1999). Opening Remarks at a Roundtable Discussion on Increasing Trust between Communities and Law Enforcement Officers, June 9, 1999. *The American Presidency Project.* Retrieved from http://www.presidency.ucsb.edu/ws/index.php?pid=57700

Clinton, William J. (2000). Remarks on Signing an Executive Order To Prohibit Discrimination in Federal Employment Based on Genetic Information, February 8, 2000. *The American Presidency Project.* Retrieved from http://www.presidency.ucsb.edu/ws/index.php?pid=58108

The Clinton Presidency: Building One America. (2018). The Clinton-Gore Administration, a Record of Progress. Retrieved from https://clintonwhitehouse5.archives.gov/WH/Accomplishments/eightyears-11.html

The Clinton White House. (1994). Statement by African-American Religious Leaders, August 16. Retrieved from https://clintonwhitehouse6.archives.gov/1994/08/1994-08-16-african-american-religious-leaders-support-crime-bill.html

The Clinton White House. (1996). Remarks by the President in Eulogy at the Funeral of Secretary of Commerce Ron Brown, April 10, 1996. Washington, D.C. Retrieved from http://historycentral.com/documents/Clinton/ClintonEulogyRonBrown96.html

The Clinton White House. (1999). President Clinton and Vice President Gore: Working on Behalf of African Americans. Retrieved from https://clintonwhitehouse2.archives.gov/WH/Accomplishments/ac199.html

CNN. (2003). Bush: Voice of Hope and Conscience Will Not be Silenced, July 8, 2003, CNN Politics, http://www.cnn.com/2003/WORLD/africa/07/08/bush.slavery.transcript/

CNN. (2009). Representative Wilson Shouts, "You lie" to Obama during Speech, September 10, 2009, CNN Politics, http://www.cnn.com/2009/POLITICS/09/09/joe.wilson/#cnnSTCText

Cockburn, Harry. (2016). DNC 2016: First Lady Michelle Obama On the Unforgettable Moment a Black Child Asked to Touch Her Husband's Hair, *The Independent,* July 26, 2016, https://www.independent.co.uk/news/world/americas/dnc-2016-michelle-obama-speech-barack-obama-child-touches-hair-photo-democratic-convention-a7156301.html

Coffman, Steve. (2012). *Words of the Founding Fathers.* Jefferson, NC: McFarland & Company, Inc.

Conlin, Joseph R. (2014). *The American Past: A Survey of American History,* Volume I: to 1877. Boston, MA: Cengage Learning.

Connolly, Ceci and Robert Pierre. (1998). African American Voters Standing by Clinton. *The Washington Post,* September 17, 1998, p. A1. Retrieved from https://www.washingtonpost.com/wp-srv/politics/special/clinton/stories/blacks091798.htm

Coolidge, Calvin. (1923). First Annual Message, December 6, 1923. *The American Presidency Project.* Retrieved from http://www.presidency.ucsb.edu/ws/index.php?pid=29564

Coolidge, Calvin. (1926). *Foundations of the Republic: Speeches and Addresses.* New York, NY: Books for Libraries Press.

Cooper, John Milton. (2009). *Woodrow Wilson: A Biography.* New York, NY: Vintage Books.

Cornell Law School. (2018). *Scott v. Sandford.* Retrieved from https://www.law.cornell.edu/supremecourt/text/60/393

Cornell Law School. (2018). *Civil Rights Cases.* Retrieved from https://www.law.cornell.edu/supremecourt/text/109/3

Cornell Law School. (2018). *Milliken v. Bradley.* Retrieved from https://www.law.cornell.edu/supremecourt/text/418/717

Cott, Nancy F., Jeanne Boydston, Ann Braude, Lori Ginzberg, and Molly Ladd-Taylor (eds.). (1996). *Root of Bitterness: Documents of the Social History of American Women, 2nd Edition.* Lebanon, NH: Northeastern University Press.

Creighton, Margaret. (2016). *The Electrifying Fall of Rainbow City: Spectacle and Assassination at the Rainbow City.* New York, NY: W. W. Norton & Company, Inc.

Cunningham, Noble E. (2003). *Jefferson and Monroe: Constant Friendship and Respect.* Chapel Hill, NC: Thomas Jefferson Foundation, University of North Carolina Press.

Cushing, Luther S. (1843). Law Magazine, From April 1838 to January 1843: During Which Period It Was Conducted and Principally Edited. Boston, Massachusetts: Charles C. Little and James Brown.

Davis, David B. (1999). *The Problem of Slavery in the Age of Revolution, 1770–1823.* Oxford: Oxford University Press.

Delreal, Jose. (2014). Obama: You Can Call It Obamacare, *Politico,* February 17, 2014, https://www.politico.com/story/2014/02/barack-obama-obamacare-103589

Devins, Neal. (1983). Tax Exemptions for Racially Discriminatory Private Schools: A Legislative Proposal. *Faculty Publications,* College of William and Mary. Retrieved from http://www.academia.edu/28479250/Tax_Exemptions_for_Racially_Discriminatory_Private_Schools_A_Legislative_Proposal

Diamond, Jeremy. (2016). Trump on black supporter: "Look at my African-American over here." CNN. Retrieved from https://www.cnn.com/2016/06/03/politics/donald-trump-african-american/index.html

Diamond, Jeremy. (2018). White House Hosts Black History Month Event, CNN, February 13, 2018. Retrieved from https://www.cnn.com/2018/02/13/politics/donald-trump-black-history-month/index.html

Dierenfield, Bruce J. (2013). *The Civil Rights Movement: Revised Edition.* New York, NY: Routledge.

Douglas, William, and Margaret Talev. 2008. McCain Defends Obama, *The Seattle Times,* October 11, 2008. Retrieved from https://www.seattletimes.com/nation-world/mccain-defends-obama/

Douglass, Frederick. (1882). *Life and Times of Frederick Douglas.* Hartford, CT: Park Publishing.

Douglas-Gabriel, Danielle and Tracey Jan. 2017. DeVos called HBCUs "pioneers" of "school choice." It didn't go over well. *The Washington Post,* February 28, https://www.washingtonpost.com/news/grade-point/wp/2017/02/28

/devos-called-hbcus-pioneers-of-school-choice-it-didnt-go-over-well
/?utm_term=.957520cd7f3b

Dred Scott v. Sandford, 60 U.S. 393, March 6, 1857.

Du Bois, W. E. B. (1912). Editorial. *The Crisis,* 5, 1, November 1912.

Du Bois, W. E. B. (1932). Herbert Hoover. *The Crisis,* 39, 11, November 1932.

Du Bois, W. E. B. (1956). Why I Won't Vote. *The Nation,* October 20, 1956. Retrieved from http://www.hartford-hwp.com/archives/45a/298.html

Dunbar, Erica Armstrong. (2017). *Never Caught: The Washingtons' Relentless Pursuit of Their Runaway Slave Ona Judge.* New York, NY: Atria Publishing.

Dupuis, Martin and Keith Boeckelman. (2008). *Barack Obama, the New Face of American Politics.* Westport, CT: Greenwood Press.

Egerton, Douglas. (1993). *Gabriel's Rebellion: The Virginia Slave Conspiracies of 1800 and 1802.* Chapel Hill, NC: University of North Carolina Press.

Ehrenreich, Barbara. (1995). *The Snarling Citizen: Essays.* New York, NY: Farrar, Straus and Giroux.

Eisenhower, Dwight D. (1953a). Annual Message to the Congress on the State of the Union, February 2, 1953. *The American Presidency Project.* Retrieved from http://www.presidency.ucsb.edu/ws/?pid=9829

Eisenhower, Dwight D. (1953b). The President's News Conference, March 19, 1953. *The American Presidency Project.* Retrieved from http://www.presidency.ucsb.edu/ws/index.php?pid=9798

Eisenhower, Dwight D. (1956). The President's News Conference, March 21, 1956. *The American Presidency Project.* Retrieved from http://www.presidency.ucsb.edu/ws/index.php?pid=10759

Eisenhower, Dwight D. (1960). Statement by the President upon Signing the Civil Rights Act of 1960, May 6, 1960. *The American Presidency Project.* Retrieved from http://www.presidency.ucsb.edu/ws/?pid=11771

Eisenhower Presidential Library & Museum. (2018). *Civil Rights: Emmett Till Case.* Abilene, Kansas. Retrieved from https://www.dwightdeisenhower.com/387/Civil-Rights-Emmett-Till-Case

Egelho, Bob. (2005). Judge Defends Writing on Affirmative Action, June 8, 2005, San Francisco Gate, https://www.sfgate.com/politics/article/Judge-defends-writing-on-affirmative-action-2629531.ph

Equal Employment Opportunity Commission. (2018). *Executive Order 8802.* Retrieved from https://www.eeoc.gov/eeoc/history/35th/thelaw/eo-8802.html

Estepa, Jessica. (2017). George H. W. Bush, George W. Bush: We must reject "hatred in all forms." *USA Today,* August 16, 2017. Retrieved from https://www.usatoday.com/story/news/politics/onpolitics/2017/08/16/george-h-w-bush-george-w-bush-we-must-reject-hatred-all-forms/572468001/

Farrakhan, Louis. (2017). Obama Is a "Murderer," an "Assassin." Huffington Post, December 6, 2017, https://www.huffingtonpost.com/2011/06/20/louis-farrakhan-obama-murderer-assassin_n_880973.html

Feagin, Joe. (2001). *Racist America: Roots, Current, Realities, and Future Reparations.* New York, NY: Routledge.

Ford, Gerald R. (1974a). Statement by the President. Washington, D.C.: The White House. Retrieved from https://www.fordlibrarymuseum.gov/library/docu ment/0248/whpr19740821–008.pdf

Ford, Gerald R. (1974b). The President's News Conference, October 9, 1974. *The American Presidency Project*. Retrieved from http://www.presidency.ucsb .edu/ws/index.php?pid=4440

Ford, Gerald R. (1975a). Remarks to Members of the National Newspaper Publishers Association, January 23, 1975. *The American Presidency Project*. Retrieved from http://www.presidency.ucsb.edu/ws/index.php?pid=5105

Ford, Gerald R. (1975b). Remarks at the Annual Convention of the National Association for the Advancement of Colored People, July 1, 1975. *The American Presidency Project*. Retrieved from http://www.presidency.ucsb.edu /ws/index.php?pid=5037

Ford, Gerald R. (1975c). Letter to the Senate Minority Leader Urging Extension of the Voting Rights Act of 1965, July 23, 1975. *The American Presidency Project*. Retrieved from http://www.presidency.ucsb.edu/ws/index.php?pid =5097

Ford, Gerald R. (1976a). Message on the Observance of Black History Month, February 1976, February 10, 1976. *The American Presidency Project*. Retrieved from http://www.presidency.ucsb.edu/ws/?pid=6288

Ford, Gerald R. (1976b). The President's News Conference, April 10, 1976. *The American Presidency Project*. Retrieved from http://www.presidency .ucsb.edu/ws/index.php?pid=5828

Ford, Gerald R. (1976c). Special Message to the Congress Transmitting Proposed School Busing Legislation, June 24, 1976. *The American Presidency Project*. Retrieved from http://www.presidency.ucsb.edu/ws/index.php?pid=6150

Ford, Gerald R. (1976d). Remarks upon Accepting the Resignation of Earl L. Butz as Secretary of Agriculture, October 4, 1976. *The American Presidency Project*. Retrieved from http://www.presidency.ucsb.edu/ws/index.php?pid =6408

Ford, Gerald R. (1999). Inclusive America, Under Attack. *The New York Times, August 8, 1999*. Retrieved from https://www.nytimes.com/1999/08/08 /opinion/inclusive-america-under-attack.html

The 43rd President; Text of Supreme Court Ruling in Bush v. Gore Florida Recount Case. (2000). *New York Times,* December 14, 2000, https://www.nytimes .com/2000/12/14/us/43rd-president-text-supreme-court-ruling-bush -v-gore-florida-recount-case.html. Accessed June 25, 2018.

Franklin D. Roosevelt Presidential Library and Museum. (2018a). *News to Archives*. Retrieved from http://www.fdrlibrary.marist.edu/archives/collec tions/acquisitions.html

Franklin D. Roosevelt Presidential Library and Museum. (2018b). *February 26, 1939: Eleanor Roosevelt Resigns from the Daughters of the American Revolution*. Retrieved from http://docs.fdrlibrary.marist.edu/tmirhfee.html

Gannon, Frank. (2010). *3.24.70*. Richard Nixon Foundation, Library and Museum. Retrieved from https://www.nixonfoundation.org/2010/03/3–24–70/

Garcia, George F. (1979). Herbert Hoover and the Issue of Race. *The Annals of Iowa (State Historical Society of Iowa, Iowa Department of Cultural Affairs),* 44, 7, Winter, pp. 507–515.

Garcia, George F. (1980). Black Disaffection from the Republican Party during the Presidency of Herbert Hoover, 1928–1932. *The Annals of Iowa,* 45, 6, 462–477. Retrieved from https://ir.uiowa.edu/cgi/viewcontent.cgi?article =8734&context=annals-of-iowa

Garfield James A. (1881). Inaugural Address, March 4, 1881. *The American Presidency Project.* Retrieved from http://www.presidency.ucsb.edu/ws/index .php?pid=25823

Gates, Henry Louis, Jr., and Evelyn Brooks Higginbotham (eds.). (2013). Hall, Prince, 1753–1807, African American, abolitionist, former slave In. *African American National Biography,* vol 5. Oxford: Oxford University Press.

Giannetti, Charlene and Williams, Jai. (2017). *Plantations of Virginia.* Lanham, MD: Rowman & Littlefield.

Giorgio, Papa. (2015). Herbert Hoover and the Changing Demographic of Black Voters. Retrieved from http://religiopoliticaltalk.com/herbert-hoover-and -the-changing-demographic-of-black-voters/

Ginzberg, Eli and Alfred S. Eichner. (1993). *Troublesome Presence: Democracy and Black Americans.* Piscataway, NJ: Transaction Publishers.

Goethals, George R. (2015). *Presidential Leadership and African Americans: "An American Dilemma" from Slavery to the White House.* New York, NY: Routledge.

Good, Timothy. (2009). *Lincoln for President: An Underdog's Path to the 1860 Republican Nomination.* Jefferson, NC: McFarland & Company, Inc.

Goodenough, Patrick. (2017). UN Experts "Disturbed" by U.S. "Failure" to Reject and Condemn Racist Demonstrations. CNSNews.com, August 24, 2017. Retrieved from https://www.cnsnews.com/news/article/patrick-goodenough /un-experts-disturbed-us-failure-reject-and-condemn-racist

Goodnough, Abby. (2009). Harvard Professor Jailed; Officer Is Accused of Bias. *New York Times,* July 20, 2009, https://www.nytimes.com/2009/07/21/us /21gates.html

Goodwin, Doris Kearns. (1994). *No Ordinary Time: Franklin and Eleanor Roosevelt: The Home Front in World War II.* New York, NY: Simon & Schuster.

Gossett, Thomas. (1997). *Race: The History of an Idea in America.* New York, NY: Oxford University Press.

Gould, Lewis L. (ed.). (2001). *American First Ladies: Their Lives and Their Legacy, Second Edition.* New York, NY: Routledge.

Grant, Ulysses S. (1869). Inaugural Address, March 4, 1869. *The American Presidency Project.* Retrieved from http://www.presidency.ucsb.edu/ws/index .php?pid=25820

Grant, Ulysses S. (1870). Special Message to the Senate and House of Representatives, March 30, 1870. Retrieved from https://www.nps.gov/ulsg/learn/his toryculture/grant-and-the-15th-amendment.htm

Grant, Ulysses S. (1873). Second Inaugural Address. Retrieved from https:// millercenter.org/the-presidency/presidential-speeches/march-4–1873 -second-inaugural-address

Gregory, David. (2007). Senator Biden Apologizes for Remarks on Obama, *NBC Nightly News,* http://www.nbcnews.com/id/16911044/ns/nbc_nightly_news _with_brian_williams/t/sen-biden-apologizes-remarks-obama/#.W4 FnTSwtFjo

Haggerty, Ryan. (2011). Farrakhan Condemns Killing of Libyan Leader Moammar Gadhafi. *Chicago Tribune,* October 25, 2011, http://www.chicagotri bune.com/news/local/breaking/chi-farrakhan-condemns-killing-of-libyan -leader-moammar-gadhafi-20111025-story.html

Hammond, Scott J., Kevin R. Hardwick, and Howard L. Lubert (eds.). (2007). *Classics of American Political and Constitutional Thought, Volume 2: Reconstruction to the Present.* Indianapolis, IN: Hackett Publishing Company, Inc.

Harding, Vincent. (1981). *There Is a River: The Black Struggle for Freedom in America.* San Diego, CA: Harcourt Brace & Company.

Harding, William G. (1921). Address to a Joint Session of Congress on Urgent National Problems, April 12, 1921. *The American Presidency Project.* Retrieved from http://www.presidency.ucsb.edu/ws/index.php?pid=126413

Harlan, Louis R. (ed.). (1972). *The Booker T. Washington Papers Volume 1: The Autobiographical Writings.* Urbana, IL: University of Illinois Press.

Harlan, Louis R. (ed.). (1975). *The Booker T. Washington Papers Volume 4: 1895–98.* Urbana, IL: University of Illinois Press.

Harris, Richard A. and Daniel J. Tichenor (eds.). (2010). *A History of the U.S. Political System: Ideas, Interests, and Institutions.* Santa Barbara, CA: ABC-CLIO.

Harris-Perry, Melissa V. 2011. *Sister Citizen: Shame, Stereotypes, and Black Women in America.* New Haven, CT: Yale University Press.

Harrison, Benjamin. (1889). First Annual Message, December 3, 1889. *The American Presidency Project.* Retrieved from http://www.presidency.ucsb.edu /ws/index.php?pid=29530

Harrison, Benjamin. (1890). Second Annual Message, December 1, 1890. *The American Presidency Project.* Retrieved from http://www.presidency .ucsb.edu/ws/index.php?pid=29531

Harrison, Benjamin. (1892). Fourth Annual Message, December 6, 1892. *The American Presidency Project.* Retrieved from http://www.presidency .ucsb.edu/ws/index.php?pid=29533

Hayes, Rutherford B. (1877). Inaugural Address, March 5, 1877. *The American Presidency Project.* Retrieved from http://www.presidency.ucsb.edu/ws /index.php?pid=25822

Hayward, Steven F. (2001). *The Age of Reagan: The Fall of the Old Liberal Order: 1964–1980.* New York, NY: Crown Publishing Group.

Hecht, Mary B. and Katherine E. Speirs. (1995). *John Quincy Adams: A Personal History of an Independent Man.* Newtown, CT: American Political Biography.

Helm, William Picket. (1947). *Harry Truman: A Political Biography.* New York, NY: Duell, Sloan, and Pearce.

Henderson, Elmer W. (1943). Negroes in Government Employment. *Opportunity Journal of Negro Life,* July 1943, pp. 118–132.

Henry, Charles P. (2007). *Long Overdue: the Racial Politics of Racial Repara-tions.* New York, NY: New York University Press.

Holt, Michael. (1999). *The Rise and Fall of the American Whig Party: Jacksonian Politics and the Onset of the Civil War.* Oxford: Oxford University Press.

Hoover, Herbert. (1930a). Message Commending the National Urban League on Its Job Training Efforts for Negroes, March 13, 1930. *The American Presidency Project.* Retrieved from http://www.presidency.ucsb.edu/ws/index.php?pid=22548

Hoover Herbert. (1930b). Message Condemning Lynching, September 23, 1930. *The American Presidency Project.* Retrieved from http://www.presidency.ucsb.edu/ws/index.php?pid=22360

Hopkins, Harry L. (1935). *Letter to the Honorable Stephen Early, Secretary to the President, June 17, 1935.* Washington D.C.: Works Progress Administration.

Jacobson, Louis. (2018). Donald Trump is partly correct in response to Jay-Z about black unemployment. PolitiFact, January 30, 2018. Retrieved from http://www.politifact.com/truth-o-meter/statements/2018/jan/30/donald-trump/donald-trump-partly-correct-rejoinder-jay-z/.

Jefferson, Thomas. (1782). *Notes on the State of Virginia.* Retrieved from https://static.lib.virginia.edu/rmds/tj/notes/index.html

Johnson, Andrew. (1867). Third Annual Message, December 3, 1867. *The American Presidency Project.* Retrieved from http://www.presidency.ucsb.edu/ws/?pid=29508

Johnson, Lyndon B. (1963). Address Before a Joint Session of the Congress, November 27, 1963. *The American Presidency Project.* Retrieved from http://www.presidency.ucsb.edu/ws/?pid=25988

Johnson, Lyndon B. (1964). Radio and Television Remarks upon Signing the Civil Rights Bill, July 2, 1964. *The American Presidency Project.* Retrieved from http://www.presidency.ucsb.edu/ws/?pid=26361

Johnson, Lyndon B. (1965). Commencement Address at Howard University: "To Fulfill These Rights," June 4, 1965. *The American Presidency Project,* Retrieved from http://www.presidency.ucsb.edu/ws/?pid=27021

Johnson, Lyndon B. (1965b). Statement by the President on the Situation in Selma, Alabama, March 9, 1965. *The American Presidency Project.* Retrieved from http://www.presidency.ucsb.edu/ws/?pid=26802

Johnson, Lyndon B. (1965c). Special Message to the Congress: The American Promise, March 15, 1965. *The American Presidency Project.* Retrieved from http://www.presidency.ucsb.edu/ws/?pid=26805

Johnson, Lyndon B. (1967). Remarks to the Nation after Authorizing the Use of Federal Troops in Detroit, July 24, 1967. *The American Presidency Project.* Retrieved from http://www.presidency.ucsb.edu/ws/?pid=28364

Jones, Jenkin Lloyd (ed.). (1919). *Unity,* 84, 1, September 4, 1919.

Journal of Executive Proceedings of the Senate of the United States of America, Volumes 25–27, From March 1837 to September 13, 1841. (1887). Volume V. Washington, D.C.: U.S. Government Printing Office, 1887.

Kaplan, Sidney. (1991). *American Studies in Black and White, Selected Essays, 1949–1989.* Amherst, MA: University of Massachusetts Press.

Katz, William Loren. (1995). *Eyewitness: A Living Documentary of the African American Contribution to American History.* New York, NY: Simon & Schuster.

Kennedy, Frances H. (2014). *The American Revolution: A Historical Guidebook.* Oxford: Oxford University Press.

Kennedy, John F. (1960). Annual Message to the Congress on the State of the Union, January 30, 1961. *The American Presidency Project.* Retrieved from http://www.presidency.ucsb.edu/ws/index.php?pid=8045

Kennedy, John F. (1963). Excerpt from a Report to the American People on Civil Rights, June 11, 1963. Retrieved from https://www.jfklibrary.org/Asset -Viewer/LH8F_0Mzv0e6RolyEm74Ng.aspx

Kennedy, Robert F. (1963). Robert F. Kennedy's Testimony on Civil Rights Act of 1963, July 18, 1963. National Archives Catalog. Retrieved from https:// catalog.archives.gov/id/193988

Khan, Huma, McPhee. (2009). Michelle Obama Defends Criticism of Cambridge Police in Arrest of Gates, ABC News, July 23, 2009, https://abcnews.go .com/Politics/story?id=8153681&page=1

Kilough, Ashley. (2013). Rangel: 'Embarrassing' Lack of Diversity in Obama Cabinet, *CNN,* January 10, 2013, https://www.cnn.com/2013/01/10/us/rangel -embarrassing-lack-of-diversity-in-obama-cabinet/index.html

Kinealy, Christine. (2016). *Daniel O'Connell and the Anti-Slavery Movement: The Saddest People the Sun Sees.* New York, NY: Routledge Publishing.

King, Martin Luther, Jr. (1957). Letter to Richard M. Nixon, on Civil Rights Act of 1957, Voter Registration. The Martin Luther King, Jr. Research and Education Institute, Stanford University. Retrieved from https://kinginstitute .stanford.edu/king-papers/documents/richard-m-nixon-1

Kinslow, Zacharie W. (2018). *Enslaved and Entrenched: The Complex Life of Elias Polk.* The White House Historical Society, Washington D.C. https:// www.whitehousehistory.org/enslaved-and-entrenched. Accessed June 18, 2018.

Kornblith, Gary J. (2010). *Slavery and Sectional Strife in the Early American Republic.* Lanham, MD: Rowman & Littlefield Publishers.

Krieg, Gregory. (2017). Rally Trump vs. Teleprompter Trump, CNN, August 23, 2017. Retrieved from https://www.cnn.com/2017/08/23/politics/comparing -donald-trump-speeches-afghanistan-phoenix/index.html

Kruzel, John. (2018). Donald Trump's misleading claim that Kanye West's praise doubled his African-American support. PolitiFact, May 7, 2018. Retrieved from http://www.politifact.com/truth-o-meter/statements/2018/may/07 /donald-trump/donald-trumps-misleading-claim-kanye-wests-praise-/

Kurtzleben, Danielle. (2016). Understanding the Clintons' Popularity with Black Voters. NPR, March 1, 2016. Retrieved from https://www.npr.org/2016/03 /01/468185698/understanding-the-clintons-popularity-with-black-voters

Kurtzleben, Danielle. (2018). FACT CHECK: Trump Touts Low Unemployment Rates for African-Americans, Hispanics, NPR, January 8, 2018. Retrieved from https://www.npr.org/2018/01/08/576552028/fact-check-trump-touts-low -unemployment-rates-for-african-americans-hispanics

Lehr, Dick. 2015. *The Birth of a Movement: How Birth of a Nation Ignited the Battle for Civil Rights.* New York: PublicAffairs.

Leiberger, Stuart, A. (2013). *Comparison to James Madison and James Monroe.* Malden, MA: Wiley Blackwell Publishing.

Lewis, Alfred Henry and Theodore Roosevelt. (2010). *A Compilation of the Messages and Speeches of Theodore Roosevelt, 1901–1905.* Washington, D.C.: Bureau of National Literature and Art.

Lewis, David L. (2000). *W. E. B. Du Bois: The Fight for Equality and the American Century, 1919–1963.* New York, NY: Henry Holt and Company.

Library of Congress. (2018). A Proclamation, Printed Ephemera Collection; Portfolio 235, Folder 26. Retrieved from http://www.digitalhistory.uh.edu /exhibits/reconstruction/section4/section4_pardon1.html

Library of Congress. (2018). Declaring Independence: Drafting the Documents. Retrieved from https://www.loc.gov/exhibits/declara/ruffdrft.html

Lincoln, Abraham. (1854). Speech on the Repeal of the Missouri Compromise, Peoria, Illinois, October 16, 1854.

Lincoln, Abraham. (1855). Letter from Abraham Lincoln to Joshua Speed, August 24, 1855.

Lincoln, Abraham. (1858). Speech at Chicago, Illinois: July 10, 1858. Retrieved from https://quod.lib.umich.edu/l/lincoln/lincoln2/1:526.1?rgn=div2;view =fulltext

Lincoln, Abraham. (1897). *Political Debates between Lincoln and Douglas.* Cleveland: Burrows Bros. Co., 1897; Bartleby.com, 2001.

Lisio, Donald J. (1985). *Hoover, Blacks, and Lily-Whites: A Study of Southern Strategies.* Chapel Hill, NC: The University of North Carolina Press.

Long, Michael G. (ed.). (2008). *First Class Citizenship: The Civil Rights Letters of Jackie Robinson.* New York, NY: Times Books.

McInerney, Thomas J. and Fred L. Israel (eds.). (2013). *Presidential Documents: Words That Shaped a Nation from Washington to Obama, Second Edition.* New York, NY: Routledge.

McKinley, William. (1897). Inaugural Address, March 4, 1897. *The American Presidency Project.* Retrieved from http://www.presidency.ucsb.edu/ws /index.php?pid=25827

Madison, James. (1794). Letter James Madison to James Madison Sr., 19 May 1794, Founders Online Archive, accessed June 15, 2018, https://founders .archives.gov

Madison, James. (1789). Memorandum on an African Colony for Freed Slaves, [ca. 20 October] 1789, *Founders Online,* National Archives, last modified June 13, 2018, http://founders.archives.gov/documents/Madison/01-12-02 -0287. [Original source: *The Papers of James Madison,* vol. 12, *2 March 1789–20 January 1790 and supplement 24 October 1775–24 January 1789,* ed. Charles F. Hobson and Robert A. Rutland. Charlottesville: University Press of Virginia, 1979, pp. 437–438.]

Malcolm X. (1963). X: Malcolm's Final Years. Retrieved from https://therealnews .com/stories/malcolmx

Malcolm X. (1964). *The Autobiography of Malcolm X.* New York, NY: Random House Publishing.

Marable, Manning and Agard-Jones, Vanessa. 2008. *Transnational Blackness: Navigating the Global Color Line.* New York: Palgrave MacMillan.

Marshall, James P. (2018). *The Mississippi Civil Rights Movement and the Kennedy Administration, 1960–1964.* Baton Rouge, LA: Louisiana State University Press.

Matthews, David. (2013). Kennedy White House had jitters ahead of 1963 March on Washington. Fox. Retrieved from http://fox13now.com/2013/08/28 /kennedy-white-house-had-jitters-ahead-of-1963-march-on-washington/

Meacham, John. (2007). *American Gospel: God, the Founding Fathers, and the Making of a Nation.* New York, NY: Random House Publishing.

Meikle, James. (2009). Dastardly Racism, Says Jimmy Carter Over "You lie" Outburst at Obama; Former US President says Interjection has Exposed "a Feeling in this Country" that an African-American Should Not Hold the Office. *The Guardian,* September 21, 2009, https://www.theguardian.com /world/2009/sep/16/jimmy-carter-you-lie-racist

Merica, Dan. (2017). Trump: Frederick Douglass "is being recognized more and more." CNN, February 2, 2017. Retrieved from https://www.cnn.com/2017 /02/02/politics/donald-trump-frederick-douglass/index.html

Miller, J. Martin (ed.). (1904). *The Triumphant Life of Theodore Roosevelt: Citizen, Statesman, President.* J. Martin Miller.

Miller, Randall, and John David Smith. (1997). *Dictionary of Afro-American Slavery.* Westport, CT: Praeger.

Montopoli, Brian. (2009). Obama: Cops Acted "Stupidly" in Professor's Arrest, *CBS News,* July 22, 2009, https://www.cbsnews.com/news/obama-cops -acted-stupidly-in-professors-arrest/

Morrison, Toni. (1998). Clinton as the first black president. *New Yorker,* October 1998. Retrieved from http://ontology.buffalo.edu/smith/clinton/morrison .html

Mosendz, Polly. (2015). Dylan Roof Confesses: Says He Wanted to Start "Race War." *Newsweek,* June 19, 2015, https://www.newsweek.com/dylann-roof -confesses-church-shooting-says-he-wanted-start-race-war-344797

Movroydis, Jonathan. (2017). RN, MLK, and the Civil Rights Act of 1957. Richard Nixon Foundation, Library and Museum. Retrieved from https:// www.nixonfoundation.org/2017/01/rn-mlk-and-the-civil-rights-act-of -1957/

Muhammad, Askia. (1987). A Mistreated Black Pioneer. *The Washington Post,* August 16, 1987. Retrieved from https://www.washingtonpost.com/archive /opinions/1987/08/16/a-mistreated-black-pioneer/f32d2785-446b-4e89 -a88a-68cd76668811/?utm_term=.c8952c3cadeb

Myre, Greg. (2013). Now Praised By Presidents, Mandela Wasn't Always Admired in the U.S. NPR. Retrieved https://www.npr.org/sections/parallels/2013 /12/09/249708436/now-praised-by-presidents-mandela-wasnt-always -admired-in-the-u-s

NAACP. (1948). *Declaration of Negro Voters.* New York, NY: Press Service of the National Association for the Advancement of Colored People. Retrieved from https://www.trumanlibrary.org/whistlestop/study_collections/trum ancivilrights/documents/pdfs/9–2.pdf

Nagourney, Adam. 2007. Biden Unwraps '08 Bid with an Oops! *New York Times,* February 1, 2007. Retrieved from https://www.nytimes.com/2007/02/01 /us/politics/01biden.html

National Archives. (2017). Black Soldiers in the U.S. Military During the Civil War, National Archives, Washington D.C., 2017. Accessed May 7, 2018, https://www.archives.gov/education/lessons/blacks-civil-war

National Archives. (2018). Executive Order 11625—Prescribing additional arrangements for developing and coordinating a national program for minority business enterprise. Retrieved from https://www.archives.gov/federal-regis ter/codification/executive-order/11625.html

National Labor Relations Review Board. (2018). Interfering with employee rights (Section 7 & 8(a)(1)). Retrieved from https://www.nlrb.gov/rights-we-pro tect/whats-law/employers/interfering-employee-rights-section-7-8a1.

Nelson, Michael. (1996). *Guide to the Presidency,* Second Edition, Volume 12. New York, NY: Congressional Quarterly

Newton, Michael. (1951). *White Robes and Burning Crosses: A History of the Ku Klux Klan from 1866.* Jefferson, NC: McFarland and Company.

Nielsen, Niels C. (2009). *God in the Obama Era: Presidents' Religion and Ethics from George Washington to Barack Obama.* New York, NY: Morgan James Publishing.

Nixon, Richard M. (1969a). Statement About a National Program for Minority Business Enterprise, March 5, 1969. *The American Presidency Project.* Retrieved from http://www.presidency.ucsb.edu/ws/index.php?pid=1943

Nixon, Richard M. (1969b). Statement About Congressional Action on the Philadelphia Plan, December 23, 1969. *The American Presidency Project.* Retrieved from http://www.presidency.ucsb.edu/ws/?pid=2382

Nixon, Richard M. (1970a). Special Message to the Congress Proposing the Emergency School Aid Act of 1970, May 21, 1970. *The American Presidency Project.* Retrieved from http://www.presidency.ucsb.edu/ws/?pid =2509

Nixon, Richard M. (1970b). Statement on Signing the Voting Rights Act Amendments of 1970, June 22, 1970. *The American Presidency Project.* Retrieved from http://www.presidency.ucsb.edu/ws/index.php?pid=2553

Nixon, Richard M. (1971a). *Letter to Representative Charles C. Diggs, Jr., in Response to Recommendations of the Congressional Black Caucus. The American Presidency Project.* Retrieved from http://www.presidency.ucsb .edu/ws/index.php?pid=3013

Nixon, Richard M. (1971b). The President's News Conference, April 29, 1971. *The American Presidency Project.* Retrieved from http://www.presidency.ucsb .edu/ws/index.php?pid=2993

Nixon, Richard M. (1972a). Proclamation 4160—National Heritage Day. *The American Presidency Project.* Retrieved from http://www.presidency.ucsb .edu/ws/index.php?pid=3612

Nixon, Richard M. (1972b). Statement About Signing the Equal Employment Opportunity Act of 1972, March 25, 1972. *The American Presidency Project.* Retrieved from http://www.presidency.ucsb.edu/ws/?pid=3358

Nobel Prize. (2002). The Nobel Peace Prize 2002. Retrieved from https://www.nobelprize.org/nobel_prizes/peace/laureates/2002/

Norton, Mary Beth, James Kamensky, Carol Sheriff, David W. Blight, Howard P. Chudacoff, Fredrik Logevall, and Beth Bailey. (2015). *A People and a Nation, Volume II: Since 1865.* Stamford, CT: Cengage Learning.

Obama, Barack. (2005). What I See in Lincoln's Eyes, CNN.com, Tuesday, June 28. Retrieved from http://www.cnn.com/2005/POLITICS/06/28/obama.lincoln.tm/

Obama, Barack. (2008). *This Is Your Victory,* delivered on November 4, 2008. CNN Politics, CNN.Com. http://edition.cnn.com/2008/POLITICS/11/04/obama.transcript/

Obama, Barack. (2009). First Inaugural Address, delivered on January 20, 2009, https://obamawhitehouse.archives.gov/blog/2009/01/21/president-barack-obamas-inaugural-address

Obama, Barack. (2015). Eulogy Delivered at the Funeral for Reverend Clementa Pinckney, One of the Victims of Deadly Shootings at Emmanuel African Methodist Episcopal Church in Charleston, South Carolina. PBS News-Hour, YouTube Video, Published on June 26, 2015.

O'Brien, Michael. (2005). *John F. Kennedy: A Biography.* New York, NY: Thomas Dunne Books.

Olson, Debbie (ed.). (2015). *The Child in Post-Apocalyptic Cinema.* Lanham, MD: Lexington Books.

Paulus, Carl Lawrence. (2017). *The Slave Holding: Fear of Insurrection and the Coming of the Civil War.* Baton Rouge, LA: Louisiana State University Press.

PBS. (2018). Freedom Riders—Meet the Players: US Federal Government. Retrieved from https://www.pbs.org/wgbh/americanexperience/features/meet-players-us-federal-government/

Peterson, Kol. (2009). A New Moment of Promise in Africa, whitehouse.gov, July 11, 2009, https://obamawhitehouse.archives.gov/blog/2009/07/11/a-new-moment-promise-africa

Pew Research Center. (2016). Demographic Trends and Economic Well Being. Retrieved from http://www.pewsocialtrends.org/2016/06/27/1-demographic-trends-and-economic-well-being/

Postrel, Virginia. (2004). The Consequences of the 1960's Race Riots Come into View. *The New York Times,* December 30, 2004. Retrieved from https://www.nytimes.com/2004/12/30/business/the-consequences-of-the-1960s-race-riots-come-into-view.html

Potter, Constance (1999). World War I Gold Star Mothers Pilgrimages, Part I. Washington, D.C.: National Archives. Retrieved from https://www.archives.gov/publications/prologue/1999/summer/gold-star-mothers-1.html

Powell, Adam Clayton, Jr. (1957). Message from Berchtesgaden, Germany on August 30, 1957. Dwight D. Eisenhower Presidential Library, Museum and Boyhood Home. Retrieved from https://www.eisenhower.archives.gov/research/online_documents/civil_rights_act/1957_08_30_Press_Release_Powell.pdf

Powell, Jim. (2003). Why Did FDR's New Deal Harm Blacks? Cato Institute, December 3, 2003. Retrieved from https://www.cato.org/publications/com mentary/why-did-fdrs-new-deal-harm-blacks

Prepared By Each Party Reporters. (1860). *Debates of Lincoln and Douglas: Political Debates between Honorable Abraham Lincoln and Honorable Stephen A. Douglas.* Columbus, OH: Columbus, Follet, Foster and Company.

Pringle, Henry F. (1939). *The Life and Times of William Howard Taft: A Biography.* New York, NY: Farrar and Rinehart.

Ragsdale, Lyn. (1998). *Vital Statistics on the Presidential Election.* Washington DC: Congressional Quarterly Press, pp. 132–138.

Reagan, Ronald. (1981a). Remarks in Denver, Colorado, at the Annual Convention of the National Association for the Advancement of Colored People, June 29, 1981. *The American Presidency Project.* Retrieved from http://www .presidency.ucsb.edu/ws/index.php?pid=44016&st=NAACP&st1=Denver

Reagan, Ronald. (1981b). The President's News Conference, January 29, 1981. *The American Presidency Project.* Retrieved from http://www.presidency .ucsb.edu/ws/?pid=44101

Reagan, Ronald. (1985). The President's News Conference, September 17, 1985. *The American Presidency Project.* Retrieved from http://www.presidency .ucsb.edu/ws/?pid=39125.

Reagan, Ronald. (1986a). Remarks to Members of the World Affairs Council and the Foreign Policy Association, July 22, 1986. *The American Presidency Project.* Retrieved from http://www.presidency.ucsb.edu/ws/?pid=37643

Reagan, Ronald. (1986b). Message to the House of Representatives Returning without Approval a Bill Concerning Apartheid in South Africa, September 26, 1986. *The American Presidency Project.* Retrieved from http:// www.presidency.ucsb.edu/ws/?pid=36504

Reagan, Ronald. (1986c). Radio Address to the Nation on Welfare Reform, February 15, 1986. *The American Presidency Project.* Retrieved from http:// www.presidency.ucsb.edu/ws/?pid=36875

Reagan, Ronald. (1988). Remarks on Signing the Fair Housing Amendments Act of 1988, September 13, 1988. *The American Presidency Project.* Retrieved from http://www.presidency.ucsb.edu/ws/?pid=36361

Rice, Condoleezza. (2017). *Democracy: Stories from the Long Road to Freedom.* New York, NY: Hachette Book Group.

Richardson, James D. (1909). *A Compilation of the Messages and Papers of the Presidents: 1789–1902,* Volume 3. Bureau of the National Literature and Art.

Ripley, Anthony. (1974). Violence Is Deplored. *New York Times,* October 10, https://www.nytimes.com/1974/10/10/archives/violence-is-deplored-ford -says-he-disagrees-with-boston-busing.html

Roberts, James. (1858). *The Narrative of James Roberts, A Soldier Under Gen. Washington in the Revolutionary War, and Gen. Jackson at the Battle of New Orleans, in the War of 1812: "A Battle Which Cost Me a Limb, Some Blood and Almost my Life."* Chicago, IL: author.

Rodriguez, Junius P. (2007). *Slavery in the United States: A Social, Political, and Historical Encyclopedia, Volume 1.* Santa Barbara, CA: ABC-CLIO.

Roosevelt, Theodore. (1906). Sixth Annual Message, December 3, 1906. *The American Presidency Project.* Retrieved from http://www.presidency.ucsb .edu/ws/?pid=29547

Roosevelt, Franklin D. (1937). Excerpts from the Press Conference, September 14, 1937. *The American Presidency Project.* Retrieved from http://www.presi dency.ucsb.edu/ws/index.php?pid=15455

Roosevelt Institute. (2010). African Americans and the New Deal: A Look Back in History. Retrieved from http://rooseveltinstitute.org/african-americans -and-new-deal-look-back-history/

Rothstein, Richard. (2016). Judge Woodrow Wilson's Racism by the Standards of His Time. *Newsweek,* May 8, 2016. Retrieved from http://www.newsweek .com/judge-woodrow-wilson-racism-standards-his-time-456232

Rowland, Kara. (2009). House Votes to Reprimand Rep. Joe Wilson, *Washington Times,* September 15, 2009, https://www.washingtontimes.com/news/2009 /sep/15/gops-wilson-faces-house-admonishment/

Samito, Christian G. (2015). *Lincoln and the Thirteenth Amendment.* Carbondale, Illinois: Southern Illinois University Press.

Sandler, Martin W. (ed.). (2013). *The Letters of John F. Kennedy.* London: Bloomsbury.

Sargent, Greg, (2012). Biden: McConnell Decided to Deny Us Cooperation before We Took Office, *Washington Post,* August 10, 2012, https://www.washing tonpost.com/blogs/plum-line/post/biden-mcconnell-decided-to-withhold -all-cooperation-even-before-we-took-office/2012/08/10/64e9a138-e302 -11e1-98e7-89d659f9c106_blog.html?utm_term=.ab9957c2e998

Scherr, Arthur. (2018). *John Adams, Slavery, and Race: Ideas, Politics, and Diplo-macy in an Age of Crisis.* Santa Barbara, CA: ABC-CLIO.

Schlesinger, Arthur M., Jr. (2007). *Journals: 1952–2000.* New York, NY: Penguin Group.

Scott, Eugene. 2018. Counterprotesters during Unite the Right rally showed there are many fine people on one side. *The Washington Post,* August 13, https:// www.washingtonpost.com/politics/2018/08/13/counterprotesters-during -unite-right-rally-showed-that-there-are-many-fine-people-one-side /?utm_term=.3d7ee8cc7f64

Sellers, Charles Grier. (1957). *James K. Polk,* Volume 1, Jackson 1795–1843. Princeton, NJ: Princeton University Press.

Severance, Frank H. (1907). *Millard Fillmore Papers,* Volume 1. Buffalo, NY: Buffalo Historical Society.

Shear, Michael D. and Liam Stack. (2016). Obama Says Movements Like Black Lives Matter 'Can't Just Keep on Yelling,' *New York Times,* April 23, 2016, https://www.nytimes.com/2016/04/24/us/obama-says-movements-like -black-lives-matter-cant-just-keep-on-yelling.html

Siegel, Josh. (2017). Paul Ryan: "We must be clear. White supremacy is repulsive." *Washington Examiner,* August 15, 2017. Retrieved from https://www .washingtonexaminer.com/paul-ryan-we-must-be-clear-white-supremacy -is-repulsive

Simmons, Althea T. L. (1984). The Civil Rights Act of 1964 Revisited. *The Crisis,* 91, 9, November, pp. 28–34.

Singer, Alan J. (1997). *Social Studies for Secondary Schools: Teaching to Learn, Learning to Teach, Third Edition.* New York, NY: Routledge.

Sinkler, George. (1969). Benjamin Harrison and the Matter of Race. *Indiana Magazine of History,* 65, 3, September, pp. 197–213.

Sitkoff, Harvard. (2010). *Toward Freedom Land: The Long Struggle for Racial Equality in America.* Louisville: The University Press of Kentucky.

Staff Writers. (2013). President Obama's Remarks on Trayvon Martin (full transcript), *Washington Post,* July 19, 2013, https://www.washingtonpost.com /politics/president-obamas-remarks-on-trayvon-martin-full-transcript /2013/07/19/

Staff Writers. (2015). President Obama's Speech on the Charleston Church Shooting, *Time Magazine,* June 18, 2015, http://time.com/3926839/president -obama-charleston-transcript/

Starks, Glenn L., and Erik Brooks. (2012). *Thurgood Marshall: A Biography.* Santa Barbara, CA: Greenwood Press.

Stockbridge, Frank Parker. (1921). The Ku Klux Klan Revival. *Current History: A Monthly Magazine of* The New York Times, 12, April–September, pp. 19–25.

Stolberg, Sheryl Gay. (2006). In Speech to N.A.A.C.P., Bush Offers Reconciliation, *New York Times,* July 21.

Sullivan, Donald Francis. (1965). *The Civil Rights Programs of the Kennedy Administration: A Political Analysis.* Norman: University of Oklahoma.

Taft, William Howard. (1909). Inaugural Address, March 4, 1909. *The American Presidency Project.* Retrieved from http://www.presidency.ucsb.edu/ws /index.php?pid=25830

Taft, William Howard. (1910). *Presidential Addresses and State Papers of William Howard Taft from March 4, 1909, to March 4, 1910, Volume 1.* New York: Doubleday, Page and Company.

Tate, Katherine. (2014). *Concordance: Black Lawmaking in the U.S. Congress from Carter to Obama.* Ann Arbor, MI: University of Michigan Press.

Thomas, Dexter. (2015). When Kanye West Told George Bush That Black Lives Matter. *LA Times,* August 28. Retrieved from http://www.latimes.com /entertainment/music/posts/la-et-ms-kanye-west-katrina-anniversary -george-bush-black-lives-matter-20150827-htmlstory.html

Thompson, Mary V. (2018). George Washington: The Only Unavoidable Subject of Regret, Mount Vernon, Mount Vernon, Virginia. Retrieved from https:// www.mountvernon.org/george-washington/slavery/the-only-unavoidable -subject-of-regret/

Tierney, Dominic. (2016). The Legacy of Obama's "Worst Mistake": There's a Problem with the American Way of War, *The Atlantic,* April 15, 2016, https://www.theatlantic.com/international/archive/2016/04/obamas-worst -mistake-libya/478461/

Tooley, Mark. (2015). *The Peace That Almost Was: The Forgotten Story of the 1861 Washington Peace Conference and the Final Attempt to Avert the Civil War.* New York, NY: Nelson Books.

Truman, Harry S. (1947). Address before the National Association for the Advancement of Colored People. *Public Papers of Harry S. Truman,*

1945–1953, Harry S. Truman Presidential Library and Museum. Retrieved from https://www.trumanlibrary.org/publicpapers/index.php

Truman, Harry S. (1952). Address at the National Convention Banquet of the Americans for Democratic Action, May 17, 1952. Harry S. Truman Presidential Library and Museum. Retrieved from https://www.trumanlibrary .org/publicpapers/index.php?pid=1296

Trump, Donald J. (2017). Presidential Executive Order on The White House Initiative to Promote Excellence and Innovation at Historically Black Colleges and Universities. Washington, D.C.: The White House. Retrieved from https://www.whitehouse.gov/presidential-actions/presidential-executive -order-white-house-initiative-promote-excellence-innovation-historically -black-colleges-universities/

Trump, Donald J. (2018a). President Donald J. Trump Proclaims February 2018 as National African American History Month. Washington, D.C.: The White House. Retrieved from https://www.whitehouse.gov/presidential -actions/president-donald-j-trump-proclaims-february-2018-national -african-american-history-month/

Trump, Donald J. (2018b). President Donald J. Trump's State of the Union Address. Washington, D.C.: The White House. Retrieved from https://www.white house.gov/briefings-statements/president-donald-j-trumps-state-union -address/

Tucker, Spencer C. (2013). *American Civil War: The Definitive Encyclopedia and Document Collection.* Santa Barbara, CA: ABC-CLIO.

Tyler, Lyon, Gardnier. (1884). *The Letters and Times of the Tylers,* Volume 1. Richmond, VA: Whittet & Shepperson Publishing.

United States Congress, Statutes at Large. (1790). 2nd Congress, 2nd Session, Ch. 7, p. 302. U.S. Senate Records, H.R. 40, a Bill to Establish an Uniform Rule of Naturalization and Enable Aliens to Hold Lands under Certain Conditions, National Archives, March 4, 1790.

U.S. Congress. (1793). Proceedings and Debates of the House of Representatives of the United States at the Second Session of the Second Congress, Begun at the City of Philadelphia, November 5, 1792, "Annals of Congress, 2nd Congress, 2nd Session (November 5, 1792 to March 2, 1793)," pp. 1414–15.

U.S. Congress. (2003). H.R. 2205, legislation to establish within the Smithsonian Institution a National Museum of African-American History and Culture: Hearing before the Committee on House Administration, House of Representatives, One Hundred Eighth Congress, first session, hearing held in Washington, D.C., July 9, 2003, Volumes 81–83. Washington, D.C.: United States Printing Office.

U.S. Congress. (2018a). H.R.1927—African American Civil Rights Network Act of 2017. Washington, D.C. Retrieved from https://www.congress.gov/bill /115th-congress/house-bill/1927

U.S. Congress. (2018b). H.R.1242—400 Years of African-American History Commission Act. Washington, D.C. Retrieved from https://www.congress.gov /bill/115th-congress/house-bill/1242

U.S. Department of Health and Human Services. (1996). The Personal Responsibility and Work Opportunity Reconciliation Act of 1996. Washington,

D.C. Retrieved from https://aspe.hhs.gov/report/personal-responsibility
-and-work-opportunity-reconciliation-act-1996

U.S. Department of Labor. (2018a). Executive Order 11478. Retrieved from https://
www.dol.gov/oasam/programs/crc/EO11478.htm

U.S. Department of Labor. (2018b). Executive Order 11246. Retrieved from https://
www.dol.gov/ofccp/regs/statutes/eo11246.htm

U.S. Department of Transportation. (2018). Transportation Equity Act for the 21st
Century. Retrieved from https://www.fhwa.dot.gov/tea21/h2400enr.htm

U.S. Equal Employment Opportunity Commission. (2018). Executive Order
10925. Retrieved from https://www1.eeoc.gov//eeoc/history/50th/thelaw
/eo-10925.cfm?renderforprint=1

U.S. House of Representatives. (2018). The Civil Rights Bill of 1866. *History, Art
& Archives,* http://history.house.gov/Historical-Highlights/1851–1900/The
-Civil-Rights-Bill-of-1866/?sf24820132=1

Vagins, Deborah J., and Jesselyn McCurdy. (2006). Cracks in the System: Twenty
Years of the Unjust Federal Crack Cocaine Law. American Civil Liberties
Union. Retrieved from https://www.aclu.org/files/assets/cracksinsystem
_20061025.pdf

Van Buren, Martin (1837). Inaugural Address: March 4, 1837. Retrieved from
http://www.presidency.ucsb.edu/ws/index.php?pid=25812

Van Buren, Martin. (1867). *Inquiry into the Origin of Political Parties in the
United States.* New York, NY: Hurd and Houghton Publishing.

VOA. (2015). Text of President Obama's Remarks at the African Union, delivered
July 28, 2015, https://www.voanews.com/a/text-of-president-obamas-re
marks-at-the-african-union-/2881236.html

Vogel, Kenneth P., Dave Levinthal, and Tarini Parti. (2012). Obama, Romney
Both Topped $1B, Both Obama and Romney Declined Public Financing
for Their Campaigns *Politco,* December 7, 2012, https://www.politico
.com/story/2012/12/barack-obama-mitt-romney-both-topped-1-billion
-in-2012–084737

Waldstreicher, David and Matthew Mason. (2017). *John Adams and Politics of
Slavery: Selections from the Diary.* Oxford: Oxford University Press.

Walsh, Kenneth T. (2014). *Family of Freedom: Presidents and African Americans
in the White House.* New York, NY: Routledge.

Ward, Walter D., and Denis Gainty. (2012). *Sources of World Societies, Volume 2:
Since 1450.* Boston, MA: Bedford/St. Martin's.

Washington, Booker. (1898). Industrial Education for Cuban Negros, in *City and
State: Commonwealth above Party,* Volume 5, September 15.

Washington, Booker T. (1901). *Booker T. Washington's Own Story of His Life and
Work.* Washington, D.C.: Library of Congress.

Waters, Robert Anthony, Jr. (2009). *Historical Dictionary of United States–Africa
Relations.* Lanham, MD: The Scarecrow Press.

Weber, Anke, Wesley Hiers, and Anaid Flesken. 2016. *Politicized Ethnicity: A
Comparative Perspective.* New York: Palgrave MacMillan.

Wheeler, Edward J., and Frank Crane. (1921). President Harding Discourses on
the Color Line. *Current Opinion,* 71, 1, July–December. New York, NY:
The Current Literature Publishing Company.

The White House. (1958). Meeting of Negro Leaders with the President: June 23, 1958. Dwight D. Eisenhower Presidential Library, Museum and Boyhood Home. Retrieved from https://www.eisenhower.archives.gov/research/online _documents/civil_rights_eisenhower_administration/1958_06_23_Meeting _of_Negro_Leaders.pdf

The White House. (2015). Office of the Press Secretary, Remarks by the President at the 50th Anniversary of the Selma to Montgomery Marches, March 7, 2015, https://obamawhitehouse.archives.gov/the-press-office/2015/03/07 /remarks-president-50th-anniversary-selma-montgomery-marches

The White House. (2015). Office of the Press Secretary, Remarks by the President in Eulogy for the Honorable Reverend Clementa Pinckney, June 26, 2015, https://obamawhitehouse.archives.gov/the-press-office/2015/06/26 /remarks-president-eulogy-honorable-reverend-clementa-pinckney

Wicker, Tom. (1968). Johnson Says He Won't Run. *The New York Times,* April 1.

Williams, Brennan. Tavis Smiley: Black Americans Have Lost Ground under Obama. Huffington Post, September 12, 2014, https://www.huffingtonpost .com/2014/09/12/tavis-smiley-black-americans-obama_n_5812020.html

Williams, Chad Louis. (2010). *Torchbearers of Democracy: African American Soldiers in the World War I Era.* Chapel Hill, NC: The University of North Carolina Press.

Williams, Edwin. (1846). *The Addresses and Messages of the Presidents of the United States,* Volume 2. New York, NY: Edward Walker Publishing.

Williams, Juan. (1988). The Harsh Message for Blacks from Clarence Pendleton. *The Washington Post,* June 12. Retrieved from https://www.washington post.com/archive/opinions/1988/06/12/the-harsh-message-for-blacks-from -clarence-pendleton/7ecb1fa6-6089-4914-aa8e-241f32c37d1f/?utm_term =.74b62fe3d115

Wilson, John K. (2016). *Barack Obama: This Improbable Quest.* New York: Routledge.

Wilson, Woodrow. (1978). *The Papers of Woodrow Wilson.* Princeton, NJ: Princeton University Press.

Windell, James O. (2015). *Looking Back in Crime: What Happened on This Date in Criminal Justice History?* Boca Raton, FL: CRC Press.

Woodson, Carter G. (1921). *Negro History.* Vol. 6. Washington, D.C.: Association for the Study of Negro Life and History.

Wolters, Raymond. (1970). *Negroes and the Great Depression: The Problem of Economic Recovery.* 1st ed., Vol. 6. Westport, CT: Greenwood Publishing.

Workneh, Lilly. (2017). Steve Harvey: "My Wife Told Me to Skip Meeting with Trump, I Should've Listened." Huffington Post, September 5, 2017. Retrieved from https://www.huffingtonpost.com/entry/steve-harvey-my -wife-told-me-to-skip-meeting-with-trump-i-shouldve-listened_us _59aee344e4b0354e440d0925

Wormser, Richard. (1933). *The Rise and Fall of Jim Crow.* New York, NY: St. Martin's Press.

Yahr, Emily. (2016). Read George W. Bush's speech at the African American Museum, 13 years after signing the bill to build it. *The Washington Post,*

September 24, https://www.washingtonpost.com/news/arts-and-entertain ment/wp/2016/09/24/read-george-w-bushs-speech-at-the-african-ameri can-museum-13-years-after-signing-the-bill-to-build-it/?noredirect=on &utm_term=.a656a47f7781

Zarefsky, David. (1991). *The Complete Lincoln-Douglas Debates of 1858.* Chicago, IL: The University of Chicago Press and Chicago Historical Society.

Zelizer, Julian. (2015). A 1965 failure that still haunts America. CNN, January 19. Retrieved from https://www.cnn.com/2015/01/19/opinion/zelizer-lbj-watts -riots/index.html

Zeleny, Jeff. (2008). Black Leader Changes Endorsement to Obama. *New York Times,* February 28, 2008, https://www.nytimes.com/2008/02/28/us/poli tics/28lewis.html

Index